# Time Off in Spain and Portugal

# Time Off in SPAIN & PORTUGAL

**Teresa Tinsley**

**Horizon Books**

**In this series**
Time Off in India and Nepal
Time Off in Turkey

*Other titles in preparation*

**British Library Cataloguing in Publication Data**

Tinsley, Teresa, *1957 –*
 Time off in Spain and Portugal –
 Time off travel guides
 1. Spain. Visitors' guides
 2. Portugal. Visitors' guides
 I. Title II. Series
 914.6' 0483

ISBN 1-85461-005-8

© *Copyright 1989 by Teresa Tinsley*

First published in 1989 by Horizon Books Ltd, Harper & Row House, Estover Road, Plymouth PL6 7PZ, United Kingdom.
Tel: Plymouth (0752) 705251  Telex: 45635  Fax: (0752) 777603.

All rights reserved. No part of this work may be reproduced, other than for the purposes of review, or stored in an information retrieval system without the express permission of the Publishers given in writing.

Typesetting and artwork by K-DEE Typesetters.
Printed in Great Britain by BPCC Wheatons Ltd, Exeter

# Contents

List of Maps 7

**Part One: Spain**

*Introducing Spain* 11
Modernisation; Abortive coup; Regional vitality; Social changes; The future

*1 Arriving & Surviving in Spain* 14
Paperwork; Getting there; Where to stay; Exchanges; Getting about; Communications and the media; Libraries; Shops and shopping; The Administration; Other key contacts; British representation; Spanish contacts in the UK

*2 Study & Work Opportunities* 43
*Study:* 'Spanish for foreigners' courses; Study visits; Other courses; Study within the State system; Validation of British qualifications; Grants and scholarships; *Work:* General situation; Work permits and other matters; Finding a job: general hints; Au pairing; Teaching English as a foreign language; Other teaching opportunities; Couriers; Casual Work; Self-employment; Other opportunities; British companies with offices in Spain; British firms with operations in Spain; Specialist employment agencies; *Voluntary work:* Work camps; Longer-term voluntary work; Missionary work

*Chapters 3 – 18 each contain the following sections:*
*What to see; Coming and going; Where to stay; What to eat and drink; Opportunities; What to do; Useful addresses*

3 *Andalucía* 74

4 *Aragón* 97

5 *Asturias* 106

6 *Cantabria* 116

7 *Castilla-León (Old Castile)* 124

8 *Castilla-La Mancha (New Castile)* 142

9 *Cataluña* 152

10 *Euskadi (The Basque Country)* 171

11 *Extremadura* 183

12 *Galicia* 191

13 *Madrid* 202

| | | |
|---|---|---|
| *14* | *Murcia* | 219 |
| *15* | *Navarra* | 224 |
| *16* | *La Rioja* | 231 |
| *17* | *Valencia* | 236 |
| *18* | *The Island Regions of Spain* | 248 |

The Balearics; The Canary Islands

*19 More Useful Information*     272
Summary of courses for foreigners; Model of letter asking for information about courses; Fiestas; What to take — a checklist; Glossary of useful Spanish words; What to read about Spain

---

**Part Two: Portugal**

*Introducing Portugal*     283
A country apart; The kingdom of Portucale; Towards an empire; Dictatorship to democracy; Portugal today

*20 Arriving & Surviving in Portugal*     286
Paperwork; Getting there; Where to stay; Food and drink; Getting about; Communications and the media; Libraries; Shops and shopping; Government ministries; Other key contacts; Portuguese contacts in the UK

*21 Study & Work Opportunities*     304
*Study:* 'Portuguese for foreigners' courses; Grants and scholarships; Study within the State system; *Work:* General situation; Work permits and other matters; Finding a job: general hints; Au pairing; Teaching English as a foreign language; Other teaching opportunities; Couriers; Casual work; Farm work; Self-employment; Other opportunities; British companies with offices in Portugal; *Voluntary work:* Work camps; Other voluntary work; Missionary work

*22 Portugal in detail*     317
Porto and the Costa Verde; The Costa da Prata; The Mountains of Portugal; The Plains; The Algarve; Lisbon and region; Madeira; More useful information

Index     349

# List of Maps

| | |
|---|---:|
| Spain | 10 |
| Andalucía | 75 |
| Aragón | 98 |
| Asturias | 107 |
| Cantabria | 117 |
| Castilla-León | 125 |
| Castilla-La Mancha | 142 |
| Cataluña | 153 |
| Street map of Barcelona | 154 |
| Euskadi | 172 |
| Extremadura | 184 |
| Galicia | 192 |
| Madrid | 203 |
| Street map of Madrid | 204 |
| Murcia | 220 |
| Navarre | 225 |
| La Rioja | 232 |
| Valencia | 237 |
| The Balearics | 249 |
| The Canary Islands | 260 |
| Portugal | 282 |
| Porto and the Costa Verde | 317 |
| Costa da Prata | 321 |
| The Mountains of Portugal | 325 |
| The Plains | 329 |
| The Algarve | 332 |
| Lisbon and region | 335 |
| Street map of Lisbon | 337 |
| Madeira | 344 |

# PART ONE
# Spain

Of the many misrepresentations regarding Spain, few are more inveterate than those which refer to the dangers and difficulties that are there supposed to beset the traveller. This, the most romantic, racy and peculiar country of Europe may in reality be visited by sea and land, and throughout its length and breadth, with ease and safety, as all who have ever been there well know, the nonsense with which Cockney critics who never have been there scare delicate writers in albums and lady-bird tourists, to the contrary notwithstanding: the steamers are regular, the mails and diligences excellent, the roads decent, and the mules sure footed; nay, latterly, the *posadas* or inns have been so increased, and the robbers so decreased, that some ingenuity must be evinced in getting either starved or robbed.

*Gatherings from Spain*, Richard Ford (1846)

# Introducing Spain

General Francisco Franco Bahamonde ruled Spain as a dictator from the end of the Civil War in 1939, until his death on 20 November 1975. Since that day, the changes have been so dramatic that many people's ideas about the country haven't been able to keep up with the pace of developments.

The idea of Spain as a rather primitive, heavily policed state, along the lines of some Latin American republic, is certainly not relevant any more. Spain is a modern western country; its democratic institutions, although newly established, are perhaps more strongly upheld for just this reason, and its accession to the EEC has reaffirmed its place among the great nations of Europe. Nor can it be seen simply as a tourist destination where you go to wonder (with misplaced romanticism) at the curious undeveloped antics of the natives, or enjoy in isolated affluence the pleasures of modern life that locals could never aspire to. Spain is now a country where you might go to enjoy doing anything that you might find worthwhile doing in this country — be it making videos, climbing mountains or working with the mentally handicapped. The bonus is that you can do it under extremely favourable conditions — in a climate that is mostly warm and sunny, among outward-looking, creative and generous people, and in an easy-going culture with an uncomplicated attitude to many of the pleasures of life.

## MODERNISATION

The economic basis for bringing Spain out of its almost medieval way of life had been laid by Franco. There were already pockets of industrialisation in Cataluña and the Basque Country, but in the 1950s and 1960s the Francoist regime was engaged in a massive campaign of modernisation, bringing tourism to tiny fishing villages, industry to sleepy towns and, belatedly, some sort of education for all. The spirit of enquiry and experimentation, however, was not allowed to grow alongside material developments. Spain remained a one-party state, whose inflexible Roman Catholic principles harked back to the supposed purity of the days of the Inquisition. Censorship was heavy, and included all forms of popular expression in the regional languages of Spain, as well as films, news items, and books deemed to be undesirable. Political dissent, needless to say, was heavily repressed by the police and the military, and most political opposition remained in exile.

However, when Franco died, his named successor King Juan Carlos, contrary to expectation, immediately set about undoing the tight knots which were strangling the country. Within a few years censorship had been lifted, political parties and trades unions legalised, an amnesty granted to (most) political prisoners and the power of the centralist regime limited by steps towards home-rule *(autonomía)* for the various regions of Spain. Suddenly, you didn't have to wrap up your copy of Sartre in a brown paper cover to read on the Metro. Suddenly there was 40 years of films, news, books and political debate to catch up on. There was a feeling of excitement, of something about to happen, the feeling that once more people were in charge of making their own futures, the feeling perhaps that it could all be short-lived.

## ABORTIVE COUP

Today, just a few years later again, attitudes have matured. In February 1981 an attempted military coup shook the country rigid as Colonel Tejero held the Spanish Parliament at gunpoint and tanks started to rumble through the streets. This, however, proved to be the last dying spasm of the Old Spain, for with the swift intervention of the King on behalf of the democratic constitution, the danger was soon past, and the following year a new Socialist government was elected to power with a sweeping majority under the leadership of the dynamic young Felipe González. The Socialist party now dominates the political scene, and a new young élite hold most of the key positions in industry and finance as well as in politics. The military and the Catholic church have receded in importance and — in parliamentary terms at least — there is effectively no opposition.

## REGIONAL VITALITY

Apart from the normalisation of life in all its senses, the most important change which has affected Spain in recent years has been a highly successful devolution programme, which means that all the regions of Spain now enjoy a fair degree of self-government. This has led to a resurgence of interest in and identification with the various regional cultures and languages which under Franco were repressed in the interests of creating a unified, monolithic state. Paradoxically this return to the roots has come at the same time as an inevitable 'Euro-isation' of Spanish culture as the barriers which had kept the country isolated for so long from international currents of thought are thrust aside.

## SOCIAL CHANGES

Many things have changed, but many things remain the same. Opportunities for women are immensely improved — many women now go out to work and a small number (probably a similar ratio to men as in Britain) have achieved high status positions. However, behind them works an army of mothers, aunts and younger sisters, who cook, and clean and iron and baby sit to make it all possible.

Many traditional Spanish customs and preoccupations have adapted very happily to more modern ways of life to produce the distinctive style of the New Spain. For instance, the evening *paseo* adapts perfectly to the big city, where it takes on greater sophistication and style. Areas of life which give the Spanish a creative outlet to their long-standing preoccupation with visual appearances — advertising, marketing, fashion, film-making, etc. — are all booming. Everything is done on a grand, unreserved scale — there are no mean measures, whether you're talking about building a new theatre or pouring a drink.

However, many foreigners complain of uncooperative attitudes and even hostility towards them on the part of Spanish people — until they get to know them. The isolation and repression suffered during the Francoist era has left people with a deep sense of conflict and mistrust which shows up in all sorts of areas of life. Once you have penetrated this initial barrier, however, and shown yourself to be on their side, their effusive generosity and willingness to do you favours can be almost embarrassing.

## THE FUTURE

Spain is a huge country, with a population substantially smaller than that of the British Isles, and with its virtually unexploited mineral wealth and agricultural potential, could have a great future ahead of it. With the Olympic Games in Barcelona in 1992, and the celebrations planned for the same year for the 500th anniversary of the discovery of America, Spain seems all set to become the fashionable place of the 1990s.

# 1
# Arriving & Surviving in Spain

## PAPERWORK

### Passports
*Passport offices:*
- Clive House, 70 Petty France, London SW1 (tel. 01-279 3434)
- India Buildings, Water St, Liverpool (tel. 051-237 3010)
- Olympia House, Upper Dock St, Newport, Gwent (tel. 0633-56292)
- 55 Westfield Rd, Peterborough (tel. 0733-895555)
- Empire House, 131 West Nile St, Glasgow (tel. 041-332 0271)
- Hampton House, 47-53 High St, Belfast (tel. 0232-232371).

A British visitor's passport — obtainable from main post offices — is valid for Spain (unless you're applying for a special visa), but at £7.50 for a year it doesn't look like as good a deal as a full passport at £15 for 10 years. You should apply well in advance for this latter, though, to your nearest passport office (see above). If you're staying for more than just a fortnight's holiday, make sure your passport's got at least 6 months left to run from date of departure — a condition for obtaining a visa/extension of residence permit.

### Visas
*Spanish Consulate:*
- 20 Draycott Place, London SW3 (tel. 01-581 5924/5)
- Suite 1a, Brook House, 70 Spring Gardens, Manchester 2 (tel. 061-236 1233).
- 63 North Castle Street, Edinburgh (tel. 031-220 1440).

No visa is required for stays of up to 90 days (3 months) for EEC, US or Canadian citizens (although Australians, New Zealanders and many other nationalities will need one). If you're working, though, you'll need a special visa in order to apply for a work permit (see section on work opportunities later in the book).

If you're not working, but want to stay longer than 3 months, you can either apply to the Spanish Consulate in London or Manchester for a (automatically extendable) 90 day visa, or wait till you get to Spain and do the necessary at your local *Comisaría de Policía*. Whichever way, you'll need mammoth amounts of documentation — 3 passport sized photos of yourself, copies of your birth certificate, proof of what you are/intend doing in the country, how you're supporting yourself, etc. An unofficial alternative would be to leave the country briefly after 3 months and re-enter with another 90 day tourist permit.

## Other documentation

*International Student Identity Card*
Useful for getting special discounts on travel, entrance to museums, etc., and in general for proving you are what you say you are — as important as ever to mistrustful officialdom in Spain. It's available from the **student travel agencies** listed on p. 17 (including the Spanish ones), costs at present £3.50, and is valid until 31 December in the year in which you bought it, although if you buy it in the period October – December it will take you through to the end of the following year.

Foreigners legally resident in Spain, and under 21-year-olds from all EEC countries, automatically get free entrance to all state-run museums, on presentation of suitable identification.

*Federation of International Youth Travel Organisations Card (FIYTO)*
If you're not a student but under 26, this card will give you access to similar discounts. It costs £3.00 and is obtainable from student travel agents, or the **Central Bureau for Educational Visits and Exchanges**, Seymour Mews, London W1 (tel. 01–486 5101) — see p. 42.

## Medical

No special vaccinations are required for travel to Spain, although if you want to be on the ultra-safe side, a combined typhoid/cholera jab might be a good idea, mainly if you're going to be in the south during the hottest months. If you're going on a dig or work camp, an anti-tetanus jab is definitely advisable. You should see your GP about these at least 2 months prior to travelling. It may also be a good idea to take with you some sort of medical certificate giving you a clean bill of health — you may well be asked to produce this if applying for work, either voluntary or paid.

## Insurance

Under EEC agreements, you're entitled to urgent medical treatment free in Spain, on production of Form E111, which you must obtain from the Department of Health *before you go*. Information about this is contained in the free leaflet *Medical Costs Abroad* produced by them, which you can get from your local office, or by writing to **Department of Health, International Relations Division**, Alexander Fleming House, Elephant and Castle, London SE1. Form E111 is only intended for use for temporary stays, but if you're working, you should in any case make sure your employer obtains medical cover *(seguro)* for you (and ensure that you're adequately covered until this comes into effect). The practicalities of claiming the free treatment covered by the form are quite complicated, so for short visits it's probably not worth bothering about.

In any case dental treatment and medicines are *not* covered by the agreement, so it's wise to take out extra medical insurance as well, which should include provision for return to the UK in the event of serious illness or injury. (Not that you'd necessarily get better treatment, but who wants to be stuck for months in a foreign hospital?)

ISIS (International Student Insurance Service, though you don't have to be a student to take out a policy) can provide a comprehensive insurance cover which includes life, medical expenses, baggage, personal liability, and cancellation or curtailment of your stay, at little more than £10 per month. There are special 'extended stay' premiums for people staying away for up to a year. To be covered for dangerous sports such as mountaineering, skiing and scuba diving, the premium will rise dramatically, but if you're thinking of doing any of these things, you could always get on-the-spot insurance cover in Spain.

ISIS is available through **Endsleigh Insurance** who have more than 40 branches throughout the country, mostly at universities. Their London office is at 97 – 107 Southampton Row, London WC1 (tel. 01-580 4311).

In general a wider range of medicines is available for sale to the general public in *farmacias* in Spain than in chemists in Britain, so for straightforward complaints you may not need a doctor's appointment. Normal opening hours are Monday to Friday 0900 to 1330 and 1630 to 2000, but when closed all display a list outside of *farmacias de guardia* which are open outside these hours.

## Money

Obviously you'll take some money with you, but make sure you have access to emergency cash in case of unforseen circumstances. If you're going to Spain to live and work, you'll have a whole host of expenses in the first few weeks: deposit on accommodation, setting up house, travel, essential items you suddenly find you need, meals out, etc. (not to mention the odd overly expensive experience before you learn to distinguish cheap places from the rip-offs). If you're working for a Spanish employer (language assistants beware!) the first month's cheque may be very slow in coming through, so even if you can persuade them to let you have an advance of some sort, you really ought to have some resources available to fall back on.

One of the best of these is the good old credit card. **Visa** and **Access** (especially the former) are accepted widely for goods and services, and are invaluable in lieu of paying deposits on car-hire. You can also get emergency cash out on them, although commission rates are quite high.

A **Eurocheque** card and cheques will enable you to write a cheque for goods or services in Spain to be drawn on your account in Britain — see your own bank for details. The card costs about £5 and can be used in automatic machines all over Spain (even the smallest town has several of these now) to draw money direct from your account, at that day's exchange rate, with no extra commission. If you're in Spain for any length of time, of course, you'll need to open an account at a bank or savings bank (*caja de ahorros*) there — the sooner the better.

You'll probably want to take a certain amount of currency with you, and possibly also **travellers' cheques**. Thomas Cook now do these in pesetas, which makes them acceptable at a wider range of places (hotels, restaurants, etc.) in Spain, and saves you the trouble of worrying what exchange rate you'll get. Commission is pretty high when you cash them, though. You can also get Girocheque travellers' cheques from the post office, exchangeable at post offices abroad — useful if you're going to very remote areas where banks are few and far between.

## Maps

Good maps are indispensable: you can get an enormous amount of information from them, and if you're hiking or climbing obviously they're going to be one of the first things on your list. The maps contained in the leaflets put out by the **Spanish Tourist Board** (57 St James St, London SW1) are improving in quality, and are good enough for a start, but if you're going to be travelling around you'll need something better. If you want to get a good map before you go, try **Stanfords**, 12 Long Acre, London WC2 (tel. 01-836 1321), or **McCarta**, 122 Kings Cross Road, London WC1 (tel. 01-278 8278).

In Spain local bookshops will be the best source — look out for maps published by **Firestone** for general purposes, and those produced by the **Instituto Geográfico Catastral** and by the **Servicio Cartográfico del Ejército** for greater detail. For very small scale maps, look out also for **Editorial Alpina**. The **Spanish Mountaineering Federation** (see p. 38) also produces some good maps, and **ICONA** (see p. 40) has some good information leaflets on the National Parks with maps included.

## GETTING THERE

### Key information
- **Spanish National Tourist Office,** 57 St James St, London SW1 (tel. 01-499 0901). Note that at the time of writing it was practically impossible to contact this office by telephone, though written enquiries were usually promptly answered. By far the best approach is to call in person; the office is just off Piccadilly (Marble Arch tube station) and is open Monday – Friday 9.30 to 4.45.

Student travel agencies:
- **STA Travel,** 74 Old Brompton Rd, London SW7 (tel. 01-581 1022), with branches at University of London Union; Kingston Polytechnic; Kent University; 25 Queens Rd, Bristol; and others.
- **Worldwide Student Travel,** 37/8 Store St, London WC1 (tel. 01-580 7733).

In Spain:
- **TIVE** offices, c/Fernando el Católico 88, Madrid (for other branches see relevant listings in regional sections).

## By air

Flying is definitely the best way of getting to Spain, unless you've got special reasons for going overland (or by boat — see below). Try to make the most of the good air connections by getting a flight as near as possible to where you want to go, or you'll spend longer on the onward journey than on the plane.

It's very easy to pick up cheap flights to tourist areas and Madrid — on average you'll pay about £100 return, depending on the time of year and the destination (out of season popular destinations can be quite a bit cheaper). Many of the cheapest flights only allow you a fortnight or 3 weeks so if you want longer or an open ticket expect to pay more — price structures tend to be absurdly complicated when you get into these realms.

The other alternative would be to buy a return ticket and attempt to sell the other half on the spot — not strictly legal but certainly possible, especially in areas with large ex-pat populations and constant comings and going from Britain.

The following agencies specialise in cheap flights to Spain, and there are plenty of others advertised in the national press:

- **Aerotour Spain,** 50a Pall Mall, London SW1 (tel. 01–839 1184).
- **Club de Vacaciones (OTA Travel),** 276 Vauxhall Bridge Rd, London SW1 (tel. 01–834 3492).
- **Intercontinental Flight Services,** Morley House, 2nd Floor, Suite 8, 320 Regent St, London W1 (tel. 01–637 4676).
- **Portugalicia Travel,** 110b Ladbroke Grove, London W10 (tel. 01–221 0333).
- **Springways,** 71 Oxford St, London W1 (tel. 01–439 0302).
- **Travel Arcade Ltd,** Triumph House, Suite 305, 189 Regent St, London W1 (tel. 01–734 5873).

If you're a student, it may be worthwhile investigating special discounted student flights offered by STA Travel and Worldwide Student Travel, listed earlier.

Spain's national airline, **Iberia**, doesn't offer particularly cheap flights, but handles a wider range of airports than are used by the charter companies. Their head office in Britain is at 130 Regent St, London W1 (tel. 01–437 9822).

For flights from Spain the TIVE Student Travel Offices (branches in various cities) offer the cheapest deals, if you're eligible — see p.39.

## By rail

There are two rail routes from London to Spain, depending on whether you want to cross the Pyrenees at Irún in the west, or Port Bou in the east. The latter route takes you down the east coast through Barcelona to Valencia and Alicante, while the former heads due south to Madrid and Andalucía. Either way it will take you 24 hours or so to reach the Spanish border, and may involve a good deal of hassle changing trains — and stations — in Paris.

If you're under 26 though, you can get some cheap deals that may make rail travel seem like a good alternative:

### Interrail
The **Interrail** card, allowing you one month's unlimited travel on most continental trains, up to 50% off rail travel in Britain, and reductions on many sea crossings, is now priced £139.00, so would work out good value if you want to travel around a lot once you're in Spain.

An extra £30 buys you the **Interrail Boat Card**, which also gives you free travel on ferries to the Balearics.

### Transalpino
Also for the under 26s, **Transalpino** offer discounted rail tickets, working out at between £50 and £70 for a single fare — good if you don't know exactly when you'll be returning. Their address is 117 Euston Rd, London NW1 (tel. 01-388 2267), or the tickets are also available through **STA** (see p.17) and other student travel agents.

Similar deals are offered by **Eurotrain**, 52 Grosvenor Gardens, London SW1 (tel. 01-730 8111).

### Rail Europ Family Card
If three or more people living at the same address are travelling together, it's possible to buy a **Rail Europ Family Card** (they don't necessarily have to be members of the same family). This costs £5; the first person pays full fare, and everyone else goes half price, or at a considerably discounted price — including 30% off Channel crossings.

The card can be bought from major BR stations, and full details can be obtained from **European Rail Travel Centre**, PO Box 303, Victoria Station, London SW1 (tel. 01-834 2345).

### Rail information
You can get information on times of trains from **British Rail Continental Enquiries** (tel. 01-834 2345), or at a **BR Travel Centre**.

You might also consider buying British Rail's *International Passenger Timetable and Rail Map of Europe* (£1.50 from main BR stations and some newsagents), or the *Thomas Cook Continental Timetable* (£4.35) and *Rail Map of Europe* (£2.85), available from Thomas Cook offices throughout the country.

Bikes are carried free on most cross-Channel ferry routes, but are charged for if you're going by hovercraft.

### By coach
You can get to most major destinations in Spain by coach. Like the train, it'll take you about 24 hours from London to the border, and anything up to 24 hours more depending on where your final destination is.

### Supabus
**Supabus** (National Express — enquire at any major bus station or ring Victoria Coach Station (tel. 01-730 3453) ) operate two routes at present, the east coast route via Gerona, Barcelona and Valencia, and the route

through the Basque country and central Spain (San Sebastián, Burgos, Madrid, Andalucía).

**Transalpino** (117 Euston Rd, London NW1 (tel. 01-388 2267) are also agents for Supabus.

### Eurolines
**Eurolines** (agents: Aerotour Spain, 50a Pall Mall, London SW1 (tel. 01-881 3252) ) run the east coast route as above, and also a west coast route to Santiago de Compostela via Bilbao, Santander and Oviedo.

These work out quite cheap — between £45 and £65 single and student discounts are available if you're under 26. Two suitcases are carried free, but you normally have to pay extra if you want to take more.

### By car
In order to drive in Spain you'll need either an **international driving licence**, obtainable from the AA and RAC, or a new EEC format pink driving licence, plus extended insurance in the form of a **green card** which you can get from your own insurance company. You must also comply with certain other regulations as detailed on p. 31. The journey through France is arduous — if you leave one of the Channel ports at the crack of dawn and drive like a maniac you might just arrive in Spain in time for dinner, but generally you'll have to plan to spend at least one night in France. If you desperately want to take your car, it may be worth considering the Plymouth – Santander ferry crossing (see below).

As a tourist you're allowed to have your car with you in Spain for 6 months, after which time it is classed as imported goods; you'll then have to pay tax on it (which can be very heavy), and get Spanish plates. You can extend this time limit temporarily by applying to a Customs Office in Spain. If you're using the car for business purposes, or if you have a work permit, you'll have to pay duty and tax anyway. The same conditions apply to motorbikes, cycles and boats.

For car hire in Spain, book from this country if possible — you'll probably get a cheaper deal and without all the hassle — but beware of the costs. Tax on car hire is currently 33% and prices start at about £100 per week. Many of the cheap flight specialists listed above will arrange car hire for you, otherwise you can do so through:

- **Transhire,** Silver House, 31 – 35 Beak St, London W1 (tel. 01-437 0951).
- **Atesa,** 7a Henrietta Place, London W1 (tel. 01-493 4934).
  There's also the possibility of picking up a lift in someone else's car and sharing costs. This can sometimes be arranged through:
- **The Lift Exchange Centre,** 14 Broadway, London SW1 (tel. 01-834 9225) the **Scala Café,** Scala Street, London SW1 (tel. 01-385 2058).

### By sea
The only direct passenger route from Britain to Spain is now the Plymouth – Santander ferry, operated by **Brittany Ferries**, Millbay Docks, Plymouth, Devon (tel. 0752-221321). The crossing takes 24 hours — no

longer than it would take overland and a lot more relaxing.
Single fares start at around £60, with subsequent additions for car, bike, etc., and cabin accommodation, so you could end up paying quite a lot. Its great advantage is that it leaves you immediately somewhere worthwhile and attractive: Santander is also a good start for exploring the north coast and (relatively) well-connected for Madrid and all of northern Spain.

## Packages

Spain is still the favourite country of package tour operators. There are some quite imaginative deals being offered now, with some built-in flexibility (like fly-drives for instance), even by non-specialist companies. Out of season you can get some ridiculously cheap deals. These may be worth looking into, as with the money you save you could easily hire a car and strike out on your own for a few days. It's pointless listing all the package tour operators covered by your high street travel agent, but there are some more specialist deals available, which combine with all sorts of special interests:

**Association for Cultural Exchange,** Babraham, Cambridge (tel. 0223–835 977). So-called 'study-tours', with an emphasis on art and history.

**Blackheath Travel Ltd,** 13 Blackheath Village, London SE3 (tel. 01–852 0025). Wine Tours.

**Brittany Ferries,** Millbay Docks, Plymouth, Devon (tel. 0752–221321). Touring holidays, motoring breaks, etc, with a heavy emphasis on *paradores* (see p. 24), and therefore somewhat expensive.

**Countrywide Holidays,** c/o Cox and Kings, 21 Dorset Square, London NW1 (tel. 01–724 6624). Walking holidays.

**Cox and Kings,** 21 Dorset Square, London NW1 (tel. 01–724 6624). Holidays catering for interests such as natural history, botany and painting.

**Explore Worldwide,** High St, Aldershot, Hants (tel. 0252–319448). Small group tours, treks and expeditions.

**Field Studies Council,** c/o Miss R. Evans, Flatford Mill Field Centre, E Bergholt, Colchester, Essex (tel. 0206–298283). Expeditions with an emphasis on botany, ornithology, butterflies and painting.

**Inter-Church Travel,** 45 Berkeley St, London W1 (tel. 01–734 0942). Tours and pilgrim routes to great religious centres.

**Mundi Color,** 276 Vauxhall Bridge Rd, London SW1 (tel. 01–834 3492). Agents for Iberia, *paradores*, fly-drive, and packages to many of the lesser known regions of Spain. Rather pricey.

**Ornitholidays,** 1–3 Victoria Drive, Bognor Regis, Sussex (tel. 0243–821230). Bird-watching expeditions.

**Ramblers Holidays Ltd,** 13 Longcroft House, Fretherne Rd, Welwyn Garden City, Herts (tel. 0707–331133). Walking holidays, combined with some sight-seeing.

**Travelscene,** 94 Baker St, London W1 (tel. 01–486 6411). City breaks, fly-drives and *parador* holidays to some of the less known regions.

**Waymark Holidays,** 295 Lillie Rd, London SW6 (tel. 01–385 5015). Small

group walking holidays.
**Wexas International,** Travel Dept, 45 Brompton Rd, London SW3 (tel. 01–589 3315). 'Packages for unpackaged people' — walking, riding, canoeing, exploring little-known areas.

The student travel agencies listed on p. 17 also do some packages, and see also the section on study opportunities for companies offering all-in study packages.

The following companies arrange 'tailor-made' group tours catering for special interests:

**Concertworld,** 6 Belmont Hill London SE13 (tel. 01–852 2035). Concert tours for orchestras and bands.
**Kestours,** Travel House, Elmers End, Beckenham, Kent (tel. 01–658 7313). Sports tours for clubs and teams.

## WHERE TO STAY

### Hotels/hostales/pensions
- Check with the tourist offices.

All this type of accommodation is very finely controlled by the tourist authorities and there is a fairly complicated system of classification which doesn't seem to bear much relation to what you get, or — necessarily — to the price you pay. Basically, all establishments display a pale blue plaque showing their official category, and a number of stars, as follows.

| | |
|---|---|
| H | — *Hotel:* from one to five stars |
| HR | — *Hotel Residencia:* the same but no meals available |
| Hs | — *Hostal:* less plush than a hotel, and going from one to three stars |
| HsR | — *Hostal Residencia:* again the same, but no meals |
| P | — *Pensión:* one to three stars |
| CH | — *Casa de Huéspedes* (guest house): no sub-categories |
| F | — *Fonda* (guest/boarding house): no sub-categories |

There is very little to choose between a P, a CH and an F. They don't usually take bookings in advance, and they're cheap. One star *hostales* and hotels are often slightly more expensive, but still within the bounds of affordability — say £5 (1,000 ptas) upwards a night for a double room. All these establishments are bound by law to display their tariffs on the back of the door of each room, and if you have any cause for complaint, you should ask for the *libro de reclamaciones* or complaints book.

There is a good scattering of all these sorts of establishments throughout the country, and tourist offices (including the London one) can let you have free lists for each province. The CHs, Fs, and lesser Ps are not usually included in these, but as a general rule you'll find these easily, either in the old central parts of towns, or on main roads going into villages and smaller towns. You will also find places just advertising *camas* (beds), which are likely to be cheapest of all. Out of season you should never run into much trouble finding somewhere with vacancies.

In season you'll have to have a bit more foresight and not leave finding anywhere to stay until too late in the day, and in certain tourist areas (San Sebastián, Santander, the more built-up parts of the Rías Bajas in Galicia, and, of course, the *costas*) you'll have to be prepared for quite a struggle to find anywhere, especially at weekends and *fiestas*. On the *costas* in particular, most accommodation tends to be block booked in advance by package companies. In these cases it's best to head inland to the nearest town.

Outside the tourist areas, and especially in the vast interior of the country, the main problem is likely to be the huge distances between towns and villages, and slow means of communication between them, so if you're touring, don't plan an ambitious day's travelling and find you're stuck in the middle of nowhere as nightfall approaches.

All these places vary incredibly in terms of what you get for your money, so ask to see the room beforehand. Bedlinen is usually scrupulously clean, but the standard of plumbing/electrical fitting may leave a lot to be desired. Noise can be a major problem with open windows, little soundproofing, and Spaniards shouting at each other until the early hours!

## Youth hostels
- **Red Española de Albergues Juveniles,** c/Ortega y Gasset 71, 28006 Madrid (tel. 91–401 1300, ex. 265 and 319).
- **YHA** (England and Wales), Trevelyan House, 8 St Stephens Hill, St Albans, Herts (tel. 0727–55215).
- **International Youth Hostel Federation,** Midland Bank Chambers, Howardsgate, Welwyn Garden City, Herts.

Spain has a good network of youth hostels *(albergues juveniles)*, although a lot of them aren't open all the year round. As a rule, they're not particularly useful for general touring, as you need to book in advance, and they're often off the major lines of communication. However, their attraction is that they tend to be well located for exploring remote or beautiful areas of the country that you wouldn't get to otherwise. Some have good sports and other facilities laid on, and they're cheap — about £6 full board, or £2–£3 bed and breakfast. However, you'll need an **International Youth Hostelling Card** (in advance, although you can join on the spot), and almost certainly you'll need to book in advance, as they're heavily used by Spanish youth groups. As in the UK, there are various rules to be observed in hostels — for instance you have to be in by around 2300, help with chores, etc.

Booking can be done either through the central Madrid office, through the regional booking offices in Spain listed in the relevant regional sections later in the book, or through TIVE student travel offices in various towns, also listed later. The Madrid office (see above) will supply you with a free map and list of hostels, or you can buy Vol. 1 of the *International Youth Hostel Handbook* (price £2.95) from the YHA here.

You can join the YHA at any youth hostel in this country, or by writing to the St Albans address given above. Despite its name there is no upper age limit on membership. The Youth Hostel Association can also arrange travel for individuals and groups.

**Paradores**
- Tourist offices:
- *Spanish Country Inns and Paradors* by Karen Brown (Harrap Columbus).
- *Paradores of Spain* by Jan Read and Maite Manjón (Macmillan, 1977).

Like youth hostels, *paradores* offer government-run accommodation, but at the other end of the scale in terms of cost, despite being fairly heavily subsidised. There are over 70 *paradores* throughout Spain, all located in glorious settings, and/or in historic buildings — castles, monasteries and palaces. The level of furnishing (all old Spanish style), service and catering (a heavy emphasis on local dishes and wines) is excellent, but at around £40 or so a night it's probably not worth dwelling on the subject here. (However, there's usually no objection to non-residents having a drink in the bar or a nose around the gardens.)

**Mountain huts**
- *Guía de Refugios de Montaña* published by the Ministry of Tourism
- Mountaineering federations (see regional sections later in the book).

In mountain areas (and there are a lot of them), you'll find some strategically located huts, or *refugios de montaña*, for the use of hikers and climbers. These vary considerably in the level of provision — some are unmanned and are little more than a roof and bare boards, others offer a respectable service.

They're run by a variety of organisations and clubs, from whom one must seek permission to use them, and they're all listed in the guide book (see above) available for consultation in tourist offices (including the London office). The guide gives you exact directions to the hut, tells you who runs it, whether meals/water are available, where to get the keys from, etc., as well as other useful information such as the best walks, climbs, views in the area.

Generally, the north of the country (Picos de Europa, Pyrenees, Montes Vascos) is better provided with *refugios* than the south.

**Monasteries**
- Tourist offices
- **Confederación de Religiosos,** c/Núñez de Balboa 99, Madrid (tel. 91-262 7696).

Spanish monasteries, especially those in the north and Old Castile, have a long tradition of offering hospitality to visitors, and those that do are listed in the regional sections later. Religious faith is by no means a requirement, but a desire for peace and a retreat from the outside world certainly is. Prices are reasonable, and despite the fact that some monasteries are suffering from depopulation and tend to have plenty of available room, as a matter of courtesy you should write or at least phone to make arrangements beforehand, not just turn up. (You'll note the monasteries listed later don't have much of an address. Don't worry about this — it's just that they're in the middle of nowhere and everyone round about knows where they are anyway.)

## University accommodation

If you're doing a 'Spanish for foreigners' course, most universities at least give you help finding accommodation — in some it is included in the price.

If you're doing some other sort of course, you can ask for a list of *colegios mayores* (residential colleges), either from the university itself or from the provincial education office. These are single-sex establishments offering reasonably priced accommodation and meals for longish-term stays, and can be approached directly.

## Camping
- **Federación Española de Campings,** Gran Vía 88, Madrid.

There are over 700 campsites in Spain, mostly on the coast, and you can get a list and map from the above organisation, or from any tourist office. They're categorised 1, 2, 3 or luxury (1 has the most facilities, after luxury), and all have basic minimum facilities of drinking water, toilets, washing facilities, rubbish collection, warden, etc. In remote areas you can camp rough, with a bit of discretion, as long as you're not within 1 kilometre of an established campsite or populated area. Camping rough is not approved of in tourist areas.

## Casas de labranza
- *Guía de Vacaciones en Casas de Labranza*, published by the Ministry of Tourism, available for consultation in tourist offices.

*Casas de labranza* are basically farmhouses or homesteads which offer cheap accommodation to visitors as a way of boosting the family income, very similar to the bed and breakfast system in Britain except that you are usually expected to stay a week or a fortnight, and often to muck in with chores about the house and farm. Sometimes accommodation is offered separately from the rest of the family.

It's an ideal way of learning the language, and getting to stay in remote rural areas which otherwise you might not visit, although it requires adaptability and an affinity with this kind of thing.

The arrangement is made directly with the owner, although the guide lists prices, so it's a question of getting a few likely looking addresses, and firing off letters — perhaps a little awkward to arrange but well worth the effort, especially for the hard-up.

## Renting/sharing

Flats to rent are advertised in the local press — look under *Se alquila* or *alquileres*. Flats are described by size (square metres), and rents quoted are per month. Spanish people complain that it's difficult to find rented accommodation, and that what there is is expensive, but they seem to end up with spacious, centrally located flats for a fraction of what you'd pay in Britain.

If you're looking for something in a particular area, one possibility is to ask the local *porteros* manning the main doors of each block of flats. They get to know of any vacancies that are coming up and put you in touch with the right people. You won't find much single-person accommodation available though, so sharing is almost a necessity. University notice boards are a good source of contacts here, as are TIVE offices, youth information offices, etc.

### Villas and holiday apartments
In tourist areas out of season you can rent these reasonably cheaply on a fairly short-term basis. Many are advertised in the British press (especially Sunday newspapers) or there is a wide variety of packages offering this type of accommodation. On the spot, you could consult the ads in local papers or estate agents, but the best and cheapest deals tend to be struck as a result of just asking around and making contact with local people who may have been given charge of the places whilst the owners are absent. In the summer, and especially during July and August, prices soar and even a 2 week package can seem exorbitant.

### Buying
Probably not a viable possibility for most, as, although house prices in some areas at least are considerably cheaper than in Britain, you're expected to put down a sizeable deposit, and mortgages tend to be for only 10 or 15 years. If you're tempted by the attractive-looking deals hawked around by the timeshare/villa salesmen of the *costas* do get a lawyer who knows what he/she is doing and can explain the ins and outs of everything to you. There are all sorts of rip-offs perpetrated on people through loopholes in the complex Spanish conveyancing law. Beware of the high-pressure salesmanship here, and if you really want to buy somewhere look to see what is available on the general market through estate agents, ads in local press, etc., to get some perspective on the prices being charged.

## EXCHANGES
If your living accommodation in the UK is reasonably attractive, a home swop can give you a very cheap holiday, and one which puts you right in the middle of things — immediately you're *living* there rather than being a tourist. Whole areas of Spain you might never have considered visiting are opened up to you, and instead of wandering around dumbly with a guide book in one hand and camera in the other, waiting for the restaurants to open, you have to cope with everyday situations, like getting on with the neighbour's dog, making the lift work or trying to buy *less* than a kilo of radishes from the local market!

The organisations listed below specialise in putting people in contact with potential home-swoppers abroad, and perhaps surprisingly you hear nothing but good reports of the experience people have had. Many advertise their services in educational magazines, so you've got a good chance of swopping with a Spanish teacher. All work basically the same way — for a small fee (£25 or so), your home is advertised in a directory/magazine which is produced two or three times a year, copies of which you also receive. It's then up to you to look through it and get in touch with the people you fancy swopping with, although lots of help and advice is provided.

If you haven't got a home to swop, but fancy renting somewhere, you can become a 'non-listed' member of the scheme. You then negotiate a suitable fee instead of swopping.

All the agencies below have a good selection of swops available in various parts of Spain:

**Home Interchange,** 8 Hillside, Farningham, Kent (tel. 0322–4527).
**Home-Swop,** 15 Benyon Gardens, Culford, Bury St Edmunds, Suffolk (tel. 0284–84315 — 24 hours). Can also arrange rents/lets, paying guest visits, youth exchanges.
**Intervac,** 6 Siddals Lane, Allestree, Derby (tel. 0332–558931). Can also arrange bed and breakfast type accommodation, lets, youth visits and exchanges, and discounts on Sealink ferries/Pilgrim air.
**The X-Change Register,** Freepost, Larkhill, ML9 1BR (tel. 0698–885672). Works slightly differently from the rest — for approximately £35 you receive 3 potential names for home-exchange, or one for a rental booking.

## Student/youth exchanges
- **Central Bureau for Educational Visits and Exchanges** (see p. 42), The Youth Exchange Centre, Seymour Mews House, Seymour Mews, London W1 (tel. 01–487 5961).

This type of arrangement, beloved by school language departments, is for young people living at home, who are 'matched' with a Spanish counterpart, and spend 2 weeks or a month in their home in exchange for inviting them back to theirs on some other occasion. Many of these types of arrangements come into being through the 'school links' department of the Central Bureau for Educational Visits and Exchanges, whereby whole classes of language students have some sort of on-going contact with a similar group in Spain. Visits may be arranged either through the school, or on an individual basis.

Spanish students wanting to come to the UK vastly outnumber British students wanting to go over there. (In Spain, English has taken over from French as the main foreign language taught in schools, while in Britain many schools have to struggle to continue offering Spanish.) If you're interested you should be able to pick and choose — look out for homes with private pools!

One of the main problems with the system is the 'matching' process, so it's best to have some sort of correspondence going with your partner to make sure you have things in common. If your language isn't up to much it helps if you can get involved in activities that don't mean constantly striving to be understood — sports, listening to music, dancing/discoing, etc. — you'll pick up an enormous amount of Spanish anyway, without attempting a 24 hour a day conversation class.

The Youth Exchange Centre provides help (including financial assistance) to groups (as opposed to individuals) wishing to make contact with their Spanish counterparts, but doesn't arrange exchanges as such. A whole range of back-up advice and information on organising exchange visits is contained in their publications *Help* (£5 a copy) and *Youth Exchange News*, a free news sheet.

There are several private organisations (listed below) which can arrange this type of contact, with or without travel, and it may well be worth while contacting the various Spanish organisations in the UK (see pp. 41–42) who, especially as summer approaches, may be in touch with people in Spain in search of exchanges — strictly on a one-off basis of course.

**Centros Europeos** c/Príncipe 12–6º A, Madrid (tel. 91–232 7230).
**El Club de Relaciones Culturales Internacionales,** Departamento Sociocultural, c/Ferraz 82–2º–D, 28008 Madrid (tel. 91–479 6303 and 91–479 6446).
**Intercambio Español,** c/o Verbatim Language Services, Grove Cottage, 1a Grove Road North, Southsea, Hants (tel. 0705–833121).
**The Robertson Organisation,** 44 Willoughby Rd, London NW3 (tel. 01–435 4907). The deal, if struck, includes escorted travel to Spain.
**Intervac** and **Home Interchange** (see Exchanges, p. 26) can also put potential 'exchangees' in contact with each other through their directory service.

The travel agents Thomas Cook provide a special travel service for groups organising youth exchanges: contact Mike Hinton, Youth Exchange, Thomas Cook Ltd, PO Box 36, Thorpe Wood, Peterborough (tel. 0733–502597).

### Homestays
- *Home from Home* published by Central Bureau, price £3.50.

If you want the experience of living with a Spanish family without actually having to receive a Spanish student in your house in return, there are various 'homestay' schemes worth investigating:

**The Experiment in International Living,** Upper Wyche, Malvern, Worcs. (tel. 06845–62577). 'A non-profit making educational association founded in 1932 to promote greater understanding, mutual respect and friendship between the nations of the world.' Arranges homestays with Spanish families for individuals and groups. Fees are about £200 for 2 weeks (excluding travel, insurance and spending money), and discounts are available for language students.

**Servas,** 6 Addison Rd, Hove, E. Sussex (tel. 0273-7287763). Also at 77 Elm Park Mansions, Park Walk, London SW10 (tel. 01-352 0203). An international movement founded in 1949 to promote peace and understanding between nations. Hosts in over 80 countries (about 70-80 in Spain) receive guests for 2 nights, who share the family's activities, offer help where needed, exchange views, and generally learn about conditions in the country, all with the idea of encouraging international understanding and good will. Prospective guests, or 'travellers' must pay a small fee for registration and hire of host lists, and be approved by the organisation. You don't necessarily have to offer to be a host in order to make use of the scheme.

**Euroyouth,** 301 Westborough Rd, Westcliff-on-Sea, Essex (tel. 0702 341434). Operates a number of schemes, including paying guest accommodation (with the option of language courses — see p. 44), and 'holiday guest stays' where applicants receive free *en famille* accommodation in return for making conversation with the host/host's children in English for several hours daily. Open to anyone with clear and correct English as a mother tongue, but demand exceeds supply, so there is no guarantee of placement. The organisation charges a fee of approximately £45 for its services.

**EuroAcademy,** 77a George St, Croydon, Surrey (tel. 01-681 2905). Arranges homestays for groups of 10 minimum between ages of 14 and 26 in the Valencia area.

**En Famille Agency** (Overseas), Westbury House, Queens Lane, Arundel, Sussex (tel. 0903-883266). Accommodation with Spanish families arranged for adults or young people (also families and couples) for any length of time, at any time of the year. £30 fee, plus about £90 per week for full board, less for half board.

**Host and Guest Service,** 592A Kings Rd, London SW6 (tel. 01-731 5340). Paying guest accommodation arranged for students, holidaymakers and business people. Prices vary according to type of arrangement, whether full board or bed and breakfast.

## GETTING ABOUT

Generally public transport in Spain is cheap but slow. The geographical problems of enormous distances and mountainous terrain mean that routes can be somewhat circuitous, and this goes for rail and road. Note that many bus and train services leave very early in the morning — in order to reach their destination in time for a good 2 hour lunch!

The frequency and efficiency of services will depend much on where you go, and some comments on this are included in the regional sections later in the book.

### By rail
The Spanish national rail company is called **RENFE** (head office at Avda.

Pio XII s/n, Madrid (tel. 91–733 6037) ). All major towns have a railway station where you can get information on times of trains and buy your ticket in advance if you want to. It's also possible to buy the *Guía RENFE* which gives train timetables for the whole of Spain and costs approximately 500 pesetas. You can also book your ticket through travel agents like the **Viajes Wagons Lits** chain.

Major railway stations have different departure notice boards for *largo recorrido* (long distance) and *cercanías* (local) trains, and sometimes *medio recorrido* (middle distance) as well. There are also different types of train: the *Talgo* (RENFE's showpiece), the *TER* and the *electrotrén* are the fastest trains (but never seem to reach their full potential!), while the *expreso* and the *rápido* are stopping trains and are neither express nor rapid.

Price structures are very complicated: there are all sorts of supplements to pay depending on the type of train, the class of ticket you buy, and when you travel. There is also a calendar of *días azules* ('blue days') when certain discounts are offered, but this is something you'll have to go into on the spot — if you've got the patience.

Generally speaking though, prices are very reasonable. Bicycles can be transported in the guard's van on most trains, provided they are labelled and stripped of any removable accessories. Larger pieces of luggage will also be transported in this way and collected at the end of the journey: the relevant term is *facturar* (to 'check in').

As well as the national railway network there are also a number of others:
- **FEVE** *(Ferrocárriles de Vía Estrecha)* — narrow gauge railways which run all the way along the north coast of Spain from Bilbao to El Ferrol in Galicia, and inland from Bilbao to León.
- There is also another narrow gauge network in the Valencia area (see p. 239).
- The Basque and Catalan governments also run their own railways: *Eusko Trenbideak* and *Ferrocarrils de la Generalitat de Catalunya*.

### By coach and bus

Almost everywhere that is approachable via an asphalted road is served by some sort of bus service, although again you'll find yourself taking some circuitous but often spectacular routes. Coach services are generally privately owned; in some towns several different companies exist using different termini, so you'll have to check this out locally.

One of the great pleasures of travelling by coach in Spain is setting out very early in the morning and then stopping around breakfast time at some wayside bar in the middle of nowhere where everyone piles out to fortify themselves with coffee and *coñac*. Such stops are a ritual on long distance journeys, but tend to spin out the travelling times.

Local buses are generally run by town councils and there is usually a good cheap service. In general, bus or coach travel is a very cheap and effective way of getting around in Spain, and can be as fast as by rail.

## By car
- **Real Automobil Club de España** (RACE! - Spain's AA or RAC) General Sanjurjo 10, Madrid 3.
- See p. 20 for information about car hire and importing your own car to Spain.

Spain uses the International Highway Code and cars drive on the right. Priority is given to cars on the right, which is especially important to remember at roundabouts. There are few motorways in Spain and you have to pay a toll to use almost all of them. Other roads are very variable — a poor road with little traffic will take you fairly speedily across the interior, but the going can be very slow in some mountain areas even on good roads.

Traffic is usually light out of towns but heavy within them. The speed limit is 130 kilometres per hour on motorways, 90-110 kmph on other roads, and 60 kmph in towns. It is compulsory to wear seat belts in the front seat and to carry a warning triangle in the car in case of breakdown or accident. It is also compulsory to use headlights (sidelights within towns) after dark, and you are required to carry spare light bulbs in the car in case the ones you are using become defective. The most common road signs are as follows:

| | |
|---|---|
| CEDA EL PASO | Give Way |
| DESPACIO | Slow |
| DESVIO | Diversion |
| PASO PROHIBIDO | No entry |
| CURVA PELIGROSA | Dangerous bend |
| DIRECCION UNICA | One way street |
| PROHIBIDO APARCAR | No parking |
| OBRAS | Road Works |
| PELIGRO | Danger |
| LLEVAR LA DERECHA | Drive on the right |
| LLEVAR LA IZQUIERDA | Drive on the left |

## Hitching
Hitching is illegal on motorways but quite possible elsewhere. Some useful information on hitching in Spain, including the best places to stand when hitching out of some of the major towns, is given in *Europe: A Manual for Hitch Hikers*, published by Vacation Work, Oxford.

Another possibility is pre-arranging lifts, and paying your share of the petrol. You can do this on an informal basis through university notice boards or Youth Information Offices, or through various agencies, as follows:

**Comparco**, c/Rivas 31–6º–1ª, Barcelona (tel. 93–246 69098)
**A Dedo**, c/Mayor 1, oficina 21, Madrid (tel. 91–231 7519)
**Veco**, María 11, Malaga (tel. 952–254584)
**Tandem**, Triumfo 4, San Sebastián (tel. 943–469370)
**Ircon**, Valencia (tel. 963–331 0062)

## COMMUNICATIONS AND THE MEDIA

**Telephones**
There are public phone boxes everywhere, but if you want to call Britain you'll have to find one which states specifically *internacional*. The code from Spain is 07-44 plus the normal code without the initial 0. (For instance if you're phoning London dial 07-44-1 and then the number you want.) Dialling instructions are given fairly intelligibly even to non-Spanish speakers.

It's also possible to make calls from telephone exchanges (*telefónicas*), found centrally in most towns, where you pay over the counter for the call afterwards. Unfortunately, though, the cheap rate for phoning abroad doesn't come into effect till 8 pm, and these offices are usually closed by then.

Telephone codes within Spain are organised provincially, as follows:

| | | | | | |
|---|---|---|---|---|---|
| Alava | 945 | Granada | 958 | Las Palmas | 928 |
| Albacete | 967 | Guadalajara | 911 | Pontevedra | 986 |
| Alicante | 965 | Guipúzcoa | 943 | Salamanca | 923 |
| Almería | 951 | Huelva | 955 | Santander | 942 |
| Avila | 918 | Huesca | 974 | Segovia | 911 |
| Badajoz | 924 | Jaen | 953 | Sevilla | 954 |
| Baleares | 971 | León | 973 | Soria | 975 |
| Barcelona | 93 | Lérida | 973 | Tarragona | 977 |
| Burgos | 947 | Logroño | 941 | Tenerife | 922 |
| Cáceres | 927 | Lugo | 982 | Teruel | 974 |
| Cadiz | 956 | Madrid | 91 | Toledo | 925 |
| Castellón | 964 | Málaga | 952 | Valencia | 96 |
| Ceuta | 956 | Melilla | 952 | Valladolid | 983 |
| Ciudad Real | 926 | Murcia | 968 | Vizcaya | 94 |
| Córdoba | 957 | Navarra | 948 | Zamora | 988 |
| La Coruña | 981 | Orense | 988 | Zaragoza | 976 |
| Cuenca | 966 | Oviedo | 985 | | |
| Gerona | 972 | Palencia | 988 | | |

If you're calling Spain from Britain, the number to dial is 01-34 plus the provincial code minus the initial 9.

For operator services in Spain dial 009.

For directory enquiries dial the provincial code plus 03 except for:

| | | | | |
|---|---|---|---|---|
| Avila | 91 + 04 | | Segovia | 91 + 02 |
| Guadalajara | 91 + 05 | | Teruel | 974 + 04 |
| Palencia | 988 + 04 | | Zamora | 988 + 01 |

Telephone directories are a useful source of information in Spain, especially the *Yellow Pages*. These are available for consultation in the *telefónicas*, and are organised provincially. Note that in Spanish alphabetical order, ch comes after all the cs, and ll after all the ls.

## Post

Post offices are *correos*, and are quite separate from the *telefónicas*, although they do deal with telegrams. Stamps are also available from tobacconists (*estancos*). Telex and Fax are widely used in Spain.

## Addressess

Spanish addresses are written 'backwards', for example:

Avda Aurora 56–6º–D = Flat D, 6th Floor, 56 Aurora Avenue

When the road is just a plain street *(calle)* this is indicated by the sign c/, which in practice is often omitted, e.g. San Bernardo 2 = 2 San Bernardo St. The letters s/n after the name of a street stand for *sin número*, indicating that the building doesn't have a street number. The postcode (if used) is written before the name of the town, and is a 5 figure number, the first 2 digits of which correspond to the province, e.g. 28008 Madrid = Madrid-8.

On envelopes men are addressed as *Sr D (Señor Don)* followed by full name, that is Christian name and both surnames (Spanish people use both parents' surnames, the father's first). Women are either addressed as *Srta Dª (Señorita Doña)* if young and unmarried, or as *Sra Dª (Señora Doña)* if married. Other titles include *Doctor/Doctora* (Dr): *Reverendo/Reverenda* (Revd, Revd Mother); *Fr* and *Sor* (Brother/Sister). People in high posts are *Ilmo Sr* or *Ilma Sra/Srta*, or, if Ambassadors and the like, *Excmo/a* etc.

It is customary politeness to write the sender's address on the back of the envelope. Bear this in mind before you throw any envelope away — the address might not be contained inside. For letter-writing formulae, see p. 274.

## Television

There are two state-run TV channels: TVE1 is on air all day, while TVE2 doesn't start until 1800 or 1900. Both shut around midnight—later at weekends and *fiestas*—and contain a mix of home-grown and imported programmes. The news is called *Telediario* and is normally on at 1500 and 2030, and again around midnight. (A classic example of the Spanish '*mañana* mentality' (which with many features of the old Spain has now disappeared) was always turning on the television around 1500 and waiting up to half an hour for the 3 o'clock news to begin.) Both channels screen lengthy sessions of adverts.

## The Press

The best known national paper is without doubt *El País*, which appeared very successfully with democracy and is widely respected. *Diario 16* is also a new publication, more popular in tone than *El País*. Both are published in regional versions as well as from Madrid.

Papers still going from the Francoist era are *La Vanguardia*, published in Cataluña; *Ya*, a Catholic paper, also published in Cataluña, and *ABC*, representing old-style culture.

Newspaper reading, although on the increase, is still not particularly widespread in Spain, but there are various weekly news magazines *(Tiempo, Cambio 16* and, nudies and all, *Interviú)* which are popular, as are the regional or local newspapers. (Newspapers are listed in each of the regional chapters later in the book.)

## LIBRARIES

Included in the regional section are the addresses of some of the best libraries in Spain for research purposes, but there are of course public libraries in most sizeable towns. Any public office will point you in the right direction locally, or you can get a complete list from the **Ministerio de Cultura** (see p. 36).

There is a difficulty with using Spanish libraries, however, in that most use the 'closed shelf' system, which means you have to order books by name from the librarian, instead of being allowed to browse at leisure. Spanish people don't have the same tradition of using public libraries as a source of information as we do but — perhaps a result of 40 years under a one-party political system — tend to seek official answers to their questions from the department concerned, and accept only these (and then with deep mistrust) as the truth.

## SHOPS AND SHOPPING

The big Spanish department stores are **El Corte Inglés** and **Galerías Preciados,** which have branches in most major towns and cities, and stay open right through the day from 0900 or 1000 in the morning till 2000 at night. They are good for browsing, and do at least have a different selection of goods from their British counterparts, but it's the smaller boutiques and shops that are the most interesting and, in general, still hold greater sway throughout Spain than the big stores. These shut for a long lunch break between about 1400 and 1700 and stay open till around 2000.

Spanish fashion design especially is coming into its own, and clothes, in particular shoes and leather accessories, can be some of the best buys. Spain's artisan traditions still survive fairly vigorously, and good buys here, varying from region to region (see the regional sections later), are pottery, wickerwork, musical instruments (especially guitars) and wrought iron work. The government-run *artespaña* shops are worth looking out for if you're looking for this type of thing. If you like the rather heavy style of traditional Spanish wooden furniture this is very well priced too.

Prices tend to be very similar to those in Britain, although you may find some toiletries more expensive (you seem only to be able to buy a litre of cheap shampoo or a tiny quantity of something outrageously expensive). Food and wine are still cheap (many Spanish people would disagree, but they don't have to pay 30p for an orange in London!), provided you go for the loose, home-produced produce rather than pre-packaged varieties.

Hypermarkets are springing up on the main roads out of major cities, and everywhere but the smallest village has its little *supermercado*. However, the traditional covered markets have in no way been supplanted, and it's here that you'll get the most value — especially in terms of entertainment.

They're absolutely buzzing with life and have an amazing selection of fruit and vegetables.

Fish is a good buy everywhere, whereas meat tends to be rather more expensive and difficult to buy, if you want anything more complicated than a *filete*, as the Spanish butcher their animals differently from us. Dried fruit and nuts (especially the delicious *turrón*) are good buys, especially for bringing back to Britain. For up-market, deli-type food, look out for the **Mantequerías Leonesas** chain.

## THE ADMINISTRATION

During Franco's time trying to deal with the highly-bureaucratised Spanish Administration was a frustrating business. The attitude that prevailed amongst its functionaries was that the public were a nuisance, to be dissuaded from having any contact with government departments if at all possible, and certainly from making too many enquiries. Fortunately since democracy there is a greater concern with the dissemination of information useful to the public, and a more relaxed attitude generally. For instance it is now common to be immediately addressed as *tu* when entering a government-run office. With the devolution of power to regional governments, staff have developed a more positive attitude towards their role in relation to the public, and there is a sense that things are being achieved.

Nonetheless, British and other foreigners' experience of Spanish bureaucracy is still often extremely negative — they complain of unhelpful staff, obstructive and complicated legal machinery, and lack of information in general. In part, this is unavoidable — there are still hangovers from Francoism both in the procedures and in the attitudes of civil servants—but there are things you can do to avoid unnecessary frustration!

- Make sure you know which department deals with whatever it is you need. At the end of this section are included a list of the various Ministries, and the addresses of the various regional departments are included in the relevant regional sections later. Be prepared to accept that the first office you go to may not be the right one, but equally, if you know it is, don't be fobbed off too easily.
- Find out your rights by seeing a copy of the relevant legislation if necessary. Many workers who deal with the public are simply uninformed themselves (in one case a doctor was told that the Canary Islands weren't part of the EEC) but nonetheless find it impossible to argue if faced with written proof of the letter of the law.
- Find out what documents are needed in advance, and take multiple copies of them with you. For official purposes photocopies are not accepted unless countersigned.
- Get your timing right, first regarding office hours (0900 to 1400 Monday to Saturday are the usual opening times, and don't turn up at the last minute as there may be a queue), secondly regarding whatever it is you're asking for (dates of application etc.). Have patience — all bureaucracies move slowly.

- If you don't speak particularly good Spanish, take someone with you who does.

## Ministries

**Presidencia del Gobierno** (Prime Minister's Office), Palacio de la Moncloa, Madrid (tel. 91–244 0200)
**Ministerio de Administración Territorial** (relations with autonomous governments), Paseo de la Castellana 3, Madrid (tel. 91–410 5190)
**Ministerio de Agricultura, Pesca y Alimentación** (Agriculture, Fisheries and Food), Paseo Infanta Isabel 1, Madrid (tel. 91–467 2400)
**Ministerio de Asuntos Exteriores** (Foreign Ministry) Plaza de la Provincia 1, Madrid (tel. 91–266 4800)
**Ministerio de Cultura** (Culture), Plaza del Rey, Madrid (tel. 91–429 2444)
**Ministerio de Defensa** (Defence), Paseo de la Castellana 109, Madrid (tel. 91–455 5000)
**Ministerio de Economía y Hacienda** (Economy and Tax), Alcalá 11, Madrid (tel. 91–460 2000)
**Ministerio de Educación y Ciencia** (Education and Science), Alcalá 34, Madrid (tel. 91–232 1300)
**Ministerio de Industria y Energía** (Industry and Energy), Paseo de la Castellana 160, Madrid (tel. 91–458 8010)
**Ministerio del Interior** (Home Office), Amador de los Ríos 5, Madrid (tel. 91–419 3900)
**Ministerio de Justicia** (Justice), San Bernardo 45, Madrid (tel. 91–479 8111)
**Ministerio de Obras Públicas y Urbanismo** (Public Works and Town Planning), Paseo de la Castellana 67 (tel. 91–253 1600)
**Ministerio de Sanidad y Consumo** (Health and Consumer Ministry), Paseo del Prado 18 y 20, Madrid (tel. 91–239 7000)
**Ministerio de Trabajo y Seguridad Social** (Employment and Social Security), Nuevos Ministerios, Madrid (tel. 91–253 6000)
**Ministerio de Transportes, Turismo y Comunicaciones** (Transport, Tourism and Communications), Nuevos Ministerios, Madrid (tel. 91–456 1144)

## The Youth Service

- Instituto de la Juventud, c/Ortega y Gasset 71, 28006 Madrid (tel. 91–401 1300).

This is the official government youth department, dependant on the Ministry of Culture. It is engaged in organising and promoting opportunities for young people in areas such as the arts, conservation, travel and contact with international youth, through competitions, workshops, conferences, exhibitions, summer camps, etc. The **Red Española de Albergues Juveniles** (Spanish Youth Hostel Association), the **Servicio Voluntario Internacional de España** (Spain's main agency for voluntary work), and the **TIVE offices** (student travel agencies — see p. 39) are all run through the **Instituto de la Juventud**.

The institute is also concerned with providing an information service for young people, and to this end publishes a fortnightly magazine *Guía*, in which the various competitions and activities are publicised. It also publishes books on youth themes, including the useful *Guía de los Jóvenes*, which provides welfare advice and outlines the rights and responsibilities of young people in Spain today.

All publications are on sale at the address given above, which is open Monday to Friday 0900–1400 and 1600–1800, and Saturdays from 0900–1400. There is also a central **Youth Information Office** at c/Marqués de Riscal 16, 28010 Madrid (tel. 91–419 7600), open at the same times, and regional youth information offices in most big towns, the addresses of which are given in the regional sections later.

## OTHER KEY CONTACTS

**Political Parties**
**Alianza Popular** (AP — ultra-conservative, strong in Galicia), Génova 13, Madrid
**Centro Democrático y Social** (CDS — small centre party formed by Adolfo Suárez who, with the King, was a key figure in the transition to democracy), Jorge Juan 30 – 5º, Madrid
**Convergencia Democrática de Cataluña** (CDC — Catalan centrist party which dominates the **Generalitat**), Valencia 231, Barcelona
**Esquerra Repúblicana de Cataluña** (ERC — left-wing Catalan party), Villarroel 45, Barcelona
**Euskadiko Ezquerra** (EE — Basque left-wing party), Plaza de Guipúzcoa 11 – 1º, San Sebastian
**Partido Comunista de España** (PCE— Spanish Communist Party), Santísima Trinidad 5, Madrid
**Partido Demócrata Popular** (PDP — small centre-right party strong in Cantabria)
**Partido Nacionalista Vasco** (PNV — traditional Basque nationalist party), Gran Vía 38 – 7º, Bilbao
**Partido Socialista Obrero Español** (PSOE — ruling socialist party), Ferraz 68 y 70, Madrid
**Unión Liberal** (UL — small liberal party), Pza de las Cortes 4, Madrid.

**Sports Federations**
The relevant national sports federation is the base line of contact for people interested in practising any particular sport in Spain, assuming that they have no contacts with local clubs. The sports federation can supply lists of such clubs, information on where to find particular facilities, who to get in touch with to arrange matches/meetings, what restrictions pertain, and a whole range of other information depending on the nature of the sport in question. (For example, in the case of sports requiring special insurance, the federation can usually arrange this.)
**Federación Española de Actividades Subacuáticas** (Underwater Sports), Santaló 15–2º, Barcelona

**Federación Española de Ajedrez** (Chess), Coslada 10, Madrid
**Federación Española de Atletismo** (Athletics), Miguel Angel 16–1º D, Madrid
**Federación Española de Automovilismo** (Rally Driving), Santísima Trinidad 30, Madrid
**Federación Española de Badminton** (Badminton), Ronda de Toledo 16–2º, Madrid
**Federación Española de Baloncesto** (Basketball), Ferraz 16, Madrid
**Federación Española de Beisbol** (Baseball), Coslada 10, Madrid
**Federación Española de Billar** (Snooker), Alcántara 48, Madrid
**Federación Española de Bolos** (Bowls), Fernando el Católico 54, Madrid
**Federación Española de Boxeo** (Boxing), Ferraz 16, Madrid
**Federación Española de Caza** (Hunting/Shooting), Ortega y Gasset 5–4º, Madrid
**Federación Española de Ciclismo** (Cycling), Ferraz 16, Madrid
**Federación Española de Colombicultura** (Pigeon Breeding), Ximénez de Sandoval 8, Valencia
**Federación Española de Colombofilia** (Pigeon Racing), Eloy Gonzalo 34, Madrid
**Federación Española de Esgrima** (Fencing), Ferraz 16, Madrid
**Federación Española de Deporte Aereo** (Air Sports), Ferraz 16, Madrid
**Federación Española de Deportes de Invierno** (Winter Sports), Claudio Cloello 32, Madrid
**Federación Española de Deporte para Minusválidos** (Sport for the Disabled), Ferraz 16, Madrid
**Federación Española de Espeleología** (Caving), Avda Francesc Cambó 14–9º, Barcelona
**Federación Española de Esquí Nautico** (Waterskiing), Sabino Arana 30–1º, Barcelona
**Federación Española de Fútbol** (Soccer), Alberto Bosch 13, Madrid
**Federación Española de Galguera** (Greyhound Racing), Barquillo 19, Madrid
**Federación Española de Gimnasia** (Gymnastics), Velázquez 10, Madrid
**Federación Española de Golf** (Golf), Capitan Haya 9, Madrid
**Federación Española de Halterofilia** (Weightlifting), Alberto Aguilera 3, Madrid
**Federación Española de Hípica** (Show Jumping/Dressage), Montesquinza 8, Madrid
**Federación Española de Hockey** (Hockey), Goya 20, Madrid
**Federación Española de Judo** (Judo), Hortaleza 108, Madrid
**Federación Española de Karate** (Karate), General Martínez Campos 15–6º, Madrid
**Federación Española de Lucha** (Wrestling), José Abascal 47, Madrid
**Federación Española de Montañismo** (Mountaineering), Alberto Aguilera 3, Madrid
**Federación Española de Motociclismo** (Motorcycling), General Pardiñas 71–1º, Madrid
**Federación Española de Motonáutica** (Motorboating), Avda de América

33, Madrid
**Federación Española de Natación** (Swimming), Conde de Peñalver 61, Madrid
**Federación Española de Patinaje** (Skating), Eduardo Dato 7, Madrid
**Federación Española de Pelota** (Pelota), Los Madrazo 11, Madrid
**Federación Española de Pesca** (Fishing), Navas de Tolosa 3, Madrid
**Federación Española de Piragüismo** (Canoeing), Cea Bermúdez 14, Madrid
**Federación Española de Polo** (Polo), Comandante Zorita 13, Madrid
**Federación Española de Remo** (Rowing), Nuñez de Balboa 16, Madrid
**Federación Española de Rugby** (Rugby), Ferraz 16, Madrid
**Federación Española de Salvamiento y Socorrismo** (Lifesaving), Goya 83–1º D, Madrid
**Federación Española de Squash** (Squash), Curta 14, Madrid
**Federación Española de Tenis** (Tennis), Avda. Diagonal 618, Barcelona
**Federación Española de Tenis de Mesa** (Table Tennis), Ferraz 16, Madrid
**Federación Española de Tiro con Arco** (Archery), Núñez de Balboa 13, Madrid
**Federación Española de Tiro de Pichón** (Clay Pigeon Shooting), Ferraz 82, Madrid
**Federación Española de Tiro Olímpico** (Shot Putting), Barquillo 21, Madrid
**Federación Española de Vela** (Sailing), Juan Vigón 23, Madrid
**Federación Española de Voleibol** (Volleyball), Valenzuela 7–1º, Madrid

The Spanish equivalent of the Sports Council is the **Consejo Superior de Deportes**, Avda Martín Fierro s/n, Madrid 3 (tel. 91–449 7300).

## TIVE Offices
These are official student travel agencies, affiliated to various international student travel associations. Addresses are given in the regional sections later. They offer the following services:

- issue of student cards, including Youth Hostel Association cards
- reservation service for youth hostels
- cheap flights, ferry crossings and rail tickets both within Spain and abroad
- package tours for groups and for individuals (see especially their cheap winter deals to the Canaries, and their skiing packages)
- educational exchange facilities for Spanish school groups.

They also serve as a general place of contact for young people. To be eligible to use their services, you must be under 26 or a student under 30, or a child or spouse of the same, or a youth leader or teacher.

## Trades unions
Organised politically in Spain, the most important are:

**Comisiones Obreras** (CCOO — nominally communist), Fernández de la Hoz 12, Madrid
**Unión General de Trabajadores** (UGT — socialist), San Bernardo 20, Madrid

The Spanish equivalent of the CBI is the **Confederación Española de Organizaciones Empresariales** (CEDE), Diego de León 50, Madrid.

## Other contacts

**ICONA (Instituto para la Conservación de la Naturaleza)**, Ministerio de Agricultura, Paseo Infanta Isabel 1, Madrid. This is the organisation which is in charge of Spain's National Parks and Wildlife Reserves, and controls fishing in many of Spain's rivers and reservoirs. It has offices in every province, the addresses of which, where relevant, are given in the regional listings. These can supply information on the restrictions pertaining to shooting and fishing (both as regards the close season for different species, and quotas of specimens), and issue licences. The institute also has a publications service, which produces some excellent information leaflets and maps on areas of particular natural interest.

**Federación Española de Universidades Populares,** Modesto Lafuente 63–2º, Madrid (tel. 91–234 7139). Federation of 'Peoples Universities' (mostly concerned with teaching literacy and basic skills to older people who missed out on educational opportunities).

**Grupo Nacional de Agencias de Viajes Españolas,** Duque de Medinaceli 2, Madrid. Spanish association of travel agents and tour operators.

**Federación de Amigos de la Tierra,** Apartado 46177, Madrid. Spanish branch of the Friends of the Earth.

**Greenpeace,** c/Barquillo 38, Madrid. Spanish branch of Greenpeace.

**Asamblea de Mujeres de Madrid,** c/Barquillo 44–2º–izq, Madrid. Madrid feminist organisation.

## BRITISH REPRESENTATION

The British Embassy is in Madrid, and there are Consulates in Barcelona, Mallorca, Bilbao, Tenerife, Santander, Las Palmas, Seville, Almería Algeciras, Vigo, Ibiza, Menorca, Tarragona, Alicante and Málaga, all listed under the 'useful addresses' headings in the regional sections. Officially you should sign on with the nearest Consulate as soon as you become resident in Spain, and inform them of any change of address. It is a good idea to do this, as for certain purposes you may have to get the Consulate to produce certification that you have been resident in the country for a certain length of time. There are British Chambers of Commerce in Madrid, Bilbao and Barcelona, and British Institutes, dependant on the British Council, in Madrid, Valencia, Barcelona, Seville and Granada.

## SPANISH CONTACTS IN THE UK

**Spanish Embassy,** 24 Belgrave Square, London SW1 (tel. 01-235 5555). General enquiries.

**Spanish Consulates,** 20 Draycott Place, London SW3 (tel. 01-581 5921), Suite 1a, Brook House, 70 Spring Gardens, Manchester 20 (tel. 061-236 1233) and 63 North Castle Street, Edinburgh (tel. 031-220 1440). Information on visas, work permits and other red tape.

**Spanish Embassy Education Office,** 20 Peel St, London W8 (tel. 01-727 2462). Information on validation of qualifications, study in Spain, etc.

**Instituto de España,** 102 Eaton Square, London SW1 (tel. 01-235 1484). Can answer general enquiries of a cultural nature. Runs a programme of lectures, film shows, recitals and exhibitions, and also has a lending library of books on Spain, and audio-visual material including videos of Spanish films available for loan. Runs lunchtime, afternoon and evening classes including GCSE and GCE A level Spanish, preparation for Institute of Linguists examinations, commercial Spanish, and Spanish shorthand. Also a course for Spanish graduates on *España Contemporanea*.

**Spanish National Tourist Office,** 57 St James' St, London SW1 (send sae if possible). Information leaflets on each of the provinces of Spain, plus lists of hotels/hostels, general information and advice on travel to Spain. Promotional posters may be available for schools and other groups.

**Spanish Embassy Commercial Office,** 22 Manchester Square, London W1 (tel. 01-486 0101). Advice and information on commercial matters.

**Wines of Spain,** 22 Manchester Square, London W1. Promotional material and information on Spanish wines.

**Hispanic and Luso-Brazilian Council,** Canning House, 2 Belgrave Square, London SW1 (tel. 01-235 2303). Organises educational and cultural activities intended to promote knowledge and understanding between the UK, Spain, Portugal and Latin America. Has a large lending library, runs courses for students and teachers, and provides an information service on opportunities abroad and in the UK. Its Education Department issues a newsletter three times a year containing details of courses in Britain, Spain, Portugal and Latin America, meetings and conferences, new publications, cultural events, etc. The council organises an annual prize examination in Spanish and Latin American studies for schoolstudents of Spanish, with a travel award of £100 as one of the prizes.

**Anglo-Spanish Society,** 5 Cavendish Square, London W1 (tel. 01-580 7537). A programme of social and cultural events designed to promote friendship and understanding between Britain and Spain.

**Association of Teachers of Spanish and Portuguese,** 50 Markham St, London SW3, and 33 North Lane, Huntington, Yorks (tel. 0904-769608). Professional body which promotes the teaching of Spanish and Portuguese in the UK. Publishes journal *Vida Hispánica* three times a year.

**Central Bureau for Educational Visits and Exchanges,** Seymour Mews House, Seymour Mews, London W1 (tel. 01-486 5101), 3 Bruntsfield Crescent, Edinburgh (tel. 031-447 8024), and 16 Malone Rd, Belfast (tel. 0232-664418). Wide range of programmes including English language assistants, study visits, teacher exchanges, exchange of students with technical experience, school links, etc. — see under specific headings above.

**International Higher Education Standing Conference,** c/o Colin Milner, Hertford College, Oxford, OX1 2DJ. Develops and encourages joint study programmes and student exchange schemes.

**The Association for Contemporary Iberian Studies,** c/o Teresa Lawlor, Polytechnic of the South Bank, Borough Road, London SE1 0AA. Recently formed association of academics concerned with Spanish and Portuguese affairs. Will organise annual conferences, publishes a journal and newsletters, and generally contributes to the furtherance of Spanish (and Portuguese) area and language studies.

**International Friendship League,** Pen Friend Service, Saltash, Cornwall. Can provide contacts with Spanish people for correspondence.

**Cyclist Touring Club,** 69 Meadrow, Godalming, Surrey (tel. 04868-7217). Publishes a useful information leaflet on cycletouring in Spain, sells maps and guidebooks, arranges insurance, etc.

**Gabriel's Book Shop,** 47 Walm Lane, London NW. Spanish bookshop (see also Foyles, Dillons and university bookshops throughout the country).

**Grant & Cutler,** 55-57 Great Marlborough St, London W1 (tel. 01-734 2012). Foreign booksellers with the largest selection of Spanish (and Portuguese) books in the UK. A catalogue and postal service is available.

**Marylebone-Paddington Institute,** Amberley Road, London W9 (tel. 01-286 1900). Evening classes in Euskera (Basque) and Catalan.

### And in the Republic of Ireland

**Spanish Embassy,** 17a Merlyn Park, Ballsbridge, Dublin 4 (tel. 691640).

**Instituto Cultural Español,** 58 Northumberland Rd, Dublin 4, Eire. Publishes *Authentik,* a summary of news articles from Spanish papers and magazines designed for use in language teaching.

# 2
# Study & Work Opportunities

## STUDY

### 'SPANISH FOR FOREIGNERS' COURSES

Fairly comprehensive listings of 'Spanish for foreigners' courses in Spain are given under the regional headings (see also p. 272). Basically they divide into two sorts — those run by universities and those run by private sector language academies and the like.

Public sector or 'official' courses tend to be cheaper, and emphasise other aspects of the culture as well as straight language acquisition. Teaching tends to follow rather traditional methods, with an emphasis on grammar and textual commentary, although there is usually plenty of opportunity for conversation too.

The advantage of the private sector courses is that groups tend to be smaller, they are more adaptable to individual needs both in terms of availability (you choose when and for how long you want to enrol), and in terms of the type and level of provision (for instance, if you're looking specifically for 'Spanish for business purposes'). Audiovisual methods and language lab techniques are more often employed in the private sector (although in the public sector, the **Escuelas Oficiales de Idiomas**, in Madrid and Barcelona are keen on these methods too).

The standard of teaching is usually good, although especially in the private sector you must obviously satisfy yourself that the institution will be able to give you the type of tuition you require — read their leaflets thoroughly. Most courses are organised on the basis of around four hours' teaching in the morning and optional or complementary activities in the afternoon/evening, which may include talks, filmshows, excursions, and social activities of various kinds.

### Duration

While courses organised by universities tend to run for a set time, say 3 weeks or a month, there is more coming and going in the private sector, and you can usually enrol at any time of the year, although many places specify a minimum of 2 weeks.

## Cost
It's difficult to generalise about cost, but you could expect to pay roughly £100 for a month in the public sector (or £250 a term, perhaps £500 for a whole academic year), and double this if the arrangements include accommodation. In the private sector, fees could be around £50 per week, excluding accommodation. There may also be a small charge for registration, or examination fee, if applicable.

## Accommodation
May or may not be included. If not some sort of help can usually be given in finding somewhere. If provided, it may be in families, or in university accommodation, or in pensions. Sometimes you may be asked to specify which you prefer.

## How to apply
Write to two or three of the most likely looking places as listed in the regional section (use the model letter given on p. 274 if necessary). As well as up-to-date information on courses, dates, prices etc., you will probably receive a *boletín de inscripción* (enrolment form), which you should fill in and return, together, usually, with a deposit and passport-sized photographs of yourself. Payment is generally by bank giro.

If you need any advice or information other than that provided in this book, two offices of the Spanish Embassy in London may be able to help you:

- **Spanish Embassy Education Office,** 20 Peel St, London W8 (tel. 01–727 2462).
- **Instituto de España,** 102 Eaton Square, London SW1 (tel. 01–234 1484).

## Study packages
If the thought of getting all this organised on your own appals you, or if you'd rather travel in a party, there are a number of organisations which offer ready-made study packages, although you'll obviously have less choice over where and when you go, and the type of course:

**Alpha Languages Services,** 2 Cottis Court, St John's Road, Epping, Essex (tel. 0378–77039 and 0279–850747). 4 week courses in a private language school in the Málaga area.

**Euroyouth (Abroad) Ltd,** 301 Westborough Rd, Westcliff-on-Sea, Essex (tel. 0702–341434). 3 and 4 week courses in Madrid, Barcelona, Salamanca and Málaga area.

**EuroAcademy,** 77a George St, Croydon, Surrey (tel. 01–681 2905). Groups only, minimum 10, ages 12 and upwards, including adults.

**International Study Programmes,** The Manor, Hazelton, Cheltenham, Glos (tel. 0451–60379). For school groups only, usually minimum of 20. Language classes are based in Spanish schools, and there is a chance to attend normal lessons as well. Also excursions and social events.

**John Galleymore,** 24 High Street, Portsmouth, Hants (tel. 0705–824095). A variety of courses for all levels from beginners to university level, and teachers of Spanish.

**The School Journey,** 48 Cavendish Road, London SW12 (tel. 01–673 4849). Easter course (14 days) in Cordoba for GCSE and A level students.

**Youth Travels,** 117 Wendell Road, London W12 (tel. 01–743 7966). 2 and 4 week courses all the year round, travel not included, although assistance given if required.

**The Educational Language Agency Ltd,** PO Box 81, Crawley, W Sussex (tel. 0293–21218). Offers free advice for schools and others organising group language trips to Spain. Can recommend schools and courses in Spain to fit specific requirements.

In Spain, the following organisations can place students on language courses at various centres:

**Centros Europeos,** c/Príncipe 12–6º A, 28012 Madrid (tel. 91–232 7230). Month long courses in July in Madrid, Valencia and Alicante.

**Centro Ibero-Americano de Difusión Cultural (CIDCU),** Molino de la Navata 12–3º B, La Navata, Madrid. Intensive summer courses (6 weeks) in Madrid, Málaga, Valencia and Santander, in Spanish language and both Spanish and Spanish American culture.

**Club de Relaciones Culturales Internacionales,** c/Ferraz, Madrid (tel. 91–479 6302).

## STUDY VISITS

The **Central Bureau for Educational Visits and Exchanges** (see p. 42) runs a study visits scheme for senior teaching staff and administrators, or youth and community workers, who wish to observe aspects of foreign educational or youth-service provision. Such visits are of 1-2 weeks in duration only, and the possibility exists of the Spanish counterpart arranging a reciprocal visit to Britain.

The **International Association for the Exchange of Students for Technical Experience (IAESTE)** is a scheme which is also handled in Britain by the Central Bureau, and involves the possibility of a work placement in Spain lasting between 6 weeks and a year. Students on courses such as engineering, science, architecture, agriculture, forestry, applied arts, commerce, economics and languages are considered, and the workplacement must obviously be course-related. For further details, apply direct to the Central Bureau.

## OTHER COURSES

A selection of other courses likely to be of interest to non-Spaniards is listed in the regional sections (see also p. 272) — mostly concerned with art and crafts or sport. Once ensconced in Spain of course, you may find all sorts of other courses which might be of interest — from Chinese to computing to psychology. These may be organised through state channels, as *cursos monográficos* (see below for study within the state system), or at a local level through the town council, or by private institutions. For information locally, the best places to contact are the provincial education departments (listed in the regional sections later) or the *ayuntamiento*.

It's also worth mentioning the **Instituto Nacional de Investigaciones Científicas y Ecológicas** (INICE — c/Consejo 9–3º–izq, Salamanca (tel. 923–219827) ), which runs an interesting selection of short courses — throughout the country, not just in Salamanca — mostly during the summer, on subjects such as self-defence, conservation, photography, etc. If you're interested in anything in the general area of science-meets-alternative-thought, they're well worth contacting.

There are also various companies in Britain which offer the chance of doing courses in Spain other than straight language courses:

**Euroyouth,** 301 Westborough Rd, Westcliff-on-Sea, Essex (tel. 0702–341434). History and Art courses based in universities and state institutions.

**Cox and Kings,** 46 Marshall St, London W1 (tel. 01–439 3380). Flower painting courses in the Aragonese Pyrenees.

**Field Studies Council,** Flatford Mill Field Centre, E Bergholt, Colchester, Essex (tel. 0206–298283). Courses for naturalists in Andalucía.

## STUDY WITHIN THE STATE SYSTEM

### Key information
- **Spanish Embassy Education Office,** 20 Peel St, London W8 (tel. 01–727 2462).
- In Spain: Provincial education departments.

### School
Education is compulsory in Spain from 6 to 16, so resident children of school age of whatever nationality must attend state schools if they're not receiving their education privately. Post-16, they will also have access to state education — either academic or technical — for which a small amount is payable in fees (negligible). After the age of 11 students from abroad wishing to enter the system will normally have to have their previous studies validated (see below) before being assigned to a class.

### University
Officially, and at the level of EEC institutions, there are moves to encourage more European students to attend universities in countries other than their own. In practice, however, British students will normally be forced to study at home, where they will be eligible for a grant, rather than in Spain, where

they won't. However, the fees at Spanish universities are not prohibitive, and if you have some means of supporting yourself or wouldn't get a grant in Britain anyway, it is possible to do your degree there. Bear in mind, however, that certain subjects like law will not be viable if you wish to return to Britain to work afterwards, and also that a full Spanish degree takes five years — a university diploma (qualifying you in areas like teaching, nursing, tourism, etc.) will take three.

To get a place in a Spanish university, you'll first have to apply to have your A levels validated, and then sit an entrance exam *(selectividad)*. You can do this in Britain by applying to: **UNED** 317 Portobello Road, London W10 (tel. 01–969 2664). Exams take place in June and September each year.

If you are interested in spending some time at a Spanish university, note that some degree courses in Britain (and not only language degrees) involve spending a portion of the time studying at a Spanish institution — a case in point is Middlesex Polytechnic's BA in European Business Administration and BA in European Economics.

**Postgraduate/research**
It's only possible to do a doctorate in Spain if you can get your British studies validated for a *licenciatura*, or full 5-year degree in Spain. A Bachelor's degree is not normally enough for this so if you're thinking of postgraduate study in Spain, you'd be wise to do a Master's here first. Apply directly to the university in the first instance (addresses given in the regional sections later).

## VALIDATION OF BRITISH QUALIFICATIONS

*In the UK:*
- **Spanish Embassy Education Office,** 20 Peel St, London W8 (tel. 01–727 2462).

*In Spain:*
- **Subdirección General de Titulos Convalidaciones y Homologaciones,** Paseo del Prado 28, Madrid (tel. 91–467 1154).

If you want to study within the Spanish state system (except at primary school level), exercise your trade or profession in Spain, or simply have your qualifications officially recognised, you'll have to go through a complex and lengthy validation procedure known as *convalidación*, or *homologación*. For this you will have to have your degree certificate (or school reports, GCSE, O and A level certificates, etc.) officially legalised in Britain before taking them to Spain. This can be done by any solicitor, whose signature must then be authenticated by the **Foreign and Commonwealth Office,** 70 Petty France, London SW1 (tel. 01–213 3397).

You will also have to supply Spanish translations of these certificates, and, in the case of degrees, a course description showing the subjects studied, duration, etc. All this, together with your birth certificate or passport, and an official application form (obtainable from the above offices) must be sent to the **Ministry of Education** in Madrid at c/Alcalá 34. A decision on the matter may take between 3 and 9 months.

Strict equivalencies are laid down for secondary school qualifications, but in the case of degrees, at the moment each case is considered individually. It is also possible to validate PhDs, in which case a synopsis of the thesis in Spanish will be required in addition to all the above.

## GRANTS AND SCHOLARSHIPS

**Key information**
- *Scholarships Abroad*, The British Council, OEAD, 65 Davies St, London W1.
- *Study Abroad*, HM Stationery Office, PO Box 569, London SE1.
- *The Grants Register*, Macmillan (see your local library — it costs £30 to buy).
- *Grants for Youth Exchanges*. Available free from the Youth Exchange Centre, Seymour Mews House, Seymour Mews, London W1.
- *Higher Education in the European Community: Student Handbook*. HM Stationery Office, PO Box 569, London SE1.
- *Sources of Financial Aid for Study Travel Abroad*. Free leaflet listing further useful sources of information, produced by Central Bureau for Educational Visits and Exchanges, Seymour Mews House, Seymour Mews, London W1 (tel. 01-486 5101).

**Sources of funding in Spain**
At present non-Spaniards are not entitled to apply for many of the normal student grants available in Spain, although the situation is under review and if you are desperate for funding and think you might qualify, or feel like being persistent, you could try the following organisations:

**Ministerio de Educación y Ciencia,** Sección de Información, Iniciativas y Reclamaciones, Alcalá 34, 28014 Madrid. Publishes a list each year of grants available, which covers a wide range of specific cases, and varies from year to year. Non-Spaniards are not likely to be eligible for any of these unless the law is changed.

**Consejo Superior de Investigaciones Científicas,** c/Serrano 117, Madrid (tel. 91-261 9800). Various research scholarships awarded annually to foreign graduates on a reciprocal basis. Application through Spanish Embassy in the student's home country (see below).

**Ministerio de Asuntos Exteriores,** Plaza de la Provincia 1, Madrid. Grants for foreign graduates available through application to Spanish Embassy in the student's home country (see below).

**Secretaría del Estado para Universidades e Investigación,** Serrano 150-3º, Madrid (tel. 91-261 5400) (Secretary of State for Universities). Possible source of information on grant-giving institutions in Spain.

**Instituto de la Juventud,** c/Ortega y Gasset 71, 28006 Madrid. Various prize competitions are held each year, some open to non-Spaniards, including the **Jóvenes Investigadores de la Naturaleza** competition, which offers substantial sums in prize money for research work undertaken by young people (15–23 years) of any nationality on themes relating to nature and conservation.

**Instituto de Estudios de Administración Local,** c/Sta Engracia 7, 28010 Madrid. Institute of Local Government Studies, offers research grants for work in this area.

**Instituto Nacional de Asistencia Social,** c/José Abascal 39, 28003 Madrid. Social Services Institute offers grants to students who have completed at least one year of their degree course in return for work or services.

**INAPE (Instituto Nacional de Asistencia y Promoción del Estudiante),** c/Torrelaguna 58, 28027 Madrid. Student welfare body and important grant-giving institution.

It may also be worth trying to get funding locally from *ayuntamientos* or regional governments, although you are likely to run into the same problems as regards nationality.

### Sources of funding in Britain

**The Spanish Embassy,** Minister for Cultural Affairs, 24 Belgrave Square, London SW1. (Note: if calling or phoning, information is available from Spanish Embassy Cultural Dept, **Instituto de España,** 102 Eaton Square, London SW1 (tel. 01–235 1484/5) ). Administers scholarships awarded by:
1. *Consejo Superior de Investigaciones Científicas.* Two research scholarships available annually to British graduates with a knowledge of Spanish for study/research in Spain, worth approximately £200 per month for 10 months, plus travel and tuition in Spain. Application forms available from the Spanish Embassy to be returned by 1st March each year.
2. *Ministerio de Asuntos Exteriores.* Approximately eight scholarships available annually for British graduates with a knowledge of Spanish for study/research in Spain, worth approximately £240 per month for 9 months, plus *seguro* and free enrolment at a Spanish university or other institution. Application forms available from Spanish Embassy, to be in by 1st March each year.
3. *Ministerio de Educación y Ciencia.* Bursaries available for teachers of Spanish wishing to attend the *Curso Superior de Filología Hispánica* at Salamanca University. Full details from the Embassy.

**Secretary of the Scholarship Committee,** Room 21a, University of London, Senate House, Malet St, London WC1 (tel. 01–636 8000, ex. 3042). Administers the 'Vicente Cañada Blanch Fellowships' awarded annually — one post-doctoral, one postgraduate, for research projects concerned with Spanish culture and civilisation to be undertaken by UK citizens. Travel and other expenses may also be paid on a discretional basis. Applications to be in by 1st February each year.

**British Council,** Overseas Educational Appointments Dept, 65 Davies St, London W1. Administers grants awarded by the following:
1. *Council of Europe:*
   — *Fellowship for European Legal Studies and Research.* For research projects to be undertaken by law graduates from member states which are deemed to contribute to a wider knowledge of European law. Applications to be made between August and October each year.
   — *Social fellowships.* To enable administrative and service personnel to undertake a short period of study in another member country. Applications to be made between October and January each year.
2. *NATO.* Research fellowships for graduates to undertake research leading to publication on topics relevant to the North Atlantic Treaty Organisation. Applications by mid-December each year.

**Local education authorities.** If you're doing a degree at a British university which involves spending a year abroad, your LEA will probably continue paying your grant if you decide to enrol at a Spanish university instead of applying for an Assistantship (see p. 58).

**Sources of funding through International organisations**
- **Council of Europe** — through the British Council (see above).
- **NATO** — through the British Council (see above).
- **European Communities Commission,** UK Office, 8 Storey's Gate, London SW1 (tel. 01–222 8122). Can provide funding for the following:
1. Development of joint study programmes in higher education between member states
2. Professional study visits in higher education
3. Youth initiatives which will assist in the transition from school to adult life
4. Grants for groups, movements, activities, congresses, etc., of a European nature
5. Grants for international non-governmental youth organisations.

Details of these and other schemes are contained in the booklet *Finance from Europe,* available from the above address, and also from offices in Belfast, Cardiff and Edinburgh, as follows:
— Windsor House, 9/15 Bedford St, Belfast (tel. 0232–240708)
— 4 Cathedral Rd, Cardiff (tel. 0222–371631)
— 7 Alva St, Edinburgh (tel. 031–225 2058).

## WORK

### GENERAL SITUATION

Despite Spain now being part of the European Community, free labour market mobility does not come into effect until the beginning of 1993, and the only group to benefit at the moment from Spain's EEC status are self-employed people wishing to set up a business (see p. 61). For those seeking a job, prospects are in general pretty poor: unemployment in Spain is exceedingly high, especially among young people, and the employment of foreigners is severely restricted by laws which are strictly applied. Nonetheless, it is possible to find work—especially temporary work — in Spain, if you are willing to be flexible over the following:

### Type of work
Opportunities are mostly restricted to the types of employment listed after the section on **Finding a job.** Ask yourself if you've got the experience/qualifications/skills necessary (knowledge of Spanish, for instance may be crucial), and if not, your time will be better spent acquiring these than firing off applications that will only get rejected.

### Putting effort into finding work
Make sure you're applying to the right people, at the right time of year. Apply to a good range of sources, be prepared to make follow up phone calls, and generally hassle.

### Pay and conditions
If you associate Spain with being on holiday, you may be put off to find that the working day tends to be longer than in Britain, and pay lower. This need not necessarily affect your standard of living, of course, but the daily grind may be much the same in Spain as in Britain, and not some wonderful alternative.

This is especially true if you work the traditional *jornada partida* with a long break in the middle of the day, which means you may not get finished until 2000. The tendency is for this to be replaced with the more familiar (to us) *jornada continua* with just a short break in the middle of the day. A 40 hour week is the legal maximum.

## WORK PERMITS AND OTHER MATTERS

### Work Permits
*In the UK:*
- **Spanish Consulates,** 20 Draycott Place, London SW3 (tel. 01–581 5921); Suite 1a, Brook House, 70 Spring Gardens, Manchester 2 (tel. 061–236 1233), or 63 North Castle Street, Edinburgh (tel. 031–220 1440).

*If in Spain:*
- **Provincial labour departments** (see regional listings).

Work permits simultaneously give you the right to stay in Spain for the period of time for which they are valid. It is your employer who is responsible for applying for these, to the Provincial Office of the Ministry of Labour, or if the employer is based in Britain, to the Spanish consulates in this country. He or she will have to provide all the details relating to your job, and evidence that it is essential to employ a foreigner rather than a Spanish national — hence the need for very specific skills, usually linked to having English as a mother tongue. You on your part will have to supply a copy of your passport, a copy of your application for a special visa (see p. 14), a medical certificate, five passport sized photos, and evidence of your academic and professional qualifications, duly validated (see p. 47) where appropriate.

For seasonal work you will be given a strictly limited non-renewable permit which commits you to leaving Spain after this time, otherwise you will probably get the Type B permit which lasts for a year and may be renewed. After several of these, you may be eligible for a Type C permit, which is valid for up to 5 years and does not restrict the type of work you do, or where you do it.

If you're self-employed, you'll have to do all the donkey-work of getting a work permit yourself — submitting all the documents listed above and more besides — and it can be a thankless task. Again, you should apply either to the consulates here or to the provincial labour departments, but you must have previously gained authorisation from the authorities on the spot to set up your business. Initial permits are for a particular locality and for 1 year only; if after this time everything is deemed to be in order, you can get a 5 year permit which doesn't restrict the type of business you can engage in, or limit you to a particular area.

Note that certain special cases, such as language assistants, people taking up teacher exchanges, entertainers whose work is not permanently based in Spain, and clergy, are exempt from needing a work permit. The Spanish consulates in Britain will be able to give full advice on this.

## Tax
- *Working Abroad?: The Guide to Fiscal and Financial Dos and Don'ts* by Harry Brown, published by Northcote House.

Spain has a double taxation agreement with Britain, which means you can't be taxed twice on the same income. It's infinitely preferable to pay tax in Spain as you'll probably end up paying less than half what you'd have to pay in Britain. However, to be excluded from paying tax in the UK you have to be resident elsewhere for at least 6 months in any tax year. This seems reasonable, but bear in mind that if you have, say, a teaching contract which starts in September, and you return to the UK in July, you'll be counted as resident in Britain for the tax year which starts in April.

You're liable to pay tax in Spain after 6 months. This is usually deducted at source by your employer, as in Britain. The relevant department is the **Ministerio de Hacienda** (c/Alcalá 9, Madrid (tel. 91–468 2000) ), which has offices in every province.

## Social Security
As stated before, you will in any case be entitled to emergency medical treatment under reciprocal social security agreements between Britain and Spain, and you can always take out additional medical insurance privately, but if you're working in Spain you should also have a *seguro,* provided by your employer. This is a card, bearing the name of your GP *(médico*

*de cabecera)* and entitling you (and your family, if applicable) to all the benefits of the Spanish Health Service. Before signing any contract, make sure the *seguro* is included, or if not (as in the case of au pair posts), who pays the cost of private insurance.

If you're working for a Spanish employer, you will not have to make British National Insurance contributions, although if you're employed by a company based in Britain, you may have to continue contributing for the first year. If you have already been contributing for a while in the UK though, you should definitely consider whether it would be worthwhile to continue paying contributions voluntarily, in order not to lose your entitlement to benefits when you return. You can get advice and assistance on this by writing to **DSS Overseas Branch,** Newcastle-upon-Tyne, NE98 1YX.

**Legal rights**
Your legal rights and obligations as an employee in Spain are laid down in the **Estatuto de los Trabajadores** of 1980. Under this legislation workers' interests are fairly well protected, and foreigners enjoy the same rights as Spaniards. Among other things it lays down the right to be paid punctually, the right to 30 days' holiday a year, and a framework for defining fair/unfair dismissal.

In practice, of course, there is little you can do to force an employer to comply with it if you are ununionised (see p. 40 for addresses of *sindicatos*) and unwilling to resort to legal action, but it helps to know what legislation does exist. If you believe you've been unfairly dismissed, you have 20 working days in which to appeal for arbitration to the **Instituto de Mediación Arbitraje y Conciliación,** which can be done through the provincial labour departments.

## FINDING A JOB: GENERAL HINTS

**Look out for advertisements**
Likely sources are the Overseas Appointments pages of the British press, professional and trade journals, and Spanish newspapers. Many colleges and universities have subscriptions to **El País,** or you can buy it from specialist newsagents. (Beware of ads in local Spanish papers for 'sauna girls'!)

**Use public services**
In Britain **Jobcentres** sometimes get enquiries from foreign employers, and **careers offices** are a good source of advice. In Spain the **Instituto Nacional del Empleo (INEM)** runs a network of careers offices (**Centros de Orientación Profesional y Laboral**) and jobcentres (**Oficinas de Empleo**), based in most sizeable towns. The latter in particular are worth approaching if you're in Spain. INEM's Head Office is at Condesa de Venadito 9, 28071 Madrid (tel. 91–408 1500).

In Madrid you could also contact the official employment agency, the **Centro Nacional de Colocación,** at General Pardiñas 5, 28001 Madrid, and in other areas the **provincial labour office** (see regional listings). There are also a number of careers centres based in universities (**Centros de Orientación e Información del Empleo**) which attempt to put graduates in touch with potential employers. These too are listed in the regional section, and are worth approaching if you're in Spain.

Other sources of information for specific enqures (but not jobs directly) are the **Ministry of Labour** (Ministerio de Trabajo, Departamento de Extranjeros, Augustín de Bethancourt 5, 28005 Madrid) and the Immigration Department of the **Spanish Emigration Institute** (Instituto Español de Emigración, Servicio de Inmigración, Paseo Rosales 44, 28008 Madrid).

### Private agencies
There are many agencies in Britain which can find you a job in Spain. These are usually specialised, and some are listed under the headings for specific jobs below, other later in the chapter. Look out for others in your particular area of employment/part of the country.

The **Federation of Recruitment and Employment Services**, 10 Belgrave Square, London SW1, can supply a list, in the form of a directory of its members. There are also agencies in Spain; some are listed below. You'll find others in the Spanish *Yellow Pages*.

### Approaching potential employers
Some British companies with operations in Spain are listed later in the chapter. Other sources of information on potential employers could be:

- **British Embassy and Consulates** — see regional listings for addresses.
- **British Chambers of Commerce** in Madrid, Barcelona and Bilbao. Can provide lists of Spanish companies with links with Britain and British companies with branches in Spain.

### Advertising your services
The agencies listed below will place advertisements for you in the Spanish press:

- **Media Universal Services,** 34-35 Skylines, Lineharbour, Docklands, London E14 (tel. 01-538 5505).
- **Publicitas Ltd,** 525/527 Fulham Road, London SW6 (tel. 01-385 7723).

### Helpful publications
*Directory of Jobs and Careers Abroad* by David Leppard, published by Vacation Work, Oxford. Good for information and advice on longer-term prospects abroad.

*Directory of Summer Jobs Abroad*, published annually by Vacation Work, Oxford.

*Opportunities Overseas in International Organisations,* booklet available from Overseas Development Association, Abercrombie House, Eaglesham Rd, East Kilbride, Scotland.

*Working Abroad* produced by the Manpower Services Commission, available from Jobcentres.

*Working Abroad, Daily Telegraph Guide to Living and Working Overseas,* by Godfrey Golzen. Good hints for finding work in the commercial sector, but mostly aimed at company executives.

*Working Holidays,* Central Bureau for Educational Visits and Exchanges, Seymour Mews House, Seymour Mews, London W1 (tel. 01 – 486 5101). Published yearly, price £4.50. Organised by countries, giving contact addresses for each, as well as useful general information. Aimed especially at young people.

*Working in Europe,* Department of Employment publication obtainable at Jobcentres.

*Work Your Way Around the World* by Susan Griffith, published by Vacation Work, Oxford. A lot of useful hints and contact addresses, especially for casual or temporary work.

## AU PAIRING

Normally to qualify for an au pair position you must be aged 18 to 27, single, female, and with no dependants. No particular qualifications are required, but normally it helps if you have at least GCSE standard education, a smattering of Spanish, and some sort of experience with children. The idea is that you get a chance to live with a Spanish family and improve your Spanish, and in return for helping with light household duties you receive a small sum in pocket money. The normal minimum stay is 6 months and you'll have more luck finding a post if you're able to stay at least this long, but it is possible to get au pair positions for 1–3 months.

You can obtain au pair work privately, through replying to ads in magazines like *The Lady*, through personal contacts, or through advertising your own services in Spain (see p. 54). Personal contacts with the family help to establish the good will on both sides that is essential to the success of the arrangement. There are also agencies which can obtain au pair placements for you (see below), and these too recommend establishing direct contact with the family before taking up a position.

Agencies in Britain can charge up to £40 for their services, legally payable only after a position has been accepted, and not as a registration fee. However you find your post, but especially if you're dealing directly with a Spanish family, make sure the following conditions are clear before you set out:

- *Hours of work.* You shouldn't be expected to work longer than 6 hours per day, 6 days per week, and either the morning or the afternoon should be free to attend classes etc.
- *Duties.* What exactly will you be expected to do: will it be mostly childcare or mostly housework?
- *Pay.* Should be at least £15 per week, paid weekly on a specified day.

- *Living accommodation.* You shouldn't have to share a room.
- *Travel arrangements.* Normally paid for by the au pair, but if you're staying for a year or longer, you may be able to get the family to agree to pay the return fare.
- *Insurance.* Very often the family will pay the insurance, but check.

When setting out to take up an au pair position, make sure you carry a letter of invitation from the family with you, essential for avoiding problems with the immigration authorities.

Among the agencies in Britain which can find au pair placements are:
**Anglia Agency,** 154 Fronks Road, Dovercourt, Harwich, Essex (tel. 0255-503717).
**Au Pair Bureau Ltd,** 87 Regent St, London W1 (tel. 01-930 4757).
**Baxter's Agency,** PO Box 12, Peterborough, Cambridgeshire (tel. 0733-62744).
**Helping Hands Au Pair and Domestic Agency,** Hertford Road, Newbury Park, Ilford, Essex (tel. 01-597 3138).
**Host and Guest Service,** 592a Kings Road, London SW6 (tel. 01-731 5340). Minimum 6 months' contracts.
**Jolaine Au Pair and Domestic Agency,** 171 High St, Barnet, Herts. (tel. 01-449 1334).
**Scattergoods Surrey Agency,** Thursley House, 53 Station Road, Shalford, Guildford, Surrey (tel. 0483-33732/66669).
**Students Abroad,** Elm House, 21b The Avenue, Hatch End, Middlesex (tel. 01-428 5823). Minimum 2 months.

Au pair agencies in Spain are harder to come by, though the following may be able to help:

**Centros Europeos,** c/Príncipe 12-6º-A, 28012 Madrid (tel. 91-232 7230).
**Club de Relaciones Culturales Internacionales,** Departamento Sociocultural, c/Ferraz 82-2º-D, 28008 Madrid (tel. 91-479 6303/6446). Recognised by the Ministry of Culture.

## TEACHING ENGLISH AS A FOREIGN LANGUAGE

This is a category for which work permits are fairly readily granted, but (with the exception of teacher exchanges and language assistant posts—see below) teaching in state schools is out. It's generally necessary to have a teaching qualification of some sort, or a degree and, preferably, some teaching experience. Posts will normally be for one academic year or more, so you'll have most success if you start hunting in spring and summer to start the following September. It's sometimes possible to get work just for the summer months. The following types of opportunity exist:

### Posts with the British Council
The British Council runs a school in Madrid for 5 to 18 year olds, with

a heavy emphasis on EFL (all children take the Cambridge First Certificate), and British Institutes in Madrid, Barcelona, Valencia and Granada, which are involved in teaching English to adults. If you're in Spain, you can apply directly to the Director of Studies of the relevant institution — the addresses are given in the regional section — but in Britain you should contact: **British Council,** Overseas Educational Appointments Dept, 65 Davies Street, London W1Y 2AA. Senior posts are generally advertised in the British press, other vacancies tend to be filled locally.

**Private language schools**
These range from internationally known and respected organisations like Berlitz to fairly disreputable fly-by-night set ups with scant respect for their employees. It's possible to get some very good posts by replying to ads in the *Education Guardian* or the *Times Educational Supplement,* but if you are willing to take a more aggressive approach to finding work you could do a mail shot of your CV. Many of the schools are listed in the regional sections later in the book, or the British Council in Madrid (c/Almagro 5) can supply an even more comprehensive list.

In Madrid there is also an Association of Language Teaching Institutions, membership of which guarantees some minimum standard of efficiency. They too can supply lists: **Asociación de Centros de Enseñanza de Idiomas de Madrid** (ACEDIM), c/Sagasta 27, 28004 Madrid.

In Britain the following make useful contacts if you're looking for work in this type of institution:

- **International House,** International Teacher Training Institute, 106 Piccadilly, London W1 (tel. 01–491 2598). The organisation has a large number of affiliated colleges in Spain (see listings), and offers 4 and 8 week teacher training courses in London which to some extent 'feed' their staff needs. The 4 week course leads to the RSA preparatory certificate, the 8 week course to the full RSA Diploma.
- **Linguarama,** 53 Pall Mall, London SW1 (tel. 01–930 7697). This organisation has 4 schools in Spain (listed under regions) and runs one-week crash courses in teaching English as a foreign language using the direct method. The course costs £122.00, and in some cases may lead to direct internal recruitment within the organisation, if places are available. Applications for the course should be sent to **TEFL Dept,** Linguarama Ltd, New Oxford House, 16 Waterloo St, Birmingham B2 (tel. 021–632 5925).
- **Dr J L Kettle-Williams,** Language Centre, School of Languages, Portsmouth Polytechnic, Wiltshire Building, Hampshire Terrace, Portsmouth PO1 2BU (tel. 0705–827681). Performs a useful service of letting potential applicants know of TEFL vacancies in a variety of institutions throughout Spain.
- The **Berlitz** organisation has a number of schools in Spain, and applications can be made centrally through the Madrid office at: **Escuelas de Idiomas Berlitz,** Gran Vía 80–4º, 28013 Madrid (tel. 91–241 6215).

- **Centros Europeos,** c/Príncipe 12–6º–A, 28012 Madrid (tel. 91–232 7230), invite applications for teaching work from graduates or suitably qualified and experienced EFL teachers who are willing to undergo a short training course beforehand.

**English-medium schools which accept Spanish-speaking children**
The British Council school in Madrid is included in this category. Again, these are listed in the regional section, and applications may be in response to advertisements or by approaching the schools directly.

**Private classes**
You won't get a work permit specifically to give private classes in Spain (unless you can prove you're already well established in this as a form of self-employment), but nonetheless it can be fertile ground, and many people make some sort of a living out of it. It can be useful in supplementing — unofficially — the allowance you get as a language assistant (see below), or other types of low-paid work.

If you have a few Spanish contacts, you'll probably actually be approached regarding the possibility of giving private classes, rather than your having to look around — people are only too keen to learn English, but on the whole rather distrustful of language schools and enjoy the status of having someone all to themselves. Usually you go to people's houses, and payment varies according to how far you have to travel, the number of hours you give a week, how well qualified you are, and whether the class is to be formal or just conversation. One thousand pesetas an hour is a reasonable starting point if you're fairly well qualified.

If you do want to advertise your services, you can do so through public noticeboards, notices in newspaper kiosks, or in local newspapers. If you are female I'd recommend NOT specifying this in the ad.

## OTHER TEACHING OPPORTUNITIES

**Language assistants**
Opportunities exist for working as conversation assistants in Spanish secondary schools or university language departments. The organisation in Britain responsible for arranging placements is the **Central Bureau for Educational Visits and Exchanges** (see p. 42) and those appointed receive official contracts from the Spanish Ministry of Education.

Priority for these places, lasting one academic year, is given to students who must spend a year abroad as part of a language degree (in which case application is normally through the language department of their university), but the scheme is also open to serving language teachers with no more than 2 years' experience, and no previous year abroad. There are also a limited number of 'junior assistant' posts, open to school leavers.

The Bureau charges a fee of £8 for its services, and applications must be received by January each year. Introductory briefings in Spain are organised before those appointed take up their places.

The work-load is light — 12 hours' teaching/conversation classes per week — but remuneration is correspondingly low. Spare time can be spent giving private classes (unofficially), or by enrolling for a course at a university.

*Note:* The Ministry of Education is notoriously slow in paying its new appointees, so it's wise to make some arrangements for obtaining emergency cash. Sometimes schools are willing to advance the money.

### Teacher exchange
This scheme too is arranged through the **Central Bureau** (see p. 42). It involves post-to-post exchanges, lasting either a term or a year between serving language teachers in Spain and Britain. (Obviously, in Spain you teach English, not Spanish.) This takes the form of a secondment on full salary, and an additional grant of £990 per year, or £330 a term is paid against expenses incurred such as travel. Availability depends on demand from Spain, but it's an excellent way of seeing the Spanish education system at first hand, and updating language skills.

### Teaching in British/US international schools in Spain
Advertisements for such posts frequently appear in the *Education Guardian*, in *The Times Educational Supplement*, or in specialised journals, and if you want to apply direct, many are listed in the regional sections of this guide. Other sources of information may be the British Council in Madrid (c/Almagro 5), provincial departments of education in Spain (addresses given in regional sections), or the **National Association of British Schools in Spain, c/o Runnymede College, Arga 9, El Viso, Madrid.**

*Note:* At a local level, you might be able to teach in Spain in ways other than those suggested here — there are all sorts of courses put on by town councils, private organisations and the *universidades populares*, which, if you speak good Spanish and have a knowledge of the local community, you might be able to get involved in.

## COURIERS
Again, this is a field for which work permits are fairly readily granted, arranged by the company that employs you. These are normally seasonal jobs — May to October, with a proportion of staff appointed for high season (July and August) only. The work is not necessarily hard, but you generally have to be on call 24 hours a day if necessary, which can be wearing.

All companies stress that a mature, outgoing personality is more important than specific qualifications, though some knowledge of Spanish is preferred. Minimum age 18–21. Applications should normally be received by December/January.

**Canvas Holidays,** Courier Department, Bull Plain, Hertford, Herts (tel. 0992–551933 or 553535). Operates camping packages on the Costa Brava. No more than four couriers are generally employed each season — and contracts are from April to July or from July to September. A good working knowledge of Spanish is required, and work involves preparing tents, organising social events, dealing with problems, etc. Accommodation, travel and insurance are all provided.

**Club Cantabrica Holidays,** 146–148 London Road, St Albans, Herts (tel. 0727–33141). Those interested in applying for courier positions are invited to send CV and covering letter for the attention of Mr Parker.

**Club Méditerranée,** Place de la Bourse, Paris 75002, France. Vacancies for couriers during the May–October period, plus the possibility of work for sports instructors, catering staff, and almost anyone with a specific skill to offer. Write to the address above for an application form, or contact the London office, 106–108 Brompton Road, London SW3 (tel. 01–225 1066).

**Club 18–30,** Overseas Personnel Dept, Academic House, 24–28 Oval Road, London NW1 (tel. 01–267 7044). Vacancies for overseas reps and 'transfer reps' (accompanying holidaymakers from airport to hotel) in mainland Spain and Balearics. Minimum age 21.

**Eurocamp Travel Ltd,** Courier Dept, Edmundson House, Tatton St, Knutsford, Cheshire (tel. 0565–50444). Vacancies for half a season or a full season for couriers, also warehouse assistants, drivers, and montage/démontage assistants to set up and dismantle tents. Pay £60 per week, travel and insurance provided.

**Ibiza Club,** Apartado 73, Es Cana, Sta Eulalia del Río, Ibiza (tel. 971–330650). Possibility of vacancies if you apply in good time and are willing to hassle.

**Solaire International Holidays,** 1158 Stratford Rd, Hall Green, Birmingham B28 8AF (tel. 021–778 5061). Some knowledge of Spanish is required. Work involves erecting and equipping tents and caravans, supervising the arrival and departure of customers, dealing with problems, organising weekly barbeques, and dismantling and cleaning equipment at the end of the season. Pay is £35–£50 per week, plus accommodation, travel expenses, insurance and an end-of-season bonus.

**Sunsites,** European Personnel Dept, Sunsites House, Dorking, Surrey (tel. 0306–887733). Only 3 vacancies per year in Spain. Pay £50–£60 per week. Duties much the same as Solaire above.

**Tentrek Expeditions,** 152 Maidstone Rd, Ruxley Corner, Sidcup, Kent (tel. 01–302 0426).

## CASUAL WORK

There seems to be a significant contradiction between the dire official threats that foreigners found working without the necessary permits in Spain are liable to be arrested and detained until arrangements can be made for their deportation, and what actually happens, especially in tourist areas during high season. Whilst not wishing to advise anyone to flout the law openly, it is possible to give some sort of idea of the money-making activities that are possible:

- *Time-share touting.* Commissions can be very high but the high-pressure sales techniques employed by the companies leave a lot to be desired.
- *Leafleting.* Discos, clubs, restaurants etc employ people to hand out leaflets to tourists advertising their services.
- *Selling* ice-creams, cold drinks, etc on the beach.
- *Street vending.* Jewellery, artefacts, anything.
- *Bar work.* In tourist areas where English-speaking staff are wanted, especially by British-owned businesses.
- *Disc-jockeying.* If you have talent in this field, and the push to persuade someone to employ you.
- *Cleaning and repairing boats.* Scour the yacht clubs on the *costas!*
- *Busking.* Not legal, but tolerated. Financial gain is normally related to musical talent.
- *Pavement artists/street portraitists.* Again dependent on your talent in this field.
- *Private classes.* See section on **teaching English as a foreign language** above.

## SELF-EMPLOYMENT

The professional self-employed can benefit immediately from Spain's joining the Common Market. You don't need a visa if you want to set up a business in Spain, although you will need the following.

1. Authorisation from the local authorities, i.e. the *Gobierno Civil* in the province where you intend setting up the business. The **Spanish Consulate** (20 Draycott Place, London SW3 (tel. 01–581 5921) ) and the **Commercial Office of the Spanish Embassy** (22 Manchester Sq, London W1 (tel. 01–486 0101) ) will be able to advise you on what sort of documentation you will need.
2. Proof that you have the qualifications necessary to practise your profession, and to have them officially validated by the Ministry of Education and Science (see p. 47). Only then will you be allowed to practise by the relevant professional body. A list is given below, but don't expect much encouragement from them!

   *Architects:* **Consejo Superior de los Colegios de Arquitectos de España,** Paseo de la Castellana 10–12, 28001 Madrid (tel.91–435 1859).
   *Lawyers:* **Consejo General de la Abogacia Española,** c/General Castaños 4, 28004 Madrid (tel. 91–419 2863).
   *Chemists:* **Consejo General de Colegios de Farmacéuticos,** c/Villanueva 11, 28001 Madrid (tel. 91–431 2560).
   *Doctors and dentists:* **Consejo General de los Colegios de Médicos de España,** c/Villanueva 11, 28001 Madrid (tel. 91–431 7780). EEC legislation exists regarding the acceptability of medical qualifications.

The General Medical Council will issue a certificate stating that your degree and training complied with it.

## OTHER OPPORTUNITIES

### Secretarial
There is a real possibility of finding work in this field for people with good skills, several years' experience, and a high level of both spoken and written Spanish. However, if you're that well qualified you'd probably be able to get a better paid job elsewhere in Europe, and avoid having to work the excessively long Spanish day.

Later in the chapter are listed some agencies that specialise in secretarial placements abroad, and a number of companies if you want to try direct contact. You may see the occasional ad in the newspapers here, but *El País* is likely to prove a richer source.

Temping exists in the larger cities in Spain, but this won't be possible immediately, as initial work permits must specify a particular job for a particular company.

### Translating
Again, possibilities exist, but mainly on a freelance basis. Not really possible unless you've first cracked the problem of getting a non-restrictive work permit, but could possibly supplement other income.

### Exchanges in the catering industry
The Employment Department of the **British Hotels, Restaurants and Caterers' Association** (13 Cork St, London W1) runs an international exchange scheme which offers students and other young people up to the age of 30 employed in catering the chance to work for several months in Spain, mostly during the high season as waiting staff. Applicants should have had at least a year's practical experience of professional training.

### Student work placements for technical experience
These are run through the Central Bureau—see p. 42.

### Opportunities in international organisations
Opportunities sometimes occur in Spain with the **Organisation for Economic Co-operation and Development**. These are 2–3 month assignments, for experts in various specialised fields such as economic programming, finance, statistics, industrial development, agriculture, marketing, tourism and regional planning. The following office deals with such posts, and keeps a file of suitable applicants for when vacancies arise: **International Recruitment Unit,** Overseas Development Administration, Abercrombie House, Eaglesham Rd, East Kilbride, G75 8EE.

### Agriculture
By time of publication the following organisation will probably be able to find 3–12 month placements on Spanish farms for young people with at

least 2 years' experience of agricultural work, with the aim of broadening their knowledge and experience of agricultural methods: **International Farm Experience Programme,** YFC Centre, National Agricultural Centre, Kenilworth, Warwicks (tel. 0203–58704).

See also the UK Sponsoring Authority for the **International Exchange of Young Agriculturalists,** Agriculture House, London SW1 (tel. 01–235 6143).

**EEC Young Worker Exchange Programme**
This is a scheme run by the **Central Bureau for Educational Visits and Exchanges,** Seymour Mews House, Seymour Mews, London W1 (tel. 01–486 5101). Short-term work placements in Spain can be arranged for young workers, or students in need of work experience.

## BRITISH COMPANIES WITH OFFICES IN SPAIN

**Madrid**
**ACROW Ibérica SA,** Ctra de Burgos km 18,200, Políg. Ind. Sur, San Sebastián de los Reyes, Madrid
**AIDS Iberia SA,** Juan Alvarez Mendizábal 3, Madrid 28008
**APV Ibérica SA,** Miguel Yuste 15, Madrid 28017
**Aikin Española SA,** Caídos División Azul 16, Madrid 28016
**Airoil Flaregas Española SA,** Colombia 63, Madrid 28016
**Alcudia,** Avda de Brasil 5, Madrid 28020
**Alexander & Alexander de España,** Paseo de la Castellana 121, Madrid 28046
**Alliance Assurance Co Ltd,** Recoletos 29, Madrid 28004
**Arquitectura Langdon SA,** Fernando el Santo 17, Madrid 28004
**Austin Rover España SA,** Crta de Madrid-Barcelona km 18,600, Políg. Ind. San Fernando de Henares, Madrid
**BOC Medishield SA,** Augustín de Foxá 27, Madrid 28027
**BP Española SA,** Cea Bermúdez 66, Madrid 28003
**BP Minera España SA,** Alberto Alcocer 46, Madrid 28016
**BP Petroleum Development of Spain SA,** Albacete 5, Madrid 28027
**BP Solar España SA,** Cea Bermúdez 66, Madrid 28003
**Bain Dawes Sagese SA,** Tambre 33, Madrid 28002
**Bank of London & South America,** Apartado 64, Madrid 28006
**Binatone SA,** Avda de Bruselas 38, Madrid 28028
**Blackwood Hodge,** Velázquez 75, Madrid 28006
**Bredia SA,** Crta de Madrid-Barcelona km 33,600, Alcalá de Henares, Madrid
**Brent Ibérica SA,** Crta de Loeches, Torrejón de Ardoz, Madrid
**British Airways SA,** San Bernardo 17, Madrid 28008
**British Caledonian Airways,** Torre de Madrid, Princesa 1, Madrid 28013
**British Rail,** Torre de Madrid 26, Madrid 28013
**British Steel Corporation Ltd,** Serrano Jover 5–5º, Madrid 28015
**British Tourist Authority,** Torre de Madrid 6–4º, Plaza de España, Madrid

**Budget Servicar SA,** Estébanez Calderón 5, Madrid 28020
**Burmah España SA,** Profesor Waksman 10, Madrid 28036
**Cadbury Schweppes de España SA,** Joaquín María López 59, Madrid 28015
**Cementos y Fibras SA,** Luchana 23, Madrid 28010
**Charter Esploraciones,** José Abascal 57, Madrid 28003
**Cía. Española de Licores,** José Abascal 42, Madrid 28003
**Cía. Española de Minas de Tharsis SA,** Núñez de Balboa 120, Madrid 28006
**Cía. General de Carbones SA,** Alfonso XII 18, Madrid 28014
**Cía. Scholl SA,** Infanta Mercedes 90, Madrid 28020
**Cierres Mecánicos Crane SA,** Cemento 1, Torrejón de Ardoz, Madrid
**Colborn Dawes Ibérica SA,** Mar Mediterráneo 5, San Fernando de Henares, Madrid
**Compair Ibérica SA,** Conde de Peñalver 47, Madrid 28006
**Construcciones y Estudios Industriales SA,** Conde de Peñalver 36, Madrid 28006
**Consultores Tillyard SA,** Paseo de la Castellana 166, Madrid 28046
**Continental Assurance Co Ltd,** Recoletos 8, Madrid 28001
**Contisa Internacional SA,** Fernando el Santo 17, Madrid 28010
**Cooper Hotworic Española,** La Maso 2, Mirasierra, Madrid 28034
**Crest Centre Hotels,** Jacometrezo 4, Madrid 28013
**Data Dynamics España SA,** Juan Pérez Zuñiga 20, Madrid 28027
**Datasense España SA,** Pedro Teixeira 8, Madrid 28020
**De La Rue Ibérica Ltd,** Claudio Coello 73, Madrid 28001
**Deloitte Haskins & Sells,** Orense 2, Madrid 28020
**Dimetronic SA,** Sierra Morena 28, Torrejón de Ardoz, Madrid
**Diseños Ibelart SA,** Fernando el Santo 17, Madrid 28004
**Dowty Meco SA,** Dracena 1, Madrid 28016
**Dunhill SA,** José Ortega y Gasset 26, Madrid 28006
**Editorial Alhambra SA,** Claudio Coello 76, Madrid 28001
**Richard Ellis SA,** Pedro Teixeira 8, Madrid 28020
**Ernst & Whinney,** Alberto Alcocer 24, Madrid
**Europistas Concesionaria Española SA,** María de Molina 37, Madrid 28006
**Expandite Asociado,** Avda General Perón 4–3º b, Madrid
**Ferodo Española SA,** Aptdo 231, Alcalá de Henares, Madrid
**Fisher Controls SA,** Sierra Nevada, San Fernando de Henares, Madrid
**Fisons,** Capitán Haya 22–1B, Madrid
**Flexibos de España SA,** Paseo de la Castellana 147, Madrid 28046
**Flexibox,** c/Canadá, Torrejón de Ardoz, Madrid
**Foster Wheeler Iberia SA,** Basílica 17, Madrid 28020
**GEC-Elliott Automation SA,** Hermosilla 8, Madrid 28001
**GKN Automotive Ibérica SA,** Cea Bermúdez 14, Madrid 28003
**Gala Cosmético SA,** Méndez Alvaro 57, Madrid 28045
**Gesinter SA,** Orfila 5, Madrid 28010
**Gestetner SA,** Príncipe de Vergara 116, Madrid 28020
**Gestión Bancaria Internacional SA,** Lagasca 88, Madrid 28001

**Gill & Duffus Chemicals SA,** Paseo de la Castellana 123, Madrid 28046
**Glaxo SA,** Paseo de la Castellana 165, Madrid 28046
**Guardian Assurance Co Ltd,** León 34, Madrid 28006
**Gyproc Ibérica SA,** Fernando el Santo 20–2º, Madrid 28004
**Haden Drysys SA,** Príncipe de Vergara 112, Madrid 28002
**Hawker Siddeley International,** Rey Francisco 8, Madrid 28020
**P C Henderson Ltd,** Capitán Haya 56, Madrid 28020
**Hispanoflex SA,** Andrés Obispo 37, Madrid 28034
**Hotel Castellana Intercontinental,** Paseo de la Castellana 49, Madrid 28046
**Thomas Howell Kiewit,** Pedro Teixeira 8, Madrid 28020
**Hydron Corlens SA,** Gral Cabrera 11, Madrid 28006
**ICI Ferma SA,** Conde de Peñalver 45, Madrid 28006
**ICL España International Computers SA,** Luchana 23, Madrid 28010
**IMACO,** Pza Lealtad 2, Madrid 28014
**Ibertanica SA,** Lagasca 88, Madrid 28001
**Indein Wrightson SA,** José Abascal 59, Madrid 28003
**Industrial de Gases Hispano-Inglesa SA,** Vallehermoso 15, Madrid 28015
**Instalaciones Maquinaria y Herramientas Industriales SA,** Hermosilla 21, Madrid 28001
**International Drilling Fluids España SA,** Paseo de la Habana 24, Madrid 28036
**International Nickel Ibérica,** Alberto Alcocer 46–3º A, Madrid
**JCB Sales,** Dr Ezquerdo 136–7º, Madrid
**Gordon Johnson Ibérica SA,** Capitán Haya 13, Madrid 28020
**Kompass España,** Avda General Perón 26–4º, Madrid 28020
**Laboratories Beecham,** Edificio Mirasierra, Costa Brava 13, Madrid 28034
**Laboratorios Liade SA,** Joaquín Costa 26, Madrid 28034
**Laing SA,** Capitán Haya 1, Madrid 28020
**Land Rover Santana SA,** Avda de Manoteras 6, Madrid 28020
**Legal & General Assurance Society Ltd,** Capitán Haya 1, Madrid 28020
**Leinster & Cia SA,** Núñez de Balboa 49, Madrid 28001
**Leo Burnett SA,** Guzmán el Bueno 133, Madrid 28003
**Letraset Esselte,** Gral Margallo 23, Madrid 28020
**Lever Ibérica SA,** Manuel de Falla 7, Madrid 28036
**Leyland Ibérica SA,** Alberto Alcocer 31, Madrid 28016
**Lintas SA,** Paseo de la Castellana 130, Madrid 28046
**Lucas Service España,** Polígono Industrial de Coslada, Avda de Fuentemar 23, Coslada, Madrid
**Macandrews & Co Ltd,** Marqués de Casa Riera 4, Madrid 28014
**Midland Bank,** Serrano 45–3º, Madrid 28001
**Midland Servicios Financieros,** José Ortega y Gasset 29, Madrid 28006
**Graham Miller España SL,** Paseo de la Castellana 143, Madrid 28046
**Minas de Gador SA,** Fortuny 51, Madrid 28010
**Mole-Richardson España Ltd,** Gustavo Fdez Balbuena 11, Madrid 28002
**Monotype de España SA,** Hermosilla 114, Madrid 28009

**Nanta SA,** Vista Alegre 4, Madrid 28019
**Nosworthy SA,** Arrieta 13, Madrid 28013
**Noudez Española SA,** Gran Vía 55, Madrid 28013
**Oxford University Press,** Campoamor 18, Madrid 28004
**Pandrol Ibérica SA,** Guzmán el Bueno 14, Madrid 28015
**Peat Marwick Mitchell & Co,** Serrano Jover 5–1º, Madrid 28008
**Pereco Euroscan SA,** Perú 3, Coslada, Madrid
**Perkins Hispania,** Hermosilla 17, Madrid 28009
**Pilas Secas Tudor SA,** Guzmán el Bueno 74, Madrid 28003
**Plessey,** Martires de Alcalá 4–3º, Madrid
**Price Waterhouse,** Princesa 3, Madrid 28008
**Pritchard Española SA,** Vicente Muzas 11, Madrid 28033
**Publinsa Kenyon & Eckehardt SA,** María de Molina 39, Madrid 28006
**Racal Survey España SA,** Paseo de la Castellana 141, Madrid 28046
**Raychem SA,** Políg. Ind. de Alcobendas, Alcobendas, Madrid
**Readymix Asland SA,** Avda de Brasil 13, Madrid 28020
**Reditune Española SA,** Manuel Luna 4, Madrid 28020
**Reed Stenhouse y Cia,** Alfonso XII 20, Madrid 28014
**Rentalauto SA,** García Paredes 57, Madrid 28010
**Rioblanco SA,** Joaquín María López 62, Madrid 28015
**Rio Tinto Minera,** Zurbano 76, Madrid 28016
**The Ritz Madrid,** Pza Lealtad 5, Madrid 28014
**Robins Davies Española SL,** Av Pio XII 47, Madrid 28016
**Rodriguez Phillips SA,** Orense 25, Madrid 28020
**Royal Assurance,** Pº de la Castellana 4, Madrid 28001
**Saccone & Speed,** Paseo de la Castellana 174, Madrid 28046
**Sarmop Ibérica SA,** Capitán Haya 56, Madrid 28020
**Schrader Bellows España SA,** Comandante Zorita 13, Madrid 28010
**Securitas España SA,** Bermúdez Cañete 1, Madrid 28016
**Sedgwick Forbes-Acebo SA,** Comandante Franco 3, Madrid 28016
**Servicios Sanitarios SA,** Rosario Pino 6, Madrid 28020
**Sharples Stokes España SA,** Rodríguez Marín 61, Madrid 28016
**Shell Española SA,** Apartado 652, Madrid 28014
**Skala Television SA,** Gral Oraa 47, Madrid 28006
**Sociedad Petrolifera Española Shell SA,** Barquillo 17, Madrid 28004
**Sotheby's,** Pza Independencia 8, Madrid 28001
**Spencer Stuart Consejeros de Dirección SA,** Oquendo 23, Madrid 28006
**Stafford-Miller de España SA,** Núñez de Balboa 118, Madrid 28006
**Stamford Ibérica SA,** Paseo de la Castellana 62, Madrid 28046
**Stone Ibérica SA,** Antonio Maura 8, Madrid 28014
**Gordon Taylor SA,** Victor Andrés Belaunde 52, Madrid 28016
**Tecalemit Iberia SA,** Bolivar 30, Madrid 28045
**Tioxide España SA,** Avda de Brasil 5, Madrid 28020
**Touche Ross SA,** Orense 2–9º, Madrid 28020
**Transmitton SA,** Alberto Alcocer 46, Madrid 28016
**Trust House Forte Hotels Ltd,** Gran Vía 88m, Madrid 28013
**Unilever Espana SA,** Manuel de Falla 7, Madrid 28045
**Union Explosivos Rio Tinto SA,** Paseo de la Castellana 20, Madrid 28046

**Unitros SA,** Mateo Inurria 23, Madrid 28036
**Velázquez SA,** Claudio Coello 17, Madrid 28001
**Wilkinson Sword,** Avda de Brasil 17, Madrid 28020
**Willis Faber & Dumas Ltd,** Villanueva 20, Madrid 28001
**Wilson Walton International,** Guzmán el Bueno 133, Madrid 28003
**Wimpey Construction Ltd,** Orense 20, Madrid 28020
**Worcester Controls Ibérica SA,** Caucho 19, Torrejón de Ardoz, Madrid
**Arthur Young & Co,** Orense 4, Madrid 28020
   Also: **The Anglo-American Hospital,** c/Juan XXIII 1, Cuidad Universitaria, Madrid

**Barcelona (and province)**
**Afora SA,** Aribau 240, Barcelona 08006
**Anglofort SA,** Rosellón 33, Barcelona 08015
**Ase España SA,** Juan Ramón Jiménez 6, San Justo Desvern (Barcelona)
**Asland SA,** Córcega 325, Barcelona 08037
**Margaret Astor SA,** Gran Vía 133, Barcelona 08014
**Belmar SA,** Ps de Gracia 11A, Barcelona 08007
**Brooke Bond Liebig España SA,** Gran Vía 497–1º, Barcelona 08015
**David Brown Sadi Español,** Angli 31, Barcelona 08017
**Burberrys Spain,** Bilbao 122–126, Barcelona 08018
**Central de Aparatos Paramedicales,** Pl F. Maciá 10, Barcelona 08004
**Centro de Calculo de Sabadell SA,** Ctra de Ripollet-Santiga km 2,750, Barbera del Valles (Barcelona)
**Centro de Trabajos Técnicos,** Aribau 185, Barcelona 08036
**Commercial Union Assurance,** Vía Augusta 23, Barcelona 08006
**Constructora de Equipos Diesel SA,** Ctra de Sardanyola, San Cugat del Valles (Barcelona)
**Croda Española SA,** Ctra de Puigcerdá km 19,800, Mollet del Valles (Barcelona)
**Danis Benton & Bowles SA,** Diagonal 512, Barcelona 08006
**EMI Odeon SA,** Guifré 728, Badalona (Barcelona)
**Enerfluid SA,** Sicilia 382, Barcelona 08025
**Eschmann Española SA,** Av Can Cabanyes, Torre Florida, Rubí. (Barcelona)
**Fullwood Comercial Española SA,** Independencia 228, Barcelona 08026
**Foseco Española,** Pedro IV 345, Barcelona 08005
**Frenos y Embragues SA,** Dolores Alameda s/n, Cornellá (Barcelona)
**Frigo SA,** Perú 84, Barcelona 08018
**General Optica SA,** Andrade 128, Barcelona 08020
**Guardian Royal Exchange,** Diagonal 523, Barcelona 08007
**Heydi España SA,** Vía Layetana 24, Barcelona 08003
**Hidracar SA,** Antigua Ctra de Manresa-Monistrol s/n, San Vicente de Castellet (Barcelona)
**Hi-Draw Española SA,** Trav de Gracia 18–20, Barcelona 08021
**Hilaturas de Fabra y Coats,** Bruch 50, Barcelona 08010
**Howard Rotavator Ibérica SA,** Ctra de Granollers-Gerona km 1,500, Granollers (Barcelona)

**Howson Algraphy SA,** Independencia 384, Barcelona 08026
**ICI España SA,** Gran Vía Sur km 2,200, Hospitalet de Llobregat (Barcelona)
**INA Rodamientos de Agujas,** Gran Vía de las Cortes 806, Barcelona 08013
**IWS Secretariado Int de la Lana,** Paseo de Gracia 111, Barcelona 08008
**Ind. del Acetato de la Celulosa SA,** Paseo de Gracia 11, Barcelona 08007
**Ind. Deslite SA,** Badajoz 5, Barcelona 08005
**Industrial Cartonera SA,** Gran Vía de las Cortes 678, Barcelona 08010
**Instron Ltd,** Paralelo 21, Barcelona 08004
**Johnston Shields SA,** Gerona 22, Barcelona 08010
**Kelly Alarm,** Vía Augusta 143, Barcelona 08021
**Kent Ibérica SA,** Gran Vía 859, Barcelona 08018
**Lasing Pares SA,** Sabino de Arana 44, Barcelona 08028
**Lloyds Register of Shipping,** Vila y Vila 19, Barcelona 08004
**Louverdrape SA,** Brasilea 4, Barbera del Valles (Barcelona)
**MSA Española SA,** Avd Diagonal 618, Barcelona 08021
**Mather & Platt,** Tuset 23–25, Barcelona
**Morgan Matroc SA,** Ctra de Sabadell-Granollers km 15, Llisa del Vall (Barcelona)
**North British & Mercantile Insurance,** Vía Layetana 41, Barcelona 08003
**Nurel SA,** Sabino de Arana 54, Barcelona 08028
**Payen SA,** Políg. Zona Franca, Barcelona 08004
**Pearl Assurance,** Vía Layetana 120, Barcelona
**Philidas Española SA,** Felipe II 33, Barcelona 08027
**Phoenix Assurance,** c/Tuset 20, Barcelona 08006
**Polydrop SA,** A Fabregada 26, Hospitalet de Llobregat (Barcelona)
**La Productora del Borax,** Tuset 8, Barcelona 08006
**K J Quinn Ibérica SA,** Gran Vía 17, Montmelo (Barcelona)
**Relampago Zipp SA,** Gral Varela 6, Rubi (Barcelona)
**Revertex Ibérica SA,** Ptrav de las Cortes 361, Barcelona 08015
**Riego Vrigta SA,** Ctra de Madrid a Francia, Cabrera de Mar (Barcelona)
**Rolls Royce de España SA,** Bailén 22, Barcelona 08010
**Royal Insurance,** Apartado 240, Barcelona 08007
**Smith & Nephew Ibérica SA,** Infanta Carlota 61, Barcelona 08029
**Sugarline SA,** San Adrián 78, Barcelona 08030
**Syamco Amiet Control Systems SA,** Palomar 58, Barcelona 08030
**TI Internacional Ltd,** Balmes 152, Barcelona 08008
**Transnatur SA,** Ausias March 26, Barcelona 08010
**Weddel SA,** Diputación 305, Barcelona 08009
**Witty SA,** Pl Medinaceli 5, Barcelona 08002
**Yorkshire de España SA,** Bergueda s/n, Sra Perpetua de Mogoda (Barcelona)

**Bilbao (including Vizcaya province)**
**Agra SA,** Autonomía 4, Lejona
**Aplicaciones Industriales de Cromo Duro SA,** Ribera Zorrozaurre 10–12, Bilbao
**Cia Española de Pinturas Internacional SA,** Pl R de Venezuela 2, Bilbao

**DCG Española SA,** Ganeta 6, Las Arenas
**Forjas y Alambres del Cadagua SA,** Aldanondo 2, Arbuyo
**Formica Española SA,** Aptdo 1031, Galdacano, Bilbao
**Marston Ibérica SA,** Talleronde Alde, Sopelana, Vizcaya
**Morganite Española SA,** Av Sabino Arana 10, Lejona
**Mure SA,** Pertexeta 22, Alonsotegui
**Reckitt & Colman SA,** Luis Power 1, Bilbao
**Roller Industrial SA,** Ctra de Bilbao-San Sebastián km 5, Galdacano
**Rotork Controls,** Mayor 25, Las Arenas-Gexto
**Sociedad General de Productos Cerámicos SA,** Bailem 1, Bilbao
**Spinks & Co,** Ribera de Azpe 28, Azpe-Erandio
**Steetley Minerales SA,** Bo Ugarte, San Salvador del Valle
**Alex Stewart Iberia SA,** Orixe 24, Bilbao
**Sun Assurance,** Alameda de Urquijo 12, Bilbao 8
**James Walker Ibérica SA,** Sta Lucia 8, Bilbao

Others
**Aranzabal SA,** Castilla 14, Vitoria (Alava)
**Aridos Asturianos SA,** San Bernabé 2, Oviedo (Asturias)
**Armstrong Amortiguadores SA,** Alton de Pumarín, Gijón (Asturias)
**Blandy Brothers & Cia,** Av Escaleritas 120, Las Palmas de Gran Canaria
**Bolton Gate Co SA,** Av Alameda Principal 4, Málaga
**Cory Brothers,** Expl Torres Quevedo, Muelle Grande, Las Palmas
**Croft (Jerez) SA,** Ctra Circunvalación km 636,300, Jerez de la Frontera (Cádiz)
**Duff Gordon & Cia SA,** Jesús Nazareno 10, Puerto de Sta María (Cádiz)
**Fabricado Inoxidables SA,** Ctra de Madrid-Cádiz, La Carolina (Jaen)
**Filtrona Española SA,** Políg. Ind. Henares, Guadalajara
**Fyffees (Canary Islands) Ltd,** Finca de los Olivos, Adeje, Sta Cruz de Tenerife
**Garvey SA,** Divina Pastora 3, Jerez de la Frontera (Cádiz)
**Girling España SA,** Ctra de Estella-Salinas s/n, Orcoyen (Navarra)
**González Byass SA,** Manuel María González 12, Jerez de la Frontera (Cádiz)
**Grupo Alimentaria Vida,** Emilio Donat 50, Carcaixent (Valencia)
**Guyatt & Sons Ltd,** Av Linares Rivas 2, La Coruña
**John Harvey & Son,** Alvar Núñez 53, Jerez de la Frontera (Cadiz)
**Hoteles Canarios SA,** Alfredo L Jones 40, Las Palmas de Gran Canaria
**Koipe SA,** Paseo del Urumea s/n, San Sebastián (Guipúzcoa)
**Lovable España SA,** Polígono El Balconcillo 57–58, Guadalajara
**Miller & Cia SA,** Muelle Sta Catalina 2, Las Palmas de Gran Canaria
**Nimes España,** Almirante Cadarso 17, Valencia
**Oilfield Hydrographic Projects,** Soler 22, Tarragona
**Productos Dolomiticos SA,** Revilla de Camargo (Cantabria)
**Productos Ortiz SA,** Ctra de Valencia-Alicante km 174,600, Vergel (Alicante)
**Rowlett & Cia,** Genaro Perlade s/n, Sevilla
**Sandeman Hermanos,** Pizarro 10, Jerez de la Frontera (Cádiz)

**Terrain Ibérica SA,** General Alava 20, Vitoria (Alava)
**Towler Hispania SA,** Entidad Zicuñaga 62, Hernani (Guipúzcoa)
**Walthon Weir Pacific SA,** Ctra de Castellón km 5,500, Zaragoza
**Wisdom & Warter Ltd,** Pizarro 7, Jerez de la Frontera (Cádiz)
**Zeltia Agraria SA,** La Rebla, Porriño (Pontevedra)

## BRITISH FIRMS WITH OPERATIONS IN SPAIN

**Acrow,** 8 South Wharf Rd, London W2 1PB (tel. 01-262 3456)
**AE Group,** Cawston House, Cawston Lane, Rugby, Warwicks (tel. 0788-812555)
**Barclays Bank International Ltd,** 54 Lombard St, London EC3P
**BICC Ltd,** 21 Bloomsbury St, London WC1B 3QN (tel. 01-637 1300)
**Blackwood Hodge,** 25 Berkeley Square, London W1A 4AX (tel. 01-629 9090)
**BL** Nuffield House, 41-46 Piccadilly, London W1 (tel. 01-734 6080)
**Brent Chemicals International,** Ridgeway, Iver, Bucks (tel. 0753-651812)
**British Mining Consultants,** Mill Lane, Common Rd, Huthwaite, Sutton-in-Ashfield, Nottinghamshire (tel. 0623-517777)
**Diamond Shamrock Europe,** PO Box 1, Eccles, Manchester M30
**Grindlays Bank Ltd,** 36 Fenchurch St, London EC3P (tel. 01-626 0545)
**Guinness Peat International,** 32 St Mary at Hill, London EC3R (tel. 01-623 9333)
**Lloyds Bank International Ltd,** 40-66 Queen Victoria St, London EC4
**Lucas Industries Ltd,** Great King St, Birmingham B19 (tel. 021-554 5252)
**McGraw Hill International Book Co,** Maidenhead, Berks
**G Watson Gray (Analysts) Ltd,** Perry Rd, Witham, Essex (tel. 0376-515050

## SPECIALIST EMPLOYMENT AGENCIES

### Key information
- **The Federation of Recruitment and Employment Services Ltd,** 10 Belgrave Square, London SW1 (tel. 01-235 6616). Can supply a list of employment agencies specialising in recruitment for overseas posts.

### Accountancy
**Brook Street Overseas,** 32 The Strand, London WC2 (tel. 01-930 7399)

### Executive
**Human Resources Management,** c/General Sanjurjo 55, Madrid 28003
**Merton Associates (Consultants) Ltd,** Merton House, 70 Grafton Way, London W1 (tel. 01-388 2051)
**Spencer Stuart and Associates Ltd,** Brook House, 113 Park Lane, London W1Y (tel. 01-493 1238)

## Secretarial
**Brook Street Overseas**, 32 The Strand, London WC2 (tel. 01-730 7399)
**International Secretaries**, 174 New Bond St, London SW1 (tel. 01-491 7100)

## Nannies
**Albermarle Nannies Ltd**, 138 New Bond St, London W1 (tel. 01-493 2441). National Nursery Examination Board Diploma essential.

## Nursing
**International Medical Personnel (London) Ltd**, 11 Hinde St, London W1 (tel. 01-486 6040)

## VOLUNTARY WORK

### WORK CAMPS

- **Servicio Voluntario Internacional de España**, Instituto de la Juventud, c/Ortega y Gassett 71, Madrid.
- **Servei Català de Camps de Treball**, (SCCT), Rambla Catalunya 5, pral 2ª, 08007 Barcelona (tel. 93-301 4281).

International work camps exist all over the world as a means of bringing young people of different nationalities together to work on projects which are of benefit to local communities. In Spain two different bodies run these, the **Servicio Voluntario Internacional de España**, which is part of the youth service in Spain and works in conjunction with the youth departments of the various regional governments, and the **Servei Català de Camps de Treball**, which is the Catalan division of the SCI (International Civic Service). Camps normally take place during July and August and last 2-3 weeks.

Most camps accept volunteers from a range of countries (although a few are organised on a bilateral basis), so you can expect to be working in a group of 20-30 young people of different nationalities. In general only people aged 18-26 are eligible, although there are a few camps for the 15-17 age group, and some will accept people up to the age of 30. Some sort of knowledge of Spanish is required, and previous voluntary work experience in the UK is preferred.

Almost all camps are located in small villages or totally rural areas, and accommodation is very rudimentary: either in tents or local schools and hostels taken over for the purpose. The group is responsible for organising the work to be done and doing its own catering on a rota basis. 6-8 hours are usually spent working each day, with the rest of the time given over to getting to know the area, visiting the local sights, taking part in community events and fiestas, and general relaxation.

Those taking part are expected to make their own travel arrangements, but accommodation and food are provided free, so there are few other expenses. Sometimes a small allowance is paid.

## Types of camp

When applying for a work camp (see below), it is useful to specify what general type of work you are interested in doing:

- *Conservation work.* This can take the form of surveys, work strengthening sea defences or river banks, bird-ringing, gardening, clearing sites of rubble, etc.
- *Reconstruction work.* Helping to rebuild historic buildings or walls, reinstating old footpaths, etc.
- *Archaeological digs.*
- *Community work.* Only through the **Servei Català de Camps de Treball**.

## How to apply

Recruiting is normally carried out through agencies in the applicant's own country, which take charge of registration (there is a small fee — about £20) and providing you with the practical details. In Britain you can apply (April–May for summer camps) as follows:

For camps organised by the **Servicio Voluntario Internacional de España**:
- **Christian Movement for Peace,** c/o Mark Roberts, Hilton's Chambers, Noushill, Shrewsbury, Shropshire (tel. 0743–66542).
- **United Nations Association International,** Youth Service, Temple of Peace, Cathays Park, Cardiff (tel. 0222–28549).

For camps organised by the **Servei Català de Camps de Treball**:
- **International Voluntary Service,** Ceresole House, 53 Regent Road, Leicester (tel. 0533–541862).

If you are in Spain, it is possible to contact the organisations themselves for information about the camps, and to apply directly through the youth departments of the regional governments whose addresses are given in the regional sections later in the book.

## Other work camps

- **The Ecumenical Youth Council in Europe** runs a programme of work camps each year throughout Europe, sometimes including one or two in Spain. For details apply to **British Council of Churches,** 2 Eaton Gate, London SW1 (tel. 01–730 9611).
- **Concordia (Youth Service Volunteers) Ltd,** 8 Brunswick Place, Hove, Brighton (tel. 0273–772086).

## LONGER-TERM VOLUNTARY WORK

- *Volunteer Work* published by the Central Bureau for Educational Visits and Exchanges (see p. 42).

There are not many opportunities for longer-term voluntary work in Spain, as most organisations working in this field concentrate their efforts on Third World countries. Nonetheless, the following may be of help:

**Archaeology Abroad,** 31–34 Gordon Square, London WC1. Can supply lists of sites requiring volunteers — some previous experience is required.
**Co-ordinating Committee for the International Voluntary Service,** 1 rue Miollis, 75015 Paris. Clearing house for requests for information on voluntary work, can supply lists of organisations concerned with voluntary service in any particular country, and produces various publications on themes related to voluntary service.
**Voluntary Service Overseas,** 9 Belgrave Square, London SW1 (tel. 01–235 5191).
**The Institute of Cultural Affairs,** 277 St Ann's Road, London N15 (tel. 01–802 2848). Community development schemes.

## MISSIONARY WORK

The following organisations can help you here, although opportunities in Spain are fairly limited:

**The Bible Churchmen's Missionary Society,** 251 Lewisham Way, London SE4 (tel. 01–691 6111). Missionary work of all kinds.

**Christians Abroad,** Livingstone House, 11 Carteret St, London SW1 (tel. 01–222 2165).

**The Evangelical Missionary Alliance,** Whitefield House, 186 Kennington Park Road, London SE11 (tel. 01–735 0421). Clearing house for information on missionary work throughout the world.

**The Medical Missionary Association,** 6 Cannonbury Place, London N1 (tel. 01–359 1313). Missionary work for medical practitioners.

**SAMS (South American Missionary Society),** Allen Gardiner House, Pembury Rd, Tunbridge Wells, Kent (tel. 0892–38647/8). Evangelistic campaigns and youth camps, with established contacts in Spain.

# 3 Andalucía

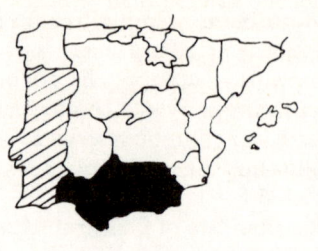

Andalucía, as the most southerly, exotic and colourful region of Spain, has traditionally provided the packagers and purveyors of Spanish culture with all those clichéd images we know so well, and which have come to stand for all Spanish culture — castanets and mantillas, scrawny 'toreadors', and proud señoritas dancing flamenco. Andalucía's power to attract outsiders goes deeper than just filling hotel rooms on the Costa del Sol though: the Moors were struck by its haunting beauty and agricultural potential, calling it the land of rivers; musicians such as Bizet (in *Carmen*) and Rossini (*The Barber of Seville*) have found inspiration in the exuberance of its culture, and many British writers and intellectuals (Gerald Brennon and Laurie Lee among the most notable) have been drawn to it, perhaps in search of the passion and sensuality which seems lacking in our own culture.

Andalucía certainly lives up to its vibrant reputation, and is an assault on the senses. The light and colour are perhaps what strike one first, then the exoticism of the landscapes: prickly pears, cactuses of tropical proportions, whitewashed Moorish style houses in the distance clinging to the rugged hills like cubes of sugar, and closer at hand the earthy smells of olives, wine casks and black tobacco. It's here in the African heat that the old Spanish habits die hard — the siesta, machismo, bullfights and flamenco.

Andalucía goes way beyond all these stereotypes though. There are great, bustling cities like Seville and Málaga, and smaller, intensely individual ones like Granada, Cádiz and Cordoba. The Arabs were here for many centuries — nearly 800 years in Granada — and their influence is evident on a grand scale in wonders of Moorish art like the Alhambra in Granada, Cordoba's Mezquita, and Seville's Alcázar, and on a popular scale all around you, in the people, the language (*Andaluz* is an Arabic-influenced dialect of Castilian Spanish) and in their way of life. There are impressive acres of olive trees and vineyards, and, in smaller concentrations, evidence of new agricultural developments — polythene-covered hillsides in Almería and on the plains whole fields of sunflowers, a dramatic sight in spring, with all faces turned to the sun, like a choir.

There are wild mountain areas and primitive hill villages, where only the weakly whine of moped engines reminds you that you're in the twentieth century. Then there is the Atlantic seaboard, with quiet seaside towns, ancient ports and sherry *bodegas*, and, of course, there is the Costa del Sol, in all its madness and magnificence, from the ugly, ill-constructed tower blocks of the seedy end of Torremolinos to the yachts and exclusive clubs of Marbella.

Finally there is the *Andaluz* character: wily, self-aware and extravagant, with an almost pagan appreciation of religious ritual and all the trappings of Catholicism — seen at its most evident in the Holy Week processions in Seville.

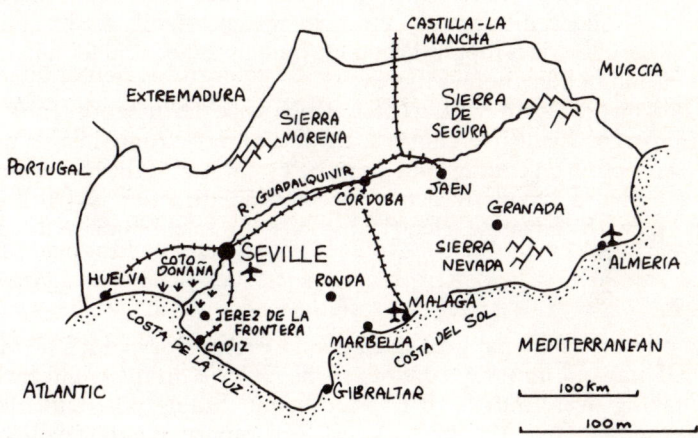

## WHAT TO SEE (FROM MÁLAGA CLOCKWISE)

### Málaga
A throbbing, vital city and port, humming with life, whose attractions remain largely unappreciated by the millions of tourists arriving at its international airport every year in search of 2 weeks in the sun. It's short on monuments (the Renaissance cathedral and the old Moorish **Alcazaba** about sum it up) but it's worth climbing the **Gibralfaro hill**, a site used for centuries as a stronghold by successive civilizations, for a bird's eye view over the bay. The *malagueños* have their priorities right, however; who needs monuments provided you've got a good supply of *tapas* bars, fried fish, wine from the barrel, a glittering sea and plenty of street life. The outlying district of **Pedregalejo** is good for all of these as well.

### Elsewhere in Málaga province
**Ronda.** A mountain town epitomising the harsh romance of Andalucía, in what must be one of the world's most dramatic natural settings. A sheer 400 foot gorge splits the town in two, and there is a walled promenade round the edge with spectacular views over the surrounding country. There are some lovely old parts, but the town's quite modern and prosperous

too. Its bullring is the oldest in Spain.
**Antequera.** Modern town in a valley, some industry.
**Mijas.** White town on the mountainside, only a short drive from the Costa, and as such a showpiece for local handicrafts etc. Pleasant nonetheless.
**The Costa del Sol.** The coast west from Málaga is very built up. What were once tiny fishing villages now merge into each other in an ugly sprawl, and in many places skyscrapers block out any view of the sea. Consult any package-tour brochure if you're interested in distinguishing between them. Marbella, and especially the yacht-infested Puerto Banus, are the most chic places to be, full of *paparazzi* snapping the celebrities. East of Málaga is less developed and until recently the road was slow and windy. The pleasant village of Nerja is rapidly becoming built up as demand for hotels, time-shares and holiday homes increases.
**Melilla.** Port on the North African coast, which since the fifteenth century has formed part of Spanish territory, accessible by ferry from Málaga and Almería (see section on **coming and going** below). There is the old walled town area, and also a modern sector, and its main attraction is that it is a free port, with Japanese electrical goods on sale beside African handicrafts.

### Cádiz
Seaport with a distinctly nautical air built on a promontory which seems already half-way out into the Atlantic. Its heyday was in the eighteenth century, taking over from Seville as the major trading port with the Americas when the Guadalquivir silted up. Still important industrially — smoking factory chimneys bear witness to this — but full of character and interest nonetheless, with old quarters like El Populo and Santa María. Good museum.

### Elsewhere in Cádiz province
**Puerto de Santa María.** Small attractive sherry-shipping port.
**Jérez (de la Frontera).** The centre of the sherry trade, giving its name to the drink (J used to be written as X in Spanish and was pronounced 'sh'). The town now has a decaying elegance reminiscent of some former *Bel Époque*, with palaces, patios and plazas all contributing to the effect. Also sherry *bodegas* and a bit of a cultural centre for other upper crust versions of Andalucian activities like equestrianism and flamenco (see listings).
**The Costa de la Luz** (also continues in Huelva province).
**Rota.** Small port with windswept beach, dominated by US naval base.
**Chipiona.** Family seaside resort, good beach.
**Sanlucar (de Barrameda).** On rather a grander scale from the other towns along this coast, with castle perched on hill overlooking the Guadalquivir estuary and Coto Doñana (see Seville). *Manzanilla* is produced in the *bodegas* here, the sea air giving it its distinctive salty flavour (see the section on **food and drink** below).
**Arcos (de la Frontera).** Inland. A higgledy-piggledy village on a hill, crowned by attractive church and square, with dramatic views over river and surrounding countryside below.

**Sotogrande.** High-class tourist development, with polo and golf featured prominently.
**La Línea (de la Concepción).** Frontier town with Gibraltar (now accessible from Spain).
**Algeciras.** Seedy port forming the crossroads between Africa and Europe, heavily used by Moroccan immigrants working in France and Northern Europe. (Some may find this type of frontier atmosphere fascinating. Personally I'd keep well away.)
**Ceuta.** Another (embattled) Spanish free port on the North African coast, with a claustrophobic atmosphere.
**Tarifa.** Walled white Moorish town with beautiful sandy beaches nearby.

## Huelva
Important port and mining town. Small crowded central area (La Placeta) with busy cafés and bars.

### Elsewhere in Huelva province
**Costa de la Luz.** Northwards from Huelva the coast is an unpretentious strip of golden sand, flanked by pine trees, with occasional resorts such as La Antilla and Isla Cristina, ending at the mouth of the Guadiana river at Ayamonte, which marks the border with Portugal. A car ferry takes about 15 minutes to cross.
**Moguer.** The poet Juan Ramón Jiménez lived here. His home is now a museum.
**Matalascañas.** New beach resort with access to Coto Doñana (see below).

## Seville
Andalucía's capital and a city of over half a million, with a striking personality, warmth and charm, all greens and whites and oranges and perpetually blue skies. It must have been a city of some splendour under the Moors, but only became truly great (and rich) after the Reconquest and the discovery of the New World, holding a virtual monopoly on trade with the Americas in the sixteenth century.

### Places of interest in Seville
**The Giralda.** A minaret from the Moorish period, now embellished as a bell tower for the cathedral, which symbolises the city itself in the popular imagination.
**The Cathedral.** Of enormous bulk, the third largest in the world, built in the fifteenth century on the site of a mosque, from which the delicate Patio de los Naranjos remains in the cathedral yard. The tomb of Columbus is contained inside.
**The Alcázar.** *Mudejar* palace built by Moorish craftsmen mainly in the fourteenth century for the Castilian King 'Pedro the Cruel'. It's the most important example of this style of architecture in existence, and a sight not to be missed, although lacking the ethereal quality achieved in the Alhambra (see Granada). The overgrown Moorish-style gardens are delightful too.

**Casa de Pilatos.** Renaissance mansion with elegant patio.
**Palacio de San Telmo.** Eighteenth century palace in Andalusian baroque style.
**Tobacco Factory.** A huge four-square building, setting for Bizet's *Carmen*, now used by Seville University.
**Plaza de España.** A magnificent example of Spanish grandiosity, opening onto the María Luisa Park, it takes the form of a huge arc of ceramic seats, each representing a Spanish province, and depicting in brightly coloured tiles an important historical event connected with that province. There are also miniature boating lakes with jauntily arched bridges, immense towers, also tiled, donkey rides, street vendors, and much coming and going by all and sundry.
**Barrio de Santa Cruz.** A labyrinth of narrow streets which made up the old Jewish quarter of the city, now a peaceful backwater from the clamour of modern Seville, although well-trodden by tourists.
**Sierpes.** A long street that winds its way through the middle of the city, and serves as a promenade and meeting place, very lively around aperitif times, which is most of the day in Seville.
**Triana.** Traditionally the 'rough' quarter, on the wrong side of the Guadalquivir, breeding all the best bullfighters and flamenco dancers.

## Elsewhere in Seville province
**Itálica** (near the village of Santiponce, 5 miles from Seville). Extensive Roman archeological site.
**Carmona.** Hill-top walled city under both Romans and Moors. Mudejar churches and Roman Necropolis.
**Osuna.** Quiet, elegant town.
**Ecija.** Supposedly the hottest place in Spain, the town is known for the baroque bell-towers of its churches, decorated with ceramic tiles.
**Coto Doñana.** National Park of salt marsh and dunes at mouth of Guadalquivir, a unique environment noted for its wild life (see listings).

## Córdoba
A sizeable city with a village-like atmosphere. The old quarter has narrow winding streets, whitewashed houses, geraniums and aspidistras, patios and fountains — all the charm you'd expect from an old Andalusian town. The capital of the Caliphate in the early days of the Moorish occupation, it was at its zenith when the rest of Europe was in the Dark Ages, and the breathtaking Mezquita is a reminder of these times.

Built during the eighth to tenth centuries, this magnificent example of Moorish architecture raises the tone of the whole city, turning quiet provincialism into high art. Inside the profusion of cool pillars topped with double arches in pink and white marble gives the impression of being in some sort of exotic palm forest. Sooner or later, and strangest of all, you come across the Christian cathedral — built right inside in the fifteenth century.

Other sights include the old Jewish quarter with fourteenth century synagogue, the Christian Alcázar with its beautiful gardens and fountains, a fair share of churches, a Roman bridge, and Arab water mills.

### Elsewhere in Córdoba province
**Medina Azahara** (just outside Cordoba). Tenth-century palace built by a Cordoban Caliph for a favourite princess, now in ruins, and still being excavated.
**Montilla.** Wine town with some interesting houses and mansions.
**Puente Genil.** Town with flourishing industries based on oil, wine and *membrillo* — a paste made from quinces which is very popular in Spain.
**Sierra Morena.** A chain of gentle mountains running across the northern parts of both Seville and Cordoba provinces, beautiful with wild flowers in the spring (see hiking below).

### Jaen
A small city on an arid plain, overlooked by its castle, now a *parador*, perched on a crag above it. Its renaissance/baroque cathedral has a beautifully carved façade by Pedro Roldán.

### Elsewhere in Jaen province
Elsewhere in the province the landscape is dry and rocky, with low scrub and olive plantations. Also worthy of note are:
**Ubeda.** The 'Salamanca of Andalucía', a beautiful old town with renaissance palaces and city walls enclosing an old quarter.
**Baeza.** Six miles away, Ubeda's twin, constructed of gold-coloured stone.
**Linares.** Lead-mining town, and the largest in the province after the capital.
**Despeñaperros.** Famous mountain pass marking the border between Castille and Andalucía.
**Sierra de Segura.** Rugged mountain area of bare crags and pine forest.
**Sierra de Cazorla.** Beautiful scenery and rich wild life. Pines, waterfalls and source of Guadalquivir.

### Granada
Another city to please the senses, but which has a more spiritual quality than earthy Málaga or sensual Seville. The light and delicate architecture of the **Alhambra**, with intimate little patios and tinkling fountains, is set off beautifully by the romantic views of the Sierra Nevada through its Moorish arches, and in its gardens (the **Generalife**) the smell of orange blossom in the clear mountain air completes the aesthetic delights of the place. The feeling the Alhambra gives to the city is strong enough to permeate the whole place, cutting through the traffic fumes and noise of modern Granada.

The city is known for its **university**, its **cathedral** where in a side chapel the remains of Ferdinand and Isabella lie, its music and dance festival (see listings), the **Albaicín** (or old Arab quarter), and the **Sacromonte** where the cave-dwelling gypsies put on flamenco shows, or *zambras*. It demands at least a visit, and would be an ideal place in which to spend longer.

## Elsewhere in Granada province
**Almuñécar.** Small friendly seaside resort with a nice promenade spilling out from the old whitewashed hill town.
**Salobreña.** Another small coastal village which has become something of a resort, with sugar cane growing on the fertile strip between village and beach.
**Motril.** Rather drab town with some industry.
**Sierra Nevada.** Mountain range with the highest peaks in peninsular Spain, snow covered all year, despite being so far south, with good skiing, climbing and hiking.
**Las Alpujarras.** Southern slopes of the Sierra Nevada, where the last of the Moors took refuge and were converted to Christianity when Ferdinand and Isabella took Granada. Some extremely remote and attractive villages, with terrace-farming on the mountainside, and the spa-town Lanjarón (you'll see its mineral water sold everywhere).
**Guadix.** Unpretentious old town, known for its whole suburb of inhabited caves.

## Almería
Former Arab city, of which little remains. A modern city of blinding light, with a port, fortified cathedral and quarter of cave-dwellings.

## Elsewhere in Almería province
**Aguadulce** and **Roquetas de Mar.** Beginnings of tourist development.
**Tabernas.** Extraordinary desert scenery, used as a location for spaghetti Westerns.
**Mojácar.** Almería's biggest resort, being developed for package holidays and second homes. Good beaches all the way along this eastern coast.
**Calar Alto.** Important observatory in the mountains.

## COMING AND GOING

### By air
Going overland from Britain is an arduous journey, so using Málaga airport is the obvious solution, since with so many package-tour charters going in and out you can pick up some very cheap flights. However, the region is huge and land communications difficult, so if you're going to Almería or Seville, it would probably be worth while paying a little more to fly direct, as both have good international airports. There are also small airports (handling internal traffic) at Granada and Córdoba.

### By sea
*Málaga.* Sailings to Melilla several times a week, with the **Compañía Transmediterranea.**
*Cádiz.* Sailings to Canary Islands (Tenerife and Las Palmas), also with **Compañía Transmediterranea.**
*Algeciras.* Ferries to Ceuta and Tangiers with **Isleña de Navegación.** Also hovercraft service to Tangiers with **Transtour.**

*Tarifa.* Hovercraft service to Tangiers with **Transtour**.
*Almería.* Sailings to Melilla with **Compañía Transmediterranea**.

Frequency of service and times of departure vary according to the time of year, so get further details on the spot, or from a tourist office or travel agent.

**Packages**
There is an immense choice of 'sun and sangria' packages to the Costa del Sol, but also quite a range with a more serious attitude towards the region (see p. 21):

**Ramblers Holidays, Explore Worldwide** and **Wexas**. Walking/adventure holidays in Sierra de Ronda/Sierra de Cazorla combined with visits to the great sights of Seville, Cordoba and Granada.
**Field Studies Council.** Courses in 'Flowers and Birds of the Coto Doñana'. Also 'Flowers and Painting in Granada/Sierra Nevada'.
**Ornitholidays.** Birdwatching holidays based at Zahara (Cadiz province).
**ACE Study Tours.** Moorish Andalusia tour taking in Seville, Córdoba, Granada and Ronda.
**Mundi Color.** Large range of holidays, including Paradors of Andalusia, the *Pueblos Blancos* (white towns), Costa del Sol, Costa de la Luz, and the 'Al Andalus Express' luxury rail tour. All high quality packages, and rather pricey.
**Travelscene.** City breaks to Seville, and 'Al Andalus Express'.
**Thomas Cook.** 'Off the beaten track' packages to Seville and the Costa de la Luz.
**Blackheath Wine Trails.** Four day tour of the sherry *bodegas*.

See also section on **horseriding** below for details of horseback excursions from Jerez or Seville.

## WHERE TO STAY

Still can be extremely cheap for **pensions** and **hostales** in remote areas. Málaga, the Costa del Sol and Seville are reasonably priced.

For information about accommodation in Granada for periods of longer than 2 weeks, contact: **Oficina de Acción Estudiantil,** c/Severo Ochoa, Jardines Universitarios de Fuentenueva, Granada.

In the Alpujarras, a local co-operative has built a small complex of holiday cottages, purpose-built in — very tasteful — traditional style. For details of lets contact: **Cooperativa Andaluza de Hostelería,** Bubion, Granada (tel. 958–763112).

**The Youth Hostels Reservations Office** for the region is at Castelar 22, Sevilla (tel. 954–216349, ex. 221).

## WHAT TO EAT AND DRINK

As all the literature on Spanish regional cooking will tell you, Andalucía is officially classed as 'the zone of the fry-ups', and to a large extent this holds true. Anything, from battered aubergines to pork chops, is flung with great style into a pan of boiling oil and a few minutes later is on the plate. It's a method which appeals to the Andalusian sense of spontaneity, and avoids both the need for long hours in a sweltering kitchen, and for having cooked food standing around in conditions where bacteria are likely to breed. The best example of the Andalusian fry up is the *gran freitura* — what others might call a seafood platter — all battered and fried in olive oil.

As well as fried food, Andalusians also do good *tapas*, although beware of the pickled fish. Look out for home-prepared olives, purplish and bitter, and flavoured with wild thyme, an excellent accompaniment to all types of sherry. There is good ham here, if you're in Huelva or Seville provinces you should have no trouble finding the famed *jamón de Jabugo*, or in Granada look out for *jamón de Trevélez*, two excellent varieties of the ubiquitous *jamón serrano*.

As far as Andalusian dishes go, *gazpacho* is by far the best known, a refreshing raw purée of tomatoes, onions, peppers, cucumber and garlic. *Huevos a la flamenca* is a substantial first course of eggs poached in stewed vegetables, or try the various dishes, especially mushrooms, cooked *al jerez* (in sherry). Sweets include sub-tropical fruits such as *chirimoyas* (rather like sweet avocadoes, with black pips distributed through the flesh), and familiar fruits like strawberries which are available at unexpected times of the year. *Torrijas* are wonderful syrupy bread creations and an Easter speciality, and other sweet things include *tocino del cielo* (rich caramel custard served in squares), and *yemas*, the candied egg yolks which you'll also see in Castille and other regions.

Andalucía's acres of vineyards produce fortified wines which can be as light as *manzanilla* or *fino* sherry, or as rich and syrupy as *málaga*. Even if you have a mental block against this kind of drink, you'll find in Andalucía — straight from the wood if sweet, and from a freshly opened chilled bottle if dry, and always accompanied by something tasty to eat — that it's quite a different experience from the dismal, stale stuff that's been standing on the pub shelf for months. Heat and winemaking traditions mean that even non-fortified wines — *montillas*, some of the *condado* wines from Huelva and other, locally produced varieties — almost always whites, have the strength and taste of a dry sherry about them, although you'll often find them served as table wines. If you ask for a red wine in Andalucía, it will usually turn out to be Valdepeñas, nicely chilled in the fridge!

## OPPORTUNITIES IN ANDALUCIA

Andalucía has the highest unemployment rate in Spain, and many people are still forced to earn a living by being hired out as day-labourers (*jornaleros*) as and when they are needed by the big landowners, which may be only a few weeks in a year. The *Junta de Andalucía* is chipping away at the traditional *latifundios*, and giving all sorts of incentives to co-operatives, but reform is slow.

Despite this sorry situation a British person's chances of finding work are fairly good. There is quite a demand for EFL teachers, and on the Costa del Sol there is both the tourist industry (opportunities for couriers, guides, etc.) and an established expatriate community, with their own 'homegrown' services such as schools, churches, estate agents and solicitors' offices which need staffing. Apart from this Málaga and Seville are big cities with many opportunities in their own right.

Seville and Granada offer good research and study possibilities, while as far as leisure goes, if you can't find anything to occupy you in this lively, varied region you could always take a tip from many an old *andaluz* and sit and watch the world go by.

## WHAT TO DO

### ARCHAEOLOGY

Important sites at **Itálica** (Roman) and **Medina Azahara** (Moorish) and a host of smaller ones throughout the region. Last year there were archaeological work camps at both the above, in which volunteers from abroad were able to take part. (See earlier section on work camps, pp. 71 – 2.)

### ART GALLERIES AND MUSEUMS

#### Málaga
**Museo Arqueológico** (in the Alcazaba). Open winter 1000 – 1300 and 1400 – 1900, and summer 1100 – 1300 and 1700 – 2000. Prehistoric and Roman material; also ceramics from the Caliphal period.
**Museo de Bellas Artes,** c/San Augustín 6. Open 1000 – 1330 and 1700 – 2000. Early works by Picasso, and nineteenth-century works by local artists. Also paintings by Zurbarán and Murillo, Roman mosaics, sculptures, etc.

#### Cádiz
**Museo de Bellas Artes,** Pza de la Mina s/n. Very interesting collection, including 21 Zurbaráns. Also an archeological section including some splendid Phoenician pieces.

#### Jérez
**Museo de Flamenco y Flamencología,** c/Quintos 1. Flamenco museum.

#### Seville
**Museo de Bellas Artes,** Pza del Museo. An exceptional collection, regarded as the second most important in Spain, containing some of the finest Murillos, as well as works by other seventeenth-century masters like Velázquez, Zurbarán and Alonso Cano.
**Museo Arqueológico,** Pza de America. Includes finds from Itálica.
**Museo de Artes y Costumbres Populares,** Pza de America. Museum of

Andalusian popular art and customs housed in a mock-*mudejar* pavilion in the Maria Luisa Park.
**Museo de Arte Contemporaneo,** Santo Tomás 5. Museum of contemporary art. Seville also has quite a number of galleries for temporary exhibitions.

### Córdoba
**Museo Arqueológico,** Pza Jerónimo Paez 7. Important collection of prehistoric, Iberian, and Roman finds, as well as some beautiful pieces from the Moorish period.
**Museo de Bellas Artes,** Pza del Potro. In a chapel of the former **Hospital de la Caridad**, and containing works by Murillo, Valdes Leal, Zurbarán, Ribera and Goya, also a section dedicated to Cordoban sculptor Mateo Inurria.
**Museo Taurino,** Pza Bulas. Bullfighting museum, including mementos of famous bullfighters, and collections of leather and silver work.

### Cazorla (Jaen)
**Museo de Artes y Costumbres Populares del Alto Guadalquivir,** c/del Rosario. Museum of popular art and customs of the Upper Guadalquivir. Interesting to visit if you're in the area.

### Granada
The **Museo Nacional Hispano-Musulman** (National Hispano-Muslim Museum) and the **Museo de Bellas Artes** are both located in the palace of Charles V — inside the Alhambra.
**Casa de los Tiros,** Pza de los Tiros. Museum of local art housed in a sixteenth-century *mudejar* house, which incidentally also incorporates the Tourist Office.

### Almería
**Museo Arqueológico,** c/Javier Sanz. Prehistoric, Greek and Carthaginian finds.

---

## BULLFIGHTS

Definitely the best region for bullfighting: the ritual was first developed in Ronda, it is here that both bulls and horses are bred (you can visit the **Los Alburejos** stockbreeding ranch on the road between Medina Sidonia and Alcalá de los Gazules, Cadiz province), and the region provides a constant stream of young hopeful *toreros*. **La Maestranza bullring** in the old part of **Seville** on the banks of the Guadalquivir is, along with **Las Ventas** in **Madrid** the most prestigious in Spain, although **Málaga, Córdoba** and **Jaen** are also noted venues, and a *corrida* forms an important part of local fiestas in monumental or makeshift plazas throughout the region.

The bullfighting season lasts from March to October, with all the major fights taking place during the summer months. A *corrida* starts at around

1700, and consists of six bulls, killed in turn by three *matadores*. Tickets vary in price from about 1,000 to about 6,000 pesetas (£5 to £30), and may be bought at the bullring *taquilla* in advance or on the spot if any remain. A seat in the sun *(sol)* costs a lot less than one in the shade *(sombra)*, for obvious reasons, and they are also graded in terms of their position in relation to the arena. As well as full-blown *corridas* you'll also find *novilladas* where apprentice *toreros* test their skill against young bulls, or ones that have been rejected by the *matadores*.

There are strong views for and against bullfighting in all strata of Spanish society, and immense vested interest tied up in its management and related industries such as horse and bull-breeding. However, it must be said that many Spanish people, especially the younger generations, are perfectly indifferent to it and don't regard it as part of their culture at all. Nevertheless, the *corrida* is a colourful, awe-inspiring spectacle which no one seriously interested in Spanish culture should miss out on.

(See also the **Museum of Bullfighting** in Córdoba (below), and the **San Fermines** in the section on Navarre.)

## CINEMA

The following organisations put on film festivals in the region:

**Cine-Club Huelva,** Hotel Tartessos, Avda Martín Alonso Pinzón 13, Huelva.

**Cine-Club Popular de Jerez,** Centro Cultural de la Caja de Ahorros de Jerez, Polígono de San Benito, Jerez.

**Ayuntamiento de Melilla,** Carlos Arellano 10, Melilla.

There is also an Andalusian Film Industry Confederation: **Confederación de la Industria Cinematográfica Andaluza**, Amor de Dios 31, Sevilla (tel. 954–381959).

## COURSES

### Public-sector courses

There is quite a choice of public-sector 'courses for foreigners' in the region:

*Granada University.* 1 and 2 month language courses for beginners and for more advanced students throughout the year. Also a year-long course lasting from October to May in Spanish studies, including history, art, literature, etc. No accommodation provided, but help given. Plenty of interest, and the possibility of getting involved in a whole range of other activities, excursions, visits, lectures, concerts, etc. Apply to: **Secretaría de los Cursos para Extranjeros**, Puentezuelas 55, Palacio de las Columnas, Granada (tel. 958–262584).

Granada University also has a college in Baeza (Jaen), where there is a month-long course available in August/September, with 2 levels, beginners and advanced. Apply: **Secretaría de la Universidad de Verano**, S Juan

de Avila 2, Baeza (Jaen) (tel. 953-740113).
*Málaga University.* 1 or 2 month language courses in July and August only, three different levels. Apply to: **Cursos de Verano para Extranjeros,** Aptdo 310, Málaga (tel. 952-214007).
*Seville University.* 1 month's course in September in Spanish language and culture, with an emphasis on Andalucía. No accommodation provided. Apply: **Secretaría de las Facultades de Filología, Geografía e Historia,** Cursos de Extranjeros, Dª María de Padilla, Sevilla.
**Escuela de Idiomas de Marbella.** Marbella town council offer a month's language course in July. There are four different levels and a programme of lectures, films and guitar recitals to go with it. Apply to: Delegación de Cultura, Huerta Chica s/n, Marbella (tel. 952-774638).
**Consejo Superior de Investigaciones Científicas.** The Spanish Scientific Research Council organises a summer course each year during July and August in Spanish philology for both Spanish and foreign graduates in Spanish. The course takes place at Málaga University and is recognised as part of the taught component of a doctorate in Spain. Information from: **Departamento de Lingüística,** Equipo de Geografía Lingüística, Duque de Medinaceli 6, 28014 Madrid (tel. 91-429 2017, ex. 141).
**Escuela Oficial de Idiomas,** Departamento de Español, Pº de Martiricos 24, 29009 Malága. Spanish language courses from February to May, with an emphasis on communicative competence.

**Privately-run courses**
*Málaga:*
**Inlingua Idiomas,** Plaza de las Flores 7-3º, Málaga (tel. 952-215752), and also at Ricardo Soriano 4, Edificio Zelim, Marbella (tel. 952-774942). A variety of language courses throughout the year to suit all needs. Minimum 2 weeks.
**Instituto Internacional Alhambra,** Avda Juan Sebastián Elcano 52, Apartado 665, Málaga (tel. 952-291509). 3 and 4 week intensive Spanish courses throughout the year. Accommodation arranged, or possibility of staying in their specially constructed 'Moorish style' club-house. Outside activities arranged, including excursions and guitar evenings.
**Centro de Estudios de Castellano,** J.S. Elcano 110, Málaga (tel. 952-290551). Full-time Spanish language courses for students, secretaries, businessmen, etc. Accommodation with Spanish families or in apartments.
**Miramar Spanish for Foreigners,** Cenacheros 123, Málaga. 3 week courses throughout the year, four different levels of ability.
**Debla Español para Extranjeros,** J Valera 27, Apartado 6.069, Málaga (tel. 952-294399). As Miramar above.
**Al Andalus Spanish for Foreigners,** c/Herrera 12, Pedregalejo, Málaga (tel. 952-291741). 4 week courses throughout the year, and four different levels of ability.
**CEP Cursos de Español,** Avda San Sebastían 4-6, 1º B, Málaga. 2, 4, 6, or 8 week courses throughout the year, different levels.
**Escuela 'La Coracha',** Pintor Sorolla 20, Málaga (tel. 952-224048). Variety of language courses throughout the year, also options for literature,

history, politics and sociology of Spain and Latin America.
**Málaga Instituto,** Paseo Salvador Rueda 7, Apartado 397, Málaga (tel. 952–223276). One of the more up-market language schools, at least from its brochure, offering 1, 2, 3 or 4 month courses and all the trimmings.

*Seville:*
**Centro de Lenguas e Intercambio Cultural,** c/Santa Ana 11, Sevilla (tel. 954–384703). 3 or 4 week courses in Spanish language throughout the year, with the possibility of enrolling for longer. Five different levels of ability, accommodation in families or *hostales,* and a full programme of outside activities.

*Córdoba:*
**ZAHR Taller de Arte y Lenguaje,** Finca Fuen Real Alto, Almodóvar del Río (15 miles from Cordoba) (tel. 957–635213). 2 week courses from May to September intended as sort of 'Andalusian workshops' for languages and arts students from abroad. As well as language work, there are opportunities of studying (and being actively involved in) painting, photography, local architecture and customs, literature, etc. Accommodation and Andalusian-style meals provided.

*Almuñecar:*
**Centro de Estudios y Vacaciones,** La Victoria 28, Almuñecar, Granada (tel. 958–633380). 2, 3, 4 and 6 week courses at Easter and from July–October. Flamenco dancing classes included in the price of a 4 week course!

*Granada:*
**Centro de Cultura y Estudios,** Cuesta de los Chinos 15, Albayzín, Granada (tel. 958–221062). 2, 3 or 4 week courses from February to October, run 'by young people for young people' with a good programme which can (optionally) include literature, flamenco, skiing and excursions as well as language work.

**From the UK**
**Alpha Language Services,** 2 Cottis Court, St. John's Road, Epping, Essex (tel. 0378–77039). Can fix you up with a Spanish language course in Málaga, if you don't fancy organising it yourself.

**Other courses**
**INICE** (see p. 46). Organises courses in mountaineering, self-sufficiency and conservation in the Cazorla National Park, and photography courses in the Córdoba area, both during the summer months. This is worth checking if you're interested, although programmes vary from year to year.
**Universidad Hispano Americana** de Sta Maria de la Rabida, Palos de la Frontera, Huelva. Course in American history which takes place every year during the last 3 weeks in August, and each year concentrates on a different aspect of American history. Open to university graduates with a knowledge of Spanish.

## CRAFTS

Many traditional Andalusian crafts are linked to the region's great traditions of horsemanship and flamenco, brought together with the flamboyant regional costume at so many fiestas (see below), which serve to keep the old techniques alive. These include the production of articles such as guitars (in Granada, Málaga, Ronda, and the village of Algodonales (Cádiz province) ), castanets, flamenco outfits for men and women, mantillas, silk shawls, jewellery, fans, etc., all of which are beautiful if you look out for the real thing as opposed to mass-produced imitations.

Córdoban leather and saddlery has been known for centuries, and is made especially in the village of Belalcázar, while Ubrique (Seville province) is famous for its embossed leatherwork.

No Andalusian house would be complete without its *rejas*, or wrought iron grilles, and 'articles of forgery' as the tourist information leaflet quaintly puts it, are produced especially in Huelva, Málaga and Ronda.

The villages of the Alpujarras weave their own brightly coloured blankets, and you'll also find these in the village of Grazalema (Cádiz province). Pottery is produced in villages all over the region, too numerous to mention, and Granada carries on the Moorish craft of copper-beating. Other crafts include wickerwork and basketwork, silverwork, embroidery and marquetry.

## CYCLETOURING

See the section on 'Hiking' on the next page for some idea of the best areas. You can hire bicycles in Granada from: **Taller Manolo,** Manuel de Falla 12.

## FIESTAS

The extreme heat of the summer months in Andalucía makes spring the favourite time for its many colourful popular fiestas, among the most impressive being the **Holy Week processions** in **Seville** and **Málaga**, and also **Granada, Jaen, Ubeda, Baeza, Puente Genil, Arcos** and throughout the region.

Those of **Seville** are astonishing for the effort, labour and time they must involve — over a hundred *pasos* or floats, heavy with ornate tableaux representing the sufferings of Jesus or the Virgin, are slowly carried around the city on the shoulders of bearers, in an emotionally charged ritual which lasts eight whole days and nights. They are accompanied by robed penitents in tall pointed headdresses which completely cover their faces, and by bands of drums and trumpets playing what are supposed to be funeral marches, but in somewhat strident tones. Many of the processions take extremely complicated routes through the city and last all night (a programme is available if you can make sense of it), but nevertheless are watched eagerly by thousands of spectators. In many ways it's more a celebration of Andalusian culture than a religious event, but the atmosphere is certainly charged with something out of the ordinary.

**Seville's April Fair** a few weeks later is a different event entirely, and shows off the city at its most colourful and flamboyant. It's an occasion for dressing up in Andalusian brimmed hats and flounced dresses, dancing, singing and clapping hands. It all takes place in brightly bedecked tents which are set up on the banks of the Guadalquivir. The sherry flows freely, accompanied by all sorts of tasty *tapas*, and the Fair lasts a week — with short breaks for siestas. Originally it was a livestock fair, something for the landowning classes, and many well-to-do *andaluces* arrive in some style on horseback or in carriages. The whole city is in a state of nervous excitement and seats for the bullfights are always sold out.

The same sort of event is repeated at the **Horse Fair** in **Jerez** in mid-May, although this is still a livestock and horse show as well. Tents are set up in the Parque González Hontoría, and there are bullfights and horseriding events.

The **Romería del Rocio** at Whitsun again brings out the horse-drawn carriages and traditional costume, when people from Seville, Huelva and Cádiz all descend on the village of **Almonte** on the edge of the **Coto Doñana** to make the annual orgiastic pilgrimage to the shrine of **Nuestra Señora del Rocío**, in the salt marshes. There is music, feasting, and again that typically Andalusian combination of the sacred and the profane.

**Córdoba's** big fiesta is in May, which is also based on a *romería*, and is of special interest for its 'best patio' competition, with the streets bright with flowers on every balcony.

In recent years **Málaga's August Fair** has been given a big boost by the city authorities — it lasts a week or more and includes spectacular firework displays, parades, horses, bullfights, musical events and much merrymaking in traditional costume along the lines of Seville's April Fair.

The **wine harvest** is celebrated with verve in **Jerez** every year in September (dates vary), with an offering to the patron saint, **San Ginés de la Jara**. There are parades, bullfights, flamenco and a livestock fair.

## HIKING

Bearing in mind that in June, July and August you won't want to do anything more energetic than take a dip somewhere to cool off, there are some areas that would make excellent hiking in spring or autumn. The **Sierra Morena** will surprise you with its greenness and freshness — there are hundreds of little streams coming down to join the Guadalquivir — and with its abundant wild life. If you're looking for a base, try **Arazena**, **La Cazalla**, or the youth hostel at **Constantina**.

In Jaen province, the **Sierra de Cazorla** is also a surprisingly green area. The **source of the Guadalquivir** is a particularly beautiful spot, while further along its course great dams have been constructed, providing excellent conditions for wildlife and lush vegetation. The Sierra includes a vast protected area for deer, mountain goat and other species. **ICONA** can provide a good information sheet and map of the area, and there are tourist offices in **Segura de la Sierra** and **Cazorla**. Cazorla itself is probably the best base here, reached by bus from **Ubeda**. There are few footpaths, however, and you'll have to stick to the mountain roads, many of which follow the course of streams.

In the Sierra Nevada, the **Las Alpujarras** region makes good walking, while the more experienced may like to try the high peak route over from **Prado Llano** and the **Solynieve** ski station to **Capileira** on the southern side, via the peak of **Veleta**. In contrast to hiking elsewhere in the region, this is only really feasible in summer (in winter it is given over to skiers) and it's so high it feels as though you're on top of the world — you're supposed to be able to see Africa on a clear day.

Andalucía is so big and wild, there are plenty of other possible places to hike, and the above are just a few suggestions.

## HORSERIDING

Andalucía must be *the* region for horse-lovers. There is show-jumping and racing at the **Club Pineda** in Seville, riding and polo at **Sotogrande** (Cádiz), and well-known clubs throughout the region, such as the **Club Hípico** in Córdoba, the **Chapín Club** in Jerez, and the **Real Sociedad Hípica** in Granada. Jerez also boasts the **Andalusian School of Equestrian Art**, where there are daily displays of horsemanship for anyone interested. The address is: Recreo de las Cadenas, Avda Duque de Abrantes, Jerez (tel. 334198). There are also minor riding schools up and down the coast.

If you fancy pony trekking in the area, contact **Aljibe Club de Viajeros**, Rui López 14, Jerez (tel. 322625), who organise expeditions in the Alpujarras and the Sierra de Cadiz (the so-called 'smugglers route'). Some are pre-arranged, or they can be organised to suit special requirements if a group of people are interested.

**Rutas a Caballo** (Augustín de Aragón 14–1º C, Madrid (tel. 91–402 9500) pick you up at Seville for a 13-day tour on horseback taking in Arcos and the Atlantic coast, or an 8-day tour of the white towns, including Ronda.

**Equitour** (Juan Güell 163, Barcelona (tel. 93–339 4100) ) also do horseback tours of the Sierra Morena, the white towns, Jerez (including visits to the sherry *bodegas*) and the Atlantic coast, again starting out from Seville.

## LIBRARIES

Seville has some important libraries, especially the **Archive of the Indies**, next to the cathedral, where records from the time of the Conquest of the New World have been dumped. See also the **University Library**, and the **Central Library for Latin American Studies** (c/Alfonso XII, 12) and the general library, next to it.

In Granada the main public library is in the **Jardines del Salón**.

## LOCAL PRESS

*El Correo de Andalucía*
*Sol de Málaga*
*El Ideal de Granada*
*Diario 16 (de Andalucía)*
*El País (de Andalucía)*

---

## MARKETS

**Seville.** Thursday morning street market in **c/Feria**. On Sundays in **Alameda de Hércules**. Also stamp market in **Plaza Cabildo**, and bird market in **Plaza de la Alfalfa**, both on Sunday mornings.

There are also flea markets in **Cádiz** — 'El Piojito' — and in **Córdoba** in the Plaza de la Corredera.

---

## MUSIC

The **Festival of Music and Dance** in **Granada** at the end of June/beginning of July stands out as the major musical event. It's a huge affair of international standing, with at least two concerts a day throughout the month, and has included such names as the London Festival Ballet, Placido Domingo and the Spanish National Orchestra, as well as jazz, religious music, Spanish guitar recitals, and a generous helping of flamenco. Some of the performances are outdoor (imagine seeing Swan Lake in the Generalife gardens!) and others take place within the Alhambra, or in the spacious 'Manual de Falla Auditorium'. There are also various peripheral events: a 'Manuel de Falla music prize', a music course, a congress of Andalusian folk music, etc. Full information from the **Festival Office**, Ancha de Santo Domingo 1, Granada (tel. 958–225201).

Other musical events include an international course in flamenco held in **Jerez** during the first 2 weeks in August (information from **Cátedra de Flamencología y Estudios Folklóricos Andaluces**, Apartado 246, Jerez, Cádiz (tel. 349702), and an international music festival in **Huelva** during August.

Apart from these special events, Andalucía is of course rich in permanent flamenco *tablaos*, although beware of some of the prices charged.

**Seville**
- El Arenal, Rodo 7
- La Trocha, Ronda de Capuchinos 23
- Los Gallos, Plaza de Sta. Cruz
- Patio Sevillano, Paseo de Colón 11

**Granada**
- El Curro, Tablas 5
- Neptuno, Jardines Neptuno, c/Arabial
- Rey Chico, Paseo del Avellano 2

- Escuela Flamenco 'Mariquilla', Pasaje Recogidas
- Various *zambras* organised in the Sacromonte district.

## SKIING

From December to April the high slopes of the **Sierra Nevada** are ideal for skiing. Accommodation (of all grades) and facilities, including bars, restaurants and shops where you can hire or buy equipment, are to be found in the resort of **Prado Llano**, and the ski-station itself, **Solynieve**, is well equipped with ski lifts, and instruction if necessary at around 2,000 pesetas an hour. There is over 40 miles of piste, for beginners and intermediate skiers rather than for experts, and travel companies advise taking a strong sun block as the light is very fierce. If you don't fancy staying on the spot it's perfectly possible to go for the day from **Granada**, either by bus or under your own steam.

All-in packages are available from travel agents all over Spain (and also from UK operators, including Thomas Cook), or for on-the-spot information and advice you could contact the Andalusian Winter Sports Federation: **Federación Andaluza de Deportes de Invierno**, Infanta Beatriz 6, Granada (tel. 958–250706).

## SPORTS

See Horseriding and Skiing. The region also offers:

*Football.* **Seville's** two teams are Real Betis and Sevilla who play at the Benito Villamarín and Sánchez Pizjuan stadia respectively — see press for details of fixtures.

*Golf.* There are some very high class courses in the region, mostly on the coast, including an exceptional one at **Sotogrande**, and a concentration in the **Málaga/Marbella area** (Málaga even has a golfing *parador*).

*Tennis.* Plenty of courts in the built up areas — you'll have no trouble finding them.

*Sailing.* Plenty of small harbours, and some flashy marinas too. The tourist offices can supply full details of facilities.

*Windsurfing.* **Tarifa** has an outstanding windsurfing school — the winds here are perfect, and it's also possible to windsurf at beaches all the way along the coast, from **Punta Umbría** to **Almería**.

An International Sports Summer School runs a variety of activities during the summer in Málaga, including courses and competitions. You can write in the spring for a full programme to: **Universidad Internacional Deportiva de Verano de Andalucía**, Pabellón de Deportes de Ciudad Jardín, Avda Jacinto Benavente s/n, Málaga (tel. 952–262300).

## THEATRE

Theatres in **Seville** are the Lope de Vega, Avda de María Luisa, and the Alvarez Quintero, Laraña 4, both closed during the hottest months of the summer. In **Granada** there is the 'Manuel de Falla auditorium', and also the Teatro Isabel la Católica.

On the whole it's not a region with great theatrical traditions. Events do include a theatre season in **Montilla** (Cordoba) towards the end of May, an Andalusian Theatre Festival in **Almería** and an International Theatre Festival in **Huelva**, details in all three cases from the respective *ayuntamiento*.

## UNIVERSITIES

Seville and Granada universities are old established institutions, while those at Cádiz, Málaga and Córdoba date from the early 1970s:

**Universidad de Sevilla**, San Fernando 4, Sevilla (tel. 954–231777)
**Universidad de Granada**, Hospital Real, Avda del Hospicio, Granada (tel. 958–278400)
**Universidad de Málaga**, Zona Universitaria 'El Ejido', Málaga (tel. 952–255054)
**Universidad de Cádiz**, Pza de Fragela, Cádiz (tel. 956–223808)
**Universidad de Córdoba**, Alfonso XIII, 19, Córdoba (tel. 957–473125).

## WILDLIFE

The **Sierra de Cazorla** is a protected area for species including the moufflon (a wild big-horned sheep), the mountain goat, and various types of deer, and is extremely beautiful, but the real area for wildlife, unique in the world, is the **Coto Doñana** at the mouth of the river Guadalquivir. You can't say it's particularly beautiful — it consists of flat salt-marshes, dunes and cork forest — but its various habitats, changing with the seasons, provide an ideal environment for many species not found anywhere else in Europe. Migratory birds in their thousands, including flamingoes and rare types of geese, descend on the salt marshes and lagoons in the spring, while the cork oaks support herons, storks and spoonbills. There are also lynx, mongoose, polecats, badgers, weasels, deer, wild boar and the great imperial eagle.

Visits are strictly supervised, and can be booked through **ICONA**, Centro de Información 'La Rocina', El Rocío, Almonte (Huelva) (tel. 955–406140). For non-tourist type information about the Coto Doñana you should contact the main research centre in **Seville**, Estación Biológica de Doñana, Paraguay 1, Sevilla.

The story of a series of Coto Doñana expeditions in the 1950s, mostly by British naturalists, is recounted — rather stolidly — in Guy Mountfort's book *Portrait of a Wilderness* (Hutchinson, 1958).

## USEFUL ADDRESSES

**Tourist offices**
**Almería:** Hermanos Machado s/n (tel. 951–234705)

**Cádiz:** Calderón de la Barca 1 (tel. 956–211313)
**Córdoba:** Hermanos González Murga 13 (tel. 957–471235)
**Granada:** Casa de los Tiros, Pavaneras 19 (tel. 958–221022)
**Huelva:** Vázquez López 5 (tel. 955–257403)
**Jaen:** Arquitecto Berges 1 (tel. 953–222737)
**Málaga:** Márqués de Larios 5 (tel. 952–312044) — also at airport
**Sevilla:** Avda de la Constitución 21 (tel. 954–221404)

**Government offices**
**Regional Government Tourist Dept,** Plaza Nueva 8, duplicado 3º, Sevilla (tel. 954–218589)
**Regional Government Office** (Junta de Andalucía), Pabellón Real, Pza de América, Sevilla (tel. 954–218860)
**Youth/Sport Department** (Dirección General de Juventud y Deportes), Consejería de Cultura, Cuesta del Rosario 8, Sevilla

**Education departments**
**Almería:** Paseo de Almería 69 (tel. 951–238533)
**Cádiz:** Pza de Minas 18 (tel. 956–223041)
**Córdoba:** Tomás de Aquino s/n (tel. 957–236313)
**Granada:** Duquesa 22 (tel. 958–279650)
**Huelva:** Alameda Sundheim 17 (tel. 955–253011)
**Jaen:** Santo Reino 2 (tel. 953–222950)
**Málaga:** Avenida Aurora s/n (tel. 952–327000)
**Sevilla:** Pabellón Real, Pza de América (tel. 954–236130)

**Labour departments**
**Almería:** Hermanos Machado 11
**Cádiz:** Acacias 2
**Córdoba:** 12 de octubre 2
**Granada:** Avda de la Constitución 21
**Huelva:** Avda de Martín Alonso Pinzón 19
**Jaen:** Paseo de la Estación 30
**Málaga:** Avda de la Aurora, Edificio 'Copyrsa'
**Sevilla:** Pza de España s/n

**University Careers Information Offices** (Centros de Orientación e Información del Empleo
**Córdoba:** Alfonso XIII s/n
**Granada:** Campus Universitario o Fuentenueva
**Málaga:** Alameda Principal 33, Colegio Universitario
**Sevilla:** San Fernando 1
**Youth information offices**
**Almería:** Hermanos Machado 4
**Cádiz:** Pza de España 19
**Córdoba:** Carbonell y Morand 9
**Jaen:** Arquitecto Bergés 11

**Jerez:** Corredera 53
**Granada:** Paseo de la Bomba 11
**Málaga:** Alarcón Luján 4
**Sevilla:** Issac Peral 2, and Cuesta del Rosario 8

**TIVE offices**
**Córdoba:** Carbonell y Morand 9 (tel. 957–472690)
**Granada:** Santa Paula 23 (tel. 958–279250)
**Málaga:** Edificio Ochoa, Huescar 2 bajo (tel. 952–213852)
**Sevilla:** Avda Reina Mercedes 53 (tel. 954–613188)

**Travel agents**
**Sevilla:**
— Viajes Ecuador, Plaza del Duque 6 (tel. 954–217858)
— Viajes Meliá, Avda de la Constitución 30 (tel. 954–228321)
— Viajes Wagons Lits, Avda de la Contitución 4 (tel. 954–218905)
— Viajes Barceló, Joaquín Guichot 5 (tel. 954–2111604)
**Málaga:** Viajes Ecuador, Duque de la Victoria 4 (tel. 952–215040)
**Granada:**
— Viajes Meliá, Angel Ganivet 7 (tel. 958–225168)
— Viajes Ecuador, Angel Ganivet 8 (tel. 958–223566)
— Viajes Wagons Lits, Cuesta de Gomérez 1 (tel. 958–222303)
**Melilla:** Wagons Lits, O'Donnell 13 (tel. 683551)

**Car Hire**
**Sevilla:**
— Atesa, Hotel Alfonso XIII (tel. 954–211293), and also at Sevilla airport
— Budget, Reyes Católicos 4 (tel. 954–224678)
**Málaga:** Atesa, Las Mercedes 11, Torremolinos (tel. 952–217493)
**Granada:**
— Atesa, Pza de Cuchilleros 1 (tel. 958–224004)
— Regente Car, Pedro Antonio de Alarcón 18 tel. (958–251435)
**Almería:** Atesa, at airport
**Melilla:** Auto–Escuela Antequera, Arturo Reyes 16 (tel. 681861)

**British consulates**
**Sevilla:** Pza Nueva 8, dpdo, 17,40 (tel. 954–228873), covering Seville, Huelva and Córdoba
**Málaga:** Edificio Duquesa, C/Duquesa de Parcent 4 (tel. 952–217571), covering Málaga, Almería, Granada and Melilla
**Algeciras:** (Vice-Consulate): Avda de las Fuerzas Armadas 11 (tel. 956–661600), covering Cádiz and Ceuta

**British representation**
**British chamber of commerce** — none in region (see Madrid)
**The British Institute,** Edificio Mecenas, Polígono Universitario, Fuente Nueva, Granada

**British Council,** Seville, c/o British Consulate
**The British Society** (ex-patriate club), Villa Luisa, Los Penones, Benalmadena-Costa, Málaga

**British schools**
**The International School at Sotogrande,** Apartado 15, Sotogrande, Cádiz (tel. 956-792902)
**Calpe College,** Carretera de Cádiz km 177, Apartado 200, San Pedro de Alcántara, Málaga (tel. 952-781479)
**The English International College,** Urbanización Ricmar, Carretera de Cádiz km196, Marbella, Málaga (tel. 952-831058)
**Sunny View School,** Cerro del Toril, Apartado 175, Torremolinos, Málaga (tel. 952-383164)
**Swans,** Capricho 1, Marbella, Málaga (tel. 952-773248)
**St. Anthony's College,** Avda Acapulco, Los Boliches, Fuengirola, Málaga (tel. 952-473166)
**Aloha College,** 'El Angel', Nueva Andalucía, Marbella, Málaga (tel. 952-784133)
**American School:** David Glasgow Farragut Elementary School, US Naval Station Box 19, Apartado 33, Cádiz (tel. 956-862780, ex. 4187)

**Language schools (TEFL)**
**Almería:** English Centre, Polígono Oliveros
**Cádiz:**
— International House, Cánovas de Castillo 33
— The English School, Pza de España 14
**Córdoba:** International House, Rodríguez Sánchez 15
**Granada:**
— Academic CEL, Antonino 6
— Idiomas Ganivet, C/Angel Ganivet 6
— Inlingua, Pza Nueva 13
— Institute of Modern Languages, Puerta Real 1
**Huelva:** International House, c/Rico 19
**Jaen:** The British Centre, Obispo Stuñiga 1–1º
**Málaga:** Inlingua Idiomas, Pza de las Flores 7–3º
**Marbella:** Inlingua Idiomas, Avda Ricardo Soriano 4–2º
**Sevilla:**
— Instituto Británico, Federico Rubio 14
— Interschool, Virgen de Consolación 20
— Academia Rolleston, Melliza 1, Dos Hermanas
— Windsor School of English, Virgen de Loreto 19

# 4 Aragón

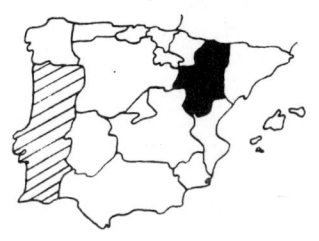

The region of Aragón forms a huge strip down the east side of interior Spain, from the Pyrenees to the border with Valencia. Administratively it is made up of three provinces, Huesca, Zaragoza and Teruel, which roughly coincide with distinct geographical zones: Huesca, in the Pyrenees, and Teruel, at the eastern end of Sistema Ibérico (Iberian Cordillera), are mountainous provinces, while Zaragoza lies between them in the Ebro Basin. Except in the Pyrenees, the region has a dry continental climate, which gives the landscape a distinctively tawny, weathered look, dotted with the silvery green of olive trees in the south, although there is a fertile agricultural zone watered by the Ebro.

Zaragoza, the capital, is Spain's fifth biggest city, with a population of over half a million, whose industrial success in recent years is largely due to its strategic position on the Ebro Valley, along which some of Spain's most important lines of communication run (linking Cataluña with the Basque country and Madrid). The rest of Aragón is something of a backwater, although it does have a very distinct character of its own.

The most obvious feature which sets Aragón apart is the wealth of *Mudéjar* architecture. Although the Moors lost control of the region progressively from the eleventh century onwards (as in Castile) many Moorish craftsmen remained, to find work in the new Christian kingdom. The Aragonese *moriscos*, however, were subject to less persecution than those in Castile, protected by the local nobility who relied on their labour and craftsmanship. Their distinctive ornamental brick and tile-work seen today on towers, churches and other buildings is one of the region's great attractions.

In medieval times the Crown of Aragón was of course an important power — its territories included Cataluña, Valencia and the Balearics (although on a fairly loose federal basis) — and its unification with Castile through the marriage of King Ferdinand to Isabella of Castile is presented as being the most important event in Spain's history. Although to some extent Aragón was the lesser partner (it was for instance the Castilian dialect of Spanish that became the standard), the Aragonese take pride in having contributed the political acumen which helped within a very few years of the union to make Spain a major world power.

Aragón itself, however, remained stuck in a traditional rural way of life for centuries, and was only brought to the world's attention once again in 1937 when the Battle of Teruel, one of the most fiercely fought of the Civil War, was fought on Aragonese soil. The loss of Aragón by the Republicans gave Franco access to the Mediterranean and cut Barcelona off from its allies in Madrid and the Basque country.

Centuries of rural isolation are supposed to have produced the distinctive Aragonese character as stereotyped in the figure of the *baturro* or peasant, who is supposed to be hardy, stubborn and somewhat anarchic. Famous Aragonese throughout history — although far from being *baturros* — have displayed something of these characteristics. They include Goya (some of his early work is to be found in Zaragoza), the pithy novelist Ramón Sender, and film directors Luis Buñuel and Carlos Saura.

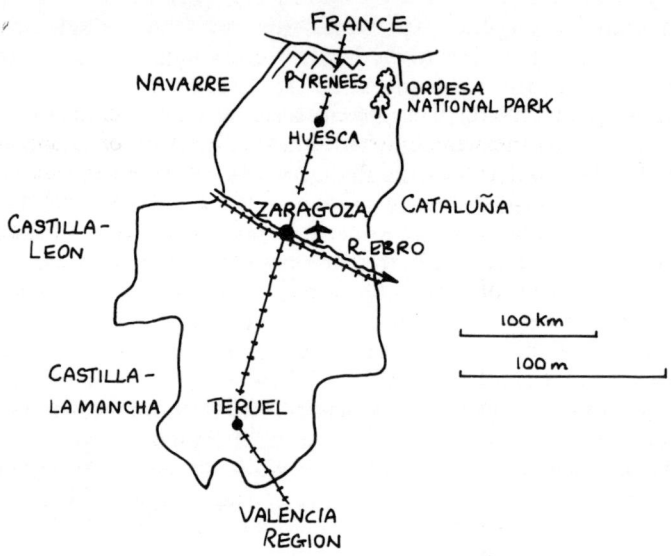

## WHAT TO SEE

### Zaragoza
An agricultural, industrial, military and religious centre which has seen rapid expansion in recent years, but still remains quite an attractive place. Its major attractions are:

**The Basilica of Nuestra Señora del Pilar.** A late seventeenth-century edifice containing the sacred image of 'Our Lady of the Pillar', the focus of one of Spain's most important cults. Thousands make the pilgrimage here each year. It's a very elegant building on the banks of the Ebro, with its four tall towers reflected in the water, and contains early paintings by Goya.

**La Seo.** Zaragoza's fourteenth-century cathedral.

**The Aljafería Palace.** The most important Moorish monument in Spain outside Andalucía, it pre-dates the Alhambra in origin, although later Christian kings also used it and made additions to it.

**The Lonja.** Very beautiful vaulted building in renaissance style, built in the sixteenth century as a Corn Exchange.
**El Tubo.** Zaragoza's liveliest district, in the streets behind the cathedral, full of bars and restaurants.

### Out of town
**Cartuja de Aula Dei.** Monastery displaying eleven works by Goya on religious themes.

### Elsewhere in Zaragoza province
**Calatayud.** Historic town on the plain, with old Moorish and Jewish quarters, quite atmospheric but otherwise rather dire.
**Tarazona.** *The* place for *mudejar* architecture.

### Teruel
Capital of lower Aragón, with some splendid *mudejar* architecture, but not a lot going for it otherwise. Outstanding are the towers of **El Salvador** and **San Martín**, built right over the street, so you pass through an arch beneath. The combination of brick and tile produces some wonderful ornamental effects. There is also a graceful sixteenth-century aqueduct over the River Turia, which incorporates a pedestrian walkway. The tragic legend of the lovers of Teruel, used by Tirso de Molina, strikes a romantic note in the town.

### Elsewhere in Teruel province
**Alcañiz.** Market town for surrounding farmland. Castle used by the Knights of Calatrava.
**Sierra de Albarracín.** A rugged, remote area of pine forests, gorges and caves.
**Albarracín.** A prosperous town in medieval times, still preserving something of this flavour.
**El Maestrazgo** (see also Valencia). Extremely remote area, which can only be visited via some precipitous roads, There are forgotten villages such as **Cantavieja** and **Valderrobles**, and the occasional lush valley, otherwise the harsh territory belongs mostly to pines and eagles.

### Huesca
Pleasant enough old town with cathedral.

**Castillo de Loarre.** One of Spain's most breathtaking castles, 12 miles from Huesca, on high ground overlooking the immense plains of Aragón. It was actually constructed by a king of Navarre, King Sancho, in the early eleventh century.

### Elsewhere in Huesca province
**Jaca.** The main centre for the Aragonese Pyrenees, and quite an interesting old town. It was the capital of Aragón in the early days, and an important stop on the Camino de Santiago (see Galicia). It has a beautiful eleventh-

century romanesque cathedral.
**The Aragonese Pyrenees.** Splendid scenery, ranging from wooded valleys to towering snow-covered peaks — including the highest in the chain — some good ski resorts, and the **Ordesa National Park**. (See also sections on Hiking, Skiing and Wildlife below.)
**Barbastro.** Town of Roman origin, with an attractive arcaded Plaza Mayor.

## COMING AND GOING

### By air

Zaragoza has an airport, with direct flights from Manchester, but if you're thinking of flying you've also got a choice between Madrid, Barcelona, Bilbao or Valencia airports, which are all about the same distance from Zaragoza. Barcelona is marginally nearer and has good road connections, although if you're heading for Teruel you'll be better off going to Valencia. If you want to go skiing, you'd probably save a lot of hassle buying an all-in deal from a travel agent in one of these cities (preferably Barcelona or Madrid), and letting someone else make the travel arrangements.

### By road and rail

There is a rail crossing from France via Pau which enters Spain at Canfranc, and then via Jaca to Zaragoza — also a useful means of getting up into the Pyrenees from the capital for walking or climbing excursions. A road follows a similar route.

As regards motorways, Zaragoza is in the fortunate position of being on the main route between Barcelona and the Basque country, with relatively easy access to places like Pamplona and Logroño en route.

The main Barcelona – Madrid road also skirts Zaragoza, although this is not yet all motorway by any means. The route through Aragón to Valencia (via Sagunto) is an interesting one, but slow, whether by road or rail.

### Packages

**Cox and Kings** offer study holidays at the Berdún Painting School and Study Centre in the Pyrenees, focussing on either flowers, natural history, birds or painting. **Ornitholidays** offer a week's birdwatching course in spring or autumn based at Jaca, **Waymark** do a walking holiday in the Pyrenees and **ACE Study Tours** do two different trips based at Berdún, one concentrating on art and architecture, the other more on walks and trails. Their 'Road to Compostela' tour also includes visits to Jaca and the Castillo de Loarre. (See also p. 21.)

## WHERE TO STAY

The main point of interest here is where to stay for excursions into the Pyrenees. The **Spanish Mountaineering Federation** (c/Alberto Aguilera 3, Madrid) runs various strategically sited huts — at Goriz at the northern end of the Ordesa Valley, at Lake Campoplano, and in the El Cinqueta

Valley. You'll also find modestly priced accommodation at the ski-resort of Candanchú, and in villages like Sallent de Gállego or Benasque (see tourist offices for full details).

There are two **monasteries** in the region which offer hospitality to visitors: **Santa Cruz** in Jaca (tel. 974–360592) (women only), and the **Monasterio de la Misericordia** (tel. 976–577834) (mixed) in Zaragoza.

Almost all the **campsites** in the region are concentrated in the Pyrenees and foothills.

The **Youth Hostel Reservations Office** is at Pza de los Sitios 7, Zaragoza (tel. 976–224858).

## WHAT TO EAT AND DRINK

The best known Aragonese dish, found also in Navarre and La Rioja, is the *chilindrón*, a way of cooking meat, usually chicken, in a sauce of ham, tomatoes and peppers. Some of Spain's best olive oil is produced in lower Aragón.

The region has a very low rainfall, and wines are typically full-bodied and alcoholic. Wines from the Cariñena region (almost always reds) can be as strong as 17% by volume, and those from Borja are similarly robust.

The many juniper trees in Teruel province provide flavouring for much of Spain's gin.

## OPPORTUNITIES IN ARAGON

You won't find much in the way of work anywhere in the region. Zaragoza, despite its size, has little to offer unless you're specifically involved with one of its major industries — car and agricultural machinery manufacturing, textiles, chemicals, etc. Study possibilities are similarly limited. Nonetheless, it's a good area to visit, and offers a lot both in the way of historical interest, and outdoor activities, especially winter sports.

## WHAT TO DO

### ART GALLERIES AND MUSEUMS

**Zaragoza**
**Museo de Bellas Artes,** Pza José Antonio 6. Paintings include works by Goya and El Greco.

**Huesca**
**Museo de Huesca,** Universidad Sertoriana, Pza de la Universidad (also an annex at the Monastery of San Juan de la Peña, near Jaca). Paintings, sculptures, and some interesting Romanesque alterpieces taken from churches.

## BULLFIGHTS

Common at fiestas throughout the region.

## CAVES

The **Callejon** and **Navazo** caves, near **Albarracín**, have some interesting prehistoric rock paintings, different in style from those of the Cantabrian coast. There are similar paintings in the **Cueva del Charco del Agua Amarga**, at **Valdealforfa**, near Alcañiz.

## CINEMA

Zaragoza has a film theatre, the **Filmoteca de Zaragoza**, at Cine Arlequin, Fuenclara 2, and it's here you're likely to find the best films being shown.

Alongside the city's **Agricultural Machinery Show** in April, there is a **competition for the best video** on an agrarian theme. Details available from the show office: Palacio Ferial, Avda Isabel la Católica 2, Apartado 108, Zaragoza.

## COURSES

Most courses in the region, it seems, are put on by the University of Zaragoza in Jaca during the summer — for university level students and above only. No previous knowledge of Spanish is required for the **language course** in August, although you'll need a degree in Spanish if you want to take the **Curso Monográfico** on contemporary Spain, which takes place during July. In both cases apply to: Secretaría de los Cursos de Verano, Ciudad Universitaria, Zaragoza (tel. 976-454648).

### Other courses
**The Painting School and Study Centre**, c/Mayor 30, Berdún, Huesca (tel. 974-377044). Offers courses in botany, natural history and watercolour painting. See packages above if you don't want to contact them directly.
**Hispalen – Oxford**, c/San Miguel 16, Zaragoza (tel. 976-221810). Language courses of optional length throughout June, July and August, open to anyone over 16. Accommodation in families.

## CRAFTS

Particularly interesting is the pottery made at **Muel** (Zaragoza province), an ancient tradition which has recently been reinstated.

## FIESTAS

Zaragoza's big celebrations are on 12th October — the day of **El Pilar** and also the day when the Spanish speaking nations of the world traditionally remember and review their hispanic origins. There is an offering of flowers to the statue of the Virgin, which is later paraded around the streets. There is a queen of the fiesta, with attendants, lots of people wearing traditional costume, and *jota* dancing in the streets.

Other fiestas draw strongly on folk traditions, especially music, dance and bulls. A **Pyrenean Folk Festival** is held in alternate years in **Jaca** and in **Oloron Ste-Marie**, across the border in France (odd years in Jaca), during the last week in July and the first in August. There is also a big fiesta in the same vein at **Graus** (Huesca province) on 12–15 September.

Outstanding among fiestas in lower Aragón is that held during **Holy Week** at **Híjar**, marked by frenetic drumming which starts at midnight on Maundy Thursday.

## HIKING AND CLIMBING

The Aragonese section of the Pyrenees is the most rugged, and offers some challenging hikes and climbs. The **Ordesa National Park** includes some really spectacular scenery. Be warned though, setting out on a hiking tour of the Pyrenees is a serious business. Make sure you're prepared physically and materially for the altitude, the roughness of the terrain, and for the sometimes long distances between villages/huts.

If you just want some good walking from a fixed base, you could make for the softer wooded valleys of **Anso** and **Hecho** to the west of the region, or **Benasque** in the east, overshadowed by **Aneto**, the highest peak of all. There is some serious climbing here too.

## LOCAL PRESS

*El Heraldo de Aragón*

## LIBRARIES

**Biblioteca Municipal** Pza de los Sitios 4, Zaragoza

## MUSIC

There is an **international festival of ancient music**, together with a course, which takes place yearly in **Daroca**, in Zaragoza province. Information from the cultural department in Zaragoza.

## SKIING

To the west of the region there is a big ski-complex around **Candanchú**, with two separate stations, **Astún** (by far the smaller) and **Candanchú**. The *pistes* are big and wide, with no trees. There are ample facilities on the spot, including hire of equipment, and good access via **Canfranc** station (4 miles from Candanchú).

If you fancy skiing cross-country, you can link up with the El Formigal ski station, a little further to the east, and further east still is **Panticosa**, a smaller resort, but with everything laid on. There is yet another station, **Cerler**, 3 miles out of Benasque — again smallish, but well equipped and linked by bus with **Zaragoza, Huesca** and **Barbastro**.

If you're thinking of doing anything more serious than just a day's skiing, you should consider buying an all-in package (**TIVE** offices have some cheap deals), or at least getting everything booked up beforehand. The tourist offices in Jaca or Huesca can be helpful here, as can the **Federación Aragonesa de Deportes de Invierno**, Casa Jiménez 1, Zaragoza (tel. 976–218338).

There is yet another option for skiing in Aragon, at the **Sierra de Gudar** ski station 40 miles from Teruel near the village of **Alcalá de la Selva**. There are 2 *pistes* amidst conifer forest, and some lifting equipment.

## SPORTS

**Jaca** has good sports facilities, including an ice rink. Shooting and fishing are possible both in the **Pyrenees** and in the mountains of **Lower Aragón**.

## THEATRE

**Zaragoza** has an international theatre festival every year towards the end of May. On the spot details from the cultural department, or *ayuntamiento*.

## UNIVERSITY

● **Universidad de Zaragoza**, Pza De San Francisco s/n, Zaragoza (tel. 976–350670)

## WILDLIFE

The **Pyrenees**, and more specifically the **Ordesa National Park**, are home to hundreds of rare species of birds (especially birds of prey), flowers (including the edelweiss) and animals such as otter, stoats, beavers, pine martens, chamoix, and a subspecies of mountain goat now unique to the park. There are also game reserves in the Pyrenees where deer and wild boar are protected. The wilder reaches of Lower Aragón also include areas such as the **Puerto de Beceite reserve,** protected by **ICONA**, where bears are still rumoured to exist.

Zaragoza province has a large natural park, the **Dehesa de Montecayo**, to the south of Tarazona.

## USEFUL ADDRESSES

**Tourist offices**
**Huesca:** Coso Alto 35 (tel. 974–212583)

Jaca: Paseo Calvo Sotelo (tel. 974-360098)
Teruel: Tomás Nogués 1 (tel. 974-602279)
Zaragoza: Torreón de la Zuda, Glorieta de Pío XII (tel. 976-230027)

**Government offices**
Regional Government Tourist Dept, Pza de los Sitios 7, Zaragoza (tel. 976-224858)
Regional Government Office (Diputación General de Aragón), Pza de los Sitios 7, Zaragoza (tel. 976-224858)
Youth/Sport Department (Dirección General de Bienestar Social y Trabajo), Pza de los Sitios 7, Zaragoza

**Education departments**
Huesca: Pza de Cervantes 4 (tel. 974-221400)
Teruel: San Francisco 31 (tel. 974-602535)
Zaragoza: Pº de Isabel la Católica 7 (tel. 976-354200)

**Youth information offices**
Huesca: Avda del Parque 9 (tel. 974-221906)
Teruel: Ronda Liberación 1-2º (tel. 974-501579)
Zaragoza: Franco y López 4 (tel. 976-451389)

**TIVE office**
Gran Vía 7, Zaragoza (tel. 976-218315)

**Travel agents**
Zaragoza:
— Rosa dels Vents, c/Legasca 10 (tel. 976-236805), specialists in youth travel
— Viajes Ecuador, Canfranc 9 (tel. 976-222695)

**Car hire**
Atesa, at Zaragoza Airport, also Avda Valencia 3, Zaragoza (tel. 976-352806)

**British representation**
British Chamber of Commerce — see Bilbao, Barcelona or Madrid
British Consulate — see Madrid, Bilbao or Barcelona
British schools — none

**Language schools (TEFL)**
Huesca: Centro de Idiomas Oxford, Coso Alto 12-2º
Zaragoza:
— The English Centre, D. Jaime 1-19-1º
— The Oxford Centre, San Miguel 16
— Inlingua, Costa 2

# 5 Asturias

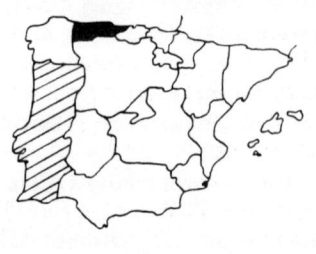

Asturias is in many ways the 'Wales' of Spain: sharing with Wales a Celtic heritage, a beautiful landscape of mountains and green valleys, and an economy split between agriculture and heavy industry. Not only that, but the title of the heir to the Spanish throne is 'Prince of Asturias', and, like Wales, it's a great place for lovers of unspoilt countryside, walking, climbing, touring, etc.

Asturias has a special place in Spanish history, starting from the Stone Age, when, as evidence from numerous caves show, the region was quite densely populated. The resistance of the Iron Age Celtic tribes to the Romans is still regarded with pride by the Asturians. However, it was their resistance to conquest by the Moors, in the eighth century AD, that really gained them a place in the history books. In 722, a local chief, Pelayo, inflicted a major defeat on the Moors at the Battle of Covadonga — their first setback since their arrival on the Peninsula some 11 years earlier — which marked the beginnings of a determination to resist the invaders which became the Reconquest. Pelayo set up court at Cangas de Onís, which thus became the first capital of the Kingdom of Asturias.

One hundred years later, Alfonso II transferred his court to Oviedo (the present provincial and regional capital), where he built the Cámara Santa (now part of the Cathedral) to house the holy relics rescued from the Visigothic capital of Toledo when it came under Muslim control. As the Reconquest spread south, the history of Asturias became linked with that of León, and later Castile, although to this day it retains its essentially Celtic character, distinct in that it lacks both the Roman and the Moorish elements which, with the exception of the Basque Country, were so influential in the rest of the Peninsula. The Asturian language, *Bable*, is still extant.

The historical ability of the Asturians to resist invaders, in which they still today take so much pride, was in part a result of geographical factors. The long coastline, and the lush green heartlands of Asturias are protected from the vicissitudes experienced by the rest of the Peninsula by the forbidding grey mountain ranges of the Cordillera Cantabrica. Geographically, therefore, Asturias is made up of three distinct zones: the coast, with its cliffs, its bays and its sandy beaches; the mountains, wild and dramatic; and between the two, beautiful green countryside, prosperous, and cultivated principally with maize, beans and cider apple orchards.

Substantial and well cared for farm houses (*casonas*) are evidence of the agricultural prosperity, the rivers team with fish — it could be something of a rural idyll! The three major towns of Oviedo, Gijón and Avilés form a wedge of heavy industry through the middle of the region. The first two were industrialised early — for Spain — taking advantage of the concurrence of coal and iron ore deposits in the area. Avilés has been developed more recently (in the 50s), and its huge steelworks complex has completely transformed the old town. Industrialisation has given the Asturians new opportunities to demonstrate their capacity for resistance: in 1934 a revolutionary committee of insurgent miners took control of Oviedo for over a week, and during the Civil War the fierce opposition to Franco's forces resulted in such destruction that Gijón had to be almost completely rebuilt.

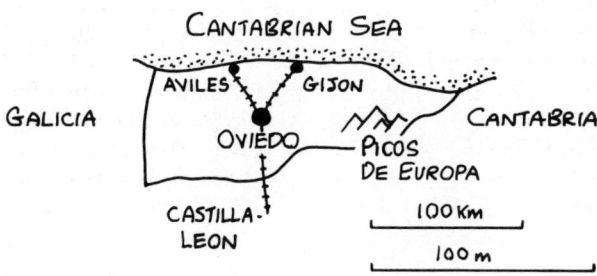

## WHAT TO SEE

**Picos de Europa.** The impressive mountain range to the east of the region, taking in the Covadonga National Park, Cares Gorge, Covadonga Lakes, etc. (See 'Hiking' below.)
**Cangas de Onís.** Centre for Picos de Europa Caves, Bronze Age dolmen.
**Llanes.** Typical walled fishing town, with good beaches. Bronze age monument, the 'Idol of Peña Tu', at nearby Vidiago.
**Ribadesella.** Beautiful spot, good beach. Prehistoric caves (see below).
**Colunga** and **Lastres.** Fishing villages, good beaches.
**Villaviciosa.** Charles V arrived here in 1517 by mistake. (He should have gone to Santander!) I would have been disappointed too.
**Gijón.** Rebuilt on a grid-plan after the Civil War, although a small old quarter with cobbled streets still exists. Impressive promenade along sea front. Birthplace of Jovellanos, the great eighteenth century liberal and man of letters.
**Oviedo.** The industrial capital of the region, with a population of about 200,000. Sights include a Gothic cathedral incorporating the ninth century *Cámara Santa* and Holy Relics, and some beautiful examples of pre-Romanesque Asturian architecture: the churches of Santullano, and, 2

miles out of the city, San Miguel de Lillo and Santa María de Naranco, the latter originally the Royal Palace of Ramiro I of Asturias (842–850 AD).
**Pajares Pass.** Breathtaking mountain scenery, ski centre.
**Salinas.** Enormous beach, sports facilities, residential area for Avilés.
**Cudillero.** Outstandingly beautiful fishing village.
**Luarca.** Lively fishing port, good atmosphere.
**Navia.** Pine woods, beach.
**Castro de Coaña.** Remains of Celtic village.

## COMING AND GOING

### By air
Asturias airport is to the west of Avilés, and has good links with other Spanish airports, but probably the best way of approaching Asturias is by land.

### By bus/coach
**Eurolines** do a coach service direct to Oviedo from London, and **Transportes Intercar** run a regular service linking Irún, on the French border, with Tuy, on the Portuguese border, passing along the coast road, and stopping at places like Ribadesella and Luarca, as well as Gijón, Oviedo and Avilés. **Alsa Autobuses** run daily services to Madrid, Barcelona, Valencia, etc., and also a comprehensive service within the region.

### By rail
Oviedo, Gijón and Avilés are linked to Madrid and the rest of Spain on a north – south route of the national rail network, but there's also a narrow gauge railway, the **FEVE**, which goes east – west along the coast from Bilbao to El Ferrol, in Galicia, a useful and pleasant way of travelling here (if slow!) as it passes through some splendid scenery. Another line takes you inland from Gijón to Pola de Laviana, through the heart of the Asturian countryside.

For a romantic, luxury rail journey, you can go on the *Transcantábrico* on an 8 day trip from León to El Ferrol or vice versa, including excursions to various 'sights' (June – September and Easter only). Enquire at any rail station in Spain, or from Britain through a major travel agent like Thomas Cook. The address of the General Sales Agent in this country is 7a Henrietta Place, London W1 (tel. 01–493 4934).

### By sea
Finally, bear in mind that the Plymouth – Santander ferry leaves you within spitting distance of Asturias. That way you can take your own bike, push-bike or car to Spain with you, or go on foot and either hitch or get public transport up the coast to your destination.

### Packages
**Ramblers Holidays** do a walking holiday in the Picos de Europa, some of the **Brittany Ferries** packages leave you well placed for exploring

Asturias, and some of the Route to Santiago packages (see Galicia) include visits or overnight stays in Oviedo. (See also p. 21.)

## WHERE TO STAY

**Hotels** and **pensions** here tend to be at the cheaper end of the accommodation market, which is useful.

There are five **youth hostels** in the region, and the **Reservations Office** is at Plaza del Sol 8, Palacio de Revillagigedo, Oviedo (tel. 985-225930).

There are at least a dozen **mountain refuges** in the Picos de Europa, and a fair number elsewhere too.

**Campsites** are reasonably numerous along the coast, and there is one at **Cangas de Onís** serving the Picos de Europa.

## WHAT TO EAT AND DRINK

The regional dish is *fabada asturiana*, which is an exceedingly filling bean stew with the addition of different varieties of sausages and meat. You will also find a coastal version of the same dish, with *almejas* (small clams) instead of meat.

Seafood in general is good here, from sardines to lobster, and the rivers are full of salmon and trout, so look out for them on the menu. Look out also for *caldereta*, which is the Asturian version of *bouillabaisse*.

Cheeses are good here, from high-fat, bland cow's cheeses to the extremely pungent *Cabrales* — a blue cheese made from a mixture of cow's, goat's and sheep's milk, wrapped in sycamore leaves and ripened in dank caves! If you like Roquefort you should certainly try it.

The regional drink is cider — you see apple orchards everywhere. It's very frothy and is traditionally poured in a long stream over the shoulder and into the glass. Try it in the local bars, or *chigres*.

## OPPORTUNITIES IN ASTURIAS

Asturias is a small region, and no particular opportunities for work or study exist. It is above all a place to spend some time off, and would make a great base for a walking/climbing/hiking holiday. Equally, it would make a pleasant long-weekend break, if you're working in Bilbao, Madrid, or even Barcelona. If you're staying in Santander, it's feasible for day trips. Its attraction is in its natural resources — lakes, mountains, uncrowded beaches, fresh air — rather than in facilities provided, although don't get the idea it's completely bereft of modern services.

## WHAT TO DO

## ARCHAEOLOGY

There are important Celtic remains in the **Coaña/Castropol** area (extreme west of the region), which are still being excavated.

## ART GALLERIES AND MUSEUMS

**Oviedo**
**Museo Arqueológico,** c/San Vicente 3, Entrance free, closed Mondays.
**Museo Provincial de Bellas Artes,** c/Santa Ana 3, Entrance free, closed Sundays and Monday mornings.
**Cámara Santa of Cathedral.** Closed in the mornings on Sundays and holidays.

**Gijón**
**Museo de la Gaita,** c/Pueblo de Asturias. Collection of bagpipes (regional instrument) from all over the world. Shut weekends.

**Luanco**
**Asturian Maritime Museum,** c/Suárez Pola.

**Mieres**
**Museum of Mining,** Alto de la Colladiella, Urbiés.

## CAVING

You should get in touch with the local **Federación de Espeleología** (Apartado 540, Oviedo) if you want to do some serious caving as they can arrange insurance, etc. If you just want to visit caves, the following are open to the public:

At Ribadesella: **Cueva de Tito Bustillo.** Prehistoric wall paintings. Open April to September. The **Cueva de les Pedroses** also has wall paintings.
At Ribadedeva: **Cueva del Pindal.** Open all the year round.
At Cangas de Onís: **Cueva de los Azules** (human remains from 7,500 BC), and nearby, at Cardes, the **Cuevas del Buxu.**
At Covadonga: The so-called **'Holy Cave' of Our Lady of Covadonga,** containing religious images.

## CINEMA

An **International Festival of Children's Cinema** takes place every year in Gijón during the first half of July. Information available from Cerinterfilm, Paseo de Begoña 24, Gijón.

## COURSES

● The University of Oviedo runs a month's Spanish language course in July at Llanes: beginners, intermediate and advanced levels. Accommodation provided. Write for further information and application form to: **Cursos de Verano — Llanes,** Universidad de Oviedo, c/San Francisco 3, 33003 Oviedo.
● The Faculty of Philology runs a course in Spanish language, culture

and civilization lasting a full academic year, with the possibility of signing up for just half a year (either October to February or February to May). It is open to anyone aged 16 or over, although some prior knowledge of Spanish is necessary, however basic. Write to: **Cursos de Invierno de Español para Extranjeros**, Facultad de Filología, Universidad de Oviedo Plaza Feijoo, 33003 Oviedo.

● Each year towards the end of July a week-long course in medieval archaeology is usually held, again at Llanes. For details of this, and also of any other courses that may be held on a 'one off' basis, write to: **Secretaria de los Cursos de Verano de la Universidad de Oviedo**, Negociado de Extensión Universitaria, Edificio Palacio de Quirós, Plaza de Riego 4, 2nd floor, 33003 Oviedo.

● There's a 'School of Co-operativism' in Arriondas which runs courses in co-operative management and organises talks and workshops on how to set up and run a co-operative. Contact them at: **Escuela de Formación Cooperativa y Trabajo Asociado**, c/del Barco 12, Arriondas (Asturias).

## CRAFTS

Jet has been mined for centuries in Asturias and in medieval times amulets and mementos made of jet were in great demand to sell to pilgrims on the Santiago de Compostela route. Asturias also found an important market for its jet jewellery in Victorian Britain. Today jet-working is undergoing a revival, especially in the town of Villaviciosa.

Other traditional Asturian crafts are metalwork of all kinds (e.g. copper cauldrons, knives, agricultural tools, bells), watchmaking, boatbuilding, wickerwork and leatherwork. The black pottery from Llamas de Mouro enjoys a certain renown in Spain.

## FIESTAS

Every year on the first Saturday in August, the **International Canoe Race** (*las piraguas*) down the river Sella, from **Arriondas** to **Ribadesella** is an excuse for a big fiesta at the finishing point. You can follow the race by car, or by special train laid on from Oviedo, which stops at strategic points en route, and returns to Oviedo in the evening. Those who don't return end up sleeping on the beach at Ribadesella. If you're interested in entering the race, contact the Spanish Canoeing Federation (**Federación Españolas de Piragüismo**) at c/Cea Bermúdez 14, 28004 Madrid.

Other festivals of note are the **Cider Festival** at **Nava** in mid-July, '**Asturias Day**' throughout the region but especially at **Covadonga** on 8th September, and '**Americas Day**' in **Oviedo** on 19th September, commemorating Asturian contacts with Latin America through emigration. In **Arenas de Cabrales** on 31st August there's a cheese festival and competition, and all the typical celebrations. In Asturias this means lots of cider-drinking, and traditional music provided by drums and bagpipes.

## HIKING/CLIMBING

There are wonderful hikes and walks all over the region, the most famous being the **Cares gorge** route in the **Picos de Europa**: a footpath has been cut into the side of the gorge (15 or so miles of it) so you can follow the spectacular course of the Cares river, many feet below!

There are mountain footpaths throughout the interior of the region, and with the help of a good map (see p. 17 earlier in the book) you should be able to plan some good routes. Try, for instance, the following areas, as well as the Picos: the **Bosque de Muniellos** (greatest extension of oak forest in the Peninsula), the **Somiedo Lakes**, or the **Las Xanas pass** (south-west of Oviedo, near Proaza) — wherever you go you can be sure of stunning scenery and a rich selection of wildlife.

If you need help planning routes, or finding out where mountain refuges are, the local tourist offices (at **Arenas de Cabrales, Panes** and **Cangas de Onís** for the **Picos de Europa**, and **Salas**, or **Gijón** or **Oviedo**, for the west of the region) will give you detailed information and advice. See also Robin Collomb's guide to walks and climbs, entitled simply *Picos de Europa*. There are also numerous guides in Spanish, which you will find in local bookshops. Another source of advice, and one which you should contact if you're intending to do any serious climbing, is the **Federación Asturiana de Montañismo**, c/Melquiades Alvarez 16, Oviedo.

The weather in Asturias is ideal for hiking, as it is unlikely to be too hot, even in August. In fact, you are likely to run into the opposite problem, especially high up in the mountains, so take warm clothes and a waterproof. If you're going to do serious walking, and camp out, it's important to take all the usual precautions, and not to overestimate your strength. Take adequate food and drink, and make sure you know where you can get help if you need it.

## LOCAL PRESS

*La Nueva España*
*El Comercio*
*La Voz de Asturias*

## NATIONAL PARKS

The **Covadonga National Park**, in the **Picos de Europa**, was Spain's first national park and offers spectacular mountain scenery, with its glaciated lakes the **Enol** and the **Ercina**, and deciduous forests. It is home to foxes, wolves, mountain cats, pine martens, otters and stoats, as well as rare species of birds of prey (see also Wildlife below).

## SPORTS

### Air sports and ballooning

There's an aerodrome at **Llanera**, where you can do parachuting, gliding or model aircraft flying. It's surprisingly cheap to go up in a balloon, and the **Aeroestación Club Astur** organises balloon trips to various fiestas in the region as well. Their address is c/Marqués de Esteban 50–A, Gijón.

### Canoeing
This is popular here (see section on fiestas above), and is practised on the rivers **Nalón, Pigueña** and **Deva**, as well as on the **Sella**. It's also possible to canoe at sea from certain points along the coast.

### Caving
See separate section above.

### Cycling
Asturias is good country for cycling enthusiasts, and has its own cyclists' touring club, where you can get good advice and useful information: **Albora Bici-Ecologista**, Avda de Galicia 86, 14–4, Gijón. Cycling clubs in Barcelona and Madrid often arrange tours to Asturias. You can hire bikes at the Naranjo de Bulnes campsite in **Arenas de Cabrales**, and here too they'll be able to point you in the right direction for the best rides.

### Climbing/Mountaineering
See section on hiking above.

### Fishing
In spring/summer you can fish for salmon and trout in most of Asturias' rivers, with a licence from **ICONA**, c/Uria 10, Oviedo (tel. 985–210231).

### Horseriding
At **Ribadesella, Llanes** and **Noreña**. In summer you can go pony-trekking in the mountains. **Ecuus Astur** offers a complete 3 day package. Get in touch with them at c/Padre Aller 3, 33012 Oviedo (tel. 985–254557).

### Sailing
Regattas, trips around the coast, etc. **Federación de Vela**, c/Foncalada 1, Oviedo.

### Skiing
Full facilities at the **Estación de Esqui Valgrande-Pajares** on the border with León. Further information from one of the tourist offices, or from the **Federación Asturiana de Deportes de Invierno**. Avda José Antonio 25, Mieres (tel. 985–471586), or just turn up, December to April.

## UNIVERSITY

There is an ancient university at Oviedo, founded in 1534, which has departments in Gijón, and also runs summer courses and other activities in Llanes, Villaviciosa, Navia and Avilés. Approaching Gijón from the east, you can't miss the huge monastery-like 'Labour University' which is actually a State Technical College. There are lectures, courses and other events going on here which might be of interest too.

**Universidad de Oviedo**, San Francisco 1 y 3, Oviedo (tel. 985–219885)

## WILDLIFE/CONSERVATION

(see also section on National Parks above)

**Somiedo National Reserve:** lonely region of high peaks and valleys. **Bosque de Muniellos:** enormous stretch of deciduous woodland, rich in mosses and lichens, and harbouring, among other species, the bear and the ibex.
**Degaña National Reserve, Reres National Reserve,** and **Sueve National Reserve.** It may be possible to get on a work camp in the region which is involved in a conservation project (see p. 72).

## YOUTH CONFERENCE

A National Youth Conference takes place every summer in Gijón, based at the Labour University. There are talks and workshops on a variety of themes relating to youth, and parallel activities such as film shows, exhibitions, youth theatre, sports, musical events. It's run by the Ministry of Culture, and they can supply information at the following address: **Centro Nacional de Información y Documentación de Juventud**, c/Marqués de Riscal 16, 28010 Madrid.

## USEFUL ADDRESSES

**Tourist offices**
**Arenas de Cabrales:** Carretera General
**Cangas de Onís:** Emilio Lara 2
**Gijón:** Marqués de San Esteban 1
**Oviedo:** Cabo Noval 5
**Ribadesella.** Carretera Piconera
**Salas:** Pza Generalisimo

**Government offices**
**Regional Government:** Consejo del Gobierno del Principado de Asturias, Palacio Regional, Fruela 17, 33003 Oviedo (tel. 985–222003)
**Education Department:** Pza de España s/n, Oviedo
**Labour Department:** Sta Teresa 15, Oviedo
**University Careers Office:** (Centro de Orientación e Información del Empleo) Rectorado de la Universidad, Oviedo
**Youth/Sport Department:** Consejería de Educación, Cultura y Deportes, Dirección Regional de Acción Cultural y Juventud, Pza del Sol 8, Palacio de Revillagigedo, 33009 Oviedo

**Youth information offices**
**Avilés:** Muralla 1, 2º–D
**Gijón:** Trinidad 6–1º
**Oviedo:** Avda Calvo Sotelo 5, Apartado de Correos 327

**TIVE office**
c/Asturias 9–4º, Oviedo (tel. 985–236058)

**Travel agents**
**Oviedo:** Viajes Wagons Lits, c/ Cabo Noval 9
**Gijón:** Viajes Altamira, c/ Fundición 2

**Car hire.**
**Atesa:** Ventura Rodriguez 8, Oviedo (tel. 985–259411)
**Hertz:** Victor Chavarri 25, Oviedo (tel. 985–215418)

**British representation**
**British Consulate:** Santander (see section on Cantabria)
**British schools** — none in this part of the world.

**Language schools (TEFL)**
**Avilés:**
— Academia de Idiomas Modernos, Generalísimo Franco 20–3º (tel. 985–564198)
— Anglo School, López Ocaña 9
**Gijón:**
— Lawton School, Cura Sama 7 (tel. 985–349609)
— Academia de Idiomas Modernos, c/ Corrida 16–3º
— Círculo de Idiomas, San Bernardo 48–2º (tel. 985–348746)
— Oxford Academy, Trinidad 4 (tel. 985–352386)
— Hibernia School, Muralla 7–1º–D (tel. 985–352230)
— Idiomas Meta, Concepción Arenal
— Inlingua Idiomas, Marqués de San Esteban 16 (tel. 985–353693)
**Oviedo:**
— Instituto IFA, San Francisco 17–2º (tel. 985–218196)
— Victoria English Speaking Club, Nueve de Mayo 18 (tel. 985–221575)
— Capel, Asturias 5–1º (tel. 985–238535)
— The Cambridge School of English, c/Independencia 7–1º (tel. 985–240283)

# 6 Cantabria

Cantabria is a much more immediately appealing region than its neighbours Asturias and the Basque Country, and if you haven't been to northern Spain before it is recommended as an attractive, comfortable introduction to 'real' Spanish culture. It's like the south of England compared to Wales or Scotland: rich, pastoral, green and beautiful — perhaps a little bland for some tastes, like the cheese it produces.

The reason why Cantabria is an island of mainstream Spanish culture between its strongly regionalist neighbours is that, until the recent division of Spain into autonomous communities, it was part of Castile, historically providing an important link with the sea for Castilian trade and defence. During the fifteenth century it became exceedingly fashionable for the Castilian nobility to own summer retreats in areas of rural Cantabria, most notably at Santillana de Mar. Driving through the countryside today you will come across these rather severe and ostentatious seigneurial mansions, emblazoned with stone family crests.

Cantabria's great industry is tourism — mainly Spanish escaping the summer heat of Madrid or the south. The coastline is less rugged here than in either Asturias or the Basque Country. Its long sandy beaches and low cliffs provide some ideal resorts. Santander, the capital, especially enjoys a magnificent natural setting, its harbour and over a mile of beaches sheltered from the force of the Atlantic rollers by a sandy promontory.

In the countryside, and right up to the cliff edge, the gentle sound of cow bells will draw your attention to herds of dairy cattle, a sight uncommon in the rest of Spain. Cantabria supplies Spain with much of its milk, butter and cows' cheese.

Further inland, beyond the rich pasturelands and woods, mountains form a natural border with the neighbouring provinces of Oviedo, Palencia and Burgos, and the scenery takes on a wilder beauty, with spectacular gorges, waterfalls, and rushing streams. The climate is mild and temperate all year round, with a fair amount of rain.

**WHAT TO SEE (from East to West)**

**Castro Urdiales.** Friendly old coastal town with narrow streets, harbour, and at the far end of an impressive promenade, a good beach.
**Laredo.** Old maritime town, which has now become a modern resort with

every facility, although not over-commercialised. An immense beach is the main attraction.

**Santander.** Elegant and lively provincial capital in a superb setting. The beaches are in the Sardinero district, a short bus ride or bracing walk from the town centre and port area.

**Torrelavega.** Prosperous town with important manufacturing industries.

**Santillana de Mar** (no longer on the coast!). A perfectly preserved village of seigneurial mansions in a totally rural setting. Chickens and farm animals roam the cobbled streets. Beautiful Romanesque church, and nearby:

**Altamira.** Its famous caves are not open to the public except through special application—see below.

**Comillas.** Dignified hill town with cobbled streets, which somehow seems to turn away from its two beautiful beaches.

**San Vicente de la Barquera.** Relaxed town and summer resort on an estuary. Beaches nearby.

Inland:

**Potes.** Centre for Picos de Europa (see section on **Asturias**).

**Reinosa.** Small mountain town and something of an industrial centre. A good base for exploring the Valle de Campóo.

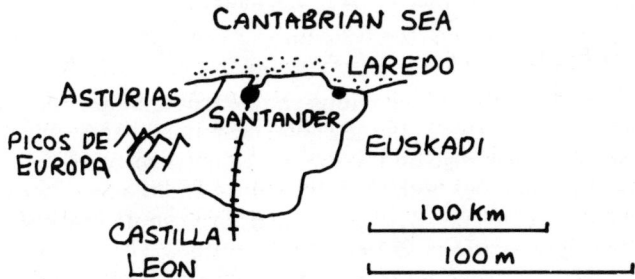

## COMING AND GOING

### By air
There's an airport at Parayas, on the Bilbao road, with internal flights only to and from Madrid, Barcelona and Pamplona.

### By sea
The twice weekly (in summer) ferry line from Plymouth is a useful means of getting to the region (see p. 20). Information and reservations (in Spain) from **Modesto Piñeiro**, Paseo de Pereda 27, Santander (tel. 942–214500). See earlier in the book for bookings from Britain.

### Boat trips
Boats leave from **Las Reginas** jetties in the port area of Santander. There is also a service which takes you to Pedreña, on the other side of the bay where there are secluded beaches, and a Golf Club.

**By train**
**RENFE** (national network) will take you to and from Madrid, Barcelona (a winding route via Burgos, Pamplona and Zaragoza) and Valladolid. The **FEVE** narrow gauge railway provides a useful link with resorts and villages along the coast in both directions. Both train stations are centrally located, next to the ferry port.

**By coach**
**Eurolines** run a twice weekly service from London to Santander via Bilbao and San Sebastián. There are also services to Barcelona, Burgos, and Oviedo and the rest of Asturias and Galicia. All services depart from either c/Castilla or Plaza Isabel II, both right next to the ferry port and railway stations. Most provincial buses also leave from this part of town. There is a motorway under construction between Santander and Torrelavega, otherwise the roads are not really designed for fast travelling, although they can be pleasant for touring as there is little traffic.

**Packages**
**Brittany Ferries** do a variety of packages as well as straight ferry crossings from Plymouth to Santander. **Ramblers Holidays'** walking holidays in the Picos de Europa are based at Potes for much of the time, as is **Travelscene's** 'Northern Spain' package.

## WHERE TO STAY

Plenty of cheap **hotels, pensions** and **boarding houses** are available. In Santillana they seem to charge a good deal more than average for a room, but outside the village on the way to Altamira many of the houses offer *camas*. In Santander both the town centre and the Sardinero district are good for places to stay. There are half a dozen **youth hostels** in the region and the **Reservations Office** is at c/Burgos 110–7º, Santander (tel. 942-238987). **Casas de labranza** are worth checking out in the area. **Campsites** are numerous all along the coast.

## WHAT TO EAT

Cantabria has good restaurants, some very up-market, and bars everywhere serving some tempting *raciones*. Like other regions on the north coast, there is a heavy emphasis on fish, especially *rabas* (fried squid) and fresh tuna. The Basque *marmitako* here becomes *marinera marmita*, that is fish stew with potatoes. Another filling dish to look out for is *cocido montañés*, a stew with flexible ingredients, containing either white beans or chickpeas, cabbage, pork and *chorizo*.

Dairy produce influences cooking, and, especially in Santillana, you'll find yourself offered buttery sponge cakes called *sobaos*, traditionally accompanied with a glass of milk. Cheeses are generally cow's milk — the rich, high-fat *Lebeña* is very typical.

Very little wine is produced in the region, but most bars keep a good stock of *Rioja* (the rosé is recommended chilled with *rabas*).

## OPPORTUNITIES IN CANTABRIA

Study possibilities are quite good. There's a university at Santander, but more importantly, the **Universidad Internacional Menéndez Pelavo** bases most of its activities here during the summer, including language courses, lectures and conferences (see next page). It's a good region in which to spend some free time too, with beach holidays in the summer, skiing in winter, hiking all the year round. Santander is pleasantly stimulating in terms of cultural interest at all times of the year, but especially in August during the International Festival (see p. 120). It's a tiny region, though, and offers few prospects of work for foreigners.

## WHAT TO DO

### ART GALLERIES AND MUSEUMS

**Santander**
**Museo Municipal de Bellas Artes,** Rubio 4. A selection of classical and contemporary art including a portrait of Fernando VII by Goya. Entrance free. Open 1000–1300 and 1700–2100 every day except Saturday afternoons.
**Museo Regional de Arqueología,** Casamiro Sainz 4. Some interesting prehistoric material uncovered locally. Open Mon–Sat, 0800–1400, entrance free.
**Menéndez Pelayo Library,** Rubio 6. Large collection of books on humanistic themes accumulated by the great nineteenth-century scholar.

**Muriedas**
**Museo Etnográfico de Cantabria.** Tools, artefacts, maps and photographs housed in an eighteenth century rural mansion. Open Tues–Sun, 1000–1300 and 1600–1800. Entrance free.

### BULLFIGHTS

The bull ring is centrally located in **Santander**, and the big *corridas* are held around St James's day, 25th July.

### CAVES

The caves at **Altamira**, with their impressive primitive wall-paintings, created world-wide excitement on their discovery in the 1870s. However, they are no longer open to the general public, and if you want to see them, you'll have to write, well in advance, to **Centro de Investigación**, Altamira, Santillana de Mar, Cantabria. A museum, a souvenir shop, and a minor cave with stalactites is otherwise all you'll get to see.

You can visit two caves at **Puente Viesgo** (on the Santander–Burgos road), one of which has traces of wall-paintings. They are open 1000–1300 and 1500–1845 every day except Mondays.

At **Ramales de la Victoria**, on the Colindres–Burgos road, there is another group of caves, open 1000–1300 and 1530–1900, except Mondays.

## COURSES

The **Universidad Internacional Menéndez Pelayo** plays the major role in 'Spanish for Foreigners' provision in Santander and is based in the Magdalena Palace (royal residence of King Alfonso XIII), on a promontory overlooking the bay. There are month-long courses of varying levels in Spanish Language and Literature in July, August and September. For those with a very good knowledge of Spanish, there is a Curso Superior de Filología Hispánica during August only. Accommodation is in the Magdalena Palace, or in university halls of residence.

There is also a summer programme of lectures on a variety of themes, with some well-known speakers. In addition there is a whole range of other activities: film shows, music classes, poetry workshops, etc. varying from year to year.

The University also welcomes suggestions and initiatives, so if you have an idea for putting something on yourself, you should get in touch with them. Their head office is in Madrid: Amador de los Ríos 1, 28010 Madrid (tel. 91–410 4901). For information about the language courses, write to: **UIMP**, Issac Peral s/n, Madrid.

The **University of Santander** runs Spanish language courses in the resort of Laredo during July and August. Various levels. Accommodation with families or in university halls of residence. Contact: Universidad de Santander, Vicerrectorado de Extensión Universitaria, Secretaría de los Cursos de Verano, Avda de los Castros, Santander (tel. 942–270400).

In the private sector, **Inlingua Idiomas** (Avda de los Castros 36, Santander) runs intensive 2 week courses in Spanish during July and August. Various levels. Accommodation with families.

There is also a School of Cookery in Santander, where you can take classes in regional and international cookery: **Escuela de Cocina Tablanca**, c/Jesús de Monasterio 25–2º, Santander (tel. 942–370261).

## FIESTAS

Santander's big event, the **International Festival**, which is on for the whole of August, can't really be classed as a fiesta, it's rather a modern cultural event put on to enhance the tourist attraction of the town. Nevertheless, it provides plenty of interest, with some excellent concerts and plays (see Music and Theatre below), exhibitions and fringe events.

If you want to see a traditional fiesta you could go to **Ampuero** in early September to see bull-running, or to **Laredo** on the last Sunday in August for the delightful **Battle of the Flowers**. At **Torrelavega** on the Sunday following the 15th August, there is another fiesta with a floral theme, but by and large it's not a region with outstanding festive traditions.

## HIKING

Good areas for hiking are the **Picos de Europa** (see also Asturias). Don't miss the ride up the mountainside in the funicular at **Fuente De** — if you're there in the spring you'll be stunned by the beauty of the wild flowers. Also the **Valle de Campóo** (based at Reinosa), where the Ebro rises amidst glorious scenery, and, directly south of Santander, the areas round the little villages of **Miera** and **Vega de Pas**.

## LOCAL PRESS

*Alerta*
*El Diario Montañés*
*National Press*

## MUSIC

There is a *Zarzuela* festival in June — details from the *Ayuntamiento* (tel. 942-212700).

The **International Festival** in August includes a programme of concerts, ballet, jazz and opera, usually with some very well-known performers. Again, information from the *Ayuntamiento*, or see the advertisements if you're there at the time. Events are held at a variety of venues, some outdoors. Booking office is in the Plaza Porticada.

## NIGHTLIFE

In August during the **Festival** the concerts, plays and filmshows usually start at 2230 and last late into the night. There are bars, discos and clubs to suit every taste, and the atmosphere is very animated. There is also a **Casino** — you can't miss the impressive building in the Sardinero district.

## SHOPPING

The main shopping areas in Santander are around the Plaza del Ayuntamiento and the Plaza Porticada (straight up from the ferry port). There is a full range of shops, stores and boutiques catering for the (fairly expensive) tastes of locals and holiday-makers.

Along the promenade in the Sardinero district they hold a **Book Fair** each year at the end of July/beginning of August.

## SPORTS

Traditional Cantabrian sports are sailing, rowing and skittles. There are also the following:

### Golf
**Santander Golf Club** (the training ground of Severiano Ballesteros) is at

**Pedreña**, on the opposite side of the bay from the town, amidst some beautiful scenery. It's possible to make the trip by boat from *Las Reginas* jetties in the port area.

**Fishing**
Trout, salmon, and other river fish can be caught in the region's many rivers (the **Miera**, the **Deva** and the **Pas**, to name a few). You'll need a licence, however, from **ICONA**, whose provincial office is at c/Rodríguez 5, Santander (tel. 942–212052).

**Skiing**
There are skiing facilities at **Fuente De, Portillo de Lunada** and **Alto Campóo**, the latter being the best equipped with six ski tows, four ski lifts and one telebaby, a hotel and restaurant, and hire or purchase of equipment. The **Winter Sports Federation** is at Isabell II, 20, Santander (tel. 942–228835).

## THEATRE

A season of some of the best productions in Spain lasts from 31 July to 31 August, during the **International Festival**. Information on the spot, or from **Fundación Pública del Festival Internacional de Santander**, Juan de la Costa 3–1, Santander (tel. 942–213508). The booking office for all events is in the Plaza Porticada.

## USEFUL ADDRESSES

**Tourist offices**
Plaza de Velarde 1, Bajo, Santander (tel. 942–211417)
Other tourist information offices are at Laredo, Santillana, Reinosa, Comillas, S. Vicente de la Barquera and other resorts. Also:
Regional Government Tourist Dept, Plaza de Velarde 1–1º Santander (tel. 942–212425)

**Government offices**
**Regional Government:** Diputación Regional de Cantabria, Casimiro Sainz 4, Santander (tel. 942–215163)
**Education Department:** Dirección Provincial de Educación y Ciencia, Vargas 53, Santander (tel. 942–372162)
**Labour Department:** Dirección Provincial de Trabajo, Vargas 53, Santander (tel. 942–374012)
**Youth/Sport Department:** Dirección Regional de Juventud y Deportes, Consejería de Cultura, Educación y Deportes, Burgos 11–7, Santander

**Youth information offices**
As above. Also:
Oficina de Información Juvenil, Marqués de Santillana 6, Torrelavega (tel. 942–882125)

**TIVE office**
Canarias 2, Santander (tel. 942-332215)

**Travel agents**
**Santander:**
— Viajes Altamira, Plaza Obispo 1 (tel. 942-229099)
— Viajes Ecuador, Lealtad 21 (tel. 942-311700)
— Viajes Piquio, Calvo Sotelo 21 (tel. 942-211309)

**Car hire**
**Atesa:** Avda Alfonso XIII s/n, Santander (tel. 942-222958)
**Europcar:** Rodriguez 9, Santander (tel. 942-214706)

**British representation**
**British Chamber of Commerce** — the nearest is in Bilbao.
**British Consulate:** Paseo de Pereda 27, Santander (tel. 942-220000)
**British schools** — none in this part of Spain.

**Language schools (TEFL)**
**Inlingua Idiomas,** Rualasal 23, Santander

# 7 Castilla-León (Old Castile)

'...solo una cruz distingue tu destino en la desierta soledad del campo.'
*Unamuno*

Castilla-León is the name given to the region whose autonomous government today controls what was in medieval times Old Castile and the Kingdom of León, and its historical roots are firmly placed in the period of the Reconquest. Before this 'Holy War' started to spread slowly southwards from Asturias, the vast plains of Castile were a depopulated no-man's-land, with, in fact very little Arab settlement. The Reconquest therefore meant not only establishing Christian control over the land, but also resettling it, and exploiting its agricultural and commercial possibilities. The tenth and eleventh centuries saw the establishment and growth of towns such as Avila, Segovia, Burgos, and Salamanca, now provincial capitals, which were peopled with Christians from further north. Sheep-herding became the major use to which the newly-conquered and unenclosed land was put, being more suited to a society at war than forms of agriculture requiring a more stable political situation.

As the Reconquest moved south, Castilian landowners started to look for ways of consolidating their profitable sheep-rearing estates, and as a result in 1273 the 'Mesta Council' gained the right to oversee the *cañadas*, or rights of way used by the herders. An important network of communications was thus safeguarded, which opened the way for the development of the Castilian wool trade with Flanders.

The ability to raise revenue through the export of wool had a decisive effect on the outlook and culture of Castile which can still be seen today. It created a powerful landowning class of absentee *conde-duques* and *hidalgos*, who, leaving the management of the trade to the small mercantile class of the Cantabrian and Basque ports, devoted their energies to 'nobler' military or monastic activities. (Orders such as the Knights Templars provided an opportunity for indulging both interests.) Castilian dedication to both warfare and religion over and above developing the economy is still very evident: from the heavily fortified castles on every rise of land, the garrison-town of Burgos, the fortified religiosity of Avila, the overwhelming number of churches, convents and monasteries throughout the region, and especially from the still impoverished and unenclosed countryside.

Castile's sense of the importance of its mission during the middle ages is reflected in the grandeur of the cathedrals at Salamanca, Burgos and León, in the ancient universities of Valladolid and Salamanca, and above all, in the spectacular castles which give Castile its name. The reign of Queen Isabella was the key period in the formation of Castile's essential character. Her marriage to Ferdinand of Aragón gave Castile the central role in a new, unified Spain. The Moors were finally driven from Spanish territory, the Inquisition persecuted heretics with deadly conviction that only they possessed the Truth, and the New World was discovered.

Castilla-León today is Spain's biggest region, yet it is very sparsely populated: a population of just over two and a half million live in an area of over 33,000 square miles, nearly half a million of them in the capital, Valladolid, the only city of any size. Apart from mining in León, the only industrial development of note is in Valladolid, and the region remains predominantly rural. You'll still see the herds of sheep, but mostly the vast plains have been put to the cultivation of cereals, which grow in great swathes across the landscape as far as the eye can see.

The high plain, or *Meseta*, is bordered by even higher mountains — the Guadarrama and Gredos ranges in the south and the mountains of Cantabria and León to the north. Through it, like a 'green arrow', flows the Duero river, tempering the otherwise austere landscape. The climate is continental, with cold, bright winters, and scorchingly hot summers.

Castilla-León is made up of nine provinces: Avila, Burgos, León, Palencia, Salamanca, Segovia, Soria, Valladolid and Zamora, with provincial capitals of the same names. It stretches from the Portuguese border in the west to Aragón in the east, from Cantabria and the Basque country in the north, to Madrid in the south. It's a vast area, and it could take you at least a day's travelling to get from one side to the other, so don't think that just because you're based in Salamanca you can do a day-trip to Soria — even Segovia is pushing it a bit. Explore the area round about, the countryside, the small villages: they almost all have something of interest — a ruined castle, a monastery, an ancient church with storks nesting in the belfry, or just a quaint old Plaza Mayor, with crumbling plasterwork.

## WHAT TO SEE

### Avila
Mountainous and very beautiful province, with green valleys. The claustrophobic religious atmosphere of the capital is maintained behind the solid medieval walls, reinforced by strong towers, that completely surround it. The Castilian combination of militarism and mysticism is given concrete expression in the cathedral: the apse itself forms part of the city walls. St Teresa and St John of the Cross both lived here, and there are numerous convents, churches and museums, all dedicated to them in some way.

**Elsewhere in the province**
**El Tiemblo.** Pre-roman sculptures known as **Los Toros de Guisando** stand in a field here.
**Valle del Tiétar.** One of the most picturesque country areas.
**Sierra de Gredos.** High mountain peaks, visible from Madrid.

### Burgos
Here you can catch the sense of what Castile was and is without feeling totally isolated from the twentieth century. The famous **Gothic Cathedral**, and the fourteenth-century **Arco de Santa María** look as if they've come from the film set of *El Cid* (this great hero of the Reconquest was born in a village locally, and is buried in the cathedral) yet twentieth-century concerns are well to the fore, with modest industrial development and a flourishing commercial sector.

Burgos is a big army headquarters, and traditionally a bastion of conservatism: Franco found strong support here during the Civil War. Refounded as early as the ninth century, the city grew as a commercial — and early tourist — centre as a result of vast numbers of pilgrims passing through on their way to Santiago. The cathedral and other sights such as the **Charterhouse of Miraflores**, the **Convent of Las Huelgas**, and the solid fifteenth century **Casa del Cordón**, in which Ferdinand and Isabella welcomed Christopher Columbus back from one of his voyages to America, still attract a fair number of tourists today.

**Outside the city**
The main sight, also on the road to Santiago, is the monastery at **Santo Domingo de Silos** (near Salas de los Infantes), famous for its eleventh century Romanesque cloister. **Lerma**, an imposing but deserted seventeenth century town, was built by corrupt court favourite the Duke of Lerma. **Miranda de Ebro** and **Aranda de Duero** are both dull crossroads towns.

## León

Small but lively city, which definitely has its place in the twentieth century, with plenty of bars, markets and street activity. The monuments left by history are well worth going there for too, for as well as being one of the first Christian kingdoms to establish itself after the Moorish invasion, it was an important stop on the Camino de Santiago.

The **cathedral** at first impresses you with its size, but once inside it is the stained glass which takes your attention: nearly 1,800 square metres of brilliant jewel-coloured glass dating from the thirteenth century in some striking designs. León's other great historic church is the **Basilica of San Isidro**, built as early as 1063. The crypt, or **Panteón de Los Reyes** is remarkable for its delightful — and extremely well preserved — wall paintings of biblical and everyday scenes, dating from the same period.

The grand, ornamental **monastery of San Marcos**, which was a hospice for pilgrims on the Santiago route, today performs a function of a similar kind — as a luxury hotel. Don't miss Gaudi's (see section on **Cataluña**) contemporary contribution to León's monuments either — the mock-gothic **Casa de Botines** which seems to house a building society.

### Out of town

**Sahagún.** Churches and monasteries in *mudejar* style, but not much else.
**Astorga.** Small market town — the last on the dry plains before the Bierzo mountains begin. Some industry. Also the traditional home of the *Maragatos*, a gypsy-type race of people, possibly of Berber origin, who have kept their own separate customs and identity, but about whom relatively little is known. The huge edifice which appears to be a gothic castle is in fact another of Gaudi's works — a **Bishop's Palace**, now used as a museum.
**Ponferrada.** A small grey mining and industrial town set in a valley in the mountains, completely atypical of Castilla-León as a whole.
**León's mountains**, which mark its borders with Galicia and Asturias, are worth mentioning: their south sides, facing Castile, are bare and dry, whereas the north-facing slopes are green and fertile, even in summer — splendid for exploring on foot or bike.

## Palencia

A large province, but not one which offers very much. The capital is another of those places where you get the impression that life was a good deal more exciting in the middle ages than it is now. There is a **cathedral**, an **archeological museum**, and the usual range of **ancient churches**. The first Spanish university, no longer extant, was founded here in 1208.

The rest of the province is typically flat, Castillian *tierra de campos*. The route to Santiago passed through the north of the province, and reminders of this may be seen at **Fromista** where there is an eleventh-century church, and at **Carrión de los Condes**, where the **Monastery of San Zoilo** is the main attraction.

## Salamanca

A small university town full of interest and history. It has two interconnecting cathedrals, the **Vieja** and the **Nueva**, one early Gothic, one late Gothic. The university was founded in 1218, and its patios in flesh-coloured stone are very reminiscent of the Oxford colleges and their quads. Other sights are the **Clerecía**, a church originally intended as a Jesuit college, the **Casa de las Conchas**, a rare example of secular architecture from the time of Ferdinand and Isabella, the **Plaza Mayor**, and museums, churches, convents and palaces too numerous to mention. A heavy emphasis on 'Spanish for foreigners' attracts many American students, but the old scholarly atmosphere of the place remains unspoilt.

### Elsewhere in the province
**Ciudad Rodrigo.** A small, quiet, fortified town guarding the Portuguese border.
**Béjar.** A small town in the mountains, the centre for the **Sierra de Béjar**, which offers skiing, climbing, lots of fresh air, and some dramatic mountain scenery.
**La Alberca.** Quaint little village stuck away in the beautiful **Sierra de Francia**, which marks the border with Extremadura.

### Segovia
The romantic pinnacles of Segovia's **Alcázar**, as seen on so much tourist literature, are supposed to sum up all that 'real Spain' has to offer. Like many of the great cities of Castile though, you can't imagine why you'd be there if it wasn't for the 'sights'. However, there is no mass-scale tourism, only a clutch of *mesones* specialising in roast sucking pig — a local speciality.

Of course, Segovia's other big sight pre-dates Castile — the **Roman Aqueduct**, a colossal piece of engineering, striding over the **Plaza Azoguejo**, and still serving its original purpose today.

Don't miss the pretty sixteenth-century **cathedral** or the atmospheric **Knights Templars' Church of Vera Cruz**, both of which have a delicacy and a finesse you tend not to expect in Castile.

### Elsewhere in the province
**Coca.** Magnificently preserved fiftenth-century castle in pink brick!
**Cuéllar.** Walled village with four parish churches.
**Sepúlveda.** Hill-town full of Castilian mansions.
**La Granja de San Ildefonso.** A change of tone here with this Bourbon palace in French Imperial style. Lovely gardens.
**Sierra de Guadarrama.** See **Madrid**, p. 205.

### Soria
Castile's most easterly province bordering on Aragonese territory, still rather remote with not much happening, but nice if you like the peace and quiet of the countryside here, made famous in the poetry of Machado and Béquer. The capital, at 3,470 feet above sea level, with reddish brown buildings blending in with the colour of the earth, has an air of quiet simplicity.

## Elsewhere in the province
**El Burgo de Osma.** An episcopal see in Visigothic times, whose cathedral is the architectural highlight of the province. The old arcaded streets and Plaza Mayor still have a distinctly medieval atmosphere.
**Numancia.** Fairly extensive Roman remains. The place is chiefly famous for its 20 year long resistance to the Roman seige. When the Roman legions finally forced their way in they found all the inhabitants had taken their own lives rather than surrender.
**Gormaz.** Impressive castle, supposed to be the biggest in Europe.
**Picos de Urbión.** Very pleasant mountain district, where the Duero rises. High up in the mountains among the pines there are glaciated lakes, the best known being the Laguna Negra.
**Medinaceli.** The famous palace of the Dukes of Medinaceli dominates the dilapidated village, set on a hill with views over the rolling countryside.

## Valladolid
The capital of the whole region, and the biggest and most industrialised city. Traditionally vying with Burgos in importance, it has undergone rapid expansion in recent years: high rise blocks and modern industries surround the old quarter. It's an archbishopric, although its cathedral, begun by Herrera, and continued by Churriguera, is still unfinished. It has a big student population (the university was founded in 1479), which makes for some lively scenes in the bars and cafés in the old university district.

## Elsewhere in the province
**Simancas.** Castle in which the archives of the kingdom of Castile are kept.
**Peñafiel.** Castle on the Duero. Ribera del Duero wine production.
**Tordesillas.** Famous for the treaty signed here between Spain and Portugal dividing the New World.
**Medina del Campo.** Old established crossroads on the Castilian trade routes, in greener countryside than much of the rest of the province. Again, there is wine production here, including the much-exalted Vega Sicilia (see below).

## Zamora
Quiet, out-of-the-way place with old stepped streets and hushed plazas. The domed cupola of the twelfth-century cathedral gives it an almost oriental air. The streets and city walls speak of romantic ballads and chivalrous deeds, but it's as if the place has had its day several centuries ago. Zamora lies on the ancient Roman road that ran north–south from Merida in Extremadura to Astorga in León, as does the second largest town of the province, Benavente.

## Elsewhere in the province
**Toro.** A dramatic red-walled hill-town, centre for the full-bodied red wine of the same name.
**Puebla de Sanabria.** Picturesque town, a centre for the Sanabresa area of mountains and lakes, with some tourism.

## COMING AND GOING

**By air, road and rail**
The region is served mainly by Madrid airport (see section on **Madrid**), and flying is a sensible way of avoiding long treks by car or train over the immense *Meseta*. Burgos and León may be exceptions here, being further north, and the Plymouth-Santander ferry would be useful for reaching them. León is an enjoyable day's drive from Santander, and Burgos is also well connected to the French border via the Basque country. All the provincial capitals can be reached fairly easily by road or rail from Madrid, but connections between them may be less easy.

If you're touring, take it slowly and enjoy the opportunity of seeing isolated villages and castles appearing on the horizon, without trying to cover vast distances. Long-distance coaches from the continent stop at Burgos. Internally the coach network provides a good means of moving from one stop to another, as long as you're prepared to accept the travelling as part of the fun — distances are great and it'll take 2–3 hours to get between neighbouring provincial capitals. If you plan to travel on one of the radial routes from Madrid towards one of the provincial capitals, by all means use the train, but you'll find it slow going if you want to crisscross your way across the country.

**Packages**
**Travelscene** does a tour which includes Segovia and Avila, as does **Mundicolor**'s 'Paradores of Castile' fly and drive tour. Packages which offer the 'Route to Compostela' (see section on **Galicia**) will visit Burgos and León, passing through the northern parts of the provinces of Burgos, Palencia and León. **Waymark** do an interesting walking holiday in the Sierra de Gredos. (See also listings later in this section for details of tours on horseback through Castile.)

## WHERE TO STAY

Don't forget the region is huge and sparsely populated. **Hotels** may be booked through the Castilla-León central reservations office at c/Vitoria 17, Burgos (tel. 947–264926).

There are twenty or so **youth hostels** in the region, in provincial capitals and in outlying areas of particular interest. The reservations office for the whole region is at c/San Lorenzo 5, Valladolid (tel. 983–340044 and 340111).

**Campsites** are fairly evenly scattered in picturesque areas throughout the region. *Casas de labranza* are worth looking into if you fancy a holiday away from it all in some remote rural area of Castilla-León — you'll find quite a few offers of this kind in the *Guía* (see p. 25). Castillian monasteries have a long tradition of offering hospitality to travellers and/or people who want a few days peace and quiet, which is kept up to this day. Write or telephone in advance if possible:

## León province
- San Pedro de las Dueñas (tel. 987-780150)
- Benadictinas de Sahagún (tel. 987-780078)
- Monasterio de Gradefes (women only) (tel. 987-333011)

## Palencia province
- San Andrés del Arroyo (women only) (tel. 988-133223)
- San Miguel de Dueñas (women only) (tel. 988-467046)
- San Isidro de Dueñas (tel. 988-770701)

## Burgos province
- Santo Domingo de Silos (men only) (tel. 947-380768)
- San Pedro de Cardeña (men only) (tel. 947-290033)
- Monasterio de las Huelgas (women only) (tel. 947-201630)
- Palacios de Benaver (women only) (tel. 947-451009)

## Soria province
- Santa María de la Huerta (men only) (tel. 975-327002)

## Segovia province
- El Parral (men only) (tel. 911-431298)

## WHAT TO EAT AND DRINK

Castilian cuisine is solid and generally meat-based to keep out the winter draughts. Roast meat is the speciality, especially the *cochinillo asado* (roast sucking pig) so typical of Segovia, and also roast lamb, but not beef. Mature veal is usually found in stews such as *olla podrida*, or various *cocidos*, which include chickpeas. As befits a noble landowning, but often impoverished race, game is often on the menu, usually partridge or quail. If you're lucky, you may also be offered trout, especially in Salamanca or Soria, and of course a whole range of highly spiced sausages and pork products.

Castilian sweetmeats are very good, especially *yemas de Santa Teresa* from Avila. Also sugared almonds (*de Santa Teresa*) and small pastry-like sweets called *mantecados* and *polverones*.

Burgos cheese makes a change from the usual *Manchego*, being fresh, white and crumbly.

The major wine producing areas of Castilla-León are Rueda in Valladolid province, centred around the town of Medina del Campo, and Ribera del Duero east of Valladolid, mostly in the province of Burgos. Rueda wines are full-bodied white wines strong in alcohol, whereas Ribera del Duero wines are usually light reds. For a strong full-bodied red, look for Toro wines, while Leonese wines from the Bierzo area are again lighter, whether classed as *claretes* or *rosados*. Vega Sicilia, produced in a small area on the banks of the Duero between Valladolid and Peñafiel, is Spain's most expensive wine, rivalling the choicest French wines in price. It also has a very high reputation as a strong, intensely flavoured red table wine almost reminiscent of port, but as it is so expensive and so rare, few people can verify this.

## OPPORTUNITIES IN CASTILLA-LEON

There's hardly anything going workwise, unless you're looking for a 2–3 week work camp. Study possibilities are good, especially in Salamanca, where you'll find everything organised for courses for foreigners in an authentically Castilian atmosphere. Castile has many ancient seats of learning, as it needed to house and make use of scholarly works captured from the Moors as the Reconquest progressed.

Above all, though, Castilla-León is a region for sightseeing, and offers so much in the way of tourist interest that other possibilities are obscured or seem pointless when history leaps out at you from every building. The Castilian plain is poor ground for hiking, offering little variety, and little shelter summer or winter. In the mountains around the edge of the region, however, you could plan some lovely walks and climbs, perhaps taking a tent with you.

## WHAT TO DO

### ARCHAEOLOGY

With so many castles, fortifications, and old buildings, you may well be able to get on a work camp of an archaeological nature in the region — almost all medieval. Some may also be dedicated to recovering or clearing the old *cañada* routes.

### ART GALLERIES AND MUSEUMS

**Avila**
**Museo de Avila,** Plaza Nalvillos 3–5, Casa de los Deanes, Avila.

**Burgos**
**Museo Arqueológico de Burgos,** Casa Miranda, c/Miranda 13, Burgos. Thirty rooms containing numerous finds of artistic and historical interest, from prehistoric times to the present day, housed in a sixteenth-century mansion
**Museo Marceliano Santa María,** Antiguo Monasterio de San Juan, Burgos. Around 150 works by Castilian painters.

**Palencia**
**Museo Arqueológico de Palencia,** Burgos 1, Palencia. Pre-Roman and Roman finds. Also a large collection of coins.

**Salamanca**
**Museo de Salamanca,** Patio de las Escuelas 2, Salamanca. Part of the university.

**Segovia**
**Museo de Segovia,** San Augustín 8, Segovia.

## Soria
**Museo Numantino,** Paseo del Espolón 8, Soria. Celto-Iberian and Roman finds, mostly from Numancia.
**Museo Medieval,** San Juan de Duero, Soria.
**Museo de Numancia,** Numancia, Soria.

## Valladolid
**Museo Arqueológico de Valladolid,** Palacio Fabio Nelli, Plaza de Fabio Nelli, Valladolid. Finds from various periods, also some interesting frescoes, housed in a former palace.
**Museo Nacional de Escultura,** Cadenas de San Gregorio, 1, Valladolid. National Museum of Sculpture. Contains an extensive and outstanding collection from the thirteenth to eighteenth centuries. Note also the fantastic Plateresque facade of the building itself.
**Museo Oriental,** Paseo de los Filipinos, Valladolid. Unusual collection of Chinese and Philippine art and porcelain, brought back by Castilian missionaries.
**Museo Casa Cervantes,** c/ del Rastro 7, Valladolid. The house where Cervantes spent the last years of his life, now a museum.

## Zamora
**Museo de Bellas Artes,** Requejo 1, Zamora.

## CINEMA

**Valladolid** is the best place in the region for film enthusiasts. As well as being a city large enough to support a number of good cinemas, an **International Film Festival** is held every autumn (end October/beginning November — further details from **SEMINCI**, Juan de Juni 4–1, 47006 Valladolid (tel. 983–339581) ), and an *Amateur Film Competition* towards the end of November. Check if you are eligible to enter with **Unión Artística Vallisoletana**, Apartado 747, Valladolid.

Throughout August the city council puts on a wide variety of cultural events, including some special film showings, which are held early evening in the **Casa Municipal de Cultura Revilla**, or late night showings outdoors in the **Plaza Herreriano**.

**Segovia** also has a special film week, at the end of May/beginning of June. Information from the cultural office: San Fecundo 3/5, Segovia (tel. 911–415791).

See also below for a film course held in Valladolid.

## COURSES

### Public-sector courses

*In Salamanca:*
- The University of Salamanca runs a whole range of courses:
— 2–3 month courses in Spanish language and culture during the autumn,

spring and summer terms, some for students in higher education (or graduates) only;
— 'Diploma in Spanish Studies' course, lasting the whole academic year, again for HE students only;
— a range of summer courses, including the Cursos Superiores de Filología Hispánica for Spanish graduates or teachers of Spanish. (There is sometimes a possibility of getting a Spanish government grant for this particular course; enquiries should be made to **Spanish Embassy Cultural Dept**, 24 Belgrave Square, London SW1).

During the summer you can also sign up for 'optional' courses in Spanish guitar, music and dance, theatre and cinema, etc., and there is a range of other activities, including excursions, laid on. Accommodation can be arranged if desired in halls of residence or with families.

Write to: **Universidad de Salamanca,** Secretaría de la Facultad de Filología, Pza de Anaya s/n, Salamanca.

*In Valladolid:*
- One month course in Spanish language and contemporary culture during August, plus optional lectures and excursions. Full board in *Colegio Mayor.*
- Also *Curso de Estudios Hispánicos* lasting from January to May.

Apply to: Prof D. César Hernández, Secretario de Estudios para Extranjeros, Facultad de Filosofía y Letras, Universidad de Valladolid, Valladolid.

*In Segovia:*
- One month's summer course in Spanish language and culture organised by the **UNED (Spanish Open University)**, Ciudad Universitaria, Madrid 40 (tel. 91–449 1923). Apply to: Director de Programas Culturales, Apdo 50487. Some prior knowledge of Spanish required.

**In the private sector**
- **Universidad Pontífica,** the private university in Salamanca, runs 1 or 3 month courses throughout the year, except in January and February. During the academic year, classes take place in the evenings, during the summer vacation in the mornings. Minimum age 14. Emphasis on Spanish for business purposes, translation, etc. Write to: Universidad Pontíficia, Cursos de Lengua y Cultura Españolas, Apartado 541, Salamanca.
- **Colegio de Estudios Hispánicos.** Bordadores 1–bajo, Salamanca (tel. 923–214837). A variety of courses throughout the year, of different durations and concentrating on different aspects of the language and culture, including Spanish for business purposes.
- **Instituto Castellano-Leonés de Lingüística Aplicada,** c/Sta María 2, 42001 Soria (tel. 975–226961). Runs 3 week courses in July and August in Avila, Segovia and Soria. Minimum age is 11 and no previous knowledge of Spanish is required. Accommodation with families or in student hostels.

*Castilla-León (Old Castile)* 135

- **Colegio de España,** Compañía 65, Salamanca. Month-long courses in Spanish language and civilization (literature, history, art) throughout the year starting on the 1st of each month. Also 3-month courses from October–December, and January–March, and a year long course from October–May. All levels from beginners to advanced.
- **Idiomas Castilla (American Institute)** c/ del Sol 9–2, Salamanca (tel. 923–217435). Individual or group classes throughout the year, tailored to individual needs.
- **Escuela Salmantina de Estudios Internacionales (SALMINTER),** Avda Alemania 81–7–D, Salamanca (tel. 923–219772). Individual or group tuition, and courses in Spanish language and culture throughout the year.
- **Instituto 'Cardenal López de Mendoza',** Pza Dr Albiñana, Burgos. A month-long summer language course during August for all levels from beginners to post-graduate. Minimum age 14.
- **Youth Travels,** 117 Wendell Rd, London W12 (tel. 01–743 7966). Can arrange study-holidays in Salamanca for 13–17 year olds, including accommodation and tuition, but not travel.
- **EuroAcademy,** 77a George St, Croydon (tel. 01–681 2905). Arranges study holidays in Zamora during the Easter vacation for school groups.
- **University of Valladolid.** Runs a course in film-studies in August of each year. Contact: Director D. Cándido Fernández, Universidad de Valladolid, Valladolid.
- **INICE** (see p. 46). Organises an 'International Convention for Young Researchers' held each year in Salamanca. Anybody between 16 and 30 who has done research in any field and would like to give a paper on it (not necessarily in Spanish) is invited to send written details of their proposal to INICE, c/Consejo 9–3º, Apartado de Correos 82, Salamanca (or, if you wish to phone for further details, the number is 923–219827).

## CRAFTS

Castilian crafts, still very locally based, and varying accordingly, include lace-making, embroidery, pottery, leatherwork, wickerwork and the making of the traditional solid oak or walnut furniture.

## FIESTAS

In **Ciudad Rodrigo,** Carnival time (February, before the beginning of Lent) is celebrated in raucous fashion with bullfights and *encierros,* dancing and merry-making in traditional costume.

**Holy Week** is an important time in Castile, with big processions in **Valladolid** similar to those in Seville, although, as you might expect, without the typically *andaluz* flavour — the Castilian version is more sombre, more introspective, perhaps more truly religious. Similar processions are held, with equal asceticism and religious fervour, in **Zamora,** where Easter morning is greeted with gunfire in the **Plaza Mayor.**

A famous fiesta of ancient, perhaps pre-Roman origin, and one that every year attracts its share of anthropologists, is the **fire-walking ritual** on St John's Eve (23rd June) in **San Pedro Manrique** in the province of **Soria**. Local men, barefoot, and carrying another on their shoulders, perform the miracle of crossing a path of hot coals without burning their feet. Visitors and tourists are prevented from trying to copy them. The week after **San Juan** sees big fiestas in **Soria** too.

On the **day of the Assumption of the Virgin Mary** (15th August), the little village of **La Alberca** (Salamanca) gives full rein to its rich folk traditions. The local costumes, some heavily embroidered and decorated with gold and silver, are brought out, and the fiestas include an offering to the Virgin, singing and dancing, and the performance of an allegorical folk play called *La Loa* in which the devil comes to sabotage the village festivities.

## HIKING

All the mountain areas, which mark the border of Castilla-León with other regions, are ideal for hiking, climbing or just walking. Some are extremely remote, but their unexplored beauty is startling, like, for instance, the **Sierra de Francia** in Salamanca, with its lush wooded valleys, its groves of fruit trees, almonds and chestnuts, its tiny villages with narrow winding streets and houses with overhanging upper floors supported on wooded stilts, and glimpses of mountain scenery.

For more serious hiking and climbing, try the **Sierra de Béjar**, also in Salamanca province. The landscape here is much more rugged, and the high peaks of the grey granite mountains are snow covered for much of the year. You could follow the track of an old *cañada* which goes from **Béjar** to **Torrejón el Rubio** in Extremadura.

In Zamora province, make for **Puebla de Sanabria**, and thence to the village of **Rivadelago**, on the shores of **Lake Sanabria**. You won't feel quite so cut off here as in some other remote areas, but there's a youth hostel, a campsite, swimming in the lake, and walks in the mountains. **ICONA** (Ronda de San Torcuato 15, Zamora (tel. 988–471350) ) put out a map/information leaflet on the area, priced 150 pts.

In the north of the region, there are the southern slopes of the **Picos de Europa** to explore (see section on **Asturias**). In Soria province, the **Picos de Urbión** are yet another remote and relatively unexplored area of great natural beauty (although the **Laguna Negra** is popular at weekends) or you could follow the old trade route, the **Cañada Real Galiana** from **Soria** to **El Burgo de Osma**.

In the south, there are the pine-forested **Gredos** and **Guadarrama Sierras**, easily accessible from Madrid but wild enough, high enough and big enough to offer challenges to the most intrepid climber.

Two areas on the plains suggest themselves for hikers/walkers/explorers: the **Duratón gorge** in Segovia province, between **Sepúlveda** and **Fuentidueña**, and along the banks of the **Duero**, perhaps based at **Tordesillas**, where poplars and holm-oaks relieve the bareness of the otherwise rather monotonous landscape. This area would be ideal for cycling too.

## LOCAL PRESS

*El Adelantado* (Segovia)
*El Adelanto* (Salamanca)
*Diario de Burgos*
*Diario de Avila*
*Diario de León*
*Norte de Castilla* (Valladolid)
*El Correo de Zamora*

## SCOUTS

The **Leonese Scouts**, Scouts de León, Apartado 49, León (tel. 987-225375) organise international scout camps during July and August for 12 to 16 year olds.

## SPORTS

The Youth Department of the **Junta de Castilla y León** (see addresses below) organises a whole range of sports courses, including parachuting, basketball and swimming.

### Canoeing
On rivers. Summer courses organised by the **Fundación Municipal Deportiva**, Joaquín Velasco Martín 9, Valladolid.

### Fishing
River fishing throughout the region (trout, barbel and river crabs), especially in the rivers of Soria and Salamanca. Contact **ICONA** for licence:

- Alonso de Ojeda 11–2º, Salamanca (tel. 923–233204)
- Ronda de San Torcuato 15, Zamora (tel. 988–513122)
- Ramón y Cajal 13, León (tel. 987–241164)
- Panaderas 14, Palencia (tel. 988–745622)
- Plaza de Alonso Martínez 7, Burgos (tel. 947–206645)
- Alonso XIII 1, Soria (tel. 975–211975)
- Plaza de Guevara 1, Segovia (tel. 911–415891)
- Méndez Vigo 6, Avila (tel. 918–221686)
- Muro 4–1º, Valladolid (tel. 983–227533)

### Horseriding
Two companies offer tours of Castile on horseback:

**Rutas a Caballo,** Augustina de Aragón 14–1º–C, 28006 Madrid (tel. 91–402 9500) do an 8-day trek, starting from Madrid airport (!), and taking you to Segovia, through some exciting country, eating in typical bars en route. April to October only. Prices include accommodation, all meals with

wine included, horse and all equipment, and bilingual guide.
**Equitour,** Juan Güell 163, entlo–1, Barcelona 28 (tel. 93–339 4100) have weekend or 4–8 day tours in the Valle del Tiétar (Avila) throughout the year.

There are also weekend courses in the Valle del Tiétar, including other sporting activities, for 14 year olds and over.

## Hunting

Many people come down from France at the start of the open season, and almost anything that moves is shot at, from song birds to wild boar. Licences are available from **ICONA** at the addresses given under fishing.

## Skiing

La Pinilla ski-station is in Segovia, with wide, clear *pistes*, hire of equipment, hotels, etc. Skiing in the Sierra de Béjar (Salamanca) is becoming very popular locally, and although as yet mostly on an *ad hoc*, cross country basis, the area is ripe for development and no doubt more facilities will be installed as time goes on. In the north of the region there is a small station at Puerto de San Isidro, León, and access to those in Santander (see Cantabria) and Asturias. Burgos boasts 2 stations, at Lunada and Valle del Sol, both superbly located among beech woods.

Further details from tourist offices or Winter Sports Federations:

**Federación Castellana de Deportes de Invierno,** Ayala 44, Madrid 1 (tel. 91–226 6174)
**Federación Leonesa de Deportes de Invierno,** Independencia 1–1º–C, León (tel. 987–230054)

Most of the ski-stations in the Gredos and Guadarrama ranges are actually in Madrid province, so see section on Madrid for details.)

---

## THEATRE

The education and culture department of the **Junta de Castilla-León** promotes a theatre season during the summer in all its provincial capitals, and other towns besides. At the end of June each year there is an important theatre festival in Burgos, laid on by the **Grupo de Teatro Tabladillo,** Pza José Antonio 1 (tel. 947–201459), and October brings theatrical events to Zamora and province.

---

## UNIVERSITIES

There are universities at Salamanca, Valladolid and León and university colleges in other provincial capitals and large towns:

**Universidad de Salamanca,** Patio de las Escuelas 1, Salamanca (tel. 923–216800)
**Universidad de Valladolid,** Palacio de Sta Cruz, Plaza de Sta Cruz 8,

Valladolid (tel. 983-291467)
**Universidad de León**, Carretera de Santander s/n, León (tel. 987-241800)

## USEFUL ADDRESSES

**Tourist offices**
**Avila:** Pza de la Catedral 4 (tel. 918-211387)
**Burgos:** Pza Alonso Martínez 7 (tel. 947-203125)
**León:** Pza de Regla 4 (tel. 987-237082)
**Palencia:** Mayor 105 (tel. 988-740068)
**Salamanca:** Gran Vía 41 (tel. 923-243730)
**Segovia:** Plaza Mayor 10 (tel. 911-430328)
**Soria:** Pza Ramón y Cajal s/n (tel. 975-212052)
**Valladolid:** Pza de Zorilla 3 (tel. 983-351801)
**Zamora:** Santa Clara 20 (tel. 988-511845)

**Government offices**
**Regional Government Tourist Dept,** García Morato 36-1º, Valladolid (tel. 983-342500)
**Regional Government** (Junta de Castilla-León) Carretera de Rueda km 3,5, 47008 Valladolid (tel. 983-279000)
**Youth/Sport Department** (Dirección General de Juventud y Deportes), Consejería de Educación y Cultura, Nicolás Salmerón 3-4, Valladolid

**Education department**
**Avila:** Cruz Roja 1 (tel. 918-221504)
**Burgos:** Vitoria 17 (tel. 947-207540)
**León:** Jesus Rubio 4 (tel. 987-202711)
**Palencia:** Lope de Vega 18 (tel. 988-747599)
**Salamanca:** Paseo de Canalejas 21 (tel. 923-236600)
**Segovia:** Pza de Colmenares 2 (tel. 911-411693)
**Soria:** Avda Valladolid 22 (tel. 975-220212)
**Valladolid:** Avda José Luis de Arese s/n, Edificio Servicios Múltiples (tel. 983-339600)
**Zamora:** Prado Tuerto s/n, Polígono Candelaria (tel. 988-522750)

**Labour departments**
**Avila:** Paseo San Roque 17
**Burgos:** Alférez Provisional 5
**León:** Avda José Antonio 1
**Palencia:** Avda de Casado del Alisal 47
**Salamanca:** Dimas Madariaga 3
**Segovia:** Covarrubias 3
**Soria:** San Vicente Tutor 6-2º
**Valladolid:** Gamazo 5
**Zamora:** Pza de Alemania 3-1º

**Youth information offices**
**Avila:** Pza Fuente de Sol 5 (tel. 918–211900)
**Burgos:** Pza San Juan s/n (tel. 947–208745)
**León:** Sierra Pambley 4 (tel. 987–236500)
**Salamanca:** Pza de la Constitución 1 (tel. 923–245411), also Casa de la Juventud, Peña Primera 19 (tel. 923–212792)
**Segovia:** Infanta Isabel 14 (tel. 911–437101)
**Soria:** Campo 6 (tel. 975–223111)
**Valladolid:** Pza Caño Argales 4 (tel. 983–390222)
**Zamora:** Avda de Reguejo 21–3º (tel. 988–512198)

**TIVE offices**
**Burgos:** Pza San Juan s/n (tel. 947–209882)
**León:** Sierra Pambley 1 (tel. 987–286314)
**Salamanca:** Pza de la Constitución s/n (tel. 923–246129)
**Valladolid:** San Blas 6 (tel. 983–354563)

**Travel agents**
**Burgos:** Viajes Ecuador, Avda Reyes Católicos 10 (tel. 947–231962)
**Salamanca:** Viajes Ecuador, Avda Mirat 11–13 (tel. 923–258379)
**Valladolid:** Viajes Ecuador, Gamazo 6 (tel. 983–306369)

**Car hire**
You'll probably want to hire a car from Madrid, Bilbao or Santander rather than locally. Otherwise try:
**Atesa,** Muro 16, Valladolid (tel. 983–301878)

**British representation**
**British Chamber of Commerce** — see Madrid or Basque country (Bilbao)
**British Consulate** — see Madrid, Basque country (Bilbao) or Cantabria (Santander)
**British schools** — None, the nearest are in Madrid.

**Language schools (TEFL)**
**Burgos:** Inlingua Idiomas, Pza Alonso Martínez 7
**León:**
— Academia de Idiomas Modernos, Avda Padre Isla 2–4
— Inlingua Idiomas, c/ Joaquín Costa 2
**Palencia:** Sonylang, Patio de Castaño 4
**Salamanca:**
— American Institute, C/del Sol 9–2º
— Centro Británico, Bordadores 1–bajo, and Espoz y Mina 17–1º
**Soria:** Eurospan, Sta María 2
**Valladolid:**
— Academia de Idiomas Modernos, c/Miguel Iscar 7–3º
— Laboratorio de Idiomas Loyola, c/Pólvora 11
— Sonylang, Paseo Isabel la Católica 7
— The English Centre, c/Santiago 13

# 8 Castilla— La Mancha (New Castile)

> Esta es mi tierra
> Una gran extensión de páramo y olivo.
> Escribo y callo.
>
> *Anon.*

Castilla-La Mancha, more popularly known as New Castile, is in geographical terms the southern half of Spain's central *Meseta*, lying between the Guadarrama mountains and Andalucía. Like its other half, Castilla-León, or Old Castile, it's a region of wide plains, open to the sky and to the elements, and presents a monotonous landscape of cereal production, shaded green, gold or brown according to the time of year. There are also olive groves, and acre after acre of vineyards, pruned desperately low to the ground to conserve moisture, which produce industrial quantities of La Mancha table wine.

Like Old Castile, Castilla-La Mancha is a region steeped in history and legend, but, whereas Old Castile bore the weight of responsibility for the political, economic and religious tasks involved in lifting Spain out of the Dark Ages, Castilla-La Mancha, in contrast, imbued with the taste of the Orient through the presence of the Moors, was the land which caught the imagination of the dreamers and adventurers of the period — members of Knightly Orders who sought glory in its vast horizons. Whilst the plains of Old Castile were well-trodden by herders and criss-crossed by trade routes, in New Castile there was nothing: the odd castle or windmill could so easily be just a mirage and melt away into the clean air. No wonder this land is bound up so tightly with the story of Don Quixote's wanderings — the very emptiness invites some sort of fantasy to fill it, and it's easy to see how the openness to the skies could lend a sense of almost transcendental importance to everyday events.

The city of Toledo is like a hinge linking the two Castiles: it was reconquered early, in 1085, and was the first major Moorish-controlled city to fall into Christian hands. From the thirteenth century onwards, as La Mancha and parts of Andalucía came under Christian control, Castile found its centre of power shifting southwards, and Toledo became the ideal city from which to wield this power. Under the Moors it was an important centre of learning, and after reconquest was able to continue in this vein for many years more, with Jews, Christians and Muslims living together in what must have been one of the most stimulating environments of the Middle Ages.

Toledo is still the capital of the region, and a jewel of a city, in stark contrast to the rest of La Mancha, where one is still thrown back on fantasy to fill this yawning hole that seems to exist in the middle of Spain, swallowing up the provinces of Ciudad Real and Albacete. Only in the north east, in parts of Guadalajara and Cuenca provinces, does the landscape become more varied, and one starts to scent the possibility of finding something of real interest.

## WHAT TO SEE (from Toledo eastwards)

### Toledo

One of the great cities of Spain, and the only one in the region worth really making an effort for. Once the Visigothic capital of Spain, its Archbishop is still head of the Catholic church in Spain.

Toledo rises out of the dust like a magical city, set higgledy-piggledy on a rocky outcrop round which the Tagus flows like a natural moat. It is densely packed with churches and palaces, hostelries and museums, all interwoven by winding cobbled streets.

For many the attraction is the paintings of El Greco, who lived and worked here and whose intense, visionary paintings are closely linked to the city itself.

Toledo has many sights to offer visitors, and attracts bus-loads of tourists throughout the year, most of whom never actually stay any length of time in the city. Basically these are the sights they're there to see:

**Church of El Cristo de la Luz.** Tiny tenth-century mosque, probably the only building dating from the Moorish period left in the city, now a church.

**Church of Santa María la Blanca.** Probably one of the most interesting religious buildings in the world — a twelfth-century synagogue, built in the style of a mosque, now a church. Inside its rows of pillars supporting Moorish arches above are reminiscent of the great Mezquita in Cordoba.
**El Tránsito.** The only other synagogue left standing in Toledo, dating from the fourteenth century. Its interior is a simple galleried hall, which houses a museum of Sephardic culture, tracing the history of the Jews in Spain.
**The Cathedral.** Imposing and Gothic in style, incorporating some *Mudejar* elements. The riches accumulated by the Catholic church here over the centuries are on display inside, including paintings, sculptures and gold and silver work of inconceivable value.
**Santo Tomé Church.** Mainly visited for the sake of one of El Greco's best paintings, *The Burial of the Count of Orgaz*, which hangs in one of its chapels.
**The Alcázar.** Toledo's fortress, and a reminder of the city's essential military role — in this century as well as in medieval times, for during the Civil War Francoist troops were holed up here for several months while Republican forces tried in vain to dislodge them. The main reason for going there, though, is the superb view over the plain from the battlements — including the present day Military Academy on the other side of the river.
**The Plaza Zocodover.** The focus of activity in the town today, as it probably was in centuries past — and a place you can hardly miss.

### Elsewhere in the province
Although nowhere can match the glory of the capital the following are of some interest:

**Talavera de la Reina.** Famous for centuries for its decorated pottery (see below).
**Oropesa** and **Ocaña.** Famous for their castles.
**Illescas** (now almost a suburb of Madrid). The Iglesia de la Caridad contains more El Grecos.

### Ciudad Real province
**Ciudad Real.** Quiet provincial capital, with only a Moorish arch surviving from its former walls.
**Almadén.** Town on the borders of Extremadura and Andalucía, noted only for its mercury mines.
**Valdepeñas.** A big centre for the wine industry. Rather dusty and drab.
**Almagro.** A quiet town, but one of the most cultured in the region, boasting the oldest theatre in Spain, the sixteenth-century **Corral de Comedias**, where Golden Age plays are still performed. It now has another theatre too, the **Teatro Principal**, a casino, and a *parador*. Almagro was the headquarters for the knightly order of Calatrava, which played a large part in the reconquest of New Castile, and was rewarded with vast tracts of land here as a result. The remains of their castle and monastery are nearby at **Calzada de Calatrava**.
**Villanueva de los Infantes.** One of the best preserved towns in the area,

with Plaza Mayor and old mansions.
**Las Tablas de Damiel National Park.** Wetlands of tiered marshes and labyrinthine canals, rich in birdlife and aquatic vegetation.

### Albacete province
**Albacete.** Modern town, once Arab.
**Almansa.** Castle of Arab origin, reconstructed by the Knights Templars in the fifteenth century.
**Sierra de Alcaraz.** Wild upland area, with fantastic views across the plain. The village of **Alcaraz** itself, and also **Yeste**, are fairly quaint.

### Cuenca province
**Cuenca.** Cuenca really is a place worth going to. Like Toledo, it's in a superb location, on a rocky crag above two rivers, the **Júcar** and the **Huécar**. If you've seen the BBC *Dígame* programmes you'll recognise the famous *cases colgadas,* houses which overhang the ravine in a way which is definitely precarious and would certainly not get passed as safe by any council in England, but, as they say, Spain is different. The rest of the town rises up behind them in a sort of anarchic harmony, and the friendly chimes of **La Mangana bell tower** mark the hours. It's certainly a place you could spend some time in, singular, but without that feeling of being miles from civilization. There is an interesting **Museum of Abstract Art** in one of the *casas colgadas.*
**Belmonte.** Outstanding castle.
**Serranía de Cuenca.** Mountainous district to the east of Cuenca, where erosion has worked some strange effects on the chalky soil. There are dramatic ravines, waterfalls, and, strangest of all, the so-called *ciudad encantada,* a 'city' of immense free-standing rocks moulded into fantastic shapes by the wind and rain.

### Guadalajara province
**Guadalajara.** A town made important by its position on the main road between Barcelona and Madrid, but of little immediate interest.
**La Alcarria.** Hilly country area, offering a varied landscape of woods, orchards, and rocky outcrops. Camilo José Cela 'rediscovered' it post-war when he set off with a rucksack from Madrid, and subsequently wrote his pleasing travelogue *Viaje a La Alcarria.*
**Atienza.** A typical village bringing some of the best features of the area together: a castle, town walls, arcaded Plaza Mayor, many churches, etc.
**Siguenza.** Now we're nearly in Old Castille here, you can tell by the Romanesque cathedral, which has beautiful rose windows. The recumbent statue of *El Doncel* in alabaster is especially to be admired.

## COMING AND GOING

### By air, road and rail
By air, use Madrid Airport. There are good bus and rail services from Madrid to Toledo (1–1½ hours). The major communications routes be-

tween Madrid and Andalucía, and Madrid and Valencia, run straight through the region, so most Spaniards are acquainted with its empty landscapes through a car or train window. Cuenca and Albacete (and the spaces in between) are accessible from the Valencian coast by road or train.

**Packages**
**Mundi Color's** 'Paradores of Castile' package includes Siguenza and Toledo, as well as paradores in Old Castile. **Travelscene** do an 8–day tour which includes Toledo (see p. 21). **Equitour** does a horseback tour which visits parts of Toledo province (see section on Castilla-León).

## WHERE TO STAY

In this region you should take very much to heart the comments made earlier in the book about distances between towns, if you're travelling about. Accommodation in Toledo is slightly more expensive than elsewhere in Spain.

There are ten or so **youth hostels** in the region, and the Reservations Office is at c/Trinidad 8, Toledo (tel. 925–223450).

## WHAT TO EAT AND DRINK

*Manchego* cheese and Valdepeñas wine are two basic products of the region which can be sampled not only here but all over Spain. It wouldn't be too difficult to find them in Britain either, if you fancy a taste before you go.

*Manchego* is a hard, full-fat cheese made from sheep's milk, pale in colour, with a characteristic woven pattern on the outside. It has a distinctive flavour and in many ways is the 'Cheddar' of Spain, tasty as a meal in itself with bread and wine, and equally good after a meal.

La Mancha wine is often loosely termed Valdepeñas, but in fact Valdepeñas is a separate *denominación*, covering a relatively small area round the town of the same name, whereas the La Mancha area proper is immense. Valdepeñas wines tend to be vigorous reds, strong in alcohol, whereas La Mancha wines are more commonly white, again, strong in alcohol, and full bodied enough to stand up to quite hearty pork or poultry dishes.

Vast quantities of wine are produced and much of it is destined for purposes other than consumption as table wine: exportation to Andalucía to be distilled as brandy, conversion to industrial alcohol, or vinegar. Strong full-bodied red wines are also produced in the Almansa and Méntrida denominated areas.

Another product typical of the region which you'll find all over Spain, especially around Christmas, is marzipan from Toledo, nicely packaged and sold as marzipan figurines. La Alcarria produces some superb honey.

As far as regional cuisine goes, there are a number of Spanish dishes described as *manchego*, including *pisto manchego*, which is a ratatouille of peppers, aubergines and courgettes, sometimes augmented by the addition of meat, fish (tuna or *bacalao*) or eggs, and *gazpacho manchego* (not to be confused with the more common *gazpacho andaluz*), which is a mixture of game, poultry and ham. In actual fact, though, you're probably more likely to find yourself eating the ubiquitous *filete con patatas* (steak and chips).

## OPPORTUNITIES IN CASTILLA-LA MANCHA

Generally the towns are dead and the villages have nothing to offer. Toledo has a great atmosphere, but mostly due to its past, and so you may have to fall back on tourist-type activities. Opportunities for study are limited, and for work practically non-existent. There is no university in the region, although there are various colleges dependent on Madrid university. Those not already acquainted with Spanish culture could possibly find the region rather grim, with the exception of Toledo and Cuenca.

## WHAT TO DO

### ARCHAEOLOGY

Archaeological work camps at various sites in the region have in the past included excavating Moorish, Roman and Visigothic remains. See general comments earlier in the book.

### ART GALLERIES AND MUSEUMS

**Toledo**
**Museo Santa Cruz,** c/Cervantes 3. An early sixteenth century hospital, and a magnificent building in itself, housing an archaeological museum and art gallery including various El Grecos. Open 1000–1800, Sundays 1000–1400. Closed Mondays.
**Museo de Cultura Visigoda,** c/San Román s/n. Museum of Visigothic culture, including jewellery and archaeological remains. Open 1000–1400 and 1600–1900. Closed Mondays and Sunday afternoons.
**Casa y Museo del Greco,** Alamillos del Tránsito, c/Samuel Levi. El Greco's house and museum. The house has been rather quaintly restored, but the main attraction is the museum, where a large collection of his work is on display, including his splendidly lurid *View of Toledo*. Open 1000–1400 and 1600–1900. Closed Mondays and Sunday afternoons.
**Museo Sefardí,** Sinagoga del Tránsito, c/Samuel Levi s/n. Museum of Jewish culture in Spain. Open 1000–1400 and 1600–1800. Closed Mondays and Sunday afternoons.

**Talavera**
**Museo de Cerámica.** Ceramics museum.

**El Toboso**
**Museo Casa de Dulcinea,** José Antonio s/n. Supposedly the house of Don Quixote's lady-love.

## Ciudad Real
**Museo de Ciudad Real,** c/del Prado.

## Segóbriga (Cuenca)
**Museo Monográfico.** Archaeological finds from Roman site.

## Guadalajara
**Museo de Guadalajara,** Palacio del Infantado, Pza de los Caídos. Museum of local art, housed in one of the most outstanding buildings in the town.

## Cuenca
**Museo de Arte Abstracto,** Casas Colgadas. Work by Saura, Muñoz, Guerrero and other Spanish abstract artists. Open 1100–1400 and 1600–1800. Closed Sunday afternoons.

## CINEMA

The **Guadalajara Film Competition** for film-makers resident in the province, is organised by the **Cine-Club Alcarreño y Agrupación Fotográfica y Cinematagráfica de Guadalajara** (Apartado de Correos 171, Guadalajara 19080, if you need to get in touch with them). Takes place in February.

## COURSES

In **Toledo** in the month of July there's a choice of courses in either Spanish language, Spanish history, art or literature — a rare opportunity for specialist courses for foreigners in something other than just language work. Minimum age 14. Various levels of proficiency in Spanish catered for. Accommodation included. Apply to: Secretaría de los Cursos de Verano para Extranjeros, Cardenal Lorenzana 1, Toledo (tel. 925–226350).

In **Cuenca** there are 2–3 week course in Spanish language during July and August, three different levels, organised by the town council. Also the possibility of guitar courses. Contact the **Casa de Cultura**, c/Hervás y Panduro, Cuenca.

## CRAFTS

Talavera pottery is famous throughout Spain, usually white decorated with popular rural scenes in green or blue tones, with a lot of contrasting yellow. It's possible to visit the factory and save a few pesetas by buying direct. Traditional terracotta pots are still made at Priego (Cuenca).

Toledo is still an important centre for metal-based crafts, knives and also damascene work. This is the art (of Arab origin) of encrusting gold or silver in decorative patterns on other metals, usually steel. It is used for jewellery and also for decorating objects such as knife handles or spoons, mostly for tourist consumption.

Other regional crafts include string instruments, wickerwork, embroidery from Almagro and lace from Lagartera, and carpets and tapestries from Casasimarro (Cuenca), and all over the region. Traditional wooden furniture is still made in the Toledan villages of Sonseca, La Puebla de Montalbán and San Pablo de los Montes.

## FIESTAS

A curious and ancient ritual takes place in the first few days of February every year in the village of **Almonacid del Marquesado**, in Cuenca province: the local men dress up as devils in an extraordinary rig-out of brightly coloured pyjamas and headdresses, with enormous cow-bells attached to their backs, and cause a great deal of commotion dancing around the town and in and out of the church, performing a ritual cleansing of the image of the saint — San Blas.

During **Holy Week** the most important events in the region take place in **Cuenca**, with silent, sober processions through the old part of the town. A festival of religious music is held in one of the churches at the same time (see below).

Two important fiestas in Toledo province celebrate the agricultural produce of the region: the **olive festival** in **Mora** on the last Sunday in April, and the **saffron festival** at **Consuegra** on the last Sunday in October.

**Corpus Christi** (June) sees a solomn festival in **Toledo**, presided over by the Spanish Primate, with processions of the various brotherhoods through the town.

**Hita** in Guadalajara sees some more light-hearted celebrations in June, with music, food, tournaments, and theatre, all on a medieval theme.

In **Albacete** province, there are 'Moors and Christians' festivals (similar to those in the Valencian region) in the village of **Caudete** during the second week in September, and **Albacete** itself celebrates its fiestas with a variety of events (concerts, sports competitions, exhibitions of local crafts, bullfights, etc.) around the same time.

**Valdepeñas** has a wine festival of passing interest to coincide with the grape harvest at the beginning of September.

## HIKING

Guadalajara and Cuenca provinces offer the best possibilities. The **La Alcarria** area is lovely in the spring and early summer for simple country walks, hilly but not too mountainous, with masses of wild flowers. **Cifuentes** is the central village here, and there are lovely walks to be had heading towards **Villanueva de Alcorón** or **Armallones**.

Around **Sacedón** there are three vast reservoirs created by damming the river Tagus for hydroelectric power, and the area is known as the **Mar de Castilla** (Sea of Castile). The area surrounding the most northerly of these artificial lakes, the **Pantano de Entrepeñas** offers perhaps the most interesting walks, with good views.

The **Serranía de Cuenca** is rougher going, but with more spectacular rugged country, with dramatic ravines, waterfalls (especially that at the source of the River Cuervo) and pine woods. Base yourself at Cuenca, and head out up the course of the Júcar river. The **Hosquillo park** here is rich in wildlife — deer, moufflon (wild sheep), and, it is claimed, bears.

## MUSIC

There is a highly acclaimed **festival of religious music** during Holy Week in **Cuenca** each year, mostly taking place in the church of San Miguel. Further information from the **Ayuntamiento**, Cultural Department (tel. 966–222651). An international festival of youth choirs also takes place in Cuenca each year during April.

For several years running, there has been a **folk music festival** in **Toledo** during the second half of April, centrally organised by the **Youth Department of the Ministry of Culture**, Pza del Rey 1, Madrid (tel. 91–419 7600). It seems likely the tradition will continue in the future.

## SPORTS

### Fishing
Fishing is permitted in the reservoirs and rivers throughout the region. Licences are available from **ICONA** provincial offices:

**Toledo:** Pza San Vicente 6 (tel. 925–227899)
**Ciudad Real:** Avda de los Mártires 31 (tel. 926–213302)
**Albacete:** Tesifonte Gallego 1 (tel. 967–213390)
**Cuenca:** c/18 de julio s/n (tel. 966–211640)
**Guadalajara:** Marqués de Villaverde 2 (tel. 911–223316)
### Horseriding
**Equitour** horseback excursions pass through Toledo — see section earlier on **Castilla–León**.

### Hunting
Various reserves throughout the region are controlled by **ICONA** — see section on fishing above for addresses to contact.

### Water sports
Being developed on the Guadalajara reservoirs.

## THEATRE

This is a surprisingly good region for events of a theatrical nature, especially in the town of **Almagro,** where there is a **festival of classical theatre** every September, centrally organised by the **Oficina de Coordinación Artística**, Pza del Rey 1, Madrid (tel. 91–232 7190). Information is available on the spot from the office at José Antonio 11, Almagro (tel. 926–860711).

Also in Almagro, there is a **Youth Theatre Festival** during the first week in July, attracting youth theatres from all over the country. Information from **Youth Office** in Madrid (c/Ortega y Gasset 71).

Other activities include:

Annual season of classical theatre in **Toledo** (information from the cultural office at c/Trinidad 8).
Annual classical theatre event in **Cuenca** (cultural office c/Hervás y Panduro).
Theatre competition on a national level at **Talavera** in March/April.
Amateur Theatre Festival at **Villacañas** (Toledo province) in May (details from **Ayuntamiento**, Pza de España 1, Villacañas).
Summer theatre festival at **Guadalajara** (early September — information Centro Civico Municipal, Pza del Concejo, Guadalajara).
'Archipreste de Hita' theatre competition at **Guadalajara** (information office c/San Esteban 7–1º, Guadalajara).
Annual theatre season in **Manzanares** (Ciudad Real province) during the third week in September. Information office: c/Carmen 10, Manzanares (tel. 926–611736).
International theatre season in **Ciudad Real** during November.

## USEFUL ADDRESSES

**Tourist offices**
**Albacete:** Rodríguez Acosta 3 (tel. 967–211658)
**Ciudad Real:** c/Toledo 27 (tel. 926–212800)
**Cuenca:** c/Calderón de la Barca 28 (tel. 966–211121)
**Guadalajara:** Travesía de Beladíez 1 (tel. 911–220698)
**Toledo:** Puerta de Bisagra (tel. 925–220843)

**Government offices**
**Regional Government** (Comunidad de Castilla-La Mancha), Palacio de Fuensalida, Pza del Conde 2, Toledo (tel. 925–224500)
**Youth/Sport Department** (Dirección General de Educación, Juventud y Deportes), Trinidad 8, Toledo

**Education departments**
**Albacete:** Avda de la Estación 2 (tel. 967–238013)
**Ciudad Real:** Avda Mártires 41, Edificio Servicios Múltiples (tel. 926–211379)
**Cuenca:** República Argentina 16 (tel. 966–222051)
**Guadalajara:** Avda de Castilla 10 (tel. 911–222800)
**Toledo:** c/Miguel de Cervantes 6 (tel. 925–227450)

**Labour departments**
**Albacete:** Avda de España (tel. 967–225200/04)
**Ciudad Real:** Dr Alarcó 28 (tel. 926–212700)
**Cuenca:** Alicante 6 (tel. 966–220212)
**Guadalajara:** Pza de Fernando Beladiez s/n (tel. 911–226000/11/40)
**Toledo:** Cuesta del Alcázar s/n (tel. 925/223507/348)

## Youth information offices
**Albacete:** Avda Estación 2
**Ciudad Real:** Paloma 7
**Cuenca:** Astrana Marín 2–2º
**Guadalajara:** Pza San Esteban 2
**Toledo:** Trinidad 8

## TIVE offices
None in the region — use the central office in Madrid.

## Travel agents
Again, it's probably better to use a specialist or national agency in Madrid, rather than go to a small local firm.

## Car hire
Use a Madrid firm.

## British representation
**British Chamber of Commerce** — none in the region, Madrid is the nearest.
**British Consulate** — see Madrid.
**British schools** — none — see Madrid.

## Language schools (TEFL)
**Albacete:** Escuela Central de Idiomas, Mayor 45
**Ciudad Real:**
— Academia de Idiomas, General Aguilera 5–2
— La Casa de Idiomas Modernos, Calatrava 4–2
— The English Academy, c/Menéndez Pelayo 1, Puertollano
**Toledo:** Anglo Centre, Pza San Vicente 4 and c/Escalona 4

# 9 Cataluña

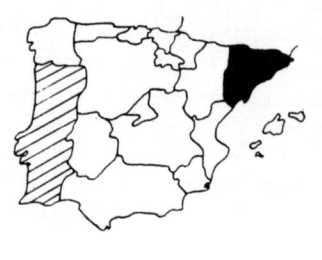

El meu amic el mar
és l'immens bressol de tots els blaus
i en el seu vaivé de so i color
aprenc el poc que tinc.

*Lluis Llach*

Cataluña includes within its four provinces an immense variety of possibilities. Its capital Barcelona is Spain's second city, a metropolitan area as big as Madrid, and, some would say, more vital — certainly it's one of the great Mediterranean cities, with a tremendous amount happening. Cataluña's coast takes in two of Spain's most famous *costas*, the Costa Brava and the Costa Dorada with tourist complexes accommodating millions of British, French, German and Scandanavian visitors every year. Every facility is laid on and there is a truly cosmopolitan air, in stark contrast to the provincial towns of Castile and other regions. Cataluña also has mountains — the eastern end of the Pyrenees, including the Aigües Tortes National Park and some good ski resorts — and a sunburnt inland plain, well developed agriculturally.

It's a region that has as much to offer as a small country in its own right, and in many ways, with its separate culture and language, it is. Throughout its history its crucial position on the Mediterranean has meant that is has always enjoyed the benefit of overseas contacts, and its open attitude towards other cultures still sets it apart from rigid, isolationist Castile. Tarragona was an important Roman town, the capital of the province of Tarraconensis as early as Julius Caesar's time, and there is evidence of even earlier Greek and Phoenician presence in the region.

The area made a quick recovery from being overrun by the Moors, and with the help of the Franks from across the Pyrenees, 'Wilfred the Hairy' managed to set up his own administration based at Barcelona in 801, and establish the 'Spanish March' or military frontier with Moorish controlled territory. The Counts of Barcelona continued independently until 1137, when they became united through marriage to the Kingdom of Aragón, and subsequently became part of the new Spain when the crowns of Castile and Aragón were merged. Like the Basques, the Catalans retained medieval rights and privileges (here called *furs*), and with them a considerable amount of autonomy and self-respect, although these were abolished by a hard-line centralist regime in Madrid in the early eighteenth century.

It was industrialisation, however — cotton mills were established in Barcelona in the eighteenth century — that really set Cataluña apart from the rest of Spain, both socially and economically, giving rise to a revival of Catalan language and literature in the 1880s called the *Renaixença*, and the birth of a separatist movement.

An autonomous Catalan government, or *Generalitat* was first set up during the Second Republic, and the Catalans, sensing this would be short-lived if Franco came to power, staunchly supported the Republican cause in the Civil War — Barcelona did not fall into Nationalist hands until January 1939. Somehow the Catalan language survived being officially prohibited during the Francoist era, and the culture remains strong and sure of itself despite the influx in the last few decades of Andalusians and 'immigrants' from other parts of Spain in search of work. Since 1980 the *Generalitat* has been restored, and Catalans are once more getting down to what they are so good at — organising their own affairs and producing a distinct, original culture which at the same time is totally accessible to outsiders.

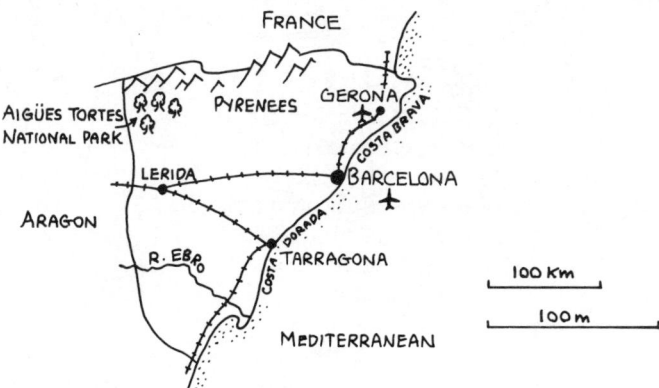

## WHAT TO SEE

### Barcelona
The thriving, elegant, fascinating capital of Cataluña. A port, a cultural centre, an industrial city, and a place with so much to offer it's impossible to do it justice here.

A gritty old **medieval quarter**, packed with interesting buildings, monuments (including the grand old gothic cathedral), museums and shops, forms the centre of the city, spreading out from the port area, and split in two by the famous **Ramblas**. These are a series of streets lined with newspaper kiosks and stalls selling flowers and birds forming a promenade for *barceloneses* and visitors alike. The liveliness and colour of the Ramblas are taken as epitomising the character of the city itself.

At the head of the Ramblas, is the **Plaça de Catalunya**, another focus

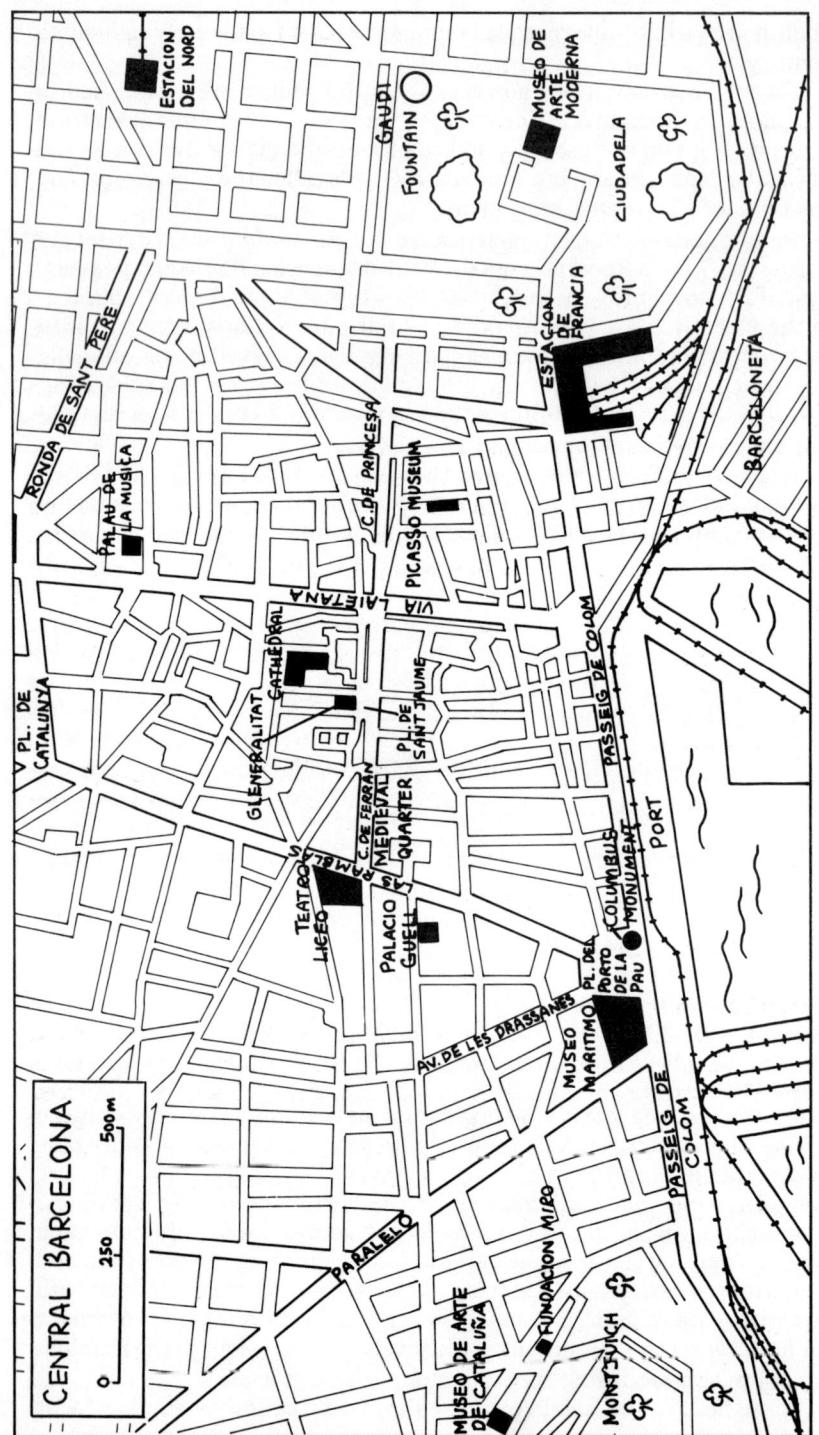

of activity in the city, forming the link between the old quarter and the rational nineteenth-century **Ensanche** area of wide avenues, residential districts, elegant shopping areas, and most of Gaudí's buildings (see below).

Beyond this again, modern developments link Barcelona proper with other manufacturing towns such as **San Feliu de Llobregat** and **Sabadell**, forming a metropolitan area of around four million inhabitants.

Three important parks give Barcelona's inhabitants a respite from their urban surroundings: **Tibidabo**, a huge tree-covered mountain with impressive views over the city; **Montjuich**, again on a rise, crowned by the old twelfth-century castle and incorporating gardens, museums, sports facilities and the famous **Pueblo Español**, a representation in miniature of Spanish regional architecture. The third park is the **Ciudadela**, which also forms part of the old fortifications of the city and now houses the headquarters of the *Generalitat,* and also a zoo.

It is to a large extent the work of Modernist architect Antonio Gaudí that gives Barcelona such an original character, and some of his buildings are so unusual, they have to be seen to be believed, incorporating elements drawn from nature (the **Casa Battlo** in the **Paseo de Gracia** is based on the idea of a wave breaking!), and a strong admixture of fantasy. His most outstanding works are the **Sagrada Familia** (an enormous temple with eight massive towers rising up into the sky like giant organ pipes to which he dedicated the latter part of his life — an incredibly ambitious project which still remains unfinished), and the **Güell Park**, in which colourful mosaics and ceramics are used to produce stunningly unusual effects. With its Plaza, pavilions, bridges, benches and Gaudí museum, it is a great centre of attraction, both for tourists and locals, who today treat it as the municipal park.

Other Gaudí buildings include the **Casa Milà** in the Paseo de Gracia, and the **Palacio Güell** off the Ramblas.

For Barcelona's museums and entertainments of various kinds, see the listings later in this section.

### Elsewhere in the province
**Montserrat.** A famous monastery high up in the mountains behind Barcelona, where the ancient image of the Black Virgin of Monserrat is kept. Perhaps more impressive is the location, where erosion has produced some strange and eerie effects on the rock face. You can take a cable-car to the top, where there are some beautiful views and mountain walks.
**Tarrassa.** One of Cataluña's main textile manufacturing towns.
**Manresa.** District capital inland.
**Vic.** Ancient town, bishopric and market town. Pretty arcaded Plaza Mayor, Romanesque cathedral.

### On the coast to the north
**Badalona.** Commercial and industrial centre with an immense but often overcrowded beach.

**Mataró.** Another large industrial town, also noted for its plantations of carnations.
Further north up the coast is package-tour country, with resorts like **Calella** and **Malgrat de Mar**.

### South of Barcelona
**Sitges.** Old seafaring town which began attracting tourists at the turn of the century, now quite a cultural centre, with plenty of activity and sophistication.

### Tarragona province
**Tarragona.** A modern, booming city with extensive Roman remains, including the Torre de los Escipios and, out of town, an impressive aqueduct and arch. There's also the inevitable 'picturesque fishermen's quarter', called **El Serrallo**.
**Salou.** Big resort.
**Cambrils.** See your package tour brochure!
**Reus.** Industrial town.
**Tortosa.** Large uninspiring town.
**Ebro Delta.** Lagoons and rice paddies — a paradise for bird life.
**Alcanar.** The beginnings of the orange groves so typical of the Valencia coast.
**Santes Creus** and **Santa María de Poblet**. Cistercian monasteries, both interesting architecturally, the former containing tombs of some of the kings of Aragón.

### Lérida province
**Lérida** (Lleida). Provincial capital on the plains, with a very different character from the coastal towns, and an administrative and market centre for surrounding agricultural area. Attractive old quarter with some interesting buildings including the **Palacio de la Pahería**, the **Town Hall** and the **Zuda**, the old citadel.
**Cervera.** Handsome old city, once the intellectual centre of Cataluña.
**Solsona.** An episcopal see since the sixteenth century, castle ruins, and some attractive old streets.
**The Pyrenees.** Lérida province includes the most spectacular part of the Catalan Pyrenees, and their foothills, the 'pre-Pyrenees', also with some splendid scenery. (See sections later on skiing, hiking, etc.)
**Seo de Urgell.** Ancient city of the Pyrenees, Romanesque cathedral.
**Aigües Tortes National Park.** See listings later in the section.
**Viella.** Charming Pyrennean resort in the Val d'Aran.

### Gerona province
**Gerona** (Girona). An ancient, very pleasant city, with a twelfth-century Benedictine monastery. Although inland, it shares with the coast a history of attacks by pirates and invaders, as its fortress-like appearance bears witness. The **cathedral**, vying with Barcelona's in importance, is remarkable for its spacious but gloomy interior.

# Cataluña 157

**Figueiras.** Centre for the wine-producing Ampurdán area, but chiefly recognised as **Salvador Dalí's birthplace**, and much visited for the crazy **museum** which the surrealist himself set up.

### Elsewhere in the province
**The Pyrenees.** Gentler peaks as the great mountain range starts to subside as it reaches the Mediterranean.
**Puigcerdá.** Beautifully located mountain resort.
**Ripoll.** Small Pyrenean town noted for its ninth-century Benedictine monastery, an important centre of learning in early medieval times.
**The Costa Brava.** This rocky coastline of bays and coves with its blue waters must be familiar to almost everyone through the pages of travel brochures, as well as the names that go with it, such as **Rosas, Palafrugell, Lloret de Mar** and **Blanes**. **Cadaqués** stands out as a particularly sophisticated — and expensive — resort that has managed to avoid the worst excesses of mass tourism. At **Ampurias** there is an important Greek and Roman archeological site.

## COMING AND GOING

### By air
Barcelona has a major international airport at El Prat de Llobregat, to the south of the city, with good train links. The airports at Gerona and Reus (Tarragona) also handle charter flights from Britain, so look out for cheap flights to them too.

There is also an hourly shuttle service *(Puente Aéreo)* between the Madrid and Barcelona airports, which is by far the most efficient solution to travelling between the two cities.

### By road and rail
Two of the major frontier crossings between Spain and France are located in Cataluña — at Port Bou and La Junquera — with excellent rail and road communications respectively. Cataluña's major land connections with the rest of Spain either follow the Ebro valley to Zaragoza and the Basque country, or continue on a north–south route along the coast to Valencia and Alicante. As yet there is no motorway link between Madrid and Barcelona.

Within Barcelona, there is a good flat-fare underground rail network, and efficient commuter train services to outlying areas. On the whole this is a region where travel should present few problems.

### Hitching
The following agency arranges for potential passengers to be put in contact with drivers going their way: **Comparco**, c/Ribas 31–6é–1a, Barcelona (tel. 93–246 6908)

### By sea
Ferries to Palma (Mallorca) and Mahón (Menorca) from Barcelona are run

by the **Compañía Transmediterranea,** Via Laietana 2, Barcelona (tel. 93–319 8212).

### Packages

All the major travel companies (see p. 21) do packages to the Costa Brava, and most also to the Costa Dorada. Here, however, are some of the more interesting packages that are available:

City breaks to Barcelona. Arranged by **Mundi Color** (7 or 14 nights, or weekend breaks), or **Travelscene** (3 or 7 nights).

Holidays in the Catalan Pyrenees are offered by **Mundi Color, Waymark** and by **Ramblers Worldwide Holidays.**

**Field Studies Council** organises a yearly trip to the High Pyrenees to study flowers and butterflies which includes several days in the Aigües Tortes National Park.

**STA Travel.** Sailing, waterskiing and windsurfing holidays arranged on the Costa Brava by Top Deck Travel bus.

**Kestours.** Sports visits arranged for groups on the Costa Brava.

## WHERE TO STAY

In Barcelona, make for the old quarter: between the cathedral and the **Ramblas** there are plenty of hotels and pensions, although be prepared to pay quite a bit more than in some other parts of Spain.

The coast is strewn with **campsites**, some heavily booked by package tour companies. In the Pyrenees, there should be no trouble camping rough in areas well away from habitation, or, if you're thinking of a trip on the higher ridges, you should check out the huts *(refugios de montaña)*, while planning your route.

There are fifteen or so **youth hostels** in the region, in the Pyrenees, on the coast and inland, and the **Reservations Office** is at c/Infanta Carlota 123–6º–B, Barcelona (tel. 93–321 0004).

As well as Youth Hostel Association hostels, there are a number of others in Barcelona run by other organisations:

**Alberg Juvenil Pere Tarrés,** c/Numancia 149–151, Barcelona (tel. 93–230 1606)
**Hostel de Joves,** Passeig Pujades 29, Barcelona (tel. 93–300 3104)
**Kabul,** Plaça Real 17, Barcelona (tel. 93–318 1590)

The following monasteries also accept guests:

**Monasterio de Poblet,** Tarragona (tel. 977-370030). Men only.
**Monasterio de Montserrat,** Barcelona (tel. 93-835 0251). Mixed.

## WHAT TO EAT AND DRINK

Catalan food is excellent, with fish and meat dishes enlivened with delicious sauces based on local products such as nuts (almonds, hazelnuts, pinenuts, etc.), saffron, olives and wine. Look out especially for dishes in *Romesco* sauce, and, as in the Balearic islands, *ali i oli* (garlic mayonaise). A classic highlight of Catalan cooking is the famous *Zarzuela*, a rich stew of different kinds of fish and shellfish in a tomato, wine and brandy sauce. Rice is important here, as it is in Valencia, and you'll find all sorts of variations on the *paella*. There are a number of typical Catalan spiced sausages, including *butifarra, longaniza, fuets* and other charcuterie produce such as patés.

Catalan wine-making came to the fore when French vineyards were hit by the pylloxera disease, and the wines produced here (denominated areas Penedés, Alella, Ampurdán and Tarragona) are generally softer and lighter than much Spanish wine, whether red, white or rosé. The Penedés region produces mainly white wines, and also a sparkling *méthode champenoise* wine known generically as *Cava*, and sold all over the world.

The most famous *bodegas* are Codorniu and Freixenet. Look out for the wines — and brandy — produced by the Torres *bodega*. Miguel Torres, the author of several books on the subject of wine, really set the standard for modernising wine production in Spain, following the French example both in terms of the types of wine produced and the methods used.

Priorato is a small denominated area in a mountainous part of Tarragona province, which is known for its strong, very distinctive red wines. The Tarragona DO also produces *rancios*, dessert wines aged in oak casks, similar to those of Valencia and Alicante.

## OPPORTUNITIES IN CATALUÑA

The region is so varied and developed economically and socially that it would be hard to think of opportunities that don't exist, if you're prepared to go out and look for them. There is a productive agricultural sector, wild mountains, developed industry, mass tourism, cultural attractions, an important financial and business sector, good universities, libraries, museums and sporting facilities, and above all a stimulating atmosphere of enterprise and self-confidence that is quite different from the sleepy insularity you find in some of the other regions. The Olympic Committee have endorsed this view in selecting Barcelona to host the 25th Olympic Games in 1992, so the next few years should show an explosion of further developments and improvement of facilities.

Work of course is difficult to come by anywhere in Spain, and in Cataluña there are plenty of unemployed *andaluces* queuing up for jobs, so when looking for work bear in mind that you must be able to offer the right skills or you won't get a look in.

## WHAT TO DO

### ARCHAEOLOGY

See section on Work Camps earlier in the book (p. 71). Ampurias is the best-known archeological site in the region, while there are a lot of Roman remains around Tarragona.

## ARCHITECTURE

Since the Modernist period Barcelona has enjoyed such renown internationally for the quality and originality of its architects, that it is fitting to include here the addresses of the Schools of Architecture, and of the College of Architects:

**Escuela Técnica Superior de Arquitectura,** Universidad Politécnica de Cataluña, Diagonal 649, Barcelona (tel. 93-334 1512)
**Escuela Universitaria de Arquitectura,** Universidad Politécnica de Cataluña, Avda Gregorio Marañón s/n, Barcelona (tel. 93-249 1680)
**Colegio de Arquitectos,** Placa Nova, Barcelona
See also the section on Gaudí's works on p. 155.

## ART GALLERIES AND MUSEUMS

### Barcelona
**Picasso Museum,** c/ de Montcada 15. One of the largest collections of his work anywhere in the world, housed in a beautiful old palace. Open 0930-1330 and 1630-2000. Closed Monday mornings and Sunday afternoons.
**Fundación Miró,** Parque de Montjuich. As well as containing a collection of Miró's work, including some outdoor sculptures, the place is a cultural centre, founded by Miró, in which exhibitions and shows are staged (see Barcelona's *Guía del Ocio).* Open 1100-2000, except Mondays.
**Museo de Arte de Cataluña,** Palacio de Montjuich, Avda Marqués de Comillas. Highly recommended collection of Catalan art, including some wonderful Romanesque frescos taken from churches. Open mornings only, except Mondays.
**Museo de Arte Moderna,** Parque de Ciudadela. Mostly by Catalan artists, from the eighteenth century onwards. Also highly recommended. Open 0930-1330 and 1630-1930.
**Museo Cambó,** Palacio de la Virreina, Rambla de las Flores. Private collection containing works by Flemish, Italian and Dutch masters. Open 0930-1330 and 1800-2100, except Mondays.
**Museo de Arqueología,** Parque de Montjuich, Paseo Santa Madrona. Good collection including finds from Ampurias. Open 1000-1400 and 1800-2000, Sundays and holiday mornings only.

See also the **Cathedral Museum** and the **Casa Gaudí** in the Parque de Güell, and the *Guía del Ocio* or the press for details of one-off exhibitions.

### Tarragona
**Museo Arqueológico,** Plaza del Rey. Extensive Roman collection.

### Figueiras
**Museo Dalí.** Surreal collection of objects set up by Dalí himself — great fun.

## BULLFIGHTS

A fairly important region for bullfights. Barcelona has two bullrings, **Las Arenas** and the **Monumental**, and for a decent *corrida* you should really go here rather than to those held on the coast for the tourists. Summer only, of course.

Perhaps the most spectacular bullfighting occasion in the region — definitely not for the easily scared — is the **Corre de Bou** fiesta in **Cardona** (Barcelona) on the second Sunday in September, when hundreds of local lads test their luck against young bulls.

## CHILDREN'S ENTERTAINMENT

**Barcelona**
Zoo in the Parque de Ciudadela, open 0930–2030.
Permanent funfairs in Montjuich and Tibidabo, open weekends only, from late morning till evening.
Special shows for children at the **Waxwork Museum** (Museo de Cera, Rambla Sta Mónica 4), open 1100–1330 and 1630–2000.

## CINEMA

Some excellent cinemas are to be found in Barcelona with a wide range of films on, some undubbed (*versión original*). See press or *Guía del Ocio*. The **Catalan Film Theatre** (*Filmoteca*) is located in the Travessera de Gracia 63 (tel. 93–201 2906), and it's well worth while checking out what they've got on. They also have a **film library** and **archive**, located, respectively at Rambla de Catalunya 81 (tel. 93–215 5450) and Pau Claris 162 (tel. 93–215 8235).

The **Catalan Federation of Film Clubs** is at Enric Granados 125, Barcelona (tel. 93–237 7431) and will be able to give you details of special events and film seasons in the whole region.

Other organisations which promote film festivals and competitions:

**Asociación de Estudios para la Promición del Cine y la Televisión,** Avda Ma Cristina Palacio 1, Barcelona (tel. 93–223 9900). International film festivals, with prizes for documentary, experimental fiction and series categories.
**Ayuntamiento de Igualada,** Apartado 378, Igualada, Barcelona (tel. 93–803 6147). Amateur film festivals.
**Sitges Fotofilm,** San Isidro 16, Sitges (Barcelona) (tel. 93–894 1306). Horror/fantasy film festival.
**Acción Super-8 Video,** Apartado de Correos 35,352, Barcelona (tel. 93–250 5441)
**Centro Cultural de la Caja de Pensiones,** Pasaje de San Juan 108, Barcelona (tel. 93–258 8907)
**Espeleo Club de Gracia,** Pau Alsina 3–bajo, Barcelona (tel. 93–257 1581). 'Speleological Film Festival'!

## COURSES

### Public sector courses
The **Escuela Oficial de Idiomas** is the only public-sector institution at the time of writing to offer Spanish for foreigners courses in the region, with a month's course during July. The standard of teaching is very good, with an emphasis on communication exercises, lab and audio-visual work. Help is given in making suitable accommodation arrangements.

Apply to: Escuela Oficial de Idiomas, Cursos de Verano de Español, Avda de les Drassanes s/n, Barcelona (tel. 93-329 3412).

### Private sector courses
In the private sector, the following Spanish language courses are available:

**Inlingua Idiomas,** Rambla de Cataluña 33, Barcelona. Wide range of courses throughout the year, all levels.

**Escuela Superior de Administración y Dirección de Empresas** (ESADE), Avda Pedralbes 60-62, 08034 Barcelona (tel. 93-203 6404). Spanish courses throughout the year, normally lasting 4 weeks. Accommodation can be arranged.

**Eurolingua,** Prats de Molló 6, 08021 Barcelona (tel. 93-201 3307). 3 week courses throughout the year. Private classes can also be arranged.

**Institutos Mangold** (Eurocentres), Rambla de Cataluña 16, Barcelona (tel. 93-301 2539). Three week courses in summer, courses from 1-3 months in duration the rest of the year. Possibility of specialising in technical, scientific or business Spanish. All levels from beginners to advanced.

**International House,** Trafalgar 14, entlo (tel. 93-318 8429). Courses throughout the year and during the summer. Very flexible, with the possibility of one-to-one teaching, Spanish for special purposes, etc. as required. From Britain **Youth Travels** (see p. 45) can arrange everything with International House for you.

**Idea Italia,** Diputación 294 pral 1ª, Barcelona (tel. 93-318 0295). Two week summer courses from June to September, using the direct method.

### Other courses
**Omnium Cultural,** Delegació de la Garrotxa, Plaça Mora 1-1er, Olot Garrotxa (Gerona). Courses in Catalan during August and September.

**Universitat de Barcelona** (Escola d'Idiomes Moderns), Plaça Universitat, Barcelona. Also puts on Catalan courses for Spanish-speakers during July, August and September.

**Centro Europeo de Estudios Internacionales,** Diagonal 441, Barcelona 08036 (tel. 93-235 4535). Short courses in natural history and geography in the Pyrenees, Catalan Romanesque art, and various others.

**Instituto Universitario de Estudios Medievales,** Condes de Barcelona 2, 08002 Barcelona. Every year this university institution organises a week-long course towards the end of June on Medieval History. It is open to history graduates and final-year students from all over the world, although some knowledge of Spanish is necessary.

For details of other courses see sections Music, Crafts, Theatre, etc., elsewhere in this section.

## CRAFTS

Cataluña offers plenty of opportunities for outsiders to get involved in arts and crafts such as pottery, engraving and painting. The following schools are worth contacting, if you're interested:

**Centre de Gravat de Barcelona,** San Lluis 63–1er, Barcelona (tel. 93–210 8101). Courses in engraving and wood-cutting techniques.
**Escola d'Estui International de Gravat,** Casa de Turisme, Sant Jaume s/n, Calella (Barcelona) (tel. 93–769 0559). International summer school in engraving and etching techniques. Beginners and specialist courses.
**Creativitat,** Bailén 126, pral–2a, Barcelona (tel. 93–207 1049). Tapestry and macramé. Children and adults accepted.
**Escola de Cerámica La Bisbal,** Ap no 13, La Bisbal de L'Empordá, Girona, (tel. 972–640794). Pottery classes.
**Escola Estil,** Campo Florido 10–12, Barcelona (tel. 93–340 4348). Courses in pottery, bookbinding, macramé and dressmaking.
**Escola Retaule AC,** Entenca 99, Barcelona (tel. 93–332 4758). Courses in painting and drawing.
**Forma, Escola de Ceramica,** Enamorats 78, Barcelona (tel. 93–245 4513). Sculpture, painting, drawing and pottery.
**Keramos, Taller de Ceramica** Mariá Cubi 68, Atic, Barcelona (tel. 93–200 6657). Pottery and decoration techniques.
**L'Argila, Escola de Ceramica,** Nápols 94, Atic, Barcelona. Pottery classes for children and adults.
**Taaniko,** Maria Teresa Pla, Barcelona (tel. 93–302 7645). Courses in *taaniko*, which is a dying techinque used by the Maoris of New Zealand.

## DANCE

The following centre runs classes in ballroom dancing, jazz, flamenco and aerobics for all ages: **Pellicer Centre**, Passatge Lluís Pellicer 10, Barcelona (tel. 93–250 2296).

On a more traditional note, the famous Catalan folk dance, the *Sardana*, can be seen performed every Sunday morning in front of the cathedral in Barcelona, a beautiful spectacle with circles of people holding hands in the sun.

## FIESTAS

Festivities in Cataluña are quite varied, ranging from ancient folk traditions to modern innovations providing a tourist attraction — and none the worse for all that. The first major fiesta of the year is that of **St Anthony Abbot**, on 17 January, celebrated in **Igualada** (Barcelona), with processions of splendid horse-drawn carriages.

On the first Sunday in Lent (February-time) there is a **vintage car rally** in **Sitges**, with cars coming from across the border with France to participate.

On Sundays during Lent, and continuing into Easter, a very ancient custom is that of performing **medieval mystery plays** representing the crucifixion and resurrection — *La Passió*. These take place especially in **Esparraguera**, about 20 miles out of Barcelona, and in the ancient town of **Cervera** (Lérida), where about 500 people take part.

A lovely fiesta in Barcelona takes place on **St George's Day**, 23 April, which is 'book day' and a sort of St Valentine's Day combined. Stalls selling roses appear all over the city and people traditionally buy a book and a rose to give their sweetheart.

*Sardanas* form an important part of many fiestas, and **Calella** (Barcelona) sees a special **Sardana festival**, on the first Sunday in June each year, with groups participating from all over the region. On the second Sunday in July there is another chance to see them performed at **Olot** in the province of Gerona.

**Corpus Cristi** (June) is celebrated in **Sitges** amongst masses of flowers and at the same time a **National Carnation Show** is held in the resort.

At **Sort** in the Pyrenees **canoe races** form the basis for popular celebrations held in mid-July.

Towards the end of September **Barcelona's** festivities in honour of its patron saint, **Nuestra Señora de la Merced**, sum up the very varied character of Catalan festivals, always changing with the times: religious, cultural and sporting activities are combined with folk dances and music to produce a really enjoyable celebration which lasts a whole week.

## FINE ARTS

There is an annual prize of a million pesetas given by the *Ayuntamiento de Barcelona* to the best contribution to art in Barcelona in that year. To be considered you must have either exhibited your work in Barcelona, or have produced it while living there. The prize, awarded in February, is called the *Premio Ciudad de Barcelona*, and you should apply to the *Ayuntamiento* directly for futher details, at c/Ciudad 6, Barcelona (tel. 93–377 6581).

## HIKING/CLIMBING

Coastal routes are really out as far as hiking goes — there's just too much development everywhere, but the **Pyrenees** offer plenty of scope for the experienced trekker and novice rambler alike. Kev Reynolds describes a **trans-Pyrenean route** from the Atlantic to the Mediterranean lasting approximately 6 weeks, and if you're an avid climber or mountaineer his book *Walks and Climbs in the Pyrenees* is recommended reading, although much of it refers to the French side. See also R. Collomb's book *The Pyrenees*.

Even without crampons, ice axes and the like, the area in and around the **Aigües Tortes National Park** (see p. 166) offers some good walks with dramatic and beautiful scenery and a rich wildlife. You could base yourself either at **Viella** or **Espot**, or, in summer, just set off with a tent, provided you are well-prepared materially and physically — it's a wild and uninhabited area. **Puigcerdá** to the east of Andorra is again a pleasant spot from which to base hikes. The **Pyrenean foothills** also offer good walking, with rich pastures and orchards.

It may be helpful to contact the following organisation, which can pass on information on huts (mountain refuges), organised excursions, and advice on weather conditions etc: **Federacio d'Entitats Excursionistes de Catalunya**, Rambla 61, 1r, Barcelona.

There is a *Guía de Refugios de Catalunya* on sale in bookshops, or which you can look at in youth information offices. The following bookshops in Barcelona specialise in mountaineering and rambling guide books:

**Llibreria Quera,** Petritxol 2
**Llibreria Montcau,** Urgell 120
**Gabernet,** Passatge del Duc de la Victoria

## HORSERIDING

**Equitour,** Juan Güell 163, Barcelona (tel. 93–339 4100). Arranges horseback excursions into the Sierra de Montseny, north of Barcelona — either weekend or short-stay tours where you stay in the same place each night, or longer treks following a route and camping or staying overnight in hostels. They need at least 15 days' notice to organise a trip, and the service is not available during August.

## LIBRARIES

**Biblioteca de Cataluña,** Carmen 47, Barcelona
**Ateneo,** Canuda 6, Barcelona
**Biblioteca Franciscalia,** Cambios Nuevos 1, Barcelona
**Biblioteca Balmesiana,** Durán y Bar 9, Barcelona

## LOCAL PRESS

*Avui* (Catalan)
*La Vanguardia* (national paper published in Cataluña)
*El País de Barcelona*
*Diario 16 de Barcelona*

## MUSIC

Barcelona's **Gran Teatro del Liceo,** on the Ramblas at c/San Pau 1, is probably Spain's most prestigious venue for opera and ballet. The opera season is from October to April, with some internationally known performers. Check their programmes in the press or *Guía del Ocio.*

The other big venue for music performances, both modern and classical, is the **Palau de la Música**, off the Via Laietana. It is here that the annual wide-ranging **International Music Festival of Barcelona** is held in October — see press for details.

Other musical events throughout the year in Barcelona include a week of **religious music** in March, and a **festival of ancient music** in May.

Major rock concerts are held in the **Palau d'Esports** on Montjuich, while various clubs and discos also engage live acts — both local and internationally known groups — see *Guía del Ocio* for details.

There are a number of organisations which run music courses and workshops in the region, especially during the summer months, which you could easily get involved in:

**Ayuntament de Llancá,** Avda d'Europa, Llancá (Gerona) (tel. 972–380181). An annual course in classical guitar, flute, violin and cello, during July. Apply by May. Also chamber music workshops.

**Audicor,** Aula de Direcció Coral, Institut Joan Llongueres, Carrer de Séneca 22, 2on, Barcelona. Course in choral direction.

**Aula Música 7,** Diagonal 327, 2on, 1a, Barcelona (tel. 93–207 4022). Guitar and chamber music.

**L'Aula de Música Moderna i Jazz,** Montornés 37, Barcelona. Contemporary music (including synthesiser) and jazz.

**Taller de Músics,** Requesens 1–3 baixos, Barcelona (tel. 93–329 5667). Contemporary music, jazz, big band.

**Taller d'Expressió Musical,** Canuda 33 pral, Barcelona (tel. 93–301 5529). Jazz, electronic music, basic harmony.

## NATIONAL PARKS

The **Aigües Tortes National Park** in the Pyrenees offers some wonderful scenery of soaring peaks, glaciated lakes and forest, with numerous rare species of wildlife including pine martens, ermines and 'snow partridges'. The park divides naturally into two areas, the **Sant Nicolau Valley**, which is accessible from the town of **Bohí**, and the **Escrita Valley**, with the **Lago de San Mauricio** accessible from **Espot**.

## SPORTS

Sports facilities are excellent, both in Barcelona and on the coast, and during the next few years will be brought up to an even higher standard for the Olympic Games in 1992, most of which will take place within the city itself. In particular the sports stadium on Montjuich is to be enlarged and improved for athletics, swimming and indoor sports. Golf, tennis and water sports are particularly well catered for in the region.

### Cycling

There is a cycle track at **Vall de Hebrón**, outside Barcelona, and a cycle touring club which organises all sorts of events, as well as offering general advice: **Amics de la Bici,** Apdo 10012, Barcelona.

## Canoeing (and other watersports)
These take place on the **Lago de Bañolas**, Gerona province, as well as along the coast. There are canoeing courses available during the summer, put on by the Catalan Federation: **Federació Catalana de Piragüisme**, Acadèmia 8, ler, Lérida (tel. 973–261800) (evenings), and hire of canoes from **La Tenda**, at Pau Claris 118–120, Barcelona and La Palma 3, Lérida, and various other branches.

## Fishing
Off-shore fishing all along the coast, and river fishing in the Pyrenees, especially in Lérida province, where **ICONA** is at General Yagüe 37 (tel. 973–235643).

## Football
Barcelona play at the Nou Camp stadium, while you can see Español, the city's other team at Sarrià stadium.

## Horseriding
See separate section earlier (p. 165).

## Sailing
**A toda vela**, Pg. de Colom 23–5e, hires out boats, and also offers sailing courses.

## Skiing
There are a dozen or so ski-stations in the Catalan Pyrenees, the biggest and best equipped being **La Molina** in Gerona province, where some of the big competitions (like the **King Juan Carlos Cup** at the beginning of March) are held. It's possible to buy packages quite easily, either from a local travel agent (try **TIVE** first if you're eligible — see p. 39) or even from Britain. Two ski-stations in Lérida province, **Sant Joan de L'Erm** and **Lles** do cross-country skiing, with circuits of from 2 to 30 kilometres.
    For advice or other contacts, the **Federación Catalana de Deportes de Invierno** is at Vía Layetana 79–3º–1ª, Barcelona (tel. 93–318 6028).

## Windsurfing
There are windsurfing courses organised, among others, by the **Ayuntament de Badalona**, Plaça de la Villa, Badalona, and **Club Nautic**, Passeig Maritim 271, Castelldefels.

# THEATRE

Catalan theatre is in fairly good shape, with a fair number of theatres and some well-known regular companies like Els Joglars, and the infamous Fura del Baus. The most notable venues in Barcelona are the **Teatro Lliure** (Leopoldo Alas 2), the **Teatro Mercat de les Flors** (c/Lérida 6) and the **Teatro Romea** (c/Hospital 51) where the Centro Dramático de la Generalitat is based.

Details of programmes are published in the press and *Guía del Ocio*, and of course many productions are in Catalan. Every couple of years there is an **International Puppet Festival** put on by the **Instituto del Teatro**, Sant Pere Mes Baix 7, Barcelona (tel. 93-301 7943).

## UNIVERSITIES

**Universidad Central de Barcelona,** Gran Vía de les Corts Catalanes 585, Barcelona (tel. 93-318 2493)
**Universidad Autónoma Campus de Bellatierra,** Barcelona (tel. 93-692 0200)
**Universidad Politécnica de Barcelona,** Avda Gregorio Marañón s/n, Barcelona (tel. 93-333 0311)

## USEFUL ADDRESSES

**Tourist offices**
Main offices:
**Barcelona:**
— Gran Vía de les Corts Catalanes 658 (tel. 93-301 7443)
— Estación de Francia (tel. 93-319 2791)
— Plaça de Sant Jaume (tel. 93-318 2525)
**Gerona:** Plaça del Vi 1 (tel. 972-202679)
**Lérida:** Avda de Madrid s/n (tel. 973-272085)
**Tarragona:** Fortuny 4 (tel. 977-233415)

There are also tourist offices at most coastal resorts, and at Puigcerdá, Ripoll and Viella, serving the Pyrenees.

**Government offices**
**Regional Government Tourist Dept,** Diagonal 341, Barcelona (tel. 93-209 2889)
**Regional Government** (Generalidad de Cataluña (Generalitat de Catalunya) ), Palau de la Generalitat, Plaça de Sant Jaume, Barcelona (tel. 93-302 4700)
**Youth/Sport Department** (Dirección General de Juventud), Presidencia de Gobierno, Viladomat 319, entlo, Barcelona

**Education department**
Consejería de Enseñanza, c/San Honorato 1, Barcelona
Provincial Offices (Servicios Territoriales de Educación):
**Barcelona:** Caspe 15 (tel. 93-301 4008)
**Gerona:** Ultonia 13 (tel. 972-214050)
**Lérida:** Pasaje Pompeyo 2, p1,7 (tel. 973-245300)
**Tarragona:** San Francisco 7 (tel. 977-239000)

**Labour departments**
**Barcelona:** Vía Layetana 16-18 (tel. 93-310 4000)

**Gerona:** Gran Vía de Jaime I, 41–4º (tel. 972–200416)
**Lérida:** Avda del Segre 12 (tel. 973–232641)
**Tarragona:** Canyellas 4 (tel. 977–233714)

**Youth information offices**
**Barcelona:** Ronda de Sant Pere 17, 5º, Barcelona (tel. 93–302 2858)
**Gerona:** Juli Garreta 14 (tel. 972–201554)
**Lérida:** Governador Montcada 4 (tel. 973–270303)
**Tarragona:** Avda de Andorra s/n (tel. 977–211300)

**TIVE office**
Gran Vía de les Corts Catalanes 615, Barcelona (tel. 93–302 0682)

**Travel agents**
**OTEJ-Moravia,** Consell de Cent 615, Barcelona (tel. 93–246 0309). Specialists in youth travel.
**Viajes Edelweiss,** Diagonal 534–4º–2ª, Barcelona (tel. 93–201 7352). Sporting and alternative-type tours.
**Viajes Barceló,** Gran Vía 640, Barcelona (tel. 93–317 0220). Student travel.
**Rosa dels Vents,** c/Jaume I, 13, Barcelona (tel. 93–315 2058). Trekking and adventure.
**Viajes Ecuador,** Pau Claris 75, Barcelona (tel. 93–301 3966), and other branches.
**Mundi Color,** c/Lauria 50, Barcelona (tel. 93–318 5628)

**Car hire**
**Atesa:**
c/Balmes 141, Barcelona (tel. 93–237 8140) also a branch at Barcelona airport
Avda Cataluña 36–A, Tarragona (tel. 977–217493)

**British (and American) representation**
**British Chamber of Commerce:** Paseo de Gracia 11, Barcelona (tel. 93–317 3220)
**British Consulate:** Edificio Torre de Barcelona 13th floor, Apartado 12111, Barcelona (tel. 93–322 2151)
**British Council:** c/Amigo 83, Barcelona (tel. 93–209 6388)
**American Club:** Via Augusta 123, Barcelona (tel. 93–209 2711)

**British (and American) schools**
**Oak House School,** San Pedro Claver 12–18, Sarria, Barcelona (tel. 93–203 8624)
**Anglo-American School,** Paseo de Garbi 152, Apartado 172, Castelldefels, Barcelona (tel. 93–665 1584)
**Kensington School,** Carretera de Esplugas 86, Pedralbes, Barcelona (tel. 93–203 5457)

**The American School,** Pje Font de Lleó s/n, Pedralbes, Barcelona (tel. 93-204 4743)

**Language schools (TEFL)**
**Barcelona** (the British Council can advise here):
**Assimil,** Rambla de Cataluña 94
**Centro Influencia Católica,** Via Augusta 205
**Dublin School of English,** Via Augusta 161-163
**Escuela de Idiomas Modernos,** Universidad de Barcelona, Gran Vía de les Corts Catalanes 585
**Berlitz,** Paseo de Gracia 59
**Escuela Superior de Administración y Dirección de Empresas (ESADE),** Avda de Pedralbes 60-62
**Eurocentre (Instituto Mangold),** Rambla de Cataluña 16
**Eurolingua,** c/Prat de Molló 6
**Glossa,** Rambla de Cataluña 78-2º-2ª
**Inlingua,** Rambla de Cataluña 33
**Instituto de Estudios Norteamericanos,** Via Augusta 123, Aptdo 12 138
**Interlog,** Enrique Granados 113
**International House,** Trafalgar 14, pral
**Linguarama,** Edificios Trade, Gran Vía Carlos III, 84, bajos
**London Language Centre,** Muntaner 184-186, pral
**St George's English School,** Carrasco i Formiguera 15
**York House,** Muntaner 479-483

There are also language schools in the following towns (write to the British Council for a complete list):

Mataró
Sabadell
Calella
Reus
Vic
Vilanova i la Geltru

Terrassa
Badalona
Gerona
Tarragona
El Vendrell
Lérida

# 10 Euskadi (The Basque Country)

> ... here there is much talk of bullocks and *fueros* or privileges, for when not digging and delving these gentlemen by the mere fact of being born here are fighting and upholding their good rights by the sword.
>
> *Richard Ford*

> "These Basques are swell people," Bill said.
>
> *Ernest Hemingway*

Euskadi, the Basque Country, is situated at the western end of the north coast of Spain, hard up against the Pyrenees, and shares many geographical features with Cantabria, Asturias and Galicia. It has a pretty coastline of bays, inlets and sandy coves, green valleys and hills watered by frequent rains and rushing streams, and a mountain range, the Montes Vascos. Frequent mists give the countryside a wash of subtle green and grey tones, whereas on sunny days the valleys can look almost Alpine. In parts of the inland province of Alava, bordering on the Castilian plain and the Ebro basin, the countryside is flatter, with more open landscapes and cereal production.

Despite sharing these natural features with the other regions of the *Cornisa Cantábrica*, culturally and linguistically, if not politically, the Basque country is a separate entity.

The Basques firmly believe they are the original inhabitants of their land, and that their language is an indigenous Iberian tongue (and indeed this may be so — it certainly shares no obvious features with Castilian or any other Romance language, being agglutinative, and, it is believed, pre-Indo-European). In the Middle Ages, during the process of the unification of Spain into a single state brought about by the Reconquest, the Basque people negotiated special rights and privileges in Royal Charters called *fueros*, and developed early democratic institutions, with representatives of local councils in each community being sent to a General Assembly of the Basque People in Guernica, in the shade of the oak tree which symbolises the Basque right to self-determination. They also developed a different and, they claim, more egalitarian social structure than the rest of Spain, together with very different cultural traditions.

The Basque Nationalist movement grew up as a result of the confiscation of the *fueros* after the Carlist Wars in the nineteenth century and the opportunities for new forms of social solidarity created by industrialisation in the coastal areas, especially around Bilbao. However, it was the devastation suffered by the Basques during the Civil War (the horror of the bombing of Guernica by Nazi aircraft is captured by Picasso in his painting of this name, on display in Madrid) and the subsequent repression of their language, customs and basic freedoms during the Francoist era which created the conditions under which an extremist nationalist group was to spring up in the late 50s, influenced by revolutionary Marxist ideas: **Euskadi ta Askatasuna (ETA)**.

Today the Statute of Autonomy has removed much oppressive centralised control over Basque affairs, but ETA's demands — if not their methods — are still widely supported. These include recognition of a separate Basque state to include Navarre and the French Pays Basque, and amnesty for all 'political prisoners'. For young people, especially, the possibility of an independent Euskadi seems to be an attractive solution to many of the problems which preoccupy them, in a context where unemployment runs at 20% — somewhat higher than the national average.

It is impossible to ignore the importance of the Basque language and cultural traditions as a source of identity and meaning for the people today. Of the two million inhabitants of the region, many of whom are 'outsiders', about half speak *Euskera* fluently. The *Ikurriña* — the green, red and white Basque flag — flies everywhere. Unpronounceable Basque names are used in preference to the Castilian versions, and the robust physicality of Basque culture is evident in demonstrations of sports involving great effort and skill: tugs of war, pelota and rowing competitions.

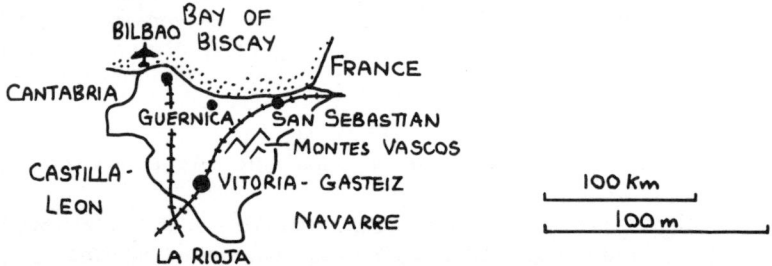

The peculiarity and separateness of Basque culture, although interesting, may perhaps be an obstacle for the outsider, especially in terms of finding your way around — the names of streets, institutions, and even whole towns have reverted to the Basque nomenclature, which is difficult to pronounce or remember — and naturally the Basques are not too keen on promoting mainstream Spanish culture, which is what might attract you to the country. Also, you'll find they function with a completely different set of assumptions from those you expect. For example, Navarre and the French Pays Basque are often treated as if they were under the Basque Autonomous Government's jurisdiction — not what is, but what, according to them it ought to be.

## WHAT TO SEE

(Note that the Castilian version of place-names is used here, as being more easily recognisable for non-Euskera speakers. The Basque version is given, where appropriate, in brackets.)

**Alava (Araba) province**
**Vitoria** (Gasteiz). Capital of the province, and an important centre on Castile's wool and iron trade routes in the Middle Ages. The old Gothic quarter is ringed by elegant eighteenth-century buildings and the whole surrounded by modern industrial developments. Beyond that there is an immense plain, and to the south and east, the Montes de Vitoria with some beautiful scenery and views. See especially the Azácata pass.
**Salvatierra.** Quaint medieval town with many old palaces and mansions.
**Laguardia.** Ancient town, and a centre for the *Rioja Alavesa* wine trade.

**Guipúzcoa (Gipuzkoa) province (from east to west)**
**Fuenterrabía.** Historic fortress town looking out over the Bidasoa river towards France. Castle, old town walls, and typical fishermen's quarter.
**San Sebastián** (Donostia). Well known as a sophisticated summer resort since the end of last century. Beautifully situated on the river Urumea, and overlooked by three hills. La Concha beach is a wide curve of golden sand, edged by an elegant promenade — very crowded in August.
**Tolosa.** Big industrial town.
**Zarauz.** Small but very popular seaside resort, with vast beach.
**Loyola.** Birthplace of St. Ignatius of Loyola, founder of the Jesuit order, whose fortified seignuerial family home is now a monument in its own right. The village is now also embellished with a magnificent baroque sanctuary cum college, built in his honour by the Jesuits.
**Arántzazu.** Village in the heart of rural Euskadi, the site of many pilgrimages to the shrine of the Virgin of Arantzazu, said to have made a miraculous apparition there. An impressive concrete basilica, in *avant-garde* style is testimony to the continued importance of the Catholic faith to Basque identity.
**Oñati.** Village in beautiful Alpine setting, with many interesting historic buildings, including a former university, built in 1548 in Renaissance style, but no longer functioning.
**Vergara.** Small industrial town. Some old mansions worth seeing.

**Vizcaya (Bizkaia) province (from east to west)**
**Lequeito.** Pretty, old fortified fishing town, now also a resort.
**Guernica.** For Basques a visit to Guernica is more a pilgrimage than a sightseeing trip, although it's possible to take a look around the nineteenth-century **Casa de Juntas** (council chamber) and see the famous **oak tree**. The rest of the town is neat and modern.
**Bermeo.** Main fishing town of the province, competing with Bilbao in importance before industrialisation took over the latter. Attractive harbour and beach.

**Durango.** Small industrial town on the plain.
**Bilbao** (Bilbo). A heavily industrialised city and port, whose air can be quite polluted at times, but spectacular mountain and coastal scenery within easy reach compensates for this — rather like Glasgow. The centre — the **Casco Viejo** — is small and really quite charming, and there's plenty happening in the nearby **El Arenal** district.

## COMING AND GOING

### By air
There are good air links between London and Bilbao and smaller airports at San Sebastián and Vitoria.

### By rail
By train the route from France takes you to San Sebastián or Vitoria. For Bilbao you must go via Miranda del Ebro, a rather circuitous route. The FEVE (narrow gauge) railway goes all the way along the coast from Bilbao westwards.

### By road
Euskadi has some of the best roads in Spain — the three provincial capitals are connected by motorways, and there is also motorway all the way to Zaragoza and Barcelona. Bus services are excellent and cheap.

### By sea
Despite Britain's historic sea links with the Basque country, and Bilbao in particular (apparently how football arrived in Spain), there is no longer any passenger line in service. If you want to go by boat though, via the Plymouth – Santander ferry, Bilbao is only a 1 – 2 hour drive along the coast.

### Packages
Some packages to other parts of northern Spain use Bilbao airport, but Euskadi itself is not touristically developed in this respect.

## WHERE TO STAY

Beware of San Sebastián in the summer. You probably won't end up sleeping on the beach, but it may take you a while to find anywhere to stay if you haven't booked in advance. Along the coast between Zarauz and Bermeo, however, there are plenty of resorts with **pensions** and **boarding houses** available. If you're staying for longer than two weeks, the following offices will help you to find **self-catering accommodation**:

**Centro de Atracción y Turismo,** c/Reina Regente s/n, San Sebastián (tel. 943–422338)

**Centro de Iniciativas Turísticas,** c/Nafarroa s/n, Zarauz (Guipúzcoa) (tel. 943–830990 or 834208)

There are a couple of **youth hostels** in the region, and the Reservations Office is at Duque de Wellington s/n, Vitoria (tel. 945-249900).
**Campsites** are plentiful all along the coast. Inland, the only two are at **Leza**, in the extreme south of Alava province, and **Zuazo**, near Vitoria.
*Casas de labranza* are a real possibility in this area: the Basque agricultural traditions and their *caseríos* or homesteads, being ideally suited to this type of arrangement. The **youth department** of the Basque government (see **Useful Addresses**) publishes a list of those available each year, or alternatively, consult the **Spanish Tourist Office** in London.
Other possibilities are:

**Refugios de montaña.** A fair number in mountain areas, but you'll have to get in touch with the various clubs which run them for the keys, see Hiking below.
**Monasteries.** There is a monastery at **Arantzazu** which takes in visitors, phone 943-781313, or write well in advance to Monasterio de Arántzazu, Arántzazu, Guipúzcoa.
**Spas.** Have a health-orientated holiday at a traditional *balneario* or health farm.
— **Balneario de Cestona,** Paseo de San Juan, Cestona, Guipúzcoa (tel. 943-867140)
— **Casa Vicente Palotti,** Baños de Molinar, Antiguo Balneario de Karrantza, Vizcaya (tel. 94-680 6002)

## WHAT TO EAT AND DRINK

Basques are enthusiastic about cookery — there is a long tradition of gastronomic societies which meet regularly to try out new recipes — and some of the most imaginative cuisine in Spain can be sampled in the region. The Basque country has long-established seafaring and maritime traditions, so it's not surprising that this cuisine is based firmly on fish. As well as fresh fish, including tuna (*bonito* or *atún*), monkfish (*rape*), and hake (*merluza*), look out for dishes made with *bacalao* or salt cod, such as *bacalao al pil pil* (with garlic and olive oil) or *bacalao a la vizcaina* (in tomato sauce).

Another typically Basque speciality is supposed to be the only black dish in the world: squid in its own ink. Look out also for the fish stews (*marmitako*), spider crab (*txangurro*) and *kokotxas*, a speciality dish made from hake 'cheeks'.

Not many people realise that a good deal of Rioja wine is actually Basque — many of the vineyards in the Rioja Alavesa district are in Alava province. The typically Basque wine, however, the *txakoli*, is much more of an acquired taste: a tart, slightly sparkling red wine. Cider is also very typical of the region, usually dry, with a low alcohol content. A word about water: the Basques have very stringent health regulations, so it is quite safe to drink water straight from the tap throughout the region.

## OPPORTUNITIES IN EUSKADI

The region has a highly developed economy, so there are work possibilities here if you've got the right skills and experience, but bear in mind that Basque unemployment is above the national average. Main industries are iron and steel, coal, textiles, paper, oil refineries, chemical, shipbuilding, and fishing, while the financial and commercial sectors are of considerable importance too. Co-operatives are being encouraged — the most famous being that at Mondragón. If you're interested in arranging work exchanges or study visits it could be a fertile area.

The region is a great place for outdoor activities — hiking, mountaineering, canoeing, horseriding, and sports of all kinds. Good also for eating and drinking, especially some of the bars in the old part of Bilbao, but a little short on cultural enjoyment for the non-Basque enthusiast.

Study possibilities are also fairly limited, and to get the most out of the region you really have to have an interest in, or a commitment to learning about, Basque culture, or you'll find the whole experience very frustrating.

## WHAT TO DO

### ARCHAEOLOGY

There are a number of fairly important archaeological sites from different periods including the Roman *oppidum* of **Iruña**, near Armentia, and, in **Alegría**, the remains of the first metal cultures in the settlement of **Hemayo**. If you're interested in going on a dig in the area, contact: **Instituto Alavés de Arqueología**, c/ San Antonio 41, Vitoria-Gasteiz (Alava) (tel. 945–230617). (See also the section on voluntary work on pp. 71–3 earlier in the book.)

### ART GALLERIES AND MUSEUMS

#### Bilbao
**Museo de Bellas Artes,** Parque Doña Casilda Iturriza, Bilbao. Includes paintings by classical Spanish painters, Flemish and Catalan Romanesque art. Also a contemporary art section. Open 10.30–1300 and 1530–1900 Monday–Saturday, mornings only on Sundays and holidays.
**The Basque Archaeological Ethnographical and Historical Museum,** c/Cruz 4, Bilbao. The museum's impressive title speaks for itself. Sited in an old Jesuit college, it is open 1030–1300 and 1600–1900 on weekdays, mornings only on Sundays. Closed on Mondays and holidays.

#### San Sebastián
**San Telmo Museum,** Plaza de Zuloaga, San Sebastián. Once a monastery, and worth seeing for its beautiful cloister. Inside, a collection of Basque memorabilia and various bits and pieces of some interest, including the sword of Boabdil, the last Moorish king. Open 1000–1300 and 1530–1730 every day except Mondays.

#### Vitoria
**Museo de Bellas Artes,** Paseo Fray Francisco de Vitoria 3, Vitoria. Works

by modern Basque artists hang alongside an El Greco and two Riberas.
**Museo de Armería**, is located in the same building. Has a collection of
weaponry and armour from all periods from 1200 onwards. Both museums
are open 1100–1400 and 1700–1900 except Mondays, when they are closed
altogether, and weekends and holidays, when they are closed in the
afternoons.

Vitoria also has a **Museum of Playing Cards** and an **Archaeological
Museum**, and there is a **Maritime Museum** at Bermeo. With the exception of the Museo de Bellas Artes in Bilbao, none of the museums charges
an entrance fee.

## BULLFIGHTS

The Basques take their bullfighting, as all sports, seriously, and it is said
that some of the best *corridas* in Spain may be seen at Bilbao Bullring, **Vista
Alegre**, especially during August. (There is also a bullring at Vitoria-
Gasteiz). Many Basque *jaiak* or fiestas include bull-running, such as that
of the San Fermines festivities in Pamplona (see section on fiestas below,
and also in the section on Navarre, p.228).

## CAVES

There are prehistoric caves to be visited all along the Cantabrian coast.
If you're touring in the Basque region look out for the ones at the following villages: **Venta de Laperra, Arenaza, Santimamiñe, Goikolau, Ekain,
Altzerri, Alkerdi, Isturitz, Etxeberriko** and **Karbia**. The one at Santimamiñe has some impressive murals of bisons and horses, and may be
visited. It is located about 3 miles north of **Guernica** on the Lequeito road.

## CINEMA

The big cinema event in the Basque country is the **International Film
Festival** at **San Sebastían** during the second half of September. It has some
unusual categories, such as Cine Submarino and Cine Médico, attracting
*aficionados* and professionals from all over the world.

The main venue is the **Teatro Victoria Eugenia** and you can get full
details from the **Fundación Pública Municipal**, Apartado de Correos 397,
20004 San Sebastián (tel. 943–429625), or if you're there at the time from
the tourist office.

**Bilbao** has its own cinema event too, the **Certamen Internacional de
Cine Documental y Cortometraje**, which takes place in early December.
Full details from the following address: Colón de Larreategui 37-4-D,
48009 Bilbao.

## COURSES

There are no 'Spanish for foreigners' courses in the region. There are, however, various schemes to encourage the learning of *Euskera*, and you may even qualify for a grant! Get in touch with the **Cultural Department of the Basque Government**, at the following address: Eusko Jaularitza, Departamento de Cultura y Turismo, Gazteentzako Informazio Zerbitzua, Duque de Wellington 2, 01011 Vitoria-Gasteiz, Alava.

If you're into cookery, the Basque Government Tourist Department (see addresses later) runs a week-long **cookery course** every other week from March to early December, including hotel accommodation and classes and meals at the '**School of Gastronomic Science**' in San Sebastián.

There is also an **International Music Course** in Bilbao — see section on Music below.

## DANCE

Strictly for enthusiasts only: learn Basque folk dances at the following school: **Euskal Dantzarien Biltzarra**, Duque de Mandas s/n, San Sebastián (tel. 943-420982).

## FIESTAS

Basque fiestas, or *jaiak*, always a medium through which the separateness of Basque culture has been expressed, have become even more animated since autonomy was granted to the region. They generally involve traditional Basque dancing, singing and music-making by *txistularis* (players of three-holed flutes), drummers and pipers. There are also demonstrations of strength and skill such as tugs-of-war, rowing races, bull-running (*encierros*) and even tree-trunk chopping competitions.

In the summer, there are *jaiak* in every town and village, too numerous to detail here and not really worth listing. It's better to take them as you find them. The famous *fueros* gave each town the right to arm its inhabitants in self-defence in the event of an invasion, and this right to a 'Home Guard' is symbolically exercised in the annual festivities of many towns (most notably that of **Irún** at the end of July) with armed parades in traditional costume.

**Vitoria-Gasteiz** has a big fiesta in honour of the Virgen Blanca starting on 4 August each year, with parades of carnival figures and bullfights. Other important times of the year for fiestas in the region are **San Juan** (24 June), **Asunción** (14/15 August), and at **Christmas**.

## HIKING

There are some good hikes in the **Montes Vascos**. If you think you need more guidance than that provided by a good map, you could get in touch with a tourist office, or with one of the hiking/mountaineering clubs in the area:

- **Club Alpino,** Carnecería Vieja 19, Bilbao
- **Federación Vasca de Montañismo,** Plaza Santa María 10, Durango

• **Sociedad Excursionista Manuel Iradier,** Pintorería 15, Vitoria-Gasteiz

These clubs also run various *refugios de montaña*.

If you're interested in organised hikes and climbs, short courses in mountaineering or cross-country skiing, contact the following travel club/agency: **Goilur Viajeros,** Aptdo 1016, San Sebastián (tel. 943-287557). The same organisation also puts on cycling expeditions — over the border into France as well. (See also details on horseriding in the section on Sports below.)

## LOCAL PRESS

*Eja*
*Egin*
*El Correo Vasco*

## MUSIC

The Basques, like the Welsh, are keen on music, and there is a **Basque Symphony Orchestra,** based in **San Sebastián,** and also one in **Bilbao,** based at the **Teatro Campos Eliseos.**

During the first half of September there is a **Choral Festival** in **Vitoria-Gasteiz,** sponsored by the Provincial Savings Bank.

The major musical event without doubt is the annual **San Sebastián Jazz Festival,** during the second half of July, cleverly timed to catch the crowds of tourists in search of further stimulus after the **San Fermines** in **Pamplona** (see section on Navarre, p. 228). For further information, contact the **Centro de Atracción y Turismo,** Ayuntamiento de San Sebastián (tel. 943-423180). There is a parallel event at **Vitoria-Gasteiz.**

Every year towards the end of September there is a music course, open to all nationalities, at the **Centro de Estudios Musicales 'Juan Antxieta',** Alda Recalde 34, Bilbao (tel. 94-424 5562).

## SHOPPING

A big antiques fair is held in Bilbao every year, usually in March. If you want to find out more, get in touch with the *Directora,* at Feria de Antigüedades, Pza de Pedro María s/n, Bilbao (tel. 94-441 5400).

## SPORTS

### Football
Enthusiastically followed and played in the region. **Bilbao Atlético** is of course the big local team.

### Golf
Golf courses are at **Fuenterrabía** and **Zarauz,** and **Algorta** and **Munguia,** near Bilbao. The Basque Government Tourist Department organises four

day **golfing holidays** in Bilbao or San Sebastián, with everything included as from your arrival on Basque soil. Contact them at the address given later for further details.

**Horse racing**
There is a race course at **Lasarte,** outside San Sebastián, with race meetings in summer.

**Horseriding**
The **pottoka**, or Basque horse, still exists in the wild, but recently they have also been bred in captivity for **pony-trekking** and **hacking**. The Basque Government Tourist Department organises special half-day or day-long excursions on horseback in the countryside around **Arantzazu**, for both adults and children (see address below). If you just want to ride, there is hire of horses at **Jaizubia** (near Irún), **Vitoria** (Club Vitoriano de Equitación Armentia), **Arántzazu, Getxo, Laukiniz, Erandio, Barakaldo, Bedia** and other villages.

**Pelota**
The Basque sport *par excellence* is a ball game called **pelota** or *jai alai*, played with great enthusiasm on special courts (you'll find them in all centres of population of any size), or against any available wall surface.

**Skiing**
In the **Montes Vascos** and in the **Pyrenees**. **Goilur Viajeros**, Aptdo 1016, San Sebastián (tel. 943–287557) can be helpful in making arrangements.

**Other sports**
Other sports facilities include **windsurfing, squash, tennis, waterskiing** and **canoeing**.
For **water sports** in **San Sebastián**, ask at the **Caseta Real**, half way along the La Concha promenade.

# THEATRE

**San Sebastián** has an annual **theatre festival,** details from **Centro de Atracción y Turismo**, Reina Regente s/n, San Sebastián (tel. 943–421002).
There is an **International Puppet Festival** held each year in **Bilbao**, organised by the cultural department of the city council: Area de Educación, Cultura y Eusquerización (*sic*), Ayuntamiento de Bilbao, Bilbao (tel. 94–445 5200).

# UNIVERSITIES

The University of the Basque Country is a new creation, and most teaching is done in Basque, whereas the old-established University of Deusto is a private institution, run by Jesuits:

**Universidad del Pais Vasco** (Udako Euskal Unibertsitatea), Avda Montevideo s/n, Bilbao (tel. 94–464 1000).
**Universidad de Deusto,** Avda Universidades s/n, Deusto-Bilbao (tel. 94–445 3100).

## WINE

If you want to visit any of the Rioja Alavesa *bodegas*, you can do so through the Casa del Vino in **Laguardia**. The Tourist Department of the Basque Government organises 4-day wine tours of the Rioja Alavesa area and will meet you at Bilbao airport and arrange everything from there on. See address below.

## USEFUL ADDRESSES

**Tourist offices**
Miramar Esquina Andia, San Sebastián (tel. 943–426282)
Paseo de la Florida s/n, Vitoria (tel. 945–249564)

**Government offices**
**Basque Government Tourist Dept.** (Viceconsejería de Turismo), Gobierno Vasco, c/ Duque de Wellington 2, Vitoria (tel. 945–246000)
**Regional Government** (Gobierno Vasco (Eusko Jaurlaritza) ), Duque de Wellington 2, Vitoria (tel. 945–247200)
**Youth/Sport Department** (Dirección General de Juventud y Acción Comunitaria), Departamento de Cultura, Duque de Wellington s/n, Vitoria

**Education departments**
Gran Vía 85–4º, Bilbao (tel. 94–442 4848)
Plaza de Lasala 2, San Sebastián (tel. 943–429906)
Avda. Gasteiz 31–1º, Vitoria (tel. 945–227800)

**Labour departments**
Gran Vía 50–2º, Bilbao
Idíaquez 6, San Sebastián
General Alava 10–2º, Vitoria

**Youth information offices**
As Youth/Sport Department above. Also:
**Oficina de Información Juvenil,** Avda. Ategorrieta 9–3º–D, San Sebastian (tel. 943–276911)

**TIVE offices**
Gran Vía 50–7º, Bilbao (tel. 94–441 4277)
Avda Ategorrieta 9–3º–D, San Sebastián (tel. 943–276934)

**Travel agents**
**Añosluz,** c/ Ledesma 7–1º–izq., Bilbao (tel. 94–424 4265)
**Bide Berriak,** c/Germikako Arbola 3, Tolosa (Guipúzcoa)

**Car hire**
Atesa:
Bilbao airport (tel. 94–453 3340)
Pza Zaragoza, San Sebastián (tel. 943–425976)
Castilla 39, Vitoria (tel. 945–249696)

**British (and American) representation**
**British Chamber of Commerce:** Alameda de Mazarredo 5, 48001, Bilbao (tel. 94–423 8605)
**British Consulate:** Alameda Urquijo 2–8º, Bilbao (tel. 94–415 7600/7711)
**British schools** — none.
**American School of Bilbao,** Apartado 38, Las Arenas, Vizcaya (tel. 94–668 0860)

**Language schools (TEFL)**
**Bilbao:**
— Assimil, Rodriguez Arias 43, Baracaldo
— Britannia Centro de Inglés, Telesforo de Aranzadi 3–6º
— Cursos de Idiomas, Camara Oficial de Comercio, Industria y Navegación de Bilbao, Rodriguez Arias 6
— Berlitz, Gran Vía 22–2º
— Inlingua, Colon de Larreategui 38–1º
**Eibar:** Inlingua, Avda Generalismimo 5
**Irún:** Inlingua, Joaquín Gamón 2–1º–A
**Mondragón:** Ahizke Idiomas, Loramendi 7
**San Sebastián:**
— Academia de Idiomas Lacunza, Urbieta 14–1º
— Centro de Idiomas Modernos, Legazpi 6–2º
— Inlingua, Hernani 29
**Vitoria:** Inlingua, Postas 6

# 11 Extremadura

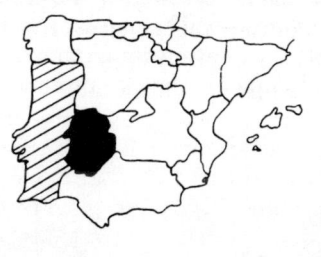

> ... desolate Extremadura ... is peopled by locusts, wandering sheep, pigs, and here and there by human bipeds.
>
> Richard Ford

Extremadura is in many ways the forgotten region of Spain, lying unvisited and undisturbed between Castile, Andalucía and Portugal. It's a huge area to ignore, however — as large as Belgium or Holland and containing within it as much natural variety and contrast as you could hope for, from the alpine to the sub-tropical, from green meadows and orchards to semi-desert. The contrast is mainly a north/south one, reflected in customs and culture — the north meshes easily with its neighbour Castile, whereas in the south the little whitewashed villages are reminiscent of Andalucía.

The contrast and variety go no further than this, however. It's a sparsely populated region (about 25 people per square kilometre) and over half its huge area remains uncultivated. Badajoz is the biggest centre, with a population of only about 120,000, and there's not a lot happening.

Despite the dearth of organised activities, the region does have its attractions. There is a good deal of history and romance attached to the place: Mérida was the capital of the Roman province of Lusitania from 25BC and it preserves an exceptional collection of Roman remains, including the great theatre where an important festival is staged every summer. In medieval times the region was dominated by the Church, by the Knightly Orders of Santiago and Alcántara, and later by the Inquisition, and a large number of interesting monuments remain from this time. Towns such as Trujillo and Medellín are closely associated with the Conquest of the New World — most of the early *conquistadores* were drawn from Extremadura, and the statues of men such as Pizarro and Hernán Cortés, now dominate the town squares of their birth. Gold from the Indies paid for the noble mansions and palaces of towns like Cáceres, and enriched the region's churches and monasteries, including the beautiful monastery of the Virgin of Guadalupe, whose cult crossed the Atlantic with the *conquistadores*.

Apart from its sense of history, Extremadura's other great attraction is its wildness and space — an immense area of Cáceres province is given over to the Monfragüe Natural Park, there are desolate mountain areas such as Las Hurdes, and a number of huge artificial lakes created by damming the two great rivers which flow through the region, the Tagus and the Guadiana, counteract the traditional barrenness of the landscape and provide a good habitat for a wide variety of flora and fauna. Nowadays the only towns of any importance are Mérida, the regional capital, and Cáceres and Badajoz, the two provincial capitals.

## WHAT TO SEE

**Badajoz province**
**Mérida.** The regional capital, with pretensions to being something of a cultural centre, but basically tiny, provincial and dusty. The Roman ruins are impressive however, including two bridges, an aqueduct, temples, baths, a triumphal arch, and an amphitheatre and circus as well as the famous theatre.
**Badajoz.** Provincial capital on the Portuguese border, and the largest town in the region (possibly the ugliest too). It was the Moors who transferred their regional headquarters here from Mérida, and the Torre de Espantaperros remains from this time.
**Medellín.** Hardly more than a village, on the Guadiana river, remarkable for being the birthplace of Hernán Cortés, who toppled the Aztec Empire in Mexico.
**Villanueva de la Serena.** Prosperous town in the fertile *vega* of the Guadiana.
**Amendralejo.** Centre for the red-earthed Tierra de Barros area, producing wine, olives and earthenware.
**Zafra.** White-walled town attracting some tourism to its Alcázar, now a *parador*, which has a smart patio designed by Herrera, of El Escorial fame.
**Jerez de los Caballeros.** Another of Extremadura's 'white towns' birthplace of Vasco Núñez de Balboa, who discovered the Pacific by crossing the isthmus of Panama.
**Llerena.** A tiny, attractive place of little importance nowadays, but which once was the seat of the masters of the Order of Santiago, supposedly the most powerful position in the Spanish feudal system. Later the Inquisition had its headquarters here, in the building which is now the Palacio de Justicia!

**Olivenza.** A village which was Portuguese until the beginning of the last century, with not a particularly Spanish atmosphere. Much of the architecture, including the twisted pillars in the parish church, is typically *manueline* (see Portugal).
**Siberia.** The name given to the arid, scrubby area in the north east of the province!

### Cáceres province
**Cáceres.** The best town in the region for staying any length of time, still small and provincial, but lively enough. Its old quarter, with its narrow streets, its noble old mansions and palaces in gold-coloured stone, and its towers with their storks' nests, is extremely attractive, and there is also a new part which manages to be fairly tasteful.

### Elsewhere in the province
**Trujillo.** Birthplace of Pizarro, Francisco de Orellana and Diego García de Paredes, *conquistadores* who between them are said to have spawned twenty American nations! There is an old walled town on a hill, and a modern part below. The interest of the former is in its Plaza Mayor, mansions, and towers, especially the *Mudejar* **Torre del Alfiler**, all given a special look by untidy storks' nests perched on top.
**Guadalupe.** Monastery in spectacular rural setting which houses the image of the Virgin of Guadalupe. It's sumptuously rich in art treasures, including paintings by Zurbarán, and has a beautiful cloister with *Mudejar* arches. The town is a quaint old place, its houses have overhanging upper storeys supported on wooden props.
**Yuste.** Quiet monastery, in pretty rural setting, where the Emperor Charles V spent his last years.
**Coria.** Small town with a cathedral, a relic of its importance in medieval times, praised by both Unamuno and Ortega y Gasset.
**Alcántara.** An immense Roman bridge, still in use, gave its name to the town through the Arabic language. Alcántara was later the headquarters of the Knights of Alcántara. Their castle and monastery are now in ruins, and the most noteworthy sight is the enormous reservoir and its great hydro-electric generating station.
**Plasencia.** A prosperous market town for the surrounding sierras on the river Jerte, and an important crossroads in medieval times. Some industry.
**Las Hurdes.** Wild mountainous region to the very north of the province, known as the 'breadless land' and inspiring all sorts of dire tales until recently. Now dams and better communications have led to greater appreciation of its natural beauty which is indeed spectacular.
**La Vera** and **Valle del Jerte.** Fertile valleys of torrential streams, small villages and above all, cherry trees, a beautiful sight in spring.

## COMING AND GOING

### By air
It's a pretty remote region, and communications are difficult. If you're

going to Cáceres and the north, use Madrid airport, and then overland. If you're going to the south or Badajoz, you might also consider using Seville airport. Badajoz itself has a small internal airport, if time is short and you can get a connecting flight.

**By train**
The railway goes north–south through the region, with a spur crossing into Portugal, but the service is incredibly slow and infrequent. RENFE offers some interesting trips round the region from Cáceres.

**By road**
Road communications are not good at all, considering the main roads between Madrid and Lisbon pass through the region. Bus services are generally better than the trains.

**Packages**
The region is not developed in this sense.

## WHERE TO STAY

Very few **campsites** or **youth hostels**, though camping rough is a distinct possibility (see p. 25 earlier in the book). You shouldn't have any trouble finding anywhere to stay in **Mérida** (except during the Theatre Festival), **Badajoz** or **Cáceres**, but if you're going anywhere else do take to heart all the comments made earlier in the book and get a list of places to stay from the tourist authorities first.

If you fancy a real retreat from modern life, the **monasteries** of **Yuste** (tel. 927–460530) and **Guadalupe** (tel. 927–367000) both take in visitors, although Yuste only caters for men. (If you're writing, note that both are in Cáceres province.)

## WHAT TO EAT AND DRINK

*Extremeño* hams are much prized — the pigs' diet of acorns is supposed to do wonders for the flavour. Also much in evidence are the *chorizos* and *salchicón*, also courtesy of the pigs. There are some supposedly regional specialities such as 'lizard in green sauce' and sheeps' testicles but it's probably best to stick to *cocido* in winter and *gazpacho* in summer!

Some wine is produced locally, notably at Montánchez, but there are no great denominated areas.

## OPPORTUNITIES IN EXTREMADURA

Very few, and the ones that do exist like hiking and retreating into nature can be enjoyed in comparatively more accessible locations throughout Spain. Cáceres could be a pleasant place to live for a while, but apart from that, the region is probably best visited from some centre like Salamanca or Seville, where you'd have a good reason for being in the first place.

## WHAT TO DO

## ART GALLERIES AND MUSEUMS

**Badajoz**
**Museo Arqueológico,** Plazoleta del Reloj
**Museo de Bellas Artes,** Palacio de la Diputación. Includes paintings by Zurbarán and Luis de Morales.

**Mérida**
**Museo Nacional de Arte Romano,** Plaza Sta Clara (National Museum of Roman Art).

**Cáceres**
**Museo de Cáceres,** Pza de las Veletas. Archaeological and ethnological collections.

## BULLFIGHTS

There are no bullrings anywhere of any size, but generally the best *corridas* are likely to be in **Badajoz**. **Coria** has spectacular *encierros* lasting for several days around San Juan in June.

## COURSES

No Spanish for foreigners courses in the region. Try Seville, Salamanca or Madrid.

## CRAFTS

There is some attractive plain **earthenware** produced in **Salvatierra de los Barros**, and other types of pottery throughout the region. Other local crafts still practised include **copper-beating, embroidery** and **wickerwork**. There are some elaborate **straw hats** produced to very ancient designs in the village of **Montehermoso**.

## EXCHANGES

Apparently there is demand in **Cáceres** for student exchanges. Interested families should contact M$^{\underline{a}}$ Dolores Maestre, Sección Provincial de Turismo, Avda Virgen de la Montaña 12–1$^{\underline{o}}$, Cáceres.

## FIESTAS

Extremadura's not a region with any big fiestas, although there are some deeply-rooted festive traditions still maintained in little villages, such as the curious ritual performed by penitents on Maundy Thursday in **Valverde de la Vera** (Cáceres province). Pieces of wood are attached to their shoulders with rope, lace petticoats donned, and the effect completed by a veil and crown of thorns on the head.

In nearby **Villanueva de la Vera**, the village made famous by the popular press for its supposed cruelty to donkeys, carnival time (February) is a signal to bring out into the village a strange figure on a long pole supposed to represent the devil, who is later beheaded and buried, amid much feasting and merrymaking.

## HIKING

There is good **hiking** all over the north of the region, in the **Valle del Jerte**, **Valle del Ambroz**, or **La Vera** areas, for all of which you could reasonably base yourself at **Plasencia**. The village of **Hervás** would also make a good starting point for some invigorating mountain walks. **Las Hurdes** and, more fertile and welcoming, the **Sierra de Gata**, on the border with Salamanca province, would also be good areas to explore, with lots of tiny villages for stocking up on provisions, and here and there a hostel or place with rooms to let.

Further south, especially south of the **Guadiana**, is very barren and inhospitable territory, not really walking country.

## LOCAL PRESS

*Hoy*

## SPORTS

**Fishing**
The Tagus and the Guadiana, and also the great artificial lakes throughout the region, provide good angling, mainly for carp, tench and barbel, also pike. Apply to **ICONA** in Badajoz or Cáceres for a licence:

Plaza de Castelar 3, Badajoz (tel. 924–225115)
Avda General Primo de Rivera 2–7º. Cáceres (tel. 927–227601)

**Horseriding**
Good country for this, though you'd have to make arrangements locally.

**Hunting/shooting**
Reputedly good for game like rabbit, hare, partridge, quail, and larger species like deer, wild boar and chamois. Again, apply to **ICONA**.

**Watersports**
**Alcántara, Borbollón** and **Gabriel y Galán lakes** in the north are regularly used for watersports such as **sailing, canoeing** and **windsurfing**, as are the **Cijara** and **García Sola reservoirs** in the extreme east.

## THEATRE

The **Theatre Festival** in **Mérida** is quite a lavish affair, lasting all of July, and spilling out into June and August as well. There are ten or so fairly prestigious productions staged throughout the period, which in the last couple of years have included Oscar Wilde's *Salomé* by the Nuria Espert Company, a Catalan version of *Antigone*, and performances of classical drama by Greek and Italian companies. They all take place in the open air, either in the Roman theatre or amphitheatre, and there is also usually a ballet performance and peripheral exhibitions as well.

Tickets can be obtained from the **Roman Theatre Box Office** (!), or from **Inprenta Rodríguez**, c/Oviedo 27, Mérida (tel. 924–311307). Further information from **Festival Office**, Conventual Santiaguista, Pza de El Rastro, Mérida (tel. 924–317612). The town hall and the *parador* also serve as information centres for the festival. The following travel agents can arrange travel and tickets to performances on an all-in basis:

**Madrid:** Viajes TP, Glorieta Ruiz Jiménez 5 (tel. 91–448 3662)
**Barcelona:** Viajes TP, Gran Vía 254 (tel. 93–321 8235)
**Seville:** Viajes Ibermar, Santo Tomás 11 (tel. 954–218707)

## UNIVERSITIES

**Universidad de Extremadura**, Avda Adolfo Díez Ambrona s/n, Badajoz (tel. 924–238800). The Law and Arts Faculties, as well as several university colleges, are in Cáceres.

## WILDLIFE

Spain's largest so-called Natural Park is **Monfragüe**, which takes up most of the area to the east of the main road between **Plasencia** and **Cáceres**. The river Tagus runs straight through it in a deep valley between two mountain ridges which create an isolated area alternating rocky crags with woodland and pasture. The wealth of bird life is immense, and includes many birds of prey such as the imperial eagle, peregrine falcon, and different types of owl and vulture. There are also stags, wild boar, foxes, badgers and lynxes, snakes and lizards, while around the rivers and the **Cornalvo Dam** area there are otters, polecats, freshwater tortoises and a whole range of aquatic birds.

Away to the east there is also the **Cijara game reserve**, where, among other species wild board and deer are protected by **ICONA**.

## USEFUL ADDRESSES

**Tourist offices**
**Badajoz:** c/Pasaje de San Juan (tel. 924–222763)
**Cáceres:** Pza General Mola s/n (tel. 927–246347)
**Mérida:** c/El Puente 9 (tel. 924–315353)

**Plasencia:** c/Trujillo 17 (tel. 927-320653)
**Regional Government Tourist Dept,** c/ Cárdenas 11, Mérida (tel. 924-313050)

**Government offices**
**Regional Government** (Junta Regional de Extremadura):
— Pza de Minayo 1, Badajoz (tel. 924-221240)
— José Fernández López s/n, Mérida (tel. 924-303343)
**Youth/Sport Department** (Dirección General de Juventud y Deportes), Avda de Huelva 2, Badajoz (tel. 924-232716)

**Education departments**
**Badajoz:** Avda del General Rodrigo 2 (tel. 924-232016)
**Cáceres:** Avda General Primo de Rivera s/n (tel. 927-224900)

**Labour departments**
**Badajoz:** Avda de Colón 2 (tel. 924-231700)
**Cáceres:** San Pedro de Alcántara 1 (tel. 927-222618)

**Youth Information Offices**
**Badajoz:** As Youth/Sport Department above.
**Cáceres:** Ancha 7 (tel. 927-246930)

**TIVE offices**
None in the region. See Salamanca, Seville or Madrid.

**Travel agents**
**Cáceres:** Viajes Sirena SA, Avda Virgen de Guadalupe 20 (tel. 927-222250)
**Badajoz:** Viajes Melia, Avda General Rodrigo 6 (tel. 924-233250)

**Car hire**
**Autos Alhambra,** Avda Colón 1, Badajoz (tel. 924-222196)

**British representation**
**British Chamber of Commerce** — see Madrid.
**British Consulate** — see Embassy in Madrid.
**British schools** — none in the region. See Madrid.

**Language schools (TEFL)**
None of the big names have branches in the region.

# 12 Galicia

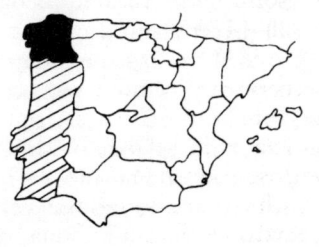

> O que nunca estivo lonxe
> non sabe o que é padecer
> de lonxe as penas aumentan
> para quen sabe querer.
>
> *Rosalía de Castro*

If you want to shatter all the usual stereotypical images of Spain, Galicia's the place to go — it's a million miles from the *costas*, and almost as far from Don Quixote. It's fresh, green and verdant (La Coruña is supposed to have as many wet days as Manchester), it has gushing rivers, a coastline more reminiscent of Scotland than Spain, and a bucolic hinterland.

Despite being remote, isolated from the rest of Spain, basically rural, and poverty-stricken for centuries, Galicia will surprise you with its sophistication. This is almost entirely due to the phenomenon of emigration: the Spaniards working in the catering and service industries throughout northern Europe (and also in Latin America, Canada, Australia, etc.) are almost all Galicians, forced to look for an income beyond that traditionally offered by the land and the sea. It is evident that at least some of their earnings have found their way back to be reinvested in small businesses and new houses, and the knowledge and experience brought back too gives Galicia a sense of being very firmly part of the twentieth century, unlike some other rural regions of Spain

Galicia shares a Celtic history with the other lands of the far west of Europe (Ireland, Wales, Cornwall and Brittany) and still looks very much towards the sea rather than towards the rest of Spain. It was occupied by the Romans, but felt very little Moorish influence except for two dramatic incursions as far as Santiago.

The 'discovery' of the tomb of St James on Galician soil in the ninth century, and the subsequent institution of the Pilgrimage to Santiago, which attracted millions of medieval 'tourists' from all over Europe, had the effect of bringing Galicia — and the other regions of Spain through which the pilgrims passed — into contact with a whole range of European ideas and influences. At the same time the scallop-shell symbol of St James (*Santiago* in Spanish) became known throughout Europe. The pilgrims entered Spain via the Pyrenean passes of Roncesvalles (in Navarre) and Somport (in Aragón), and the *Camino de Santiago* took them over Castilian plains and Leonese mountains, passing through such places as Pamplona (see section on Navarre), Logroño (see Rioja), Burgos, and León (see Castilla-León), before arriving on Galician soil, and eventually at the great cathedral of Santiago de Compostela. The Galician part of the route passes through some remote and beautiful rural areas (villages in the heart of Galicia such as Samos, Sarria, Puertomarín, Mellid and Arzúa), and the way is still littered today with Romanesque churches, shrines, monasteries, stone crosses and hospices.

The cult of St James was very strong in Spain during the period of the Reconquest, and numerous 'sightings' were recorded of him, mounted on horseback and slaying Moors by the hundred, thus earning him the title *Santiago Matamoros*. Santiago remains today a symbol of national unity and strength, and every year on St James's day a ceremony of national offering is held in the cathedral, attended by members of the Royal Family, politicians, representatives of the armed forces and other dignitaries.

It is unlikely that the medieval pilgrims had much appreciation of Galicia's other great tourist attraction, it's magnificent coastline, indented by *rías* like the sea lochs of Scotland or the fjords of Norway. Those on the north coast and continuing down as far as Finisterre are known as the *rías altas*, and south of Finisterre down to the Portuguese border as the *rías bajas*. On the north coast, the land is fairly low lying, wild, and forested with pines and eucalyptus right down to the water. The landscape around Finisterre is bleak, exposed to the full force of the Atlantic gales, while the *rías bajas* are Galicia's real tourist area, the climate is warmer and sunnier, and there are some pleasant resorts. Everywhere, by the way, is stunningly beautiful: the water of the *rías* is clear and blue, and icily cold, even in August!

Galician vegetation offers a strange mix of northern and southern species: roses alongside cactuses, potatoes and palms, vines and cabbages, and all over you see the typical coffin-shaped granaries on stilts (*hórreos*), stone crosses, and here and there an elegant *pazo*, or Galician country manor house.

Galician regionalism, is strong, and the language *Gallego*, which incorporates elements of Portuguese, is widely used. The autonomous government has its seat at Santiago, the capital of the region, and there are four provinces: Lugo, La Coruña, Pontevedra and Orense, with provincial capitals bearing the same names.

# WHAT TO SEE

*Note*: Bear in mind that the *Gallego* version of place names may be used on road signs, maps and the like, for instance Sanxenxo for Sangenjo, A Coruña for La Coruña, etc.

## La Coruña province
**La Coruña** (Corunna in English). Big industrial port. Many houses have attractive glazed-in balconies. Sights include the **Torre de Hércules**, the only Roman lighthouse still in use (you can go up it and get a good view of the city, entrance free, opening hours 1000–1300 and 1600–1930, Monday to Saturday), and the **San Carlos Gardens**, where you can see the tomb of Sir John Moore.
**El Ferrol.** Franco's birthplace. Large naval base and dockyard.
**Betanzos.** Old-fashioned hill town with more glazed balconies.
**Santiago de Compostela.** A breathtaking city, but friendly and on a human scale, except for the impressive cathedral itself, with its towering baroque facade. Behind this the twelfth-century **Portico de la Gloria** is a stunning piece of sculpture in stone, its central pillar worn smooth where for centuries pilgrims have grasped it to signify safe arrival, and to make their wish. St James sits high above the altar, surrounded by mounds of soaring gold fancy-work, like a buddha in an Eastern temple, while long queues form to file past and kiss his image.

Outside though, the cathedral is given a homely feel by the lichens and rock plants growing out of its stones, as if out of the cliff face, and the simplicity of the stone squares surrounding it offsets the richness of the visual fare within,

Elsewhere the city is a delight, with its old porticoed *ruas* and university atmosphere. There are plenty of places to eat and drink and indulge after the rigours of some of the country districts, as no doubt the medieval pilgrims appreciated too.
**Padrón.** The remains of St James are supposed to have arrived on Spanish soil here, now a fairly prosperous village, which boasts the **Rosalía de Castro museum** (she was a nineteenth-century poet who wrote in *Gallego*).

## Lugo province
**Lugo.** 2 kilometres of Roman walls, cathedral.
**Sierra de Ancares.** Remote protected area for wildlife.
**Ribadeo.** Pretty hill town on the first of the *rías altas*.
**Foz.** Up and coming resort — some extremely beautiful beaches round about.

## Orense province
**Orense.** Famous for its *burgas*, not the MacDonald variety, but thermal springs, otherwise pleasant enough, but unremarkable.
**Ribadavia.** Quaint old place with its own former Jewish quarter of narrow, winding cobbled streets. Beautiful position on the bank of the Miño river, and a centre for the Ribeiro wine-producing area.

**El Barco (de Valdeorras).** A prosperous small town on the beautiful River Sil, at the heart of a wine producing area and looking very much towards León.

### Pontevedra province
**Tuy.** Border town on a hill overlooking the Miño river. Fortress-cathedral and just a trace of Portuguese influence.
**Bayona.** Old fortress-city, good views and beaches.
**Vigo.** Modern and prosperous port, with lively old *Berbés* fishing district.
**Cíes Islands.** Pretty unspoilt little islands at the mouth of Vigo Ría. You can do a day trip to their fantastic beaches from Vigo, or stay overnight and camp.
**Marín.** Commercial, military and fishing port.
**Sangenjo.** Lively summer resort.
**El Grove.** Summer resort and fishing village. Lively tourist atmosphere but don't go exploring too far beyond the harbour area or you'll end up in the sardine factory!
**La Toja.** Exclusive summer resort.
**Cambados.** Elegant stone fishing town. *Fefiñanes bodega* (see section on **Food and Drink** below), *Figueroa pazo*.
**Villanueva.** *Rua Nova pazo*. Ferry to the **Isla de Arosa**, with its fine sand beaches.
**Villagarcía de Arosa.** Harbour, boat club, sailing school.
**Pontevedra** (*Pontevedra e boa vila, ninguen a ve que n'o diga*). Attractive small provincial capital, with arcaded streets.

## COMING AND GOING

### By air
There's an international airport at Labacolla, outside Santiago (incidentally the medieval pilgrims used to stop here to have a bath and freshen up before making the final step of their journey to Santiago — hence the name). Cheap flights are available from London, as Spanish emigrants use the route to return home — try some of the specialist travel agents mentioned earlier in the book. La Coruña also has its own airport at Alvedro.

### By sea
Unfortunately there are no direct passenger lines between Britain and Galicia, so you can't follow in Laurie Lee's footsteps and arrive in Vigo by boat. Once there, however, there are boat trips you can take — to the Islas Cíes, for instance. Contact: **Ría de Vigo Cruises**, Estación Marítima Ría s/n, Vigo.

### By train
There are twelve trains a day from the rest of Spain to Galicia, but it'll take you all day. Nevertheless, it's a good way of seeing the interior of the region. The **FEVE** (narrow gauge) railway goes along the Cantabrian coast as far as El Ferrol, where the station and ticket office is in the Avda Com-

postela (tel. 981-316855). The *Transcantábrica* luxury train also starts/terminates at El Ferrol (see section on Asturias).

**By road**
Again, it'll take you at least a day to get from anywhere else in Spain. There's no traffic, but the roads wind about up hill and down dale, and there's no getting over the fact that the region covers an immense area. The stretch from La Coruña to the Portuguese border is exceptionally good, although if you use the motorway you'll have to pay a toll.

**Packages**
A number of companies offer a 'Route to Santiago' package, with emphasis on varying aspects. For instance **Interchurch Travel** stresses the pilgrimage aspect, **ACE Study Tours** lay most emphasis on art history and architecture, while **Waymark** do a walking holiday, following the old pilgrims' way from Ponferrada in León all the way to Santiago.

**Brittany Ferries** offer the chance to follow most of the route via Oviedo and returning through León and Burgos. You take your car on the Plymouth–Santander ferry and stay in their recommended hotels.

**Mundi Color** also do up-market holidays in La Toja, La Coruña and Santiago, while **Explore Worldwide** strike an offbeat note with their 'Unknown North' exploratory holiday starting from Santiago and taking in northern Portugal as well as Galicia. (Addresses: p. 21.)

## WHERE TO STAY
There are plenty of **hotels, pensions** and the like in the *rías bajas* vicinity, although you should bear in mind in August that it is a tourist area, for Spaniards as well as foreigners, and not leave it till late in the evening to start room-hunting. The *rías altas* are less well served, but have correspondingly less tourists, so you should have few problems. There are several **youth hostels** in the region, both inland and on the coast, and the Reservations Office is at Plaza de Pontevedra 22, La Coruña (tel. 981-220043).

The coastal areas are fairly well served with **campsites**, and there are two at Santiago. Inland they are few and far between (Orense province only has one), so it would be a question of *acampada libre* (see p. 25 earlier). The **monastery** at Poyo, just outside Pontevedra, may well take you in, and is worth visiting anyway for its beautiful views over the *ría*.

## WHAT TO EAT AND DRINK
Galicia boasts that it is the gourmet region of Spain, and there are some excellent restaurants serving some very good food. However, the cuisine is based on good ingredients plainly prepared rather than on any culinary art. Fish is the highlight, especially turbot (*rodaballo*) and sole (*lenguado*), both generally served *a la plancha* (griddled). In the cheaper restaurants you can have either *merluza* (hake) or *rape* (monkfish), either fried (*a la romana*) or stewed with potatoes (*a la gallega*). The variety of seafood caters for all budgets, from oysters and lobster to varieties of baby squid and

shellfish you've never heard of, complicated of course by their local *gallego* names.

There are some typically *gallego* dishes to try too: *lacón con grelos* (hand of salt pork with turnip tops), *caldo gallego* (cabbage soup), and *empanadas* (pasties filled with fish or meat and sold by the slice — individual ones are called *empanadillas*). A typically *gallego* tradition is the *churrasco* or barbeque — if you order a *churrasco* it will probably be a large pork chop. In Padrón and surrounding area, look out for the tiny green peppers stewed in olive oil known as *pimientos de Padrón*. The attraction is that *unos pican, otros no* — some are hot and some are not — you can't tell until you taste them!

Galician vines, like those over the border in the *vinho verde* region of Portugal, are trained high above the ground on trellises to prevent contact with the often wet ground. A wide range of wines is produced for local consumption — mostly much more demanding on the palate than *vinho verde* — including some fizzy, yeasty white wines, traditionally served straight from the barrel in white cups, and some rather acidic reds.

There are also some excellent denominated wines which are among the best in Spain. Ribeiro wines from the area around the town of Ribadavia are the most famous: the whites are pale, dry and sometimes slightly *pétillant*, and the reds are sharp and flinty. The Valdeorras region produces some pleasant, fresh tasting whites, while the Albariño wines come from a specific *bodega* — Fefiñanes in Cambados. These wines are highly prized and produced in very small quantities, with the result that they are rather expensive.

## OPPORTUNITIES IN GALICIA

Galicia's long-standing unemployment problem is far from resolved, and if you're looking for work you will also have to compete with children of returned emigrants from England for jobs requiring English. Unless you have some special interest in Galicia, or your work is linked to shipbuilding, the naval industry or the sea, you would be better off concentrating your efforts on finding employment in some other, more economically favoured region.

For universities per square kilometre, Galicia is badly served: it only has one, at Santiago, but this is more than made up for by the fact that it is a large, ancient and prestigious institution, so study possibilities are reasonably good.

Touring, cycling, hiking, beachcombing, are favoured activities in the region as far as leisure goes. There are good sports facilities in the La Coruña and *rías bajas* areas. La Coruña, and Vigo are sizeable cities, with all sorts of leisure activities going on. Santiago is more culturally orientated, while Pontevedra, Orense and Lugo are big enough to offer all the basic facilities.

## WHAT TO DO

## ARCHAEOLOGY

Regional archaeological remains from 2000 BC to 300 AD are preserved at **La Guardia**, at the mouth of the Miño river looking out towards Portugal. They include semicircular huts, ceramics and prehistoric paintings.

## ART GALLERIES AND MUSEUMS

**La Coruña**
**Museo Histórico-Arqueológico,** Castillo de San Antón
**Museo de Bellas Artes,** Panaderas s/n

**Santiago**
**Museo de Peregrinaciones,** San Miguel 4, Museum of the Pilgrimage to Santiago. See also an important **Tapestry Museum** inside the cathedral.

**Lugo**
**Museo de Lugo,** Pza de la Soledad 6

**Orense**
**Museo Arqueológico,** c/ Obispo Carrascosa 1

## BULLFIGHTS

Not an important part of this region's culture, but nonetheless you'll find them laid on at summer fiestas.

## CINEMA

There's an **international film week** towards the middle of September in **Lugo**, and the **Cine-Club Carballino** in **Orense** run a good programme of films, including a video week at the beginning of August.

## COURSES

Spanish language courses are organised by the **University of Santiago** in July, August and September. Minimum age 16. No prior knowledge of Spanish required. Also a year long course from October to May for people with some prior knowledge of Spanish only. Contact: Secretaría de los Cursos para Extranjeros, Facultad de Filología, Universidad de Santiago de Compostela, Pza de Mazarelos, Santiago de Compostela (tel. 981–580011, ex. 45).

  **INICE** (Instituto de Investigaciones Científicas y Ecológicas) organises summer courses in a variety of fields, varying from year to year, based at the **Gandario-Sada Youth Hostel** outside **La Coruña**, which has very good sports and other facilities. Subjects range from self-defence, biology and photography to deep-sea diving. Obviously you would need to speak some Spanish. Contact INICE at their head office in Salamanca: c/ Concejo 9–3 izq.

(See also section on Music below for an **international music course** held at **Santiago University**).

## CRAFTS

**Pottery,** both decorative and functional, traditional and modern is made in Galicia, as in most other regions of Spain. The most famous is the **Sargedelos pottery**, from the village of that name near Cervo on the Lugo coast.

Santiago is traditionally a city of **silversmiths**, and you will also see on sale enormous **copper pans** — 'for octopus or jam'.

**Lacemaking** is still a popular craft, and is said to have been introduced by sixteenth-century Irish immigrants. **Camariñas** (near Finisterre) is *the* lace-producing village, where the lace-makers are called *palilleiras*.

## FIESTAS

Many Galician fiestas have to do with 'exalting' the produce of the land and the sea. For example in **Ribadavia** at the end of April there is a fiesta in honour of the Ribeiro wine produced in the region, with free tastings, music and dancing, and plenty of local goodies to eat.

The Albariño wine festival in **Cambados** takes place on the first Sunday in August, and in **El Grove** there is a shellfish festival, normally on the second Sunday in October, again, with music and dancing. An octopus festival takes place in **Carballino** (Orense) on the second Sunday in August.

Another typical Gallician fiesta is **A Rapa das Bestas**, of ancient origin involving local males going off into the mountains at dawn and capturing numbers of wild horses which are brought down into the village to undergo various rituals such as branding, or having their manes and tails cut before they are finally released into the wild. Fiestas of this type take place at **San Lorenzo de Sabucedo-La Estrada**, in Pontevedra province, and at **Vivero**, on the Lugo coast, on the first weekend in July.

Most fiestas in Galicia are held during the summer, as the weather at other times of the year is bad. If you are there then you'll find fiestas in villages and towns everywhere, mostly involving parades in regional dress, bagpipes, and the dancing of *muñeiras* — colourful, somewhat jerky country dances.

## FINE ART

Every August there's an **art festival** in **Pontevedra**, organised by the provincial authorities and held in the **Palacio-Museo Provincial**. Information from **Diputación Provincial**, Avda Montero Ríos s/n, 36001 Pontevedra.

See also the **Finis Terrae gallery** in **La Coruña** (c/ Juan Canalejo 39, bajo) and the **Novecento gallery** in **Santiago** (Rua Nueva 30).

## HIKING

The north coast is lovely country for **hiking**, although you may find you've taken all day to get to the other side of the *ría*. There's not much traffic, even on the main roads, and villages are nicely spaced. In the interior, don't strike off into the unknown with no supplies; villages can be thin on the ground, and offer few facilities.

It would be interesting to try **walking** a section of the **Camino de Santiago**. In some places the modern road follows the route almost exactly (although near **Puertomarín** the old village of **Belesar**, through which the pilgrims passed, has been submerged by a reservoir). All you really need are good maps (see p. 17 earlier) and good shoes. The tourist offices can supply you with useful information — in English — about the route the pilgrims took.

For hiking combined with **birdwatching** or **wildlife spotting**, go to the **Sierra de Ancares** — see section on Wildlife below.

## LOCAL PRESS

*La Voz de Galicia*
*El Ideal Gallego*

## MUSIC

There is an **international course on Spanish music** which takes place every year in August at the **University of Santiago**. Apply before May to Secretaría de 'Música en Compostela', Pablo Aranda 6, 28006 Madrid.

Towards the end of July each year there is often a **Festival of Celtic Music** near the remote village of **Ortigueira** on the north coast. Take your pan pipes and a tent!

## SHOPPING

Look out for **lace** and **pottery**, and take home some **Albariño** or **Ribeiro wine**. It is possible to find it in the UK, but it's a rarity, as they say it doesn't travel. You might like to take home some **jet** from **Santiago**, as the medieval pilgrims did.

For **non-regional products, Vigo** and **La Coruña** are the best shopping centres, and **La Coruña** has an **open air antiques/craft market** in the **Plaza de María Pita** on Sunday mornings.

The wholesale **fish markets** in **La Coruña** and **Berbes de Vigo** are worth visiting for the experience, even if you've no intention of buying 10 kilos of conger eel. Get up really early, and be prepared for an assault on all your senses: it's noisy, smelly and you've never even heard of half of the varieties of fish being auctioned off to be shipped all over the world.

## SPORTS

**La Coruña** has a big sports complex near the **Torre de Hércules**, and the two **youth hostels** between **Sada** and **Gandario** have excellent sports facilities (ice rink, swimming pools, water sports, indoor sports hall and the like).

There's a ski-station with all the facilities including hire of equipment at **Cabeza de Manzaneda**, in the extreme south-east of the region, accessible from Orense. It's worth a visit in summer too, as there's good hiking and facilities for other activities such as horseriding and tennis. On the Leonese border there's a smaller ski-station at **Peña Trevinca**. The **Galician Winter Sports Federation** is based at Habana 105–5º, Orense (tel. 988–22891), in case you want to contact them.

There is fishing both in the many rivers, and off the coast. The provincial offices of **ICONA**, where you should apply for a licence are:

- **La Coruña:** Linares Rivas 30–8º (tel. 981–226949)
- **Lugo:** Ronda General Primo de Rivera 38 (tel. 982–216152)
- **Orense:** Calvo Sotelo 20–5º (tel. 981–212624)
- **Pontevedra:** Michelena 1 (tel. 986–851754)

See also the courses of a sporting nature organised by the **INICE**.

## UNIVERSITIES

**Universidad de Santiago,** Pza de Obradoiro s/n, Santiago de Compostela (tel. 981–581329).

## WILDLIFE

The **Ancares Park**, in the **Sierra de Ancares** near **Lugo**, is a fantastic area for wildlife such as deer and wild boar — if they're not being shot at by Spanish 'wildlife' enthusiasts.

## USEFUL ADDRESSES

**Tourist offices**
**La Coruña:** Dársena de la Marina s/n
**Santiago de Compostela.** Rúa del Villar 43
**Lugo:** Plaza de la Soledad 15
**Orense:** Curros Enríquez 1
**Pontevedra:** General Mola 1, bajo
**Vigo:** Jardines de Elduayen

**Government offices**
**Regional Government** (Junta de Galicia), Palacio de Rajoy, Santiago de Compostela (tel. 981–580033)
**Youth/Sport Department** (Consejería de Turismo, Juventud y Deportes de la Junta de Galicia), Pza de Pontevedra 22, La Coruña

**Education Department** (Consejería de Educación de la Junta de Galicia), Pza Vigo 2, Santiago de Compostela

**Labour departments**
**La Coruña:** Emilio Pardo Bazán 27
**Lugo:** Ronda da Moralla 58
**Orense:** Parque de San Lázaro 14
**Pontevedra:** Avda de Cánovas de Castillo 18, Vigo
Also:
**Centro de Orientación e Información del Empleo** (university careers office), Ciudad Universitaria, Santiago.

**Youth information offices**
**La Coruña:** Durán Lóriga 9–2º
**Orense:** Avda de La Habana 205–3º
**Pontevedra:** Benito Corbat 47–1º
**Vigo:** García Barbo 12 bajos

**TIVE offices**
**Santiago:** Rúa del Villar 35
**Vigo:** García Barbón, 12, bajo

**Travel agents**
**Viajes Ecuador,** Juana de Vega 10, La Coruña (tel. 981–220926)
**Viajes Wagon Lits,** Avda de la Marina 35, La Coruña (tel. 981–222884)

**Car hire**
**Atesa,** Ramón de la Sagra 22, La Coruña
**Hertz,** Estación Ferrocarril, La Coruña

**British representation**
**British Consulate:** Pza de Compostela 23–6, Apartado 49, Vigo (tel. 986–417133)
**British schools** — none.

**Language schools (TEFL)**
Lugo:
**Centro Audiovisual de Idiomas,** Pza Comandante Manso 11 (tel. 982–220374)
Vigo:
**Centro Internacional de Aplicación Lingüística,** Montero Ríos 22–1 (tel. 986–224342)
**The English Institute,** Gran Vía 54 (and also Marqués de Valladares 17) (tel. 986–411878 and 226745)

# 13 Madrid

Madrid was just a small Castilian town which happened to be in the geographic centre of Spain until 1561, when Felipe II transferred his court there from Valladolid, in an action typical of the Spanish preference for symbolic significance over practicality. Even after becoming the capital of what was a highly centralised, powerful and bureaucratic state, it remained something of a backwater for centuries.

One of the most dramatic events in Madrid's history took place on 2nd May 1808, when its population took to the streets in a violent and bloody uprising against Joseph Bonaparte. The sufferings of Madrileños at the hands of French troops are vividly depicted in Goya's paintings *El Dos de Mayo* and *El Tres de Mayo*, on display in the Prado Museum.

In the early part of this century, Madrid was the scene of a cultural revival in Spain, when the so-called *Generación del 98* (a group of writers and thinkers determined to improve Spain's standing and self-respect after the shock loss of Cuba, the last colony, in 1898), conducted their *tertulias* (sort of intellectual coffee-breaks) in Madrid cafés like the Café León — still in business today. Among these the novelist Galdós based much of his work on his observations of life and society in Madrid at the time. In the 20s Salvador Dalí, the poet Federico García Lorca, and (later to be) film director Luis Buñuel were all students at Madrid University. A fascinating and uproarious account of their exploits is to be found in Buñuel's autobiography *My Last Breath*, which really brings out the contrast between modern ideas in a traditional setting that is still part of the attraction of Madrid today.

During the Civil War the people of Madrid once more took to the streets in defence of their city, and successfully held out for over two years against Franco's troops besieging it, after the Republican government had fled in terror to Valencia.

The highly centralised nature of the Franco régime, combined with the dramatic economic growth of the 50s and 60s, made Madrid the grand and rich city it is today — at the expense of the impoverished and depopulated rural areas of Spain. Today the *Comunidad de Madrid* extends beyond the — still fairly well delimited — city area as far as the Guadarrama mountains to the north and taking in attractive towns to the south and east such as Aranjuéz, Chinchón and Alcalá de Henares. It houses the seat of Government (the *Cortes*), the Bank of Spain, and the impressive Royal Palace, and is still managing to hold economic and political sway over the rest of Spain today, despite devolution.

Madrid culture is basically Castilian, enlivened by all the sights and sounds of a big city: bustling crowds, bright lights, the tooting of car horns, and also by the fact that it is in many ways a melting-pot for many other regional cultures of Spain. Its major period of expansion was in the last three decades, and most older people are not native Madrileños. You'll come across quaint throwbacks to rural origins in combination with the hardness and sharpness typical of Latin urban culture — shops with sacks of beans and *chorizo* from the *pueblo* just round the corner from up-front designer boutiques.

At over 2,000 feet above sea level, Madrid has beautiful clear mountain air most of the time; you do get the occasional day when the air pollution is very bad. The sun is bright and the sky blue, even in winter, when temperatures can be quite nippy, and the surrounding mountains are snow-covered. Rain tends to take the form of occasional torrential storms, sometimes causing quite severe flooding.

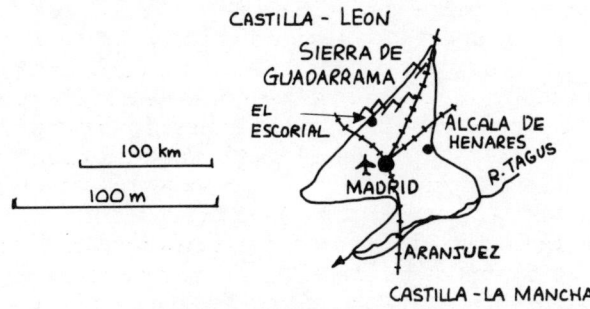

Madrid is a fascinating place to visit — and would make a great place to live — but don't go expecting all the sights and monuments of a major European capital: you will be disappointed. Spanish people may love their Telephone Building and the Monument to Cervantes, but you are unlikely to feel the same emotional pull. Perhaps the best way to appreciate its charm is just sitting at a pavement café in the bright November sunshine. . .

## WHAT TO SEE

Madrid can be best appreciated by simple street wandering, so don't waste too much time organising specific sight-seeing trips. Here, however, are some of the major places to make for.

### Madrid
**The Austrian Quarter** (Barrio de los Austrias). The Plaza Mayor and the older streets adjoining it were built when Spain was under Hapsburg rule: the capital of a huge empire taking in most of Latin America and a large part of Europe. The Plaza Mayor is especially evocative of the past, with its arched gateways leading on to the enclosed square, once the scene of *autos de fe*, early bullfights, proclamations and canonisations.

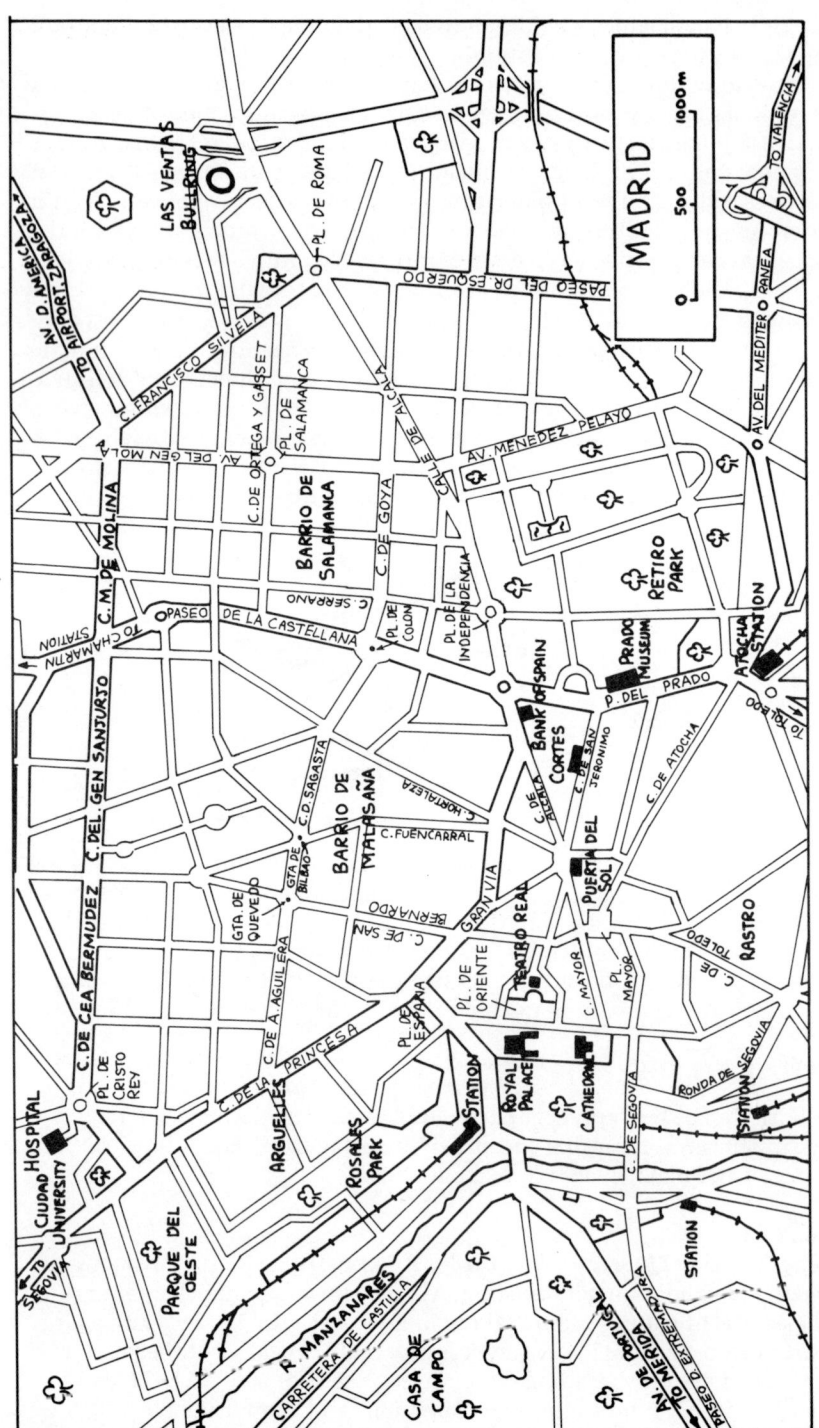

**Malasaña.** This is the tangle of streets to the south of the c/ Carranza and c/ de Sagasta where Madrid youth hangs out. Loud and lively, especially after dark.
**Barrio de Salamanca.** North of the Retiro Park, the grid of streets leading down to Recoletos and the Castellana is the stamping ground of Madrid's 'Sloanes', full of exclusive boutiques and trendy bars and clubs.
**Arguelles** (between Arguelles and Moncloa Metros). Busy student quarter, full of interest.
**Prado Museum** and **Royal Palace** — see Art Galleries and Museums on p. 208.
**Retiro Park** and **Casa de Campo** — see Parks and Gardens on p. 214.
**Rastro.** See Shopping on p. 214.

### Out of town
**Alcalá de Henares.** Small town with beautiful old university buildings. Birthplace of Cervantes.
**Aranjuez.** Madrid's (mini) Versailles: parks, gardens and palace on the river Tagus.
**Chinchón.** Where the famous *anís de Chinchón* is made (aniseed liqueur in *dulce* or *seco* varieties). Pretty country town/village and a favourite destination for young Madrileños wanting to get out of the hubbub of the city. Church, Plaza Mayor, country strolls and visits to the *anís* factory.
**El Escorial.** Felipe II's dour but incredibly impressive monastery cum palace, built by Herrera at the time of the Spanish Armada. The mausoleum contains the remains of practically all Spanish monarchs since.
**Valle de los Caídos.** Franco's tomb and monument to the Civil War dead (the ones that fought on his side). A massive mausoleum carved out of the mountain side (in the exact geographical centre of Spain) by political prisoners, marked by a huge cross which is visible for miles around. The ceiling is decorated with pictures of saints and angels welcoming Falangist leaders into heaven(!). Worth a visit if only to boggle at the ugliness and totalitarian monumentality of the whole thing.
**Sierra de Guadarrama.** More and more Madrileños are spending their free time up in the *sierra*, especially in the summer months when the harsh mountain peaks are free of snow and ice and burst into green life — a welcome change from the sweltering city below. The mountain villages are without exception clean and pleasant and generally offer good facilities.

## COMING AND GOING

### By air
It's sensible to travel to Madrid by air: you can get some good deals and it's only 1½ to 2 hours travelling time from Britain. Barajas airport is a joy after the crush of Heathrow or Gatwick, and there is a bus link into the city (10 miles) which takes you to the subterranean coach station beneath the Plaza Colón, right in the centre.

### By road
Be warned if you're travelling overland, Madrid, stuck on Spain's central *Meseta*, will take perhaps a full day's journey from any of the frontiers. Nonetheless, land communications in Spain radiate out from Madrid, and plenty of options exist, even if they are slow.

Roads radiate from Madrid towards the other major cities of Spain, although not always in straight lines, as there are major mountain ranges in almost every direction. Also, the motorway you left Madrid by has a nasty habit of petering out as you leave civilisation . . .

If you're travelling *from* Madrid, you might like to contact **A Dedo** (c/Mayor 1, oficina 21, Madrid 13 (tel. 91–231 7519) ), an agency which puts drivers in touch with potential passengers, so they can share petrol.

### By train
Trains from the north and Europe arrive at the big modern Chamartín Station, in the north of the city. The older and more central Atocha Station serves Andalucía and the south, and also Portugal. Both stations link in with the *metro* network (see below).

### By coach
The main coach station is the Estación Sur de Autobuses, away to the south of the city near Palos de Moguer Metro. There's a direct service from London, and a comprehensive network around Spain.

### Within Madrid
Madrid's a big city, but not impossibly so, and with the aid of short bus or metro hops it's very easy to get around. The main arteries of the city lead to recognisable landmarks, and these are the routes along which both metros and buses tend to run. The *metro* is cheap and efficient, if a bit dirty and uncomfortable, with no great distances between stops. As well as normal buses there is also a microbus service (yellow minibuses) which is a bit more expensive, but more comfortable and often slightly quicker. Taxis are very cheap compared to London, and almost always available.

### Packages
**Travelscene** and **Mundi Color** are among the companies which offer package tours to Madrid.

## WHERE TO STAY

Providing you're not thinking of actually buying a flat (house prices in Madrid are currently rocketing), you shouldn't have much trouble finding anywhere to stay at any time of the year. There are literally hundreds of cheap **pensions** and **hostales**: look in the back streets off the Gran Vía, or Carrera de San Jerónimo.

There are two **youth hostels** in Madrid itself: one at c/ Sta Cruz Marcenado 28 and the other in the Casa de Campo (Lago Metro). The Youth Hostels Reservations Office is at c/ Sagasta 13 (5th and 6th floors) (tel. 911–445 0800 and 445 8847). There are also youth hostels in the mountains to the north and east of Madrid.

The **monastery of El Paular** offers hospitality to visitors (men only). Its telephone number is 91–869 3141.

## WHAT TO EAT AND DRINK

Madrid cuisine is basically Castilian (see Castilla-León), but there are some typically *madrileño* dishes, such as *cocido madrileño*, made out of chick peas, meats and sausage, with the juice served separately as a soup course. *Madrilène*, or *consomé* as it is known in Spain, is of course famous throughout the world. Another typical dish is *callos a la madrileña* — tripe with onions, tomatoes, garlic and paprika.

There are also restaurants in Madrid offering the best of all the regional cuisines, especially Basque and Andalusian. You'll also find the odd Asturian *chigre*, and plenty of *mesones* run by Galicians. In addition to this of course, there are restaurants specialising in all varieties of international cuisines, from Chinese to Argentinian, and *pizzerías*, *crêperies*, ice cream parlours, hamburger joints, vegetarian restaurants . . . the list is endless.

As far as drinks go, there's a local wine called Sierra de Gredos, and of course *anís de chinchón* (see above), but as with food, Madrid brings together a comprehensive range of what is available in the different regions of Spain, as well as all the internationally known varieties.

## OPPORTUNITIES IN MADRID

If opportunities for work exist for you at all in Spain, they must surely do so in Madrid, with its feverish activity in commercial, financial and industrial fields. Most British companies with representations in Spain have their offices here, and there are a large number of Spanish and multinational companies, cultural or scientific organisations which have links with Britain and the US, and an Anglo-American Hospital, which may all require the services of English-speaking staff. Teaching is an area especially in which, with the right qualifications, you could easily find work.

Madrid has two large universities, a Polytechnic university, a further university at Alcalá de Henares, 20 miles out of town, as well as some of the best libraries in Spain, so study possibilities are good too.

For leisure time, Madrid has all the space and opportunities of a large city: shops and sports facilities, museums and parks, and bars, restaurants, clubs and nightlife to suit every taste — without spending a fortune. Don't think the nightlife just consists of the 'flamenco clubs' or discos of the package tour *costas* either: there are good theatres and cinemas, and live music of all varieties (see listings).

Some of Spain's best known sights are within easy reach of Madrid for a day's outing: towns like Toledo, Segovia and Avila (see section on Castilla-León), as well as attractions within the Madrid region (see below) such as Aranjuez and El Escorial.

## WHAT TO DO

*El País* carries a good deal of information about what's on in Madrid on a day-to-day basis, and for weekly listings, you should buy the small format magazine *Guía del Ocio*, on sale in kiosks.

### ART GALLERIES AND MUSEUMS

**In Madrid**
Here is a selection of some of the most interesting:

**The Prado.** One of the foremost art collections in the world: you could spend a whole week here. As well as some of the best paintings by classic Spanish artists (Goya, Velázquez, Murillo, El Greco, etc), other works you shouldn't miss are those by Rubens, Van Dyck, Titian and Hieronymus Bosch's *Garden of Earthly Delights*. There is also a sculpture section, and collections of coins, and gold and silver work. Located in the Paseo del Prado and open every day except Mondays and Sunday afternoons. Admission free with student card.

In the nearby **Casón del Buen Retiro**, which houses Spanish nineteenth century art, Picasso's *Guernica* is now on display — under strict security. Again, closed on Mondays and Sunday afternoons.

**Contemporary Art Museum,** Avda Juan de Herrera 2 (by the university). The permanent collection is rather dull, but there are frequently some interesting temporary exhibitions.

**Open Air Sculpture Museum,** Paseo de la Castellana, under the Eduardo Dato/Juan Bravo bridge.

**Lázaro Galdiano Museum,** c/ Serrano 122. Large collection of Spanish, early Flemish, Italian, French and English paintings. Open 1000–1400, Tuesdays to Sundays, and closed during August.

**Sorolla Museum,** General Martínez Campos 34. House and works of the Valencian impressionist Joaquín Sorolla. Open 1000–1400 except Mondays.

**Royal Palace,** Plaza de Oriente. Said (by the Spanish) to be one of the best palaces in Europe, its collections of Flemish tapestries, Rococco furniture, Sèvres and Saxony porcelain, paintings and other works of art are certainly impressive. There is also an Armoury, and Museum of Carriages. Times of opening: Summer: 1000–1330 and 1600–1815; Winter: 1000–1245 and 1530–1645; Sundays and fiestas, mornings only.

**The Convent of Las Descalzas Reales,** Plaza de las Descalzas Reales. Rich collection of tapestries and paintings. Open every day except Friday, Saturday and Sunday afternoons.

**Real Fábrica de Tápices,** Fuenterrabia 2. Royal Tapestry Factory where you can watch tapestries being made, some still to Goya's designs. Open Monday to Saturday, mornings only, and closed during August.

**Waxwork Museum,** Paseo de Recoletos 41. Open daily.

**Archaeological Museum,** Serrano 13. Open mornings only.

For details of temporary exhibitions — see *Guía del Ocio*.

## Out of town

**Alcalá de Henares.** Cervantes' house, c/ Mayor 48. Open afternoons only.
**Aranjuez.** Royal Palace, Jardín de la Isla. Open every day.
**El Escorial.** The monastery (see What to See above) is open 1000–1300 and 1500–1900 daily. The art collection, library, mausoleum, chapter houses, and royal lodges are all included on the entrance ticket.

## BULLFIGHTS

Madrid's main bullring is at **Las Ventas**, to the east of the centre, and there is a smaller one at **Vista Alegre**, a suburb in the south-west of the city. There are *corridas* from early spring through till the autumn, the most important being during Madrid's **San Isidro** festivities in May. (see below) Tickets in advance from the bullring, or from booth in c/ Preciados.

## CHILDREN'S ENTERTAINMENT

There is a **zoo** and permanent fairground in the **Casa de Campo** (Batán Metro). The zoo is open daily, and not prohibitively expensive. The fairground is closed on Mondays.

There is also a **Safari Park** 15 or so miles out to the west at **Aldea de Fresno**, again with its own fairground, plus minigolf, swimming pool, horseriding, and a whole host of other facilities. Closed Mondays.

**Playparks** can be found throughout the city. (See also sections on Parks and Gardens, and Sports below.)

## CINEMA

For cinema listings, see *Guía del Ocio* or papers. For films in English look for 'VO' (*versión original*). Tickets are relatively cheap, and there is always a wide range of films showing.

Madrid's official **Film Theatre** (*Filmoteca*) is at c/Princesa 1, and their office address is Filmoteca Española, Carretera Dehesa de la Villa s/n, 28040 Madrid (tel. 91–449 0011).

The **Federation of Spanish Film Clubs** is based in Madrid, at Paseo de la Castellana 210, 5–9, 28046 Madrid (tel. 91–458 1238).

The **Festival International de Cine de Madrid (IMAGFIC)**, with prizes in various categories, takes place every year the week before Holy Week (i.e. two weeks before Easter). For information contact: DICREFILM, Gran Vía 62, 8º–izq, 28013 Madrid (tel. 91–241 5545).

**Alcalá de Henares** also has its own **Film Festival** at the end of April/beginning of May, again with prizes in various categories. Contact **Cine-Club Nebrija**, Plaza de Atilano Casado 2, Alcalá de Henares (tel. 91–881 0297). Again at Alcalá de Henares, there is an **Ecological Film Festival** towards the end of May. Contact: Grupo GUEFILOS, Pza de la Juventud, Alcalá de Henares, or Fundación Colegio del Rey, Libreros 15, Alcalá de Henares (tel. 91–881 3934).

## COURSES

**Public-sector courses**
The following state-run Spanish language courses are at present on offer in Madrid:

- **Escuela Oficial de Idiomas,** Departamento de Español para Extranjeros, c/Jesús Maestro s/n, 28003 Madrid. 6 week summer courses from mid-June to end-July. Beginners, intermediate and advanced levels. Mostly language work, with an increased cultural content at the higher levels. Accommodation in *Colegios Mayores*. There are also 4 month courses available, which run from October to February, or February through to June.
- **Facultad de Filosofía y Letras,** Secretaría de los Cursos para Extranjeros, Universidad Complutense, Ciudad Universitaria, 28040 Madrid (tel. 91–243 3448). A year-long very comprehensive course in *Estudios Hispánicos*, including language, literature, history, art, geography, and history of ideas, as well as visits and excursions to places of interest. There is also the option of taking just a term (October – December, January – March or April – June), or just a month or 2 week course over the summer.

**Private-sector courses**
In the private sector, choose from the following:

- **Nueva Escuela,** Pedro Muguruza 1, 28036 Madrid. A school specialising in the audio-visual method, courses all the year round, commencing on the first day of each month.
- **Centro de Idiomas Sagasta,** Sagasta 27, 28004 Madrid. Courses in Spanish for Business Purposes, certified by the Madrid and London Chambers of Commerce. Three-month courses from June – September, October – December or January – March.
- **Estudio Internacional Sampere,** Castelló 50, 28001 Madrid (tel. 91–275 4025). Courses in Spanish language and civilization run throughout the year, max. nine students per group.
- **International House,** Zurbano 8, 28010 Madrid (tel. 91–410 1314). Flexible courses for six different levels of ability throughout the year, emphasising communicative competence.
- **EASO,** Gran Vía 64–7º and 8º, 28013 Madrid (tel. 91–242 3183). 'Immersion' courses for all levels of ability lasting upwards of a week (July and August only) with accommodation in special student residences if required.
- **Centro Cooperativo de Idiomas,** Gran Vía 64–1º D, 28013 Madrid (tel. 91–241 3902). Summer courses for 1, 3 or 4 weeks in July and August with an emphasis on activities involving Spanish people, designed for people who need to learn Spanish but have little time available to spend in Spain. Accommodation provided.
- **Fundación Ponce de León,** Lagasca 16, 28001 Madrid. A variety of Spanish language and culture classes throughout the year — no previous

knowledge required. Also courses in subjects such as contemporary Spanish society and politics, literature, history, etc., lasting 6 weeks and available between September and April.
- **Linguacenter,** c/Caracas 10–1º–D, 28010 Madrid (tel. 91–419 1616). Month-long courses starting at the beginning of each month throughout the year. Anyone over 16 accepted, no previous knowledge of Spanish required.
- **Centros de Estudios Hispánicos,** Antonio de Nebrija, Zurbano 41, 28010 Madrid (tel. 91–419 5972). Three-month courses throughout the year. Also 3-week summer courses.
- **Language Studies SA,** Luchana 31, 28010 Madrid (tel. 91–446 2299). Four-week courses throughout the year, either part-time (3½ hours daily) or full-time (5 hours daily).
- **Washington Institute,** Juan Hurtado de Mendoza 11, 28036 Madrid (tel. 91–250 1858). Month-long courses from March to September, catering for six different levels of ability.
- **Dinámica,** Francisco Silvela 21, 28005 Madrid (tel. 91–401 7522; telex: 23955 DADI-E). Courses run throughout the year. Emphasis on grammar and textual analysis. Max. five students per group.
- **Inlingua Idiomas,** Arenal 24, 28013 Madrid. Wide range of courses throughout the year. Again, emphasis on grammar. Small groups.
- **Institutos Mangold,** Gran Vía 32–2, 28013 Madrid (tel. 91–222 3800). A range of courses at different levels throughout the year (see *Eurocentre* below).
- **Iberlengua,** Avda Alfonso XIII, 122, 28016 Madrid (tel. 91–250 7297). Spanish language and culture course for students with a good basic knowledge of Spanish, lasting from January to June. Also intensive one-month language courses starting on the first day of each month.

## Package deals

If you'd prefer to buy an all-in package including travel, accommodation and language tuition (see p.44 earlier) you can do so through the following agencies:

- **EuroAcademy Outbound,** 77a George St, Croydon, CR0 1LD (tel. 01–686 2363). 'Crash courses' available all the year round, starting any Monday, minimum 1 week.
- **Eurocentre** courses bookable through **STA Travel,** 74 Old Brompton Rd, London SW7 (tel. 01–581 1022). 4 or 12 week courses available.
- **Youth Travels,** 117 Wendell Rd, London W12 9SD (tel. 01–743 7966). Courses all the year round for all levels, including courses for interpreters, translators, and teachers of Spanish.

## Other courses

- Weekend courses in Astronomy, organised by **Consejería de Educación y Juventud de la Comunidad de Madrid,** Sagasta 13, 28004 Madrid (tel. 91–447 0800).
- Courses in video-making techniques, organised by **Centro de Estudios**

de Animación y Promoción Sociocultural, c/ San Bartolomé 7–2º, 28005 Madrid (tel. 91–231 6354).

## FIESTAS

Not a region which is particularly rich in traditional fiestas — there's too much else going on. San Isidro is the patron saint of Madrid, and the local authorities and groups of individuals organise a whole range of entertainments, lasting a week or more in mid-May. These include cultural events, bullfights, and jamborees in the Casa de Campo — greasy-pole climbing and the like! Summer — especially August — is the time to catch fiestas in the mountain villages of the *Sierra*.

## HIKING

There is good hiking in the **Sierra de Gredos** and the **Sierra de Guadarrama** — see section on Castilla-León.

## LIBRARIES

The National Library is located in Madrid, as well as four other important libraries:

**Biblioteca Nacional,** Paseo de Recoletos 20
**Biblioteca Municipal,** c/ Fuencarral 78
**El Ateneo,** c/ del Prado 21
**Biblioteca Real,** Palacio Real

## LOCAL PRESS

National papers
*Guía del Ocio*

## MUSIC

**Key information**
- **Instituto Nacional de Artes Escénicas y de la Música,** Ministerio de Cultura, Pza del Rey 1, Madrid (tel. 91–229 8216). This office can supply full details of performances of opera, ballet, jazz, flamenco, *zarzuela*, etc.

**Classical**
The big venue for classical music and opera is the beautiful nineteenth-century **Teatro Real**, in the Plaza de Oriente. Concerts are given by the **National Orchestra** on Fridays and Sundays, and the **Spanish Radio and Television Orchestra** also puts on weekly performances. In summer there are sometimes **open air concerts** of classical music in the Plaza Mayor.

## Flamenco

The above department will give you information about flamenco performances, especially those in the **Teatro Alcázar** which take place as part of a **National Flamenco Season** during the second half of April. Apart from this, there are authentic flamenco *tablaos* at the following venues:

- **Arco de Cuchilleros,** Arco de Cuchilleros 7 (off the Plaza Mayor)
- **Café de Chinitas,** c/Torrija 7 (Santo Domingo Metro)
- **Los Canasteros,** c/ Barbieri 10 (Chueca)
- **Corral de la Morería,** c/Morería 17 (La Latina)
- **Corral de la Pacheca,** c/ Juan Ramón Jiménez 26
- **Torres Bermejas,** c/Mesonero Romanos 11 (Callao).

They usually open about 2000 and continue until the early hours. Check the entrance fee doesn't include dinner if you've already eaten.

The local authorities organise flamenco evenings every Thursday from 2030 onwards at **Puerta Real**, c/Arrieta 7, Madrid.

## Jazz

There is a **jazz festival** in Madrid every November, the main venue being the **Teatro Alcalá**. Again, get in touch with the Department of the Ministry of Culture indicated above for full details of programmes.

The *Guía del Ocio* will give you up to date information on **jazz clubs** and **jazz bars** operating in the city. Look out for:

- **Clamores,** c/Albuquerque 14 (Bilbao Metro)
- **Whisky Jazz Club,** c/Diego de León 7 (Nuñez de Balboa)

## Latin American

Such venues come and go, and again check on the spot, but look out for:

- **Barrio Latino 2,** c/ Tetuan 27 (Sol Metro)
- **Baranquilla,** c/ Marqués de Villamejor 8 (Ruben Darío)

## Rock

There are any number of bars and clubs with live or recorded music, especially around the **Plaza Dos de Mayo** in the **Malasaña** district.

## Zarzuela

*Zarzuela* is a colourful, very typically Spanish type of light opera — good entertainment even for non-Spanish speakers. The **National Zarzuela Theatre** is at c/Jovellanos 4, and it is very well worth while checking out their programme.

## NIGHTLIFE

As well as music, theatre and cinema, dealt with under other headings, there are any number of specialist bars: video bars, disco bars, bars specialising in hamburgers, cocktails, exotic coffees, board games, floor shows, strip shows, gay bars, bingo, bier kellers . . . the list is endless and constantly changing as fashions come and go. You'll always find plenty of traditional *tascas* and *mesones* though, and these are here to stay. Try the following streets for a good selection: c/ de la Victoria, c/Espoz y Mina, c/Núñez de Arce, c/Echegaray, c/ de Postas, and the Plaza Mayor area.

There are also still a number of old fashioned cafés in existence, retaining something of their original ambience: the **Café Comercial** in Bilbao, the **Café Gijón** (Paseo de Recoletos) and the **Café León** (c/Alcalá). The best thing about night life in Madrid, though, is the fact that the streets themselves are animated until very late: you can wander about and take it all in, or sit outdoors on a *terraza* and just watch the street life.

## PARKS AND GARDENS

**Retiro Park.** Pretty in the spring when the flowers are out. Lake, with hire of rowing boats. Also hire of horse-drawn buggies.
**Botanical Gardens.** Entrance next to Prado Museum.
**Rosales** and **Parque del Oeste.**
**Casa de Campo.** Huge estate originally bought and re-forested by Felipe II, now a Sunday afternoon venue for all of Madrid. Access via funicular in the Paseo Rosales, or Batán Metro. Zoo, fairground, amusement park and boating lake.
Out of town — the **palace gardens at Aranjuez.**

## SHOPPING

In Madrid you'll find the best of Spain's handicrafts and manufactured goods on sale (see p. 34 earlier for best buys), as well as food produce, antiques, and, if you're so inclined, works of art.

For ordinary shopping there are many possibilities, mostly centred around the big department stores **El Corte Inglés** and **Galerías Preciados**, in the c/Princesa, c/Preciados del Carmen, and around Goya and Quevedo metro stations. Among the boutiques, or down a back street, you'll still find **traditional shops** selling *bacalao*, pottery or strings of garlic — and doing a roaring trade. One thing you'll notice is the number of *street sellers*, some even dodging the traffic to sell their wares to drivers through the car window.

For a real street market though, you mustn't miss the **Rastro** — at its height on Sunday mornings in the area round the Ribera de Curtidores, south of the Plaza Mayor. Much of what's on sale is just junk, but nonetheless it's greatly entertaining, and who knows, you might find just what you'd always been looking for — whether it's a silk scarf or an antique brass bedstead.

For real **antiques**, try some of the shops in the Rastro area during normal shopping hours, or those in the c/ del Prado, or Carrera de San Jerónimo.

Also on Sunday mornings, there is an open-air second-hand **book market** on the Cuesta de Moyano, and a **stamp and coin collectors market** under the arches in the Plaza Mayor.

If it's **food or wine** you're after, there is everything from tiny hole-in-the-wall shops to great hypermarkets like **Jumbo** in the Avda Pío XII, which is perhaps the most central. The selection of fresh fish and seafood is particularly remarkable, considering Madrid's distance from the coast.

## SPORTS

### Football
You can watch **Real Madrid** play in the **Bernabeu Stadium** (off the Plaza de Lima, at the far end of the Paseo de la Castellana), or **Atlético Madrid** at their ground, the **Estadio Vicente Calderón**.

### Skiing
There are three well-equipped ski-stations in the province, at **Valcotos**, **Valdesquí** and **Puerto de Navacerrada** in the **Guadarrama mountains**. You can make arrangements through a travel agency in Madrid or just turn up — equipment is available for hire.

The relevant sports federation in the region is the **Federación Castellana de Deportes de Invierno**, Ayala 44, Madrid 1 (tel. 91–226 6174).

### Swimming
Probably the only sporting activity you'll have the time or inclination for in Madrid, especially during the summer, is a dip in a pool. Here are some of the public baths:
**El Lago Pool,** Avda de Valladolid 37 (near the Puente de los Franceses)
the Casa del Campo Pool (Lago Metro)
**Piscina de La Elipa,** Avda de la Paz (special children's area, with organised activities during the summer holidays)
**Moratalaz Pool,** Encomienda de Palacios
**Piscina Playa Victoria** (off the c/ Bravo Murillo, Tetuan metro)
**Plaza de la Cebada Pool** (La Latina metro)
There is also a pool on the c/José Martínez Velasco (Sainz de Baranda metro), built for the 1986 world championships.

### Other facilities
Other sporting facilities include the **Palacio de los Deportes** in the c/Goya, and the **university sports halls**.

## THEATRE

(See also section on Music above.) The main theatres for classical Spanish drama are the **Teatro Español** (Plaza de Santa Ana) and the **Teatro María Guerrero** (c/ Tamayo y Baus 4). More modern productions tend to be staged at the **Centro Cultural de la Villa** (underneath the Plaza Colón) and the **Círculo de Bellas Artes** (Marqués de Casa Riera 2). The **Carlos III**

**Theatre** in **El Escorial** is one of the oldest in Europe, and it's worth checking out their programme too.

The best times of the year for theatre in Madrid are March, when there is an annual theatre festival organised by the Ministry of Culture, and July and August, when special productions are put on as part of the Los Veranos de la Villa entertainments organised by the City Council.

## UNIVERSITIES

**Universidad de Madrid-Complutense,** Ciudad Universitaria, Pabellón de Gobierno, 28003 Madrid
**Universidad de Madrid-Autónoma,** Carretera de Colmenar Viejo km 15, Madrid
**Universidad de Madrid-Politécnica,** c/ Ramiro de Maeztu s/n, 28003 Madrid
**Universidad de Madrid-Alcalá de Henares,** Carretera de Barcelona km 33, Madrid

## USEFUL ADDRESSES

**Tourist offices**
Barajas Airport
Maria de Molina 50
Torre de Madrid, Plaza de España

**Government offices**
**Regional Government** (Comunidad Autónoma de Madrid), c/Miguel Angel 25, 28010 Madrid (tel. 91–441 9222)
**Education Department:** c/Vitruvio 4, 28006 Madrid (tel. 91–411 4017)
**Labour Department:** Princesa 3 (tel. 91–248 9600)
**Youth/Sport Department** (Dirección General de Juventud), Consejería de Educación y Juventud, Sagasta 13, 28004 Madrid
**University Careers Offices** (Centros de Orientación e Información del Empleo)
**Universidad Complutense,** Escuela de Estomatología, Ciudad Universitaria, Madrid
**Universidad Autonoma,** Pabellón B, piso 1º, Cantoblanco, Madrid
**Universidad Politécnica,** Ramiro de Maeztu s/n, Madrid
**Universidad de Alcalá de Henares,** Facultad de Ciencias Económicas y Empresariales, Pza de la Victoria, Alcalá de Henares

**Youth information office**
**Centro de Información y Documentación Juvenil,** Sagasta 13, 28004 Madrid (tel. 91–445 0800)

**TIVE office**
Fernando el Católico 88, 28015 Madrid (tel. 91–449 6800)

## Travel agents
**Añosluz,** Carrera San Jerónimo 18–1º–C, 28014 Madrid (tel. 91–458 1534)
**Viajes Transalpino,** Plaza de España 9, 28008, Madrid (tel. 91–241 3478)
**Viajes Edelweis,** c/Serrano 63–2º–D, 28001 Madrid (tel. 91–431 7724)

## Car hire
**Atesa:**
— Madrid airport
— Capitán Haya 7 (tel. 91–455 4106)

## British representation
**British Embassy:** c/Fernando el Santo 16, 28004 Madrid (tel. 91–419 0200)
**British Chamber of Commerce:** c/Marqués de Valdeiglesias 3, 28003 Madrid (tel. 91–221 9622)
**British Council:** c/Almagro 5, 28004 Madrid (tel. 91–419 1250)

## British schools
**The British Council School,** Martínez Campos 31, 28010 Madrid (tel. 91–442 4300)
**Kings College,** Paseo de los Andes s/n, Urbanización Soto de Viñuelas, El Goloso, Carretera de Colmenar Viejo km 15, Madrid (tel. 91–803 4733)
**Runnymede College,** Arga 9, El Viso, Madrid (tel. 91–457 2327)
**St. Anne's School,** Pinar 22, 28006 Madrid (tel. 91–261 2717)
**Hastings School,** Paseo de la Habana 204, 28036 Madrid (tel. 91–259 0621)
**International Primary School,** Rosa Jardon 3, 28016, Madrid (tel. 91–259 2121)
**Numont PNEU School,** c/Parma 16, 28043, Madrid (tel. 91–200 2431)
**St. Michael's Prep School,** Camino Ancho 89, La Moraleja, Alcobendas, Madrid (tel. 91–650 2115)
**The English Montessori School,** Triana 65, 28016 Madrid (tel. 91–457 4222)
**Kensington School,** Avda de Bulares s/n, Urbanización los Alamos de Bulara, Pozuelo de Alarcón, 28023 Madrid (tel. 91–715 4797)
**Fairy Land,** Comandante Franco 6, 28016 Madrid (tel. 91–259 2321)

## American schools
**The American School of Madrid,** Apartado 80, Madrid (tel. 91–207 0641)
**Torrejón American High School,** Base Aérea de Torrejón, Torrejón de Ardoz, Madrid
**Hill House (American) Montessori School,** Avda Alfonso XIII 34, 28002 Madrid (tel. 91–416 0952)

## International schools
**International College Spain,** c/Vereda Norte 3, La Moraleja, Alcobendas, Madrid (tel. 91–650 2398)

**International Special School.** Study Center Foundation, Valentín Robledo 2, Pozuelo de Alarcón, Madrid (tel. 91-715 5138)

**Language schools (TEFL)**
There are about a hundred private English-teaching establishments in Madrid, and it would obviously be impossible to list them all here. The British Council in Madrid can supply you with a complete list. The best known are:

- **Berlitz Idiomas,** Gran Vía 80-4º, Madrid 13
- **International House,** c/ Zurbano 8, Madrid 4
- **Linguarama Ibérica SA,** c/Orense 34, Madrid 20
- **Nueva Escuela,** Pedro Muguruza 1, Madrid 16

# 14 Murcia

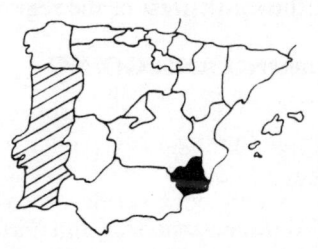

Murcia is a smallish coastal region in the south-east corner of Spain, forming with Valencia what is still known as the 'Levant'. In the fertile valley of the river Segura, which crosses the region, there is a *huerta* similar to Valencia's, with citrus groves, rice paddies, palms and cultivation of a rich variety of vegetables. Further north, around the towns of Jumilla and Yecla, there are extensive vineyards, while around the port of Cartagena there is mining (lead, iron and zinc), and a big oil refinery. Tourist development is mostly around the Mar Menor, a huge salt-water lagoon enclosed by a spit of sand, and at Mazarrón, but there's nothing on the scale seen just up the coast in Alicante province.

Although the region became part of Castile more than two centuries before neighbouring Andalucía, a large Arab population remained until the early part of the seventeenth century, when they were finally expelled. Murcian culture is therefore a mixture of Castilian and Arab elements, and the language too is Castilian with the odd dialect word or pronunciation derived from Arabic. There is no separate language as in Valencia.

A southern exuberance is definitely evident in the region, but somehow — and perhaps this is due to the sobering Castilian influence — Murcia seems overshadowed by the enormous vitality of its neighbours Valencia and Andalucía.

## WHAT TO SEE

**Murcia.** The capital of the one-province region, and a city of over a quarter of a million. A cluster of old streets expands out into a more modern area of wide avenues, producing quite an attractive — if rather stolid — city. The cathedral façade is acclaimed as one of the most brilliant examples of Spanish baroque, although the building itself incorporates a mixture of styles from *mudéjar* to churrigueresque.
**Cartagena.** An ancient settlement, which takes its name from the time it was under Carthaginian occupation. Now an important naval base, port and industrial centre.
**Cabo de Palos.** Tasteful resort stretching out along the sand bar (La Manga) enclosing the Mar Menor.
**Puerto de Mazarrón.** New development of villas and apartments.
**Aguilas.** Beach and more tourist development.

**Lorca.** Ancient town of historical importance, full of character and a centre for the south-west of the region.

## COMING AND GOING

There are **direct flights** from London to Murcia airport, but if you have trouble finding a cheap one, you could easily get one to Alicante, which is an hour's drive away on good roads.

**Bus and coach services** also link up well with the east coast route from Alicante and Valencia, and Cartagena is at the end of one of the radial lines of communication spreading out from Madrid (both road and rail). In general the region tends to look away from Andalucía, and communications are not particularly good in this direction.

The region is also now beginning to be exploited as a **package-tour** destination.

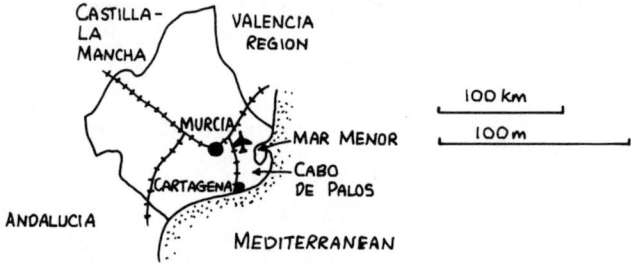

## WHERE TO STAY

**Campsites** get much less numerous as soon as you leave Alicante province, and there is just one **youth hostel** in the region, at **Los Narejos** on the Mar Menor (tel. 968 575189). For accommodation in **monasteries** in the region, contact Convento de los Padres Capuchinos, Totana (Murcia) (tel. 968–420237). There are a number of offers of *casa de labranza* holidays in the region — see p. 25 earlier.

## WHAT TO EAT AND DRINK

Food here is very similar to Valencia — a preponderance of rice, and lots of good fruit and vegetables.

There are two great wine producing areas — Jumilla and Yecla — which adjoin each other in the north of the region. The wines are known more for their strength (13.5–18% by volume) than for their finesse.

## OPPORTUNITIES IN MURCIA

Very limited possibilities for work, although the University of Murcia offers some possibilities for study. The region could appeal to you for touring, for one of the festivals or for water sports, but the best beaches are further north in Alicante province.

## WHAT TO DO

### ARCHAEOLOGY
Bronze Age site at **Cerro de las Viñas**, near the village of **Coy**.

### ART GALLERIES AND MUSEUMS
**Museo Salzillo,** Ermita de Jesús, Murcia. Open 0930–1300 and 1500–1900, 1800 winter; closed afternoon on Sundays and holidays. Museum containing religious wood sculptures or *pasos* (as used in Holy Week processions) by local eighteenth-century artist Francisco Salzillo, reckoned to be some of the best in Spain.
**Museo Arqueológico,** Alfonso X, 7, Murcia. Provincial archaeological museum, including finds from the Punic era, Arab coins and the like.
**Museo de Bellas Artes,** Obispo Frutos 12, Murcia. Fine arts museum.
**Museo Nacional de Arqueología Marítima,** Dique de Navidad, Cartagena, Maritime Archaeological Museum, and national centre for underwater archaeological investigations.

### COURSES
The **University of Murcia** puts on a 3-week intensive Spanish course in July, based at **Cartagena**, and catering for three levels of ability. There is also a 2-week course for teachers or student teachers of Spanish, also during July. This course is intended to improve both language and teaching skills and lays special emphasis on the 'communicative method'. For further details and application forms, apply to: **Cursos para Extranjeros**, Universidad de Murcia, 30071 Murcia (tel. 968–249200, ex. 307 and 338).
For courses in sailing, underwater fishing, windsurfing, etc. see section on Sports below.

### FIESTAS
**Murcia's Holy Week** processions are highly rated as being distinct from both the Andalusian and Castilian varieties, and Salzillo's *pasos* (see section on Museums above) get an airing. There are also important processions in **Jumilla** at this time.
The week after Easter sees more fiestas in Murcia, with a **cavalcade in traditional dress** on the Tuesday, and the **'Burial of the Sardine'** on the Saturday — a popular tradition from the **huerta** marking the end of spring. The third week in August is a good time to be in **Jumilla**, when there are fiestas celebrating the beginning of the wine harvest.
Murcia has its own variety of flamenco, the **Cante de las Minas**, and every year brings together its best performers in a **festival** held in the coastal town of **La Unión**. This usually takes place in mid-August in the old market building — a delightful construction in modernist style.
During the first half of September there is a **Festival of Mediterranean**

**Folklore** held in **Murcia**, with special emphasis on music and dance. There are contributions from a range of different countries — each year one is designated as being of particular interest, and there are film shows, lectures, exhibitions, etc. in its honour.

## LOCAL PRESS

*La Verdad*
*La Línea*

## MUSIC

See section on Fiestas above for the **Fiesta del Cante de las Minas**.

There is also a **Folk Music Festival**, in **San Pedro del Pinatar** on the Mar Menor, in mid-August.

There are open-air performances by bands in the **Jardines de San Esteban** in **Murcia** on Saturdays in June and July.

## SPORTS

It's a good place for water sports: there's a sailing school on **La Manga del Mar Menor** which offers water skiing and windsurfing as well as sailing (contact **Escuela Internacional de Vela de la Urbanización Veneziola** (tel. 968–563142) ), and there are also sailing clubs at **Aguilas, Mazarrón** and **Cartagena**.

There are sailing courses organised by the **Club de Regattas de Mazarrón** (tel. 968–594011) and by **Aguilas town council** (ask at the *Ayuntamiento*). The latter also offers a course in underwater fishing during the summer.

## THEATRE

There are a number of theatre festivals in the region, mostly taking place during the summer, which try to bring culture to towns which otherwise don't see much of it, like **San Javier** on the Mar Menor, **Cienza** (mid-August), **Molina de Segura** (this one has in other years included the infamous punk theatre group La Fura del Baus), and **Cehegín** (first week in September).

## UNIVERSITIES

**Universidad de Murcia,** Santo Cristo 1, Murcia (tel. 968–249200).

## USEFUL ADDRESSES

**Tourist offices**
**Murcia:** c/Alejandro Seiquer 4 (tel. 968–213716)
**La Manga:** Pza Bohemia (tel. 968–563096)

**Government offices**
**Regional Government Tourist Dept,** c/Isidoro de la Cierva 10, Murcia (tel. 968-217157)
**Regional Government** (Comunidad Autónoma de la Región de Murcia), Avda Teniente Flumista s/n, Murcia (tel. 968-216141)
**Education Department,** Pza de Fontes 2, Murcia (tel. 968-217683)
**Labour Department,** Avda del General Primo de Rivera, Edfo 'Alba', Murcia (tel. 968-234714)
**Youth/Sport Department** (Dirección Regional de Juventud y Deportes), Manresa 5, entlo, Murcia

**University Careers Office** (Centro de Orientación e Información del Empleo) Santo Cristo s/n, Murcia

**Youth information office**
Avda de la Libertad 10, Murcia (tel. 968-246212)

**TIVE office**
Manresa 4, Murcia (tel. 968-213261)

**Travel agents**
**Viajes Ecuador,** Pza Circular 7, Murcia (tel. 968-237234)

**Car hire**
**Atesa:** At San Javier airport

**British representation**
**British Chamber of Commerce** — none.
**British Consulate** — see Alicante.
**British Schools** — see Alicante.

**Language schools (TEFL)**
Murcia:
**Academia Climent,** Jaime I El Conquistador 9
**Inlingua,** Alejandro Seiquer II

# 15 Navarra

> The dancing kept up, the drinking kept up, the noise went on. The things that happened could only have happened during a fiesta. Everything became quite unreal finally and it seemed as though nothing could have any consequences. It seemed out of place to think of consequences during the fiesta. All during the fiesta you had the feeling, even when it was quiet, that you had to shout any remark to make it heard. It was the same feeling about any action. It was a fiesta and it went on for seven days.
>
> *Ernest Hemingway*

Navarra (Navarre) lies at the western end of the Pyrenees, and stretches down to the Ebro Valley, which marks its border with La Rioja to the south. It comprises a single province, administered from the city of Pamplona, and is a small but varied region, a sort of transitional zone between the Basque country and mainstream northern Spain, between well-watered mountains and arid plain.

Two versions of its history exist — the Basque version, which concentrates on Navarre's historical links with Euskadi, and the official Spanish version, stressing Navarre's role in creating a unified Spain, and its own regional distinctness within that. There is no doubt, however, that Navarre was one of the first Christian kingdoms to emerge after the Moorish occupation of the Peninsula. Early in their history the *navarros*, rebelling against the interference of the powerful Frankish King Charlemagne in their affairs, forced him to retreat to his own side of the Pyrenees. The famous defeat they inflicted on him at Roncesvalles is recorded in the French epic poem, *The Song of Roland*.

The kingdom grew to include what are now parts of France, Aragón and La Rioja, reaching its height under the powerful and astute King Sancho, early in the eleventh century. During the Middle Ages the Pyrenean pass of Roncesvalles was a key communications link with the rest of Europe. Navarre was the first place in the Peninsula to feel the rejuvenating influence — on the culture, the language and on religion — of the reforming Benedictine monks from Cluny in France, who built great abbeys such as that of San Salvador de Leyre. Pilgrims too passed through on their way to Santiago (see Galicia), bringing Navarre into contact with currents of thought from all over Europe. For over three centuries, Navarre continued to look towards France and away from medieval Spain, as its throne was occupied by French dynasties, until it finally became linked with Castile in 1512. As in the case of the Basque Country, the union was based on respect and observance of Navarre's traditional *fueros*, and the two regions thus had a parallel relationship with Castile for many centuries.

When the system of *fueros* came under threat from a centralising liberal regime in Madrid, the reactionary Carlist movement found strong support amongst the rural, conservative and strongly Catholic populations of northern Spain. However, after the Carlist Wars (1833–1839 and 1872–1875), whereas in the Basque Country and Cataluña Carlism dissolved into the respective nationalist movements, in Navarre, which was economically backward and still predominantly rural, it remained strong, although something of an anachronism. Thus, when Franco initiated the rebellion against the Republican government in 1936, Carlist supporters in Navarre led a popular uprising in support of him — the only place in Spain where this happened. After the Civil War, Franco attempted to drive a final wedge between Navarre and the Basque Country by rewarding Navarre with *fueros*, while confiscating those of the Basques.

Today Navarre is vociferously claimed as part of Euskadi by the Basques, and there is a noticeable split between *navarros* who identify with Basque culture (especially those from the mountain districts to the west, where Euskera is commonly spoken), and those who don't. (Navarre to the Basques is Nafarroa, and Pamplona is Iruñea or Iruña.) They are a vigorous and idealistic people, perhaps more expansive than the Basques, who welcome strangers warmly, especially during the world-famous San Fermines (see section on Fiestas below).

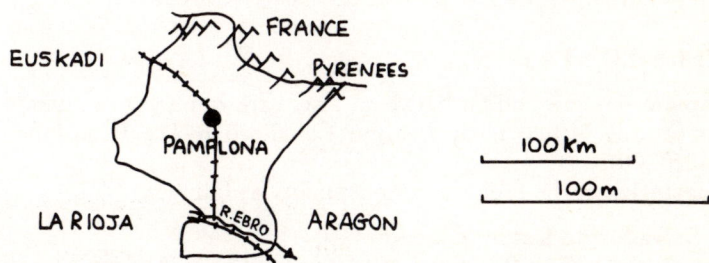

## WHAT TO SEE

**Pamplona.** City of just under 200,000, with relaxed, lively atmosphere, if rather provincial.
**Tudela.** Navarre's second city, and the only one with any industry to speak of. Also an agricultural centre for the surrounding Ribera district (the Ebro plain).
**Tafalla.** Market town.
**Estella.** Important town on the Camino de Santiago still with a medieval feel about it.

**Olite.** Known as the 'gothic town' — a reference to its many ancient buildings, including the former fortress – castle of the Kings of Navarre, now a *parador*.
**Monasterio de Leyre.** Important monastery in a stunning position overlooking the Yesa reservoir. The eleventh-century crypt is reckoned to be the most important piece of Romanesque architecture in Spain.
**Castillo de Javier.** Castle built around the birthplace and home of St Francis Xavier (San Francisco Javier), who is supposed to have converted two million Buddhists to Christianity.
**Sangüesa.** Ancient town on the river Aragon.

## COMING AND GOING

### By air, road and rail
Pamplona's airport has no links with Britain, so it would be best to fly to Bilbao, and catch a bus — a 3 or 4 hour ride.

By road the region's well connected via the Irún – Hendaye frontier crossing. A motorway links Pamplona with Barcelona via Zaragoza, and there are good roads to the Basque country and La Rioja.

There is an important rail crossroads at Alsásua, where the line which passes through the region joins the main France–Madrid line.

### Packages
Visits to Pamplona, Roncesvalles and the monastery of San Salvador de Leyre are frequently included in packages which offer the 'Route to Santiago' (see p. 195). **STA Travel** offer a fortnight in Pamplona to see the running of the bulls at a really rock-bottom price.

## WHERE TO STAY

**Campsites** are few and far between. There are 2 or 3 **youth hostels**: the Reservations Office is at Paulino Caballero 6–1º, Pamplona (tel. 948–227200).
**Monasteries** in the region offer hospitality as follows:
**San Salvador de Leyre** (tel. 948–884011)
**Monasterio de San Benito,** Estella (tel. 948–550882) Women only.
**Monasterio de Oliva** (tel. 948–725006)
**Monasterio de Santa María Magdalena,** Lumbier (tel. 948–880043) Women only.

## WHAT TO EAT AND DRINK

Navarre is well known for its good food, perhaps the most famous product being the *chorizo* from Pamplona, more finely minced than other varieties, which is sold throughout Spain. Meat, fish and fresh vegetables are all good, and as in neighbouring regions Aragón and La Rioja, the *chilindrón* is a favourite way of preparing meat and chicken. Trout from Navarre's rivers are often served *a la navarra* — stuffed with *jamón serrano*.

The sheep's cheese produced in the Roncal valley in the Pyrenees is one of the few Spanish cheeses which have been given *denominación de origen* status (similar to wine DOs). It's a hard, close textured, yellowish-white cheese given its characteristic aroma and flavour by the high quality milk produced in the area by local breeds.

As for wine, the Navarra denominated area is huge, taking up the best part of the region and, as would be expected of a neighbour to La Rioja, produces some excellent table wines — mostly red, and some rosé. Pacharrán, Navarre's version of sloe gin, is rapidly becoming a fashionable drink throughout Spain.

## OPPORTUNITIES IN NAVARRE

Limited, but nonetheless you could spend time here very enjoyably as long as you're not in search of bright lights and city living.

## WHAT TO DO

### ART GALLERIES AND MUSEUMS

**Museo de Navarra,** c/Santo Domingo, Pamplona. Open 1000–1330, admission free. A range of exhibits and pictures from the Iron Age onwards, including an ivory coffer made for a Cordoban caliph in the eleventh century, and pieces from a Romanesque church which stood on the site of the present cathedral.

### BULLFIGHTS

It's the bull-running (*encierros*) rather than the fights as such which the region has a name for. See section on Fiestas below.

### COURSES

The (private) University of Navarre has an **Instituto de Lengua y Cultura Española** which offers courses as follows:

2 week course for teachers of Spanish (mid–end July)
2 week course for A level standard students (mid–end July)
A month-long course in September, and a course lasting from October–February, both for students with some knowledge of Spanish.

Apply to: **Secretaría del ILCE,** Edificio Central, Universidad de Navarra, Pamplona.

Other courses in the private sector:
- **Hispalen–Oxford,** Pza Príncipe de Viana 2, Pamplona (tel. 948–230917). Courses of optional length throughout June, July and August. No previous knowledge required — anyone over 16 can apply. Accommodation in families.

## FIESTAS

Clichéd though it is to say so, Pamplona's **San Fermines** really are one of Navarre's main attractions, promoted by Hemingway as a macho frolic worth experiencing in his book *Fiesta*. Considerable numbers of Americans and other foreigners still come on the basis of this to drink large quantities of cheap wine and *anis del mono*, and soak up the intense festival atmosphere which lasts a whole week (7–14 July each year).

Apart from being a test of staying power as far as drinking and going without sleep, the fiesta's main interest for those who want to prove their masculinity (women are not allowed to participate) is the bull-running. Each morning at 0800 a rocket sounds, announcing the release of the bulls — to be fought later the same day — from their enclosures. To the sound of further rockets, attesting their progress, they charge through the middle of Pamplona to the bullring, with those who dare running before them. A final rocket is sounded when they are secured in the bullring's corrals, and the drinking starts again — for those who have escaped unscathed — along with processions of carnival figures, dancing, sporting competitions, tests of strength, incessant piping and drumming, and, of course, the religious element, the procession of San Fermín's statue round the town. For drama, excitement and sheer festive spirit, it's got to be classed as one of Spain's great fiestas, along with Seville's April Fair and Valencia's Fallas.

Later in the month, around the 24th, **Tudela** has its fiestas in honour of St Anne, and at the beginning of August, **Estella** has its, with many of the same elements present, including bull-running. There are smaller affairs throughout the region, mostly in the summer, which involve hearty *navarros* in such rural jollifications as pig racing!

## FINE ART

A painting competition, open to artists of any nationality, is held each year in August. The **Institución Principe de Viana**, c/Ansoleaga 10, Pamplona, will let you have full details of this, and of any other cultural events. Their telephone number is 948–227200.

## LOCAL PRESS

*Diario de Navarra*

## SPORTS

As in the Basque country, *pelota* is widely played, and there are courts in most towns. Other sports are fishing (especially trout, apply for permits to **Delegación de Turismo**, c/Arrieta 11, Pamplona (tel. 948–230622) ), mountaineering (seek advice from the National Federation — see p. 38 earlier), and winter sports in the Pyrenees (there are small ski-runs at Isaba and Burguete). The region would also offer good cycling or hiking.

## THEATRE

There is a **theatre festival** every year in **Pamplona** during August, organised by the **Institución Principe de Viana**, c/Ansoleaga 10, Pamplona.

## UNIVERSITIES

The University of Navarre is something of an oddity, an institution set up by the Opus Dei (an influential and somewhat sinister Catholic organisation) in 1952, breaking the state monopoly on higher education. Its degrees are fully recognised.

- **Universidad de Navarra,** Ciudad Universitaria, Pamplona (tel. 948–252700).

A new, public University of Navarre is currently being established and some faculties are now functioning.

## USEFUL ADDRESSES

**Tourist office**
Duque de Ahumada 3, Pamplona (tel. 948–124424)

**Government offices**
**Regional Government Tourist Dept,** Arrieta 11–5º, Pamplona (tel. 948–230622)
**Regional Government** (Diputación Foral de Navarra), Avda de San Ignacio 1, Pamplona (tel. 948–227200)
**Education department,** Paulino Caballero 4, Pamplona (tel. 948–223303)
**Labour department,** Monasterio de Cilvetí 4, Pamplona (tel. 948–261750)
**Youth/Sport Departments,** Institución Principe de Viana, Departamento de Educación y Cultura, c/Ansoleaga 10, Pamplona

**Youth information office**
See TIVE office.

**TIVE office**
Carlos III, 55–2º, Pamplona (tel. 948–233722)

**Travel agents**
**Viajes Ecuador,** Pza del Castillo 6, Pamplona (tel. 948–225606)

**Car hire**
**Atesa:** c/Sangüesa 24, Pamplona (tel. 948–235462)

**British representation**
**British Chamber of Commerce** — see Bilbao.
**British Consulate** — see Bilbao.

**British schools** — none.

**Language schools (TEFL)**
Pamplona:
**International House Study Centre,** Pza de las Merindades 3–1º–D
**Idiomas Navarra SA,** Pza Principe de Viana 1–4º

# 16 La Rioja

Compared with the vast expanses of the other regions of Spain, La Rioja is tiny; in fact it's the smallest region on the mainland, wedged between Navarre, Aragón and Castile in a productive stretch of land alongside the river Ebro, and extending southwards as far as the mountains of Soria.

A distinction is generally made between the Rioja Alta, which has a comparatively wet and mild climate, and the Rioja Baja, which has more in common with the burning plains of Aragón. Linking the two, on the Ebro, is the capital Logroño, a prosperous town of some 200,000 inhabitants.

Rioja's prosperity, and of course fame, come directly from its wine, with sales increasing dramatically worldwide during the last ten years or so, and likely to continue rising. However, the region is rich agriculturally in other products, especially peppers, asparagus and artichokes, which are the basis for an important canning industry.

Historically it's a region which has formed part of, first, Navarre and later Castile, and bears much resemblance to these two regions today in terms of culture and way of life.

## WHAT TO SEE

**Logroño.** A market town given a certain importance through the wine trade, and especially since decentralisation through being the regional capital. Lively and very pleasant, if rather provincial.

**Haro.** The real wine town, again on the Ebro, with a clutch of *bodegas* surrounding it, much smaller than the capital, but with a really authentic feel about it.

**Calahorra.** A noble old town, already in existence before the Roman occupation, in the heart of the Rioja Baja. Some buildings show the *mudejar* style features typical of Aragón.

**Santo Domingo de la Calzada.** A walled town built around the one-time hermitage of St Dominic 'of the causeway', so called because he dedicated his life to repairing roads and bridges to ease the way of pilgrims on the road to Santiago (see Galicia). Places of interest include the eleventh-century cathedral, the church of San Francisco, built by Herrera, and the old pilgrim hospice which has been converted into a *parador*. It's strictly for visiting only though, and rather a dull place otherwise.

**Monasteries of Yuso and Suso.** Two monasteries built to celebrate the local cult of San Millán de la Cogolla, who is supposed to have made a Santiago-like appearance in defence of the Christians from the Moors. The church at Suso is in tenth-century Mozarabic style, while Yuso, built much later, is dubbed the 'Escorial of La Rioja'.

**Nájera.** Once a capital of the Kings of Navarre, who extended its importance by diverting the pilgrim route through it. However, now it's little more than a village. The monastery of Santa María la Real contains, among others, the beautifully carved tomb of Doña Blanca, a Queen of Navarre.

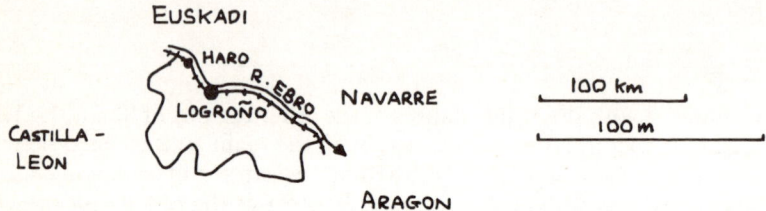

## COMING AND GOING

### By air and road
The nearest major airport is Bilbao, only 2 or 3 hours from Logroño by road. Coming overland through France the region is also fairly accessible, and the third possibility is via Santander on the ferry from Plymouth. Again, you could cover the distance to Logroño in a morning.

The motorway linking Bilbao to Zaragoza and Barcelona runs straight through La Rioja, following the course of the Ebro, so road communications are generally good, although it's a bit of a haul to or from Madrid.

### Packages
**Blackheath Wine Trails** organise a week-long trip to the region, via Madrid, visits to *bodegas* included.

**Travelscene** offer a 'fly-drive' trip to northern Spain (Cantabria) and the Rioja country, and of course the companies which offer the 'route to Santiago' include visits to Logroño and Santo Domingo de la Calzada (see p. 195).

## WHERE TO STAY

There are only a couple of **campsites** in the region and no youth hostels, though you'll have little trouble finding cheap accommodation in Logroño.

## WHAT TO EAT AND DRINK

Local cuisine shares features of Castilian, Navarre and Aragonese cooking, and you can eat very well here. Look out for the *chilindrones* (see Aragón), and as far as meat goes, lamb is likely to be a good choice. A notable Riojan dish is *huevos revueltos a la riojana* — scrambled eggs with *chorizo*, which turns out to be very tasty.

The number of people who appreciate the round oakiness of a good Rioja wine is growing steadily, but generally people are less aware of the many different styles of riojas available. There are three sub-areas within the rioja denominated region, Rioja Alta, Rioja Baja, and Rioja Alavesa which is in Euskadi. Rioja Alta wines are deemed to be the finest. Reds range from light and fruity young wines to grand old *reservas* that have spent ten years or more in oak casks and present quite a challenge to the taste-buds. White riojas have traditionally been aged in oak too, producing some surprisingly hefty wines which can hold their own against any chicken or pork dish, but more recently the trend has been towards fresh dry white wines more in common with modern tastes. You'll also find *semi-dulce* whites which are great to drink on their own, a range of *rosados* — some quite oaky as well — and even a sparkling rioja made by Bodegas Bilbainas.

## OPPORTUNITIES IN LA RIOJA

The region is small, with an economy revolving around the wine industry, so don't expect to find much in the way of work opportunities here — unless you're in the wine trade of course! Logroño is a small town, and there's not much happening — it's more a region to visit than to attempt to make any sort of life here. But who knows? If an opportunity came up, it could be quite pleasant for a while.

## WHAT TO DO

### ARCHAEOLOGY

A Roman site, the town of **Varea**, which dates from the first century is being excavated just outside Logroño. Volunteers from various countries participate in an archaeological work camp here — see p. 71 earlier.

### ART GALLERIES AND MUSEUMS

**Museo Arqueológico**, Palacio de Espartero, San Agustín 23, Logroño. Provincial museum containing paintings as well as archaeological exhibits.

### CINEMA/FILM

The cultural department of the local government promotes a course in film and video held every year for a week during August. Further information from **Consejería de Cultura de la Comunidad Autónoma de La Rioja**, Calvo Sotelo 15, Logroño (tel. 941–246990).

### COURSES

**Instituto Castellano–Leonés de Lingüística Aplicada**, c/Sta Maria 2, 42001 Soria (tel. 975–226961). Three-week courses in Hispanic studies in Logroño during July and August. Anyone over 11 may apply. Accommodation is either with families or in student hostels.

See also section on Cinema above.

## FIESTAS

There is a strongly religious note to most local fiestas, which involve *romerías*, processions and the dancing of *jotas*. The most notable are at **Santo Domingo de la Calzada** (10–13 May), **Haro** (where there is also a wine fight!) on 29 June, and in the village of **Anguiano**, where there is a spectacular stilt-dance (21 and 22 July). **Logroño's** fiestas are around St Matthew's day, September 21.

## LOCAL PRESS

*La Rioja*

## SPORTS

**Caving**
Caves at **Ortigosa de Cameros, Nestares, Torrecilla** and **Peñamiel**.

**Fishing**
For trout, in the **Najarilla** and **Iregua** rivers. Licences from **ICONA**, Belchite 2–1º, Logroño (tel. 941–237211).

**Mountaineering**
In the **Sierra de Cameros**, south of **Logroño**.

**Skiing**
There is a fully-equipped ski-station at **Valdezcaray**, on the border with Burgos province.

## UNIVERSITIES

None, although there are one or two university schools (nursing, teacher training, etc.) which depend on the University of Zaragoza (see section on Aragón).

## WINE

A main attraction of the region is the possibility of visiting *bodegas*. Visits are generally welcomed, and you don't have to make any arrangements beforehand, just turn up during normal working hours, say between 0900 and 1300 or between 1630 and 1900. What you see will depend very much on the time of year — late October is interesting as you can witness the first tumultuous fermentation of the must — and also on whether you visit a *bodega* which uses traditional methods or more modern techniques.

Jan Read (*A Guide to the Wines of Spain and Portugal* — also something of a travel guide) suggests a visit to one of each, for instance López de Heredia at Haro representing the traditional, and Federico Paternina at Ollauri for an example of a big new *bodega*. Wherever you go, it's likely the tour will end with a chance to sample the product — and also to buy, if this is your intention, but in any case there are some good outlets selling wine at discount prices in Haro itself. (See section on Packages above, and also the section on Euskadi for details of organised tours.)

## USEFUL ADDRESSES

**Tourist office**
Miguel Villanueva 10, Logroño, (tel. 941-215497)

**Government offices**
**Regional Government Tourist Dept**, General Mola 1, Logroño (tel. 941-211261)
**Regional Government** (Comunidad Autónoma de La Rioja), General Vara del Rey 3, Logroño (tel. 941-257599)
**Education Department**, Gran Vía de Carlos I, 1, Logroño (tel. 941-222179)
**Labour Department**, Avda de Pío XII, 33 Logroño (tel. 941-231411)
**Youth/Sport Department** (Dirección Regional de Deportes y Juventud), Calvo Sotelo 15-2º, Logroño

**Youth information office**
As for Youth/Sport Department above.

**TIVE offices**
See Pamplona, Bilbao or Zaragoza.

**Travel agent**
**Viajes Ecuador**, Avda España 2, Logroño (tel. 941-227225)

**Car hire**
See Bilbao.

**British representation**
**British Chamber of Commerce**—see Bilbao.
**British Consulate**—see Bilbao.
**British schools**—none.

**Language schools (TEFL)**
**Logroño:**
**Idiomas Oxford**, Calvo Sotelo 8-3º-D
**Inlingua**, General Mola 47

# 17  Valencia

Valencia is one of Spain's sunniest, happiest, most colourful regions, a southern Mediterranean culture relatively untouched by the hardships and unemployment which temper Andalucía's gaiety.

Its prosperity is largely based on the produce of the rich agricultural land, including the famous *huerta*, just outside the city of Valencia, whose alluvial soil allows cultivation of several crops of the highest quality fruit and vegetables each year. Rice, a legacy of the Moors, is also intensively produced in the area, in specially irrigated paddy fields. So important is the irrigation system to Valencia's economy that the institution of the Water Court, or Tribunal de las Aguas, is still preserved, meeting every Thursday at noon to resolve disputes among farmers over the question of irrigation.

There is also a good deal of industry (mostly textiles and engineering) both in Valencia itself and further up the coast in Castellón, and traditional industries like furniture making, shoes and ceramics still make an important contribution to the economy of the region. A major feature of the Valencian landscape, especially along the coast north of the capital, is its citrus groves, which stretch for miles, and give their name to this coast, the Costa del Azahar, or Orange Blossom Coast. The Alicante coast, the Costa Blanca, is of course already familiar to millions of British people, and resorts like Benidorm are evidence of Valencia's other great industry — tourism.

Valencia is Spain's number one tourist destination, both for foreigners and Spaniards, with excellent beaches, typically with wide curving bays and shallow waters, and resorts to suit all tastes. Many guides to the 'real Spain' recommend avoiding the region as being too touristy, but this really underestimates the resilience and sheer vivacity of Valencian culture, as well as ignoring the many opportunities that are available simply because it is a tourist area (see below). If you don't like crowds, though, they can be a problem on the coast in July and August, and there is a lot of residential development as well as hotels, but inland it's easy to find peace and solitude in wild and remote areas like El Maestrazgo (see What to See below).

Today the Comunidad Valenciana, as the region is called, is made up of three seaboard provinces: Castellón, Valencia and Alicante, with Valencia (the city) as its capital. It is historically a distinct region, and has its own language, Valencian, which is similar to Catalan. However, you are not likely to find yourself addressed in anything but Castilian Spanish, although the Valencian version of many place names is taking over (e.g. Castelló for Castellón, Xátiva for Játiva).

Historically Valencia is famous for the exploits of El Cid in wresting it from the Moors in the eleventh century. After his death, however, it reverted once more to Arab rule until 1238 when it finally became a Christian kingdom in its own right. The centuries of battles between Moors and Christians have passed into popular legend, and are symbolically re-enacted each year in festive celebrations organised by almost every town and village in the area (see section on Fiestas below). Valencia was later absorbed into the Crown of Aragón, and the capital became an important port through which the Aragonese conducted their overseas trade. It continued to prosper both through its rich agriculture, already well established under both Romans and Moors, and through industries such as pottery and tile-making, and silk production.

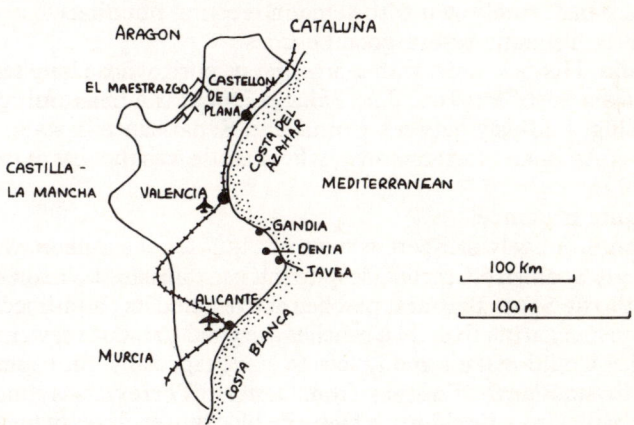

## WHAT TO SEE

**Valencia**
Capital of the region, and Spain's third city. It's a busy, fun-loving city, whose inhabitants are convinced it's the most wonderful place on earth. It seems in many ways to be built with its back to the sea, although the port is still busy, and there is a lively seaside *barrio* called La Malvarrosa, where a lot of the nightlife is centred. Valencia is famous for its flowers and parks, especially the roses in the **Jardines de los Viveros**, and the presence of the nearby *huerta* imbues the city with its luxuriance. Its principal places of interest are as follows:

Splendid examples of Spanish baroque, culminating in the elaborately fanciful facade of the **Palacio del Marqués de Dos Aguas** where the ceramics museum is housed (see listings below).
**El Miguelete.** Octagonal tower which is identified with the city itself in the popular imagination — you can go up it for a view over the city.

**La Lonja de la Seda.** Former Silk Exchange building in unusual Gothic style.
**Palau de la Generalitat.** An impressive Gothic palace which is now the seat of the Valencian regional government.
**The Cathedral.** Important Gothic building with a baroque facade.
**El Jardín Botánico,** c/Beato Gaspar Bono. The first botanical gardens to be established in Spain, containing many exotic species, including an interesting palm collection.

### Valencia province
**La Albufera.** An enormous fresh-water lake to the south of Valencia. A beautiful spot, surrounded by orchards and paddy fields, with fishing, birdwatching and rowing.
**Sagunto.** A Roman town, famous for its resistance to the Carthaginians. Roman remains including an amphitheatre, plus crumbling Moorish castle. Good beaches.
**Liria.** Small rural town with some interesting buildings.
**Cullera.** Teeming resort, good beaches.
**Gandia.** Historic town with a prosperous port, whose long sandy beach attracts a lot of tourism. The **Palacio Ducal** is a beautiful, clean-lined building, mid-way between Gothic and Renaissance in style.
**Játiva.** An inland fortress town, whose castle was the seat of the Borgias.

### Alicante province
**Alicante.** A lively prosperous town of a quarter of a million, with its own strongly Spanish character, despite intense tourism. Its main sight is the **Castillo de Santa Barbara,** perched above it and its palm-lined esplanade is extremely attractive. The beaches are good too, but very crowded. All in all it would make a good place to stay, especially out of season.
**The Costa Blanca.** The coast from **Denia** to **Torrevieja** is almost all built up, ranging from **Benidorm's** high-rise blocks to enclaves of luxury holiday homes, and with such beautiful weather and beaches, and fairly attractive towns, you can see why.
**Elche.** Ancient town, remarkable for its **Palm Forest**, first planted by the Phoenicians, and still being cultivated for dates and palm fronds. Just outside is one of the most important Iberian archaeological sites, where the pre-Roman sculpture of a woman known as the *Dama de Elche* was discovered. Elche also has a famous mystery play which attracts many visitors each year (see section on Fiestas below).
**Orihuela.** More palm forests, and subtropical plantations of citruses, cotton, etc.
**Alcoy.** Industrial town in a mountain setting.

### Castellón province
**Castellón (de la Plana).** Fishing and industrial port, with little to interest the visitor.
The **Costa del Azahar.** Again, a lot of tourist development, mostly centred on **Benicasim, Oropesa** and the attractively situated **Peñiscola.** Further

north **Benicarló** and **Vinaroz** (famed for its king prawns) are fishing towns which also attract a fair bit of tourism.

**El Maestrazgo.** This is the name given to the wild mountain area occupying the northern (inland) part of Castellón province and the southerly part of the neighbouring Aragonese province of Teruel. This is El Cid country, a backwater forgotten by the twentieth century, a rugged and austere landscape with gorges, pine woods, and such rare species as the ibex and wild boar. From time to time a well-watered valley provides a lush contrast to the arid mountain scenery and the area is ideal for hiking, or simply getting away from it all. Places to make for, if you really want to catch the sombre magic of the middle ages, are the district capital **Morella**, perched on a crag and encircled by fourteenth-century walls, and the little atmospheric village of **Ares del Maestre**.

## COMING AND GOING

### By air
You should have no trouble getting cheap flights to either Valencia or Alicante. Valencia airport is 5 miles out of the centre, at Manises, and there are train and bus links into the city, or taxis at the ready.

### By train
The region is directly connected by rail with the rest of Europe via Barcelona and there are good rail links with Madrid. The 'Aragonese' line to Teruel is slow but goes through some spectacular country. For travel within the region, there is a network of narrow gauge railways linking Valencia, Alicante, and many resorts and small towns.

### By road
The Autopista del Mediterráneo, or A7, zooms straight down the coast to Valencia and Alicante from the French border, making road communications easy. Bear in mind that from the border to Valencia you will have to pay a toll of approximately 3,000 pesetas. There are coach services direct from London and Dover, as well as from most major cities in Spain.

### By sea
The **Compañia Transmediterránea** (c/ Manuel Soto 15, Valencia) runs ferries throughout the year to Ibiza, Mallorca and Menorca, and to Sete, in the South of France, twice a week from June to September.

### Packages
Package tours to this area abound, and certainly out of season, they make a really cheap way of seeing the region. After all, you don't have to do what you're expected to do on a package tour. **Ramblers Holidays** do a walking holiday in spring and autumn, based in Gandia. **Mundi Color** offer some luxury packages to the region. (See p. 21.)

## WHERE TO STAY

More possibilities in Valencia and Alicante or in towns inland than in the resorts, where **hotels** get block-booked.

There are a few **youth hostels** on the coast, and the **Reservations Office** is at: Pintor Sorolla 25–5º, Valencia (tel. 96–3523159).

**Campsites** are extremely numerous all the way up and down the coast.

## WHAT TO EAT AND DRINK

The regional dish is of course the *paella Valenciana* and variations abound on the theme of rice with fish and/or seafood and/or meat and/or vegetables. The quality of produce, the green vegetables and salads of the *huerta* and the various fruits in their season (cherries, pears, peaches, figs, apricots, grapes, melons and, naturally, the citrus fruits) is excellent. The fish is also good and fresh, and tends to be simply cooked. The inland mountain areas have a separate cuisine, which is heavier and more meat-based.

Junket (*cuajada*) is the local speciality as far as sweets go, although in practice fresh fruit or ice cream is all you usually get offered. At fiesta time *buñuelos* appear for sale on stalls pitched on every street corner. These are doughnuts fried on the spot and traditionally eaten with sticky liqueurs. *Turrón* is a local sweet made from nuts, half-way between halva and nougat, and eaten all over Spain at Christmas time. There is a toffee-hard version, *turrón Alicante*, and a soft crumbly version, *Jijona*. Buy some to bring home wherever you are in Spain, it's a real delicacy.

Look out for *horchata* (a light milky drink made from a tuberous plant called an 'earth almond') as a soft drink here, or ask for *zumos naturales* (fresh fruit juices).

The area has three denominated areas as far as wine production goes, Utiel Requena (light reds and rosés), Valencia (whites and dessert wines) and Alicante, which produces *rancio* dessert wines (aged in oak casks) and muscatels.

## OPPORTUNITIES IN THE VALENCIA REGION

The enormous numbers of British people here, ex-patriots as well as holidaymakers, create certain work opportunities — courier work, casual work, teaching in British schools, etc. The area is fairly prosperous, so if you're interested in au pairing or nannying, you may find yourself some opportunities here. Equally, if you're au pairing or nannying for a Spanish family based in some other part of Spain, you may very well find yourself spirited away to some resort on this coast for a month or so's summer vacation. Resorts like Cullera and Javea (north of the Benidorm area) are very popular holiday destinations for Spanish families.

The degree of tourist development means that the area is provided with excellent leisure facilities. Sports, especially water sports, are well served with facilities here, and the Alicante authorities particularly are eager to help you find them, arrange meetings with Spanish teams/clubs, etc.

Valencia, as Spain's third city, has much to offer in the way of provision for cultural interests — galleries, theatres, concert halls and the like, although not on the same scale as Madrid or Barcelona. The coastal areas are strewn with bars, restaurants, discos and other facilities, and Valencia and Alicante both offer good study opportunities.

## WHAT TO DO

### ARCHAEOLOGY

There are a good number of interesting sites from all periods in the region, so applying for an archaeological work camp here could bear fruit.

### ART GALLERIES AND MUSEUMS

**Valencia**
**Museo de Bellas Artes,** c/ San Pio 9. An important collection containing works by Goya, Murillo, Velázquez, and also the Valencian impressionist Joaquín Sorolla. Closed in the afternoons in summer.
**Museo Nacional de Cerámica y Artes Suntuarias,** Palacio del Marqués de Dos Aguas, Poeta Querol 2. Spain's national museum of ceramics containing some splendid *azulejos* and ceramics of all kinds.
**Museo Fallero,** Plaza de Monteolivete 4. A collection of the best *ninot* of each year's Falla saved from the flames (See section on Fiestas below).

**Sagunto**
**Museo Arqueológico,** c/Castillo. Iberian and Roman sculptures, mosaics, etc.

**Castellón**
**Museo de Bellas Artes.** Small but impressive collection of paintings, including some good sixteenth- and seventeenth-century works.

### BULLFIGHTS

The Spanish bullfighting season is inaugurated in Valencia during the Falla festivities in March, but the biggest bullfights are held during the July Fair (15th–31st July). The **Plaza de Toros** is in the c/ Játiva. There are other smaller rings in resorts up and down the coast.

### CAVES

The area is a good one for caves — there are prehistoric wall paintings in the **Cueva de la Araña** near the village of **Bicorp** (Alicante province), and at **Morella la Vella,** in El Maestrazgo. At **El Val de Uxó,** in Castellón province, there is a spectacular underground river, known as the **Grutas de Sant Josep,** which can be visited by boat.

## CHILDREN'S ENTERTAINMENT

There is a zoo in the **Viveros park** in Valencia (c/ San Pio V). On the main road out of Benicasim, going towards Castellón, there is the **aquarama water park**, with wave machines, slides, etc.

Children take an active part in Valencian fiestas, having their own special Fallas, and each year on St. Vincent Ferrer's day (7 April) stage dramatic representations of the 'miracles' of the patron saint.

The **Scouts Association** in Valencia organises a variety of activities for young people between 7 and 18 (summer camps, bike excursions, etc). They may be contacted at the following address: **Scouts de España**, Zona XV–Valencia, c/ Don Juan de Vilarasa 12, 1st floor, 46001 Valencia.

## CINEMA/FILM

There is a **Mediterranean Film Festival** each year in **Valencia** at the beginning of October. For information contact **Mostra del Cinema del Mediterrani de Valencia** c/ Salvador Giner 14, Valencia (tel. 96–332 1504).

**Elche** has a thriving film club, the **Cine–Club Luis Buñuel**, which also holds festivals and special film seasons.

## COURSES

### In Alicante

In July the University of Alicante organises a variety of summer courses, including Spanish for foreigners, but also short courses on Spanish history, art, geography, literature and anthropology. There is also a month's course in Hispanic literature for teachers of Spanish. The same institution also puts on an International Course in Benidorm on social scientific topics. Contact: **Cátedra Rafael Altamira**, Cursos Internacionales, Universidad de Alicante, San Vicente del Raspeig, Alicante.

### In Valencia

There are a number of private-sector institutions running language courses:

- **Escuela de Traductores,** (School of Translating and Interpreting — of some repute), San Vicente 55–4º, Valencia (tel. 96–351 5228). 2–4 week language courses throughout the year. All levels. No previous knowledge of Spanish required. Also summer courses (July and August) in Spanish language and culture. There are also translating courses available, both for one month during the summer, and for the whole academic year.
- **FICDE Colegio Ausias March,** Tancat de L'Alter, Picassent, Valencia. Flexible courses (minimum 2 weeks) from April to July, all levels. Also a 3-month course from September–November.
- **Hispania Universalitas,** Martín Mengod 3, 1st floor, Valencia. A 3-month language course from June to August. All levels, no previous knowledge of Spanish required. Also a 3-month history and literature

course from March to May.
- **Inglingua Idiomas,** Ribera 13, Valencia. Flexible courses (minimum 2 weeks) throughout year. All levels, no previous knowledge of Spanish necessary.
- **Instituto de Estudios Españoles,** c/El Bachiller 13, Valencia (tel. 96–369 6168). 2- and 4-week summer courses and whole academic year. Bookable through John Galleymore — see below.
- **John Galleymore** (24 High St, Portsmouth), and **Youth Travels** (117 Wendell Rd, London W12) can both arrange courses in Valencia from Britain.

**In Denia (Alicante):**
- **Inlingua Idiomas,** Carlos Sentí 7, 03700 Denia (tel. 965–787975). Offers courses lasting a minimum of 2 weeks during July, August and September. Beginners are accepted on the first and third Mondays of each month, others on any Monday. Language work and optional activities including films. Accommodation with families.

## CRAFTS

The great tradition of pottery and tile-making in the region continues in the village of **Manises,** outside Valencia, which produces brightly coloured crockery in bold designs. Spain's main **pottery school** is located here, at Guillermo de Osma 3. Other regional crafts are glass-blowing in the village of **L'Olleria,** fan-making, basketwork, woodwork and embroidery.

## DANCE

**Benidorm** has three dance schools: **Escuela de Danza Mª. José Sánchez,** c/ Puente 4, Edif. Las Tejas; **Escuela de Danza Pedro Martín,** c/ Tomás Ortuño 6; and **Escuela de Danza Paco Beltrán,** c/ Mirador 8, Edif. Acacias IV.

## FIESTAS

Valencia is a great region for fiestas, which are celebrated in typically enthusiastic style in almost every village. A common theme is that of 'Moors and Christians' with villagers dressing up in medieval costume and re-enacting the struggles of the Reconquest. These take place in the village of **Bocairente** (early February), **Alcoy** (around St George's day — 23 April), **Petrel** (third week in May), and **Villajoyosa** (late July) where the ritual battles are fought in boats at sea, as well as on land.

The most exciting fiestas in the region are by far and away the **Fallas of Valencia** which take place in the week leading up to St Joseph's day, 19 March. The Fallas are floats of enormous carnival-like figures, or *ninots* which depict, often with cutting satire, the various famous 'faces' of the year, TV personalities, sportsmen, politicians, etc. About 300 of these are constructed at great expense (and, it must be said, with a considerable amount of artistic talent), sponsored by different neighbourhood groups. They are paraded around the streets for a week, amid mounting excitement fuelled by the deafening gunpowder shots and firecrackers which are let off at intervals, day and night, before being symbolically burned at midnight on St Joseph's day. With a typically Spanish sense of drama, the best *ninot* each year is rescued from the flames and put on permanent display (see section on Art Galleries and Museums above).

Of course, there is a lot more going on throughout Falla week besides the Fallas themselves: loud music, parades of 'Falla girls' in traditional costume, firework displays, religious ceremonies, including the offering of flowers by the ton (literally) to the Patroness of Valencia, eating and drinking, staying up late and getting no sleep, etc., etc. The bustle and excitement of Falla week is incomparable, and well worth experiencing — if you can stand the pace. The Tourist Office can supply you with further details, as well as an interesting leaflet tracing the history of the Fallas.

As mentioned above, the whole population of Valencia turns out again on **St Vincent Ferrer's day** (April 7) to see scenes from the life of the saint performed by children in the Valencian language on make-shift stages set up in the street — 'a popular and living echo of medieval ecclesiastical drama'.

In **Alicante** the big fiestas, which also contain all the elements typical of Valencian festivities — fireworks, bonfires, carnival figures — are the **Hogueras de San Juan**, culminating on the night of 24 June.

In **Elche** the festivities take on a more religious note, with the performance, in the church of Santa María, of a thirteenth-century mystery play depicting the death, and assumption into heaven, of the Virgin Mary. Entrance is free on 14 and 15 August. Tickets for other performances on 11, 12, and 13, may be obtained from the **Tourist Office** in Elche (in the Parque Municipal).

Finally, in **Castellón** the **Fiestas de la Magdalena** are held during Lent, with processions, bullfights, and a *romería* to the shrine of St. Mary Magdalene, outside the city.

## HIKING

The coast is too built up for hiking, even out of season, but it's very easy to find good walking country inland (See section on Packages on p. 239 for a holiday specialising in this). The **Júcar valley** with its gorges, and, for more serious excursions, **El Maestrazgo**, are particularly recommended, but almost any of the little *sierras* away from the coast will make good walking, with spectacular scenery and views.

## LOCAL PRESS

*Levante*
*Las Provincias*

## MUSIC

During the second half of September an **International Contemporary Music Festival** is held in **Alicante**. For further information contact: **Centro para la Difusión de la Música Contemporánea**. Teatro Real, Plaza Isabel II, Madrid (tel. 91–247 3573).

At the same time of the year, **Peñiscola** organises a **Classical Music Festival** — details from the *Ayuntamiento* or Tourist Offices.

There is a range of other musical events throughout the summer in the region, varying from year to year, and there are any number of local bands, choirs and music groups of all varieties in the area. If you want to be put in touch with any of them, the tourist authorities are only too happy to oblige.

## SPORTS

The tourist authorities boast that you can practice any sport you care to name in the Valencia/Alicante region, and, if you have a passion for a particular sport, be it roller hockey or Tai Kwon Do, it's certainly worth getting in touch with them. If you want to arrange matches or meetings with Spanish teams, write to the provincial tourist office (addresses below — you'll probably find Alicante the most helpful) in good time with details of when you are arriving, for how long, how many people you are bringing, etc., and they will do their best to arrange something for you. It's worth bearing in mind, however, that during July and August many clubs' normal activities are brought to a standstill due to holidays.

The most commonly available sports are:

- **Golf.** There are eleven golf clubs in the region, the most famous being the **El Saler** club just outside Valencia.
- **Tennis.** Courts abound, belonging to clubs, hotels and housing developments.
- **Water sports.** There is windsurfing and water-skiing all the way up the coast (Benidorm has a water-skiing school and eleven windsurfing schools), as well as opportunities for deep-sea diving and sea-fishing. You can hire both sailing and motor boats at Moraria, Basetes, Altea and Benidorm (get in touch with the harbour authorities), and there are sailing schools in all of the major resorts (23 in all).

## THEATRE

Look out for the **Puppet Week** held every November in the **Teatro Buffo**, c/ Misser Mascó, **Benidorm**.

During the summer plays are staged in the **Roman Theatre** at **Sagunto**.

**Valencia** (city) has a number of theatres, the most important being the **Teatro Principal**, in the c/ Barcas. Its **Drama Centre**, which is at Avenida Campanal 32, organises a number of activities, including courses and workshops for people working in the fields of theatre and dance.

## WILDLIFE/CONSERVATION

See also the earlier section on the **El Maestrazgo** region on p.239. The **La Albufera lagoon** is an important stop off point for many migratory birds, especially ducks and waders, and a paradise for bird life in general. There is a wildlife reserve for mountain goat and wild boar at **La Muela de Cortes**, near **Ayora** on the border with Albacete province.

## USEFUL ADDRESSES

**Tourist offices**

**Alicante:** Explanada de España 1
**Castellón:** Plaza Mayor
**Valencia:** Paz 46

**Government offices**
**Regional Government Tourist Dept** (Dirección General de Turismo), Isabel la Católica 8, Valencia (tel. 96–352 6177)
**Regional Government** (Generalitat de la Comunidad Valenciana), Palau de la Generalitat, Caballeros 2, Valencia (tel. 96–332 0203)
**Youth/Sport Department,** Pintor Sorolla 25, 5º, Valencia

**Education departments**
**Alicante:** Carratalá 1 (tel. 965–102255)
**Castellón:** c/ Mayor 109 (tel. 964–225586)
**Valencia:** Navarro Reverter 2 (tel. 96–373 8811)

**Labour departments**
**Alicante:** Pintor Lorenzo Casanova 6 (tel. 965–122211)
**Castellón:** María Agustina 1–2º (tel. 964–221716)
**Valencia:** San Vicente 85 (tel. 96–351 2710)

**University Careers Office** *Centro de Orientación e Información del Empleo*
Universidad Politécnica, Campus del Comino de la Vera, Valencia

**Youth information offices**
**Alicante:** Avda Aguilera 1 (tel. 965–227442)
**Castellón:** Avda del Mar 23–20 (tel. 99964 232911)
**Valencia:** Avda Campanar 32–34 (tel. 96–349 0244)

**TIVE office**
Mar 54, Valencia (tel. 96–352 2801)

**Travel agents**
**Valencia Tours,** Camino de las Moreras 27, Valencia
**Wagons Lits Viajes,** Marqués de Sotelo 7, Valencia
**Viajes Ecuador,** Gran Vía Fernando el Católico 6, Valencia; Ramón y Cajal

1, Alicante, and other branches.

**Car hire**
**Atesa:** Avda del Cid 64, Valencia, and Valencia and Alicante airports.
**Hertz:** Segorbe 7, Valencia

**British representation**
**British Chamber of Commerce** — see Barcelona
**British Consulate:** Pza Calvo Sotelo 1–2º, Alicante (tel. 965–216190)
**British Council:** General Sanmartín 7, Valencia (tel. 96–351 8818)

**British and American schools**
Alicante:
**Sierra Bernia School,** Alfaz del Pi
**Edge Hill School,** Carretera de Benidorm km 53, La Nucia
Valencia:
**El Plantio International School,** calle 233 s/n, Urbanización El Plantio
**English School Los Olivos,** Avda de Pino Panera s/n, Campo Olivar
**Colegio Hispano Norteamericano,** Urbanización Valle de los Monasterios, Puzol, Valencia

**Language schools (TEFL)**
Alicante:
**Centros de Estudios Superiores,** Avda Denia s/n, Apartado 306
**Inlingua,** Avda Méndez Núñez 45
**Instituto de Idiomas Modernos,** Avda de Denia 60
Benidorm:
**Inlingua,** Alameda 7–2º
Calpe:
**Laboratorio de Idiomas,** Avda Ifach 5–7º
Elche:
**Lenguas Attika,** Mariano Benlliure 6
**The English Centre,** c/Canónigo Torres 4–1º
Valencia:
**Centre of English Studies,** Jai Alai 5
**Centro Estudios Norteamericanos,** San Bernardo 5
**Club de Idiomas,** Calvo Sotelo 9
**English School,** Avda Barón de Cárcer 31–1ª
**Escuela de Traductores e Intérpretes,** Cirilo Amoros 14
**Escuela de Idiomas Berlitz,** Lauria 20
**Global School,** Pascual y Genis 17
**Inlingua,** Ribera 13
**International House,** Pascual y Genis 16
**The Mangold Institute,** Avda Marqués de Sotelo 5, Pasaje Rex (also branches in Gandia, Buñol, Sagunto, Liria and Alcudia de Carlet)
**Kings Idiomas,** Guillém de Castro 57–5ª
**Lenex Centre,** Martínez Cubells 2
**The Oxford Centre,** Alvaro de Bazán 18

# 18
# The Island Regions of Spain

## THE BALEARICS

Tourism provides the life force for these four idyllic Mediterranean islands: last year a total of nearly five million people spent their holidays there — a massive figure considering that the total population of the islands is only 700,000. Once one of Spain's poorest regions, the Balearics now have the highest per capita income in the whole country — more than double that of Extremadura for example.

It's easy to see the attraction, for the islands of Mallorca, Menorca, Ibiza and Formentera really are beautiful and remain so despite pockets of heavy tourist development where the local population is swamped. The Mediterranean climate is delicious, with over 300 sunny days a year, and there are hundreds of enticing bays or *calas*, their waters clear and sparkling.

Mallorca, the biggest island, is the site of the Balearics' capital, Palma, and it's here that you're likely to be based if you're teaching or doing a language course. It's a good-sized attractive city and port and, although some of the heaviest tourist developments in the islands are around its bay, it's big enough to have a real life of its own, and in any case most holidaymakers stick to the immediate vicinity of their hotels. A chain of mountains runs down the north side of the island, providing some attractive scenery, and at least for nine months of the year it is possible to enjoy the magnificent coastline unhindered by crowds. Even at the height of the season if you have your own transport you can find quiet beaches to the north and east of the island.

On Menorca you'll find it quiet at all times of the year. It is not built up to anything like the same extent and life is generally slower and more traditional. A brilliant light illuminates the whitewashed houses and vivid greens of the landscape, which, however, is generally flat and less varied than Mallorca, offering little shelter from the high winds which sometimes sweep the island. Menorca was under British control for nearly a century (1713 to 1802) and perhaps this has contributed to the restrained rather conservative atmosphere of the place.

Ibiza in contrast had a reputation for tolerance and liberalism even under Franco, attracting a sizeable hippy population which is still in evidence. Today though it takes pride in a much more up front image — anything goes, as long as it's fashionable. It's a place where if you're one of the beautiful people you go to flaunt yourself, and if you're not, you go for the spectacle. It also has some superb beaches and scenery.

Formentera is the smallest of the islands and has little to offer except the solitude of its splendid beaches.

The islands have a long history of being inhabited and exploited by various peoples. Menorca is dotted with curious prehistoric stone structures, variously called *talayots*, *taulas* and *navetas*, the purpose of which is a mystery. Ibiza was important for its salt production in ancient times, and the Carthaginians, who founded Ibiza town, have left many traces of their presence, now mainly in archaeological museums. The beauty of the islands was praised by Latin authors, and Formentera takes its name from the Latin word for granary, as it is thought to have produced wheat for the Roman Empire. Later all the islands came under Moorish occupation and they were responsible for providing many of the most basic elements of the culture (the type of crops grown, food consumed, the way houses and streets were built. . . ). During the thirteenth century the islands were brought under Christian control by the Aragonese, and thus became incorporated into Spain. Today, although there is great pride in local culture, the islands are very much a part of mainstream Spain, and there is no sense of isolation or marginalisation.

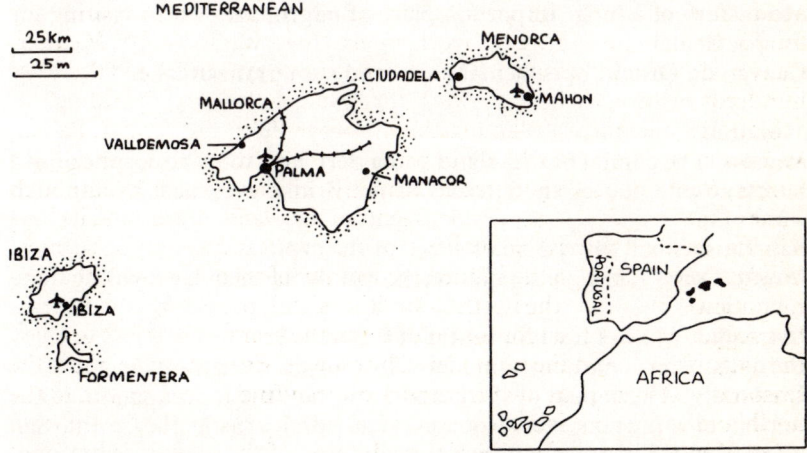

## WHAT TO SEE

### Mallorca
**Palma**. Palma is a notable city of some quarter of a million people and its airport is the busiest in Spain in terms of passenger traffic. The built-up area stretches all round the beautiful bay on which it is set, but the old part is just a cluster of steep narrow streets around the cathedral — many of them now bright with modern boutiques. The cathedral itself is one of Spain's great Gothic constructions, looking out over the bay and providing the main feature of the view if you arrive by sea.

The size of the city, combined with the need to provide tourist entertainment, ensures that there's always plenty to do, with plenty of scope for eating, drinking and enjoying oneself, whether you go for coke, hamburgers and disco dancing or the local alternatives (see below).

**Castillo de Bellver.** Thirteenth/fourteenth-century Gothic castle now housing the archaeological museum (see below).

### Elsewhere on Mallorca

**Valldemosa.** One of the islands main tourist sights, a monastery known simply as **La Cartuja** is located here, between the mountains and the sea. It's a beautiful spot, made famous by the French novelist George Sand, who stayed here with Chopin from 1838–9 and wrote *A Winter in Mallorca*.

**Deia.** Mountain village in a beautiful setting where Robert Graves lived.

**Soller.** Outstandingly attractive bay with attendant resort.

**Puerto Pollença.** Port and tourist resort.

**Alcudia.** Once a Roman town, the ruins of a small theatre remain. There is tourist development around the harbour, known as **Puerto de Alcudia**.

**Manacor.** Mallorca's second town, which also has something of a life beyond tourism, although its main industry is cultivating the famous Mallorcan pearls. Some good traditional furniture is also produced here.

**Felanitx.** Town producing wine, pearls, and ceramics.

**Monastery of Lluch.** Important place of pilgrimage, worth visiting for its spectacular site.

**Cuevas de Drach.** Spectacular caves and subterranean lake.

### Menorca

**Mahón.** The capital of the island and a port with some atmospheric old streets. Some houses show traces of the British presence, having sash windows.

**San Luis.** Small town 2 miles south of the capital.

**Monte Toro.** The highest point on the mainly flat island, providing some good views.

**Mercadal.** Market town in centre of island.

**Fornells.** Pretty harbour famed for its sea food restaurants.

**Ciudadela.** The capital of the island until the British occupation, it has some interesting houses and squares, a cathedral, a castle, the Castillo San Nicolás, and a distinct Moorish feel about it.

### Ibiza (Eivissa in local dialect)

**Ibiza Town.** The old town, known as **D'alt Villa**, is completely surrounded by ancient walls which seem to rise up out of the rock and give the place a good deal of character. They enclose the cathedral and some interesting old streets and squares.

Outside the walls the **Sa Penya** district, the old fishermen's quarter, is the scene of much of the town's activity, especially at *paseo* time. The more modern part is known as **La Marina**, and this is lively too, with lots of shops, bars and traffic.

During the day Ibiza's beaches, **Las Salinas** and **Figueretas**, become an extension of its scene, and nudism or at least toplessness is common.

**Santa Eulalia (del Río).** Small town on the Balearics' only river. There is an established hippy market at nearby Es Cana.
**San Antonio (Abad).** Major package tour resort.
**Portinatx.** Resort on the stunningly attractive north coast of the island.

### Formentera
Situated very close to Ibiza, it's accessible by boat from Ibiza harbour, and would make a good day trip. The beaches are beautiful — white sand backed by pine trees — and are free from crowds. Both the capital, **San Francisco Javier**, and the next largest place, **San Fernando**, have a few basic services, and there's a bit of a resort at **Es Pujols**, but there's little scope for anything else.

## COMING AND GOING

### By air
Palma, Ibiza and Mahón all have busy international airports, and you should have no trouble getting cheap flights.

### By sea
Alternatively, you can go by sea from the mainland: the **Compañia Transmediterránea** (Muele Viejo 5, Palma (tel. 971–726740) ) operates ferries as follows:

| | | |
|---|---|---|
| Barcelona–Palma | Valencia–Palma | Alicante–Palma |
| Barcelona–Ibiza | Valencia–Ibiza | Alicante–Ibiza |
| Barcelona–Mahón | | |

A different company, **Isleña de Navegación**, which runs the ferry between Ibiza and Formentera, also runs a service between Denia and Ibiza. Services vary according to the time of year (and logically are more frequent in the summer months), so check times of sailing with a travel agent.

You'll also have no trouble getting inter-island ferries, although it's a good idea to check prices against the cost of local flights, which can be surprisingly cheap.

### By road and rail
Although the islands are small, getting around can prove a problem: taking a car over is expensive and car hire, although readily available locally, is pretty expensive too. Buses can be infrequent and don't give you much flexibility.

Mallorca is the only island with any railway service, and there is a wonderful old track which passes through the mountains from Palma to Soller. This certainly makes a scenic ride, but is not an efficient means of transport.

The solution, as many tourists find, is to hire a moped. You shouldn't have any difficulty finding these, but if so, try:

**Jaybee**, Avda Joan Miró, Terreno, Mallorca (tel. 971–238930)

**Gelabert**, c/J A Clave 12, Mahón, Menorca (tel. 971–360614)
**Extra Bikes**, C/Ignacio Wallis, Figueretas, Ibiza (tel. 971–302125)

**Packages**
Buying a 2-week package can often work out cheaper than a flight, so especially out of season it's well worth looking into, even if you don't intend to use the hotel. As well as an immense selection of sun-and-sea deals to the various resorts, there are some good 'special interest' packages available to the islands, as follows (see p. 21 for addresses):
**Ornitholidays.** 1 or 2-week bird watching holidays in lesser known areas of Mallorca.
**Ramblers Holidays.** Walking holidays in Mallorca; birdwatching holidays in Menorca.
**The Field Studies Council.** Bird watching in Mallorca.
**Waymark Holidays.** Walking holidays in Mallorca.
**Cox and Kings.** Special interest holidays in Mallorca for botany and wild flower enthusiasts.
**Kestours.** Specially arranged sports tours for clubs or groups.
**Travelscene.** City breaks to Palma.
**Mundi Color.** Up-market packages to Mallorca, Menorca and Ibiza.

## WHERE TO STAY

Accommodation can be really hard to come by at the height of the season, with every available room/corridor/broom cupboard packed tight with package tourists, but at other times of the year finding somewhere to stay shouldn't be a problem — although you may end up paying slightly more than on the mainland.

Ibiza is the island which is best provided with **campsites**; Mallorca has one (at Muro) and Menorca none. With a little discretion you can camp rough, especially on Formentera, although getting fresh water is a problem.

The two Balearic **youth hostels** are on Mallorca, at **Alcudia** (open mid-June to August only) and **Palma** (open all year). You can book through the **Reservations Office**, at San Felio 8–A–3º, Palma (tel. 971–211140). The **Monastery of Lluch** (tel. 971–517025) accepts overnight visitors.

## WHAT TO EAT AND DRINK

Probably the first time you have breakfast in the Balearics (and especially in Mallorca) you'll come across *ensaimadas*, pastries made out of deliciously light dough coiled, supposedly, in the shape of a Moorish turban. They may be plain, or filled with custard or *cabello de ángel*, a jam-like substance made from pumpkin or squash. On Sundays and fiestas the bakeries produce especially large *ensaimadas* to be shared by whole families, and these are packed in distinctive flat boxes like enormous pizzas.

The Balearics have their own distinctive cuisine, and typical dishes are *sopa mallorquina*, a substantial vegetable soup thickened with bread; *tumbet*, a kind of baked ratatouille; dishes made with the local sausages, *butifarra* and *sobresada*; and of course sea food of all kinds. The town of Mahón gave its name to mayonnaise, which was invented on Menorca, but this is not particularly in evidence. Menorca also produces a highly acclaimed cheese, *queso de mahón*, a yellow-coloured cows' milk cheese with a distinctively salty taste.

There are some very drinkable local wines produced on Mallorca, Menorca and Ibiza, although none have DO status. It being a tourist area, you'll often find the wine mixed with lemonade and fruit as *sangría*. Menorca also produces gin - another British hangover!

## OPPORTUNITIES IN THE BALEARICS

Anything connected with tourism is well starred, whether it's enjoying the facilities laid on for tourist enjoyment, or finding some means of making money out of it (for example working as a courier or setting up your own moped-hire business). However, activities which depend on the participation of Spanish people, like teaching English or learning Spanish, will be restricted to the one major centre of population — Palma.

If you're going on holiday, bear in mind that the islands are a little short on sights of historical interest, at least compared to some of the wonders of the mainland, and those that exist are well trampled by the tourist hordes. For sun, sports, sea and entertainment though (in any combination), the region would be hard to beat, although keep away in July and August if possible, as the crowds can easily overwhelm all the positive things the region has to offer.

## WHAT TO DO

## ARCHAEOLOGY

The **Deia Archaeological Museum and Research Centre** (c/o Dr W H Waldren, Deia, Mallorca) seeks volunteers for excavating an important Copper Age site near **Valldemosa**. The work is for 2-week periods between April and September and in December and January. No fares or wages are paid, although board and lodging is provided.

Other archaeological sites being excavated on the islands are the Roman city of **Pollentia** (Mallorca) and a Punic site at **Cap Llabrell**, on Ibiza.

## ART GALLERIES AND MUSEUMS

### Ibiza
**Museo de Baleares**, Pza de la Catedral 3, Ibiza (open mornings only). Archaeological museum with some really interesting Punic finds from a Carthaginian necropolis discovered locally, one of the most important ever found.
**Museo 'Puig des Molins'**, vía Romana 31, Ibiza (open afternoons only). An extension of the above.

## Mallorca
**Museo de Mallorca**, Portella 5, Palacio Desbrull, Palma. Provincial arts museum.
**Archaeological Museum**, Castillo de Bellver.

## BULLFIGHTS

Palma's bullring is quite prestigious, and is situated to the north of the city, on the Avda del Arquitecto Bennassar. There are bullfights every Sunday during July and August. There is also a bullring in Ibiza town, which in season holds fights every other week, and another ring on Mallorca at Inca, with only occasional fights.

## CINEMA

Film lovers won't find an awful lot to see here, but **Ibiza** does have a **film festival**, held in October in the **Cine Cartago**.

## COURSES

The **Estudio General Luliano** in Palma (an ancient Mallorcan university institution) runs a 2-week summer course in Spanish language and culture (history, literature, etc.) during the last fortnight in July, and some years during August or at Easter too. The minimum age is 16, and hotel accommodation is provided. Write to: **Cátedra Ramón Llull**, Curso de Español para Extranjeros, c/San Roque 4, 07001 Palma de Mallorca (tel. 971-211988).

The same institution also puts on summer courses in Catalan language and culture. Write and ask them for further information if you're interested. **John Galleymore** (24 High St, Portsmouth (tel. 0705-824095) ) can book everything up for you, including flight, from the UK if you wish.

If you want to learn Spanish in Mallorca at any other time of the year, you'll have to fall back on the private sector: **Inlingua Idiomas**, c/31 de Diciembre 7, Palma (tel. 971-293422) runs courses all through the year for different levels of ability, beginning on any Monday.

On a different level, the **Universidad Internacional del Mediterráneo** offers a varied programme of lectures and cultural events during July and August in **Ibiza's Art School**. Further information may be obtained from: **Fomento de Turismo de Ibiza-Formentera**, H. José Clapés 4, Ibiza (tel. 971-302490).

## FASHION

There are fashion shows in Ibiza during the first week of June, organised by **IFEBAL**, c/Federico García Lorca 17, Ibiza (tel. 971-455500).

## FIESTAS

The tourist department of the Balearic Islands produces an exhaustive booklet entitled *Festivales, Ferias y Fiestas en Baleares* which details every conceivable festive event taking place on the islands, and especially if you're going to be there some time, it's well worth asking for a copy. Here are brief details of the most outstanding:

- **15 January.** Fiestas in honour of **Sant Antoni Abat** (St Anthony Abbot). These are very ancient festivals which take place at various locations on Mallorca, the most important being at **La Puebla**. Enormous bonfires are lit in the streets and the people dress up and sing and dance around them, playing traditional instruments called *ximbombes*.
- **17 January. Processó d'els Tres Tocs** in **Ciudadela** (Menorca). Procession which commemorates the Christian takeover of the town on 17 January 1287 after the defeat of the Moors. On the same day there are also parades and celebrations in **Palma, Manacor, Pollensa**, and other villages.
- **Good Friday.** Religious processions in **Palma, Pollensa** and other villages.
- **23/24 June. St John's day** celebrations in **Ciudadela, Muro** and all over Mallorca.
- **23/24/25 August.** Celebrations in honour of **St Bartholomew**, especially at **Capdepera** and **Montuiri** (Mallorca) and **Ferreríes** (Menorca).
- **31 December. Palma** commemorates Jaime I of Aragón wresting the city from the Moors in 1229, incorporating both religious and civic celebrations, together with folk music and dancing.

## LOCAL PRESS

*Ultima Hora*
*Diario de Mallorca*
*El Día de Baleares*
*Baleares*
*Majorca Daily Bulletin*
*Sun*
*Diario de Ibiza*
*Menorca*

## MARKETS

Palma's **Rastro**, or flea market, is held on Saturday mornings in the streets around the Avda de México. There is also a **handicraft market** on Monday, Fridays and Saturdays (mornings only) in the Plaza Mayor.

A **book fair** is held in Palma every year towards the end of May in the Paseo del Born.

## MUSIC

Palma has an impressive **concert hall**, the Auditórium (on the Paseo Marítimo), which as well as a reasonable programme of music and ballet, is the venue for regular recitals by the Orquesta Sinfónica Ciudad de Palma between October and April. There are also open-air concerts (rock, jazz, folk and traditional) held during the summer in the **Parc de la Mar** (between the old town and the sea) — watch out for them locally or ask for a programme from a tourist office.

There are also numerous small music festivals held at various sites around the islands at different times of the year. The *Festivales, Ferias y Fiestas en Baleares* booklet (available from tourist offices) will give you an exhaustive list, and addresses where you can get full information, but here is a taste of the sort of thing to expect:

**Mahón Opera Week** in the Teatro Principal in Mahón, held during March or April each year.
**Flamenco Festival** held in Palma towards the end of April.
**Concerts** of classical music held during Holy Week in various churches on the island of Ibiza.
**Classical music recitals** held every Tuesday in July in San Francisco church in Palma.
**Concerts** of classical music held every Tuesday from July to September in the castle of Son Mas, in Andratx, Mallorca.
**Jazz festival** held in July and August in Palma's Auditorium.
**Jazz festival** in Ibiza at the beginning of August, held in the Plaza Vara del Rey.
**Classical music festival** held in Ciudadela Seminary, Menorca, with concerts every Monday and Wednesday in July and August.
A **festival of Mallorcan music**, held in the Teatro Cine Municipal, Paseo Mallorca, Palma, from October–December.

## SPORTS

This is a good region for both spectator and participatory sports:

### Cycling
The country and climate is good for cycling, and during September there is a cycle race around Mallorca. For details of this and other events, contact the **Federación Balear de Ciclismo**, Fco Fiol y Juan 2–1º, Palma (tel. 971-253288).

### Dog racing
There is a greyhound racetrack at Cno de Jesús s/n in Palma, with races every day except Wednesdays from 1630.

### Fishing
The Balearics are ideal for sea fishing: you can hire boats from the **Real**

**Club Náutico de Palma**, Muelle San Pedro s/n, Palma (tel. 971–226848). The temperature of the waters makes underwater fishing an attractive proposition almost all the year round, if you're keen on this.

### Football
You can see Real Mallorca play in the Luis Sitjar Stadium in Palma.

### Golf
You can play golf at one of several clubs in Mallorca: Santa Ponça, Magalluf, Palma, Son Severa or Alcudia. In Menorca there is a course at Son Parc, just outside Mahón and Ibiza has one at Sta Eulalia. There are also various golfing events organised throughout the year: for details contact the **Federación Balear de Golf**, Av Jaime III, 17, Palma (tel. 971–222753), or ask at a tourist office.

### Hiking
You may not think of Mallorca as hiking country, but in fact out of season it can be great. Not only is the countryside beautiful, with some lovely sea views, but the weather is ideal: clear, dry and not too hot.

### Horseracing
You can see trotting races every Sunday afternoon at Palma Hippodrome, and there are others at Manacor, Mahón or Ciudadela.

### Horseriding
You can ride, among other places, at the **Club Escola d'Equitació de Mallorca**, Carretera de Sóller km 12 (tel. 971–613157), or the **Club de Hípica de Manacor**. Both these clubs also put on various events of interest to horse lovers throughout the year (dressage, show jumping, etc).

### Running
An international marathon takes place in and around Palma on the last Sunday in March. For details contact the **Club Peñalver**, c/Cannes 27, Palma (tel. 971–266106).

### Sailing
There are excellent sailing facilities, with marinas or harbour facilities all round Mallorca, and in Menorca at Ciudadela, Mahón and Fornells, and in Ibiza at Ibiza, San Antonio and Sta Eulalia. There are also numerous regattas, sailing competitions and festivals held throughout the year, including the Princess Sofia Trophy during Holy Week, the King's Cup (*Copa de S.M. el Rey de Vela*) in mid-August, and a spectacular tall ships race, also during August.

For details of these and other events, or just advice and general information, contact the **Federación Balear de Vela**, Avda Joan Miró s/n, Palma (tel. 971–402412).

## Other facilities
Palma has a major sports centre, the **Polideportivo Municipal** (Cno Vecinal la Vileta), which as well as offering good facilities, puts on all sorts of spectator events and competitions, from synchronised swimming to volleyball. The **sports department** of the **Palma town council** is the place to contact for details, at Pl Cort 1 (tel. 971–227744).

## THEATRE
In Palma various productions are staged in the Auditorium (see section on Music) or in the Teatro Principal — see locally for details. The best time of the year for theatre is from mid-June to the end of July, when there is a special theatre season organised by the city council.

## USEFUL ADDRESSES

**Tourist offices**
**Palma**:
— Av Jaime III 10 (tel. 971–212216)
— c/Almudaina 7–A (tel. 971–224090)
**Mahón**:
Pza del Generalísimo 13 (tel. 971–363792)
**Ibiza**:
— Vara del Rey 13 (tel. 971–301900)
— Cayetano Soler 10 (tel. 971–301293)

**Government offices**
**Regional Government Tourist Dept**, Av Jaime III, 8, Palma (tel. 971–21202)
**Regional Government** (Govern Comunitat Autónoma), Marina 3, Palma (tel. 971–216092)
**Education Department**: Pasaje Guillermo de Torella 1, Palma (tel. 971–214146)
**Labour Department**: Plaza Mayor 10–1º, Palma (tel. 971–225901)
**Youth/Sport Department**: San Felio 8–A–3º, Palma

**Youth information office**
Venerable Jerónimo Antich 5 bajo, Palma (tel. 971–212914)

**TIVE office**
Venerable J. Antich 5 (tel. 971–211785)

**Travel agents**
**Viajes Ecuador**, Pza Madrid s/n, Palma (tel. 971–281853)

## Car hire
**Atesa:**
— Palma, Mahón and Ibiza airports
— Borne 6, Palma (tel. 971-215009)
— c/Virgen del Carmen 3, Ciudadela (tel. 971-384736)

## British representation
**British Chamber of Commerce** — none.
British Consulates:
— Plaza Mayor 3-D, Palma (tel. 971-212425)
— Avda Isidoro Macabich 45-1º, Ibiza (tel. 971-301818)
— Torret 28, San Luis, Menorca (tel. 971-366439)
**British American Club of Mallorca** (ex-patriate club), Soldada Marroig, Son Armadams 8, Palma

## British schools
**The Academy English Preparatory School**, San Amethier Vell Pont Dluca, Apartado 1300, Palma
**Bellver International College**, c/ José Costa Ferrer 10, San Matet, Marivent, Cala Mayor, Palma
**Baleares International School**, Camino Cabo Mateu Coch 17, San Agustin, Palma
**Kings Palma**, Juan de Saridakis 64, Genova, Palma
**Norma Valley School**, Apartado 95, San Carlos, Ibiza

## Language schools (TEFL)
**Mr Robert Toole**, Apartado 34, Santa Eulalia del Río, Ibiza
**Academia de Idiomas**, Isaac Peral 72, C'an Picafort, Palma
**Berlitz**, Via Alemania 3, Palma
**Instituto de Lenguas Modernas**, c/San Roque 4, Palma
**Escuela de Idiomas del Mediterraneo**, Montesión 24, Palma
**Inlingua Idiomas**, 31 de Diciembre 7, Palma

---

## THE CANARY ISLANDS

The Canaries are a group of seven volcanic islands off the west coast of Africa, as far away again from Madrid as Madrid is from London. Administratively they form an autonomous region, divided into two provinces, that of Tenerife, which takes in the islands of Tenerife, La Palma, Gomera and Hierro and has its capital at Santa Cruz de Tenerife, and the province of Las Palmas, administered from the city of Las Palmas de Gran Canaria and consisting of the islands of Gran Canaria, Fuerteventura and Lanzarote.

The islands seem to hold a special attraction for northern Europeans, both holiday makers and ex-patriates, due no doubt in large part to the subtropical climate, which is always warm with very little noticeable difference between the seasons and hardly any rain. In terms of natural features too the islands can satisfy anyone's thirst for the exotic, ranging from stark volcanic landscapes to luxuriant banana plantations.

The islands belong in many ways to the New World rather than to the Old, having only been discovered in the fifteenth-century. Until then they had been inhabited by the Guanches, a tall, fair skinned race of people with, as far as can be gauged, a fairly primitive culture. Once under Spanish control, however, the race all but died out, and very little trace of their presence remains. The islands were mainly used by the Spanish as a stopover on the way to the Americas, first by Columbus on the voyages of discovery, and subsequently as important ports on trade routes.

The beginnings of tourism came to the islands as luxury cruise liners too began to use the Canaries as ports of call, and as time passed manufactured attractions began to be added to the natural ones, and mass tourism took off. As a consequence the islands (especially Gran Canaria and Tenerife) now boast miles of artificial beaches, skyscraper hotels, bungalow complexes, lidos, pools and marinas, pubs, clubs and restaurants, and above all duty free shopping — there are no customs barriers on the islands. In commercial terms, it's a great success, but as with so many 'new' countries, the culture seems a little vapid, despite the popular re-discovery of Guanche roots that has accompanied the devolution of power to a regional government.

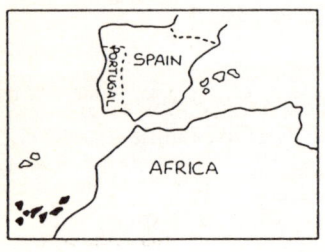

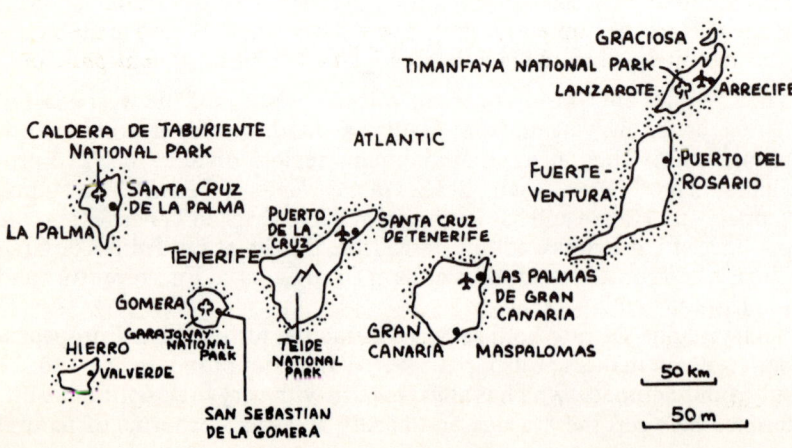

## WHAT TO SEE

**Tenerife**
The largest of the islands with a soaring mountain range running through its centre and substantial tourist developments both in the arid south around **Playa de las Américas** and in the north centred on **Puerto de la Cruz**. Spain's highest mountain, **Teide**, provides a distinctive landmark, and in its shade the valleys are rich with luxuriant vegetation.

**Santa Cruz de Tenerife.** Modern city which is important as a free port, with some considerable industrial development too. Tourism is mainly concentrated on the two nearby beaches: **Las Gaviotas** and **Las Teresitas**.
**La Laguna.** Perhaps the most historically interesting place in the Canaries, this is the former capital of Tenerife, founded in 1496. It's a university city, and also a bishopric.
**La Orotava.** Town set in one of the most beautiful valleys in the islands, giving access to the **Cañadas del Teide** (see below). It is famed especially for its ancient 'Drago' or 'Dragon' tree, distinctively formed and supposedly thousands of years old.
**Puerto de la Cruz.** Tenerife's main tourist centre, and well set up for tourist enjoyment. Attractions include the spectacular lido, with its cascading fountains, and just outside the city, a **parrot park** and a **botanical garden**.
**Icod de los Vinos.** Old town at the foot of Teide, displaying some exuberant vegetation, and famed, as its name suggests, for its wines.
**Los Cristianos.** Coastal resort, with access to Gomera via ferry.
**Granadilla de Abona.** Agricultural town which is growing in importance touristically since the new Reina Sofía airport was built nearby.
**Güímar.** Major town.
**Playa de las Américas.** Big tourist developments.
**Cañadas del Teide National Park.** Set on a huge crater, the main features of the park are its altitude and its aridity. Volcanic activity has created a unique environment where, although practically the only specimens of animal life are lizards, some rare species of plants survive and even flourish. The *cañadas* are the impressive gorges which have been formed in the side of the mountain, and the whole area bears the name of *mal país*, or badlands.

**La Palma**
La Palma is an attractive island with higher rainfall and consequently a greener aspect than the other islands. Its interior is mountainous and is occupied by the gigantic **Caldera de Taburiente**, supposedly the world's biggest volcanic crater, and now a National Park.

**Santa Cruz de la Palma.** Capital of the island, it's a peaceful, pleasant town with some interesting old houses displaying the old wooden balconies which once were typical of Canary architecture.
**Los Llanos de Aridane.** The other main centre on the island.

## Gomera

A mountainous island, whose slopes have been carefully terraced to allow cultivation of crops such as bananas, grapes and vegetables. Its soil is very fertile and date palms form an important feature of the landscape. Columbus stopped off in the capital, **San Sebastián**, before setting sail for America, and his stay is much vaunted by the tourist authorities. Many tourists visit the island as an excursion from the big resorts in Tenerife. In the interior the **Garajonay National Park** is densely forested with Canarian laurel, and mosses and lichens in rich variety cover the trunks and branches of the trees.

## Hierro

The smallest of the Canary islands, Hierro has a population of only 7,000 and an area of little over 100 square miles. It does have some spectacular scenery however, both coastal and mountain, and has a rich agriculture. The main town is **Valverde**, which has a tranquil village-like atmosphere.

## Gran Canaria

Despite its name, Gran Canaria is only the third largest of the islands, although it is first in importance, as its capital **Las Palmas** is the seat of the autonomous Canary Government. The island is heavily developed for the tourist trade, but offers a rich variety of possibilities. The landscape ranges from rugged cliffs around **Puerto de las Nieves** to the undulating sand dunes of **Maspalomas**, and there are many luxuriant valleys rich with subtropical vegetation.

**Las Palmas.** The biggest city on the island. Las Palmas has a population of about a third of a million and its port handles the largest volume of trade in Spain. It's an extremely lively modern city, with every facility, and also has an interesting old quarter, known as **Vegueta**. Here you'll find old mansions with wooden balconies, the cathedral, and the **Casa de Colón**, which was the residence of the first governors of the island. Las Palmas' beach, **Las Canteras**, is over a mile and a half long.

**Playa del Inglés.** Important tourist development to the south of the island.
**Maspalomas.** An immense beach, several miles long, which runs into Playa del Inglés and offers a desert-like landscape of sand and dunes. Nearby there is a natural 'oasis' and a small lagoon, around which the tourist developments have been centred.
**Guía.** Prosperous town.
**Gáldar.** Town interesting for the remains of Guanche culture left in the area, including the **Cueva Pintada**, or painted cave. Nearby another group of caves, known as the **Cenobio de Valerón**, are thought to have been used for instructing young Guanche women in religious rites.
**Puerto Rico.** Modern tourist development.
**Agaete.** Attractive coastal city amidst lush vegetation.

## Fuerteventura

Despite being a large island with a long coastline, Fuerteventura has relatively little tourist development and would make a good destination if you want to enjoy Canary scenery and exotica away from the crowds. The most 'African' of the Canary islands, it is bare and undeveloped and only goats graze the bare sides of the volcanoes in the interior. There are some excellent sandy beaches, however, and the coast is recommended for fishing. The capital, **Puerto del Rosario**, has 14,000 inhabitants and is growing steadily.

## Lanzarote

Lanzarote's volcanic aspect was created by a series of catastrophic eruptions during the eighteenth and nineteenth centuries which formed the distinctive lunar landscape you see on every travel brochure. The Canaries as a whole are unique, but Lanzarote is remarkable: as it hardly ever rains farmers give their crops the necessary moisture by spreading them with volcanic ash which absorbs the night dew. By this surprisingly effective method melons, watermelons, grapes, figs and tomatoes are produced in abundance.

**Arrecife.** The capital of the island, a pleasant port and commercial centre.
**Puerto del Carmen.** Good beaches and the main tourist development on the island.
**Timanfaya National Park.** Unlike national parks on the mainland, the Timanfaya celebrates not the profusion of wildlife but rather pure geology — much of it consists of solidified lava on which nothing will grow. Underneath the ground the 'Mountain of Fire', **Montaña del Fuego,** still retains an intense heat, as is demonstrated by tourist guides who pour water down vents in the earth, causing great artificial geysers to shoot up.

The island has other wonders too: to the north, at the foot of **La Corona volcano**, are miles of underground galleries which have been formed by cooling lava, and one of the largest caves has been turned into a concert auditorium. The **Jameo del Agua** nearby is a huge underground lagoon with caves which serve as a night club.

## COMING AND GOING

### By air

All the islands, with the exception of Gomera (which can be reached by sea relatively easily from Tenerife), have airports. Most of the charter flights available are either to one of the two airports in Tenerife (Los Rodeos in the north, Reina Sofía to the south), to Gran Canaria (Gando airport) or to Lanzarote. Less frequently there are flights available to Fuerteventura. Flying time is approximately four hours from the UK, and you can expect to pay about £20 more than for charter flights to the mainland. Alternatively Iberia operate scheduled services to all of the airports, from either London or Manchester. If you're based on the Spanish mainland by the way, and you fancy a few days in the Canaries, you should be able to fix this up really quite cheaply through local travel agents.

**By sea**
It is possible to go by sea from Cadiz to either Tenerife or Las Palmas (the service is run by the **Compañía Transmediterránea**) but this is a 2 day journey and can work out very expensive.

Sea connections *between* the islands are much more feasible, however, starting at about £12. Between Tenerife and Gomera the **Ferry Gomera** company (Muelle Los Cristianos, Tenerife (tel. 922–790556) ) runs two services daily in each direction, taking approximately 4½ hours. The **Compañía Transmediterránea** runs ferry services between all the islands and operates a hovercraft between Tenerife and Las Palmas which takes about 80 minutes. For full details contact a travel agent, or the company's offices, as follows:

**Tenerife:** Marina 59, Sta Cruz de Tenerife (tel. 922–287850)
**Gran Canaria:** Muelle Santa Catalina, Las Palmas (tel. 928–273774)
**Lanzarote:** José Antonio 90, Arrecife (tel. 929–811019)
**Fuerteventura:** León y Castillo 46, Puerto Rosario (tel. 928–850877)

**Public transport**
Public transport on the islands varies enormously, from the excellent on Tenerife and Gran Canaria to the practically non-existent on Fuerteventura, where car hire is almost essential.

**Packages**
Apartment, villa or hotel holidays to the islands abound throughout the year. There doesn't seem to be much in the way of more original packages available.

## WHERE TO STAY

Accommodation can be very difficult to come by in the tourist areas as everything tends to be block booked by the big package companies. Unfortunately this applies all the year round, as the Canaries are always in season for holidays, winter and summer. **Tourist offices** can supply complete lists of **hotels** and **pensions** though, so ring ahead first, and go for the older-established villages and towns inland rather than the big new tourist developments.

**Camping** is not an established means of accommodating oneself on the islands — the terrain is not really suitable — and there are only two official campsites: at **Aguimes** and **Mogan** on **Gran Canaria**.

Gran Canaria also has the monopoly on **youth hostels** in the islands: one at **Arinaga** (open July and August only) and one at **Sta María de Guía** (open all the year round except September). The **Reservations Office** is at Cano 24, Las Palmas (tel. 928–370179).

If you have the money, there is a nicely situated **parador** on every island except Lanzarote.

## WHAT TO EAT AND DRINK

Canary cuisine is quite distinct from cooking on the mainland, making use of the variety of exotic fruits and vegetables that can be cultivated in the subtropical conditions — especially bananas, but also pumpkins, guavas and avocados. Of particular note is the fact that bread — of primordial importance on the mainland — tends to be substituted by corn meal or other cereals. *Gofio* (ground toasted wheat) for instance is a basic ingredient, in use since Guanche times, which is eaten as a breakfast cereal or used in baking.

One of the most typical dishes is *patatas arrugadas* or 'wrinkled' potatoes, which are served with a special hot sauce called *mojo picón*. You may also come across *mojo verde* which is made with coriander leaves.

There is a red wine produced around Tacoronte on Tenerife, while the wines from Icod and La Orotava tend to be white. The islands also produce rum and a malmsey wine made from Malvasia grapes.

## OPPORTUNITIES IN THE CANARIES

In the Canaries, wherever there are concentrations of population, tourism dominates, so if you are looking for the sort of opportunities which are provided by people and in towns, you'll have to put up with exposed northern European flesh and the smell of Ambre Solaire. Nevertheless both Sta Cruz de Tenerife and Las Palmas are sizeable cities with a good variety of things happening of interest to people who're looking for a bit more than tourist fodder. There are also important British ex-patriate communities on Gran Canaria, Tenerife, and to a lesser extent Lanzarote, which means that work opportunities, like teaching in British schools, are quite good. If you want to avoid the tourist crush and mix with the locals, either head for one of the smaller islands or for the more authentic inland towns on Tenerife and Gran Canaria — La Laguna would make a good choice for example.

## WHAT TO DO

### ARCHAEOLOGY

Work camps on the islands (see p. 71 earlier) generally include at least one of an archaeological nature each year investigating Guanche sites.

### ART GALLERIES AND MUSEUMS

**Las Palmas**
**Museo Canario,** c/Doctor 2 (closed Sundays, fiestas and Saturday afternoons). If you're at all interested in the Guanches, you'll find the best demonstration of what their culture was like here.
**Museo Néstor,** Pueblo Canario (closed Wednesdays). Museum dedicated to the works of the Canarian painter Néstor (1888–1938).

**Galdos' House,** c/Cano 6 (open mornings only, every day except Sundays and fiestas). Benito Pérez Galdós, the Spanish Hardy or Dickens, is perhaps the most famous son of the Canaries, so it's fitting that his house should be open as a museum.

**Sta Cruz de Tenerife**
**Museo Municipal,** c/Ruiz de Padrón. Municipal Museum.

## CINEMA

There is an **international ecological film festival** held in **Puerto de la Cruz** each November, with films shown in the Cine Timanfaya and the Cine Chimisay, and a parallel programme of lectures and discussions in the Universidad Popular Municipal. Many of the films shown are original versions subtitled in Spanish and you can get a programme from the youth information offices whose addresses are given at the end of this section.

## COURSES

**Public-sector courses**
The only publicly subsidised Spanish for foreigners course in the Canaries is held from mid-January to mid-March in the **Instituto de Estudios Hispánicos de Canarias**, Quintana 18, Puerto de la Cruz, Tenerife. It caters for three levels of ability, and is open to anyone over 18.

**Private-sector courses**

- **Inlingua Idiomas,** Paseo Tomás Morales 28, Las Palmas de Gran Canaria (tel. 928–360671). Month-long courses are run throughout the year, as follows:
  — for beginners: in April, July, October and January;
  — for intermediate students: in May, August, November and February;
  — for advanced students: in June, September, December and March.

- **Inlingua** also have a school at Playa del Inglés: Edificio Mercurio, Torre 11, 1A, Avda de Tirajana (tel. 928–763361), which offers courses organised in a similar way.
- **Gran Canaria School of Languages,** Tomás Morales 54, Las Palmas de Gran Canaria (tel. 928–371957). Courses all the year round, minimum 1 week. Beginners start the first Monday in April, July, October or January, others any time throughout the year.
- **Spanish Institute,** Tomás Zerolo 17, La Orotava, Tenerife. Four-week courses throughout the year for beginners, pre-intermediate, intermediate and advanced, using the direct method.

## FIESTAS

At carnival time **Sta Cruz de Tenerife** turns into a mini Rio, and all stops are pulled out to put on a good show with fancy dress parades, music and dancing. A brilliant spectacle at a time when northern Europe is enduring the drabbest part of the winter.

The town of **Garachicho** (Tenerife) celebrates San Roque (16 August) with a *romería* and a tremendous outpouring of popular enthusiasm, with fireworks, poetry competitions, etc.

Towards the end of August **Arrecife de Lanzarote** puts on a big show in honour of San Ginés. This includes demonstrations of Canarian wrestling (a local sport), fishing competitions, bowls, children's games, and singing.

Every five years (the next time will be in 1990) **Sta Cruz de La Palma** has its ancient **Fiestas de la Bajada de la Virgen** during August, involving allegorical plays enacted on specially constructed stages.

At **Santa Lucía** on Gran Canaria there is a religious event in honour of this saint on 13 December each year, with offerings of local produce, processions in local costume, dancing and music.

## HIKING

If you're interested in getting off the beaten track in **Gran Canaria** or **Tenerife**, and want more orientation than good maps can provide, Noel Rochford's books *Landscapes of Gran Canaria* and *Landscapes of Tenerife* between them provide over a hundred suggestions for long and short walks on the islands.

## LOCAL PRESS

*La Provincia* (Las Palmas)
*El Día* (Sta Cruz de Tenerife)
*El Diario de Las Palmas*
*Diario de Avisos* (Sta Cruz de Tenerife)
*Jornada* (Sta Cruz de Tenerife)

## MUSIC

Every year from the first week in January to the first week in February there is a prestigious **Music Festival** held in the Canaries, with concerts and recitals in both **Las Palmas** and **Sta Cruz de Tenerife**. One year the London Philharmonic Orchestra was among those taking part. Seats can be reserved in advance from the UK and a programme obtained from: **Festival de Música de Canarias**, Consejería de Cultura del Gobierno de Canarias, c/Cano 24–3º, 35002 Las Palmas de Gran Canaria.

An important **opera festival** is traditionally held in **Las Palmas** every year from February to March, with names like Pavarotti and Plácido Domingo amongst the performers.

There are a number of **music competitions** for young people open to anyone resident in the Canaries. These are organised each year by the **Cultural Department** of the Canarian Government (c/Cano 24–4º, Las

Palmas), and include prizes for folk music, jazz, rock, youth choirs, and songwriting.

## SPORTS

Sports of all kinds are particularly well catered for in the Canaries; the combination of mass tourism and the benign climate ensures this. Here are some of the main possibilities:

### Fishing
Both deep sea and underwater. For deep sea fishing you can join an excursion either from **Santa Catalina Wharf** in **Las Palmas** or from **Puerto Rico**. There are over 1,500 species of fish in Canary waters, and the climate is suitable for underwater fishing all the year round.

### Golf
There are two golf courses on **Gran Canaria**, one near **Las Palmas** and one in the south at **Maspalomas**. The address of the **Club de Golf de Gran Canaria** is: PO Box 183, Santa Brígida, Gran Canaria.

### Horseriding
There are riding schools on **Gran Canaria** at **Marzagán**, **Bandama** (near the golf club) and **Maspalomas**.

### Parachuting
You can parachute onto the dunes at **Maspalomas** from the **Aero-Club de Gran Canaria** at **Tarajalillo**, near Maspalomas — a course lasts about 3 hours.

### Sailing
There are harbours and good facilities for sailing on all the islands, but especially **Gran Canaria** and **Tenerife**. Full details are contained in a leaflet produced by the tourist authorities entitled *Instalaciones Náuticas en las Islas Canarias*.

### Skygliding
The **Tamarán School-Club**, based in **Las Palmas** at León y Castillo 244–1º (tel. 928–243540) will take you skygliding over the dunes at **Maspalomas**.

### Swimming
The temperature of the water in the Canaries stays around 65–70°F winter and summer, so it is ideal for swimming throughout the year. You might also like to try the over-the-top **Aguapark Octopus**, 'Tenerife's water fun park in the heart of the island's sunny south', near **Playa de las Américas**.

### Tennis
The tourist areas are extremely well supplied with tennis courts.

## Watersports

Waterskiing, scuba-diving, wind surfing (the latter especially in the south of Gran Canaria) and other water sports are all widely available in the tourist areas. There are various important motorboating trials held in Las Palmas bay throughout the year.

## THEATRE

The university town of **La Laguna** on **Tenerife** is the site of a modest **Theatre Festival** each year. Details from the **Palacio Insular**, Pza de España 1, Sta Cruz de Tenerife (tel. 922–242090).

The **Cultural Department** of the Canary Government (c/Cano 24, Las Palmas) organises a festival for **youth theatre groups** each year.

## UNIVERSITIES

- **Universidad de La Laguna,** Avda de la Universidad, La Laguna, Tenerife (tel. 922–258219).
- **Universidad Politécnica de Las Palmas,** Paseo Tomás Morales 70, Las Palmas de Gran Canaria (tel. 928–242340).

## YOUTH

Every year around the beginning of September a **youth conference** is held in **Sta Cruz de Tenerife**, with lectures on a range of subjects involving young people, craft and technology workshops, video and film shows, rock/jazz concerts, sports, etc., varying a little from year to year. If you're interested in finding out more, contact the **Cultural Departments** at c/Cano 24, Las Palmas (tel. 928–370399), and Betancourt Alfonso 9–1º, Sta Cruz de Tenerife (tel. 922–241426).

## USEFUL ADDRESSES

**Tourist offices**
**Tenerife:**
— Palacio Insular, Sta Cruz de Tenerife (tel. 922–242227)
— Plaza de la Iglesia, Puerto de la Cruz (tel. 922–371928)
**La Palma:** Plaza de España, Sta Cruz de La Palma (tel. 922–411641)
**Gran Canaria:** Casa del Turismo, Parque Santa Catalina, Las Palmas (tel. 928–264623)
**Lanzarote:** Parque Municipal, Arrecife (tel. 928–811860)

**Government offices**
**Regional Government Tourist Dept,** Casa del Turismo, Parque Sta Catalina, Las Palmas de Gran Canaria (tel. 928–270790)
**Regional Government** (Gobierno de Canarias), Plaza de San Bernardo 27, Las Palmas de Gran Canaria (tel. 928–372377)

**Youth/Sport Department,** Cano 24, Las Palmas de Gran Canaria

**Education departments**
Las Palmas: León y Castillo 226 (tel. 928–244740)
Sta Cruz de Tenerife: de la Marina 26, Edificio de Servicios Múltiples (tel. 922–283800)

**Labour departments**
Las Palmas: Luis Doreste Silva 64–1º (tel. 928–234456)
Sta Cruz de Tenerife: Marina 26 (tel. 922–284350)

**Youth information offices** As Youth/Sport Department above and Bethencourt Alfonso 9, Sta Cruz de Tenerife

**TIVE offices**
Avda Heraclio Sánchez 52, La Laguna (tel. 922–259630)
Cano 24, Las Palmas de Gran Canaria (tel. 928–370399)

**Travel agents**
Viajes Ecuador:
— Galicia 13, Las Palmas de Gran Canaria (tel. 928–231011)
— A Grimo s/n, Puerto de la Cruz, Tenerife (tel. 922–382663)
— El Pilar 6, Sta Cruz de Tenerife (tel. 922–242124)

**Car hire**
Atesa:
**Gran Canaria:**
— Avda Tirajana 22, Playa Inglés (tel. 928–765199)
— Lois Morote 42, Las Palmas (tel. 928–276852)
**Tenerife:**
— Bethancourt Alfonso 1, St Cruz de Tenerife (tel. 922–242240)
— Avda Generalísimo 23, Puerto de la Cruz (tel. 922–384252)
— Complejo Residencial Sansofe, Avda Marítima, Playa de las Américas (tel. 922–790720)
**Lanzarote:**
— At the airport
— Avda de las Playas s/n, Puerto del Carmen (tel. 928–326225)

**British representation**
**British Chamber of Commerce** — none.
**British Consulates:**
— Edificio Cataluña, c/Luis Morote 6, Las Palmas (tel. 928–262508)
— Edificio Marichal Suárez Guerra 40–5º, Sta Cruz de Tenerife (tel. 922–242000)

**British and American schools**
Colegio Hispano Británico, Apartado 228, Arrecife, Lanzarote
British School of Lanzarote, José Antonio 80, Arrecife, Lanzarote

**Canterbury School,** c/Juan XXIII 44, Las Palmas de Gran Canaria
**The British School of Gran Canaria,** PO box 11, Tafira Alta, Las Palmas de Gran Canaria
**Wingate School,** Mirador de las Cumbritas 10, Cabo Blanco (Arona), Tenerife
**British Yeoward School,** Parque Taoro, Puerto de la Cruz, Tenerife
**The American School of Las Palmas,** Apartado 15, Tafira Alta, Las Palmas de Gran Canaria

**Language schools (TEFL)**
**Escuela Benedict,** Tomás Morales 54, Las Palmas de Gran Canaria
**Inlingua Idiomas,** Tomás Morales 28, Las Palmas de Gran Canaria

# 19
# More Useful Information

**SUMMARY OF COURSES FOR FOREIGNERS**

|  | Spanish Language and Culture | | | | Other Courses |
|---|---|---|---|---|---|
|  | Summer courses | Term or ½ year | Whole year | Short courses throughout year |  |
| **ANDALUCIA** | | | | | |
| Almuñecar | ✓ | | | | |
| Baeza | ✓ | | | | |
| Córdoba | ✓ | | | | Photography & various |
| Granada | ✓ | ✓ | ✓ | ✓ (Feb–Oct) | |
| Málaga | ✓ | | | ✓ | |
| Marbella | ✓ | | | ✓ | |
| Palos de la Frontera | | | | | American history |
| Seville | ✓ (Sept) | | | ✓ | |
| **ARAGON** | | | | | |
| Berdún | | | | | Painting, Natural history |
| Jaca | ✓ | | | | |
| Zaragoza | ✓ | | | | |
| **ASTURIAS** | | | | | |
| Llanes | ✓ | | | | Archaeology |
| Oviedo | | ✓ | ✓ | | |
| **BALEARICS** | | | | | |
| Palma | ✓ | | | ✓ | |
| **CANARIES** | | | | | |
| Playa del Inglés | ✓ | | | ✓ | |
| Las Palmas | ✓ | | | ✓ | |
| Puerto de la Cruz | | ✓ | | | |
| La Orotava | | | | ✓ | |

|  | Spanish Language and Culture | | | | Other Courses |
|---|---|---|---|---|---|
|  | Summer courses | Term or ½ year | Whole year | Short courses throughout year |  |
| **CANTABRIA** | | | | | |
| Laredo | ✓ | | | | |
| Santander | ✓ | | | | International university |
| **CASTILLA-LEON** | | | | | |
| Burgos | ✓ | | | | |
| Salamanca | ✓ | ✓ | ✓ | ✓ | |
| Segovia | ✓ | | | | |
| Valladolid | ✓ | ✓ | | | Film |
| **CASTILLA-LA MANCHA** | | | | | |
| Cuenca | ✓ | | | | |
| Toledo | ✓ | | | | History, Art, Literature |
| **CATALUNA** | | | | | |
| Barcelona | ✓ | ✓ | | ✓ | Catalan & various |
| Olot | | | | | Catalan |
| **EUSKADI** | | | | | Euskera (Basque) |
| **EXTREMADURA** | | | | | |
| **GALICIA** | | | | | |
| Santiago | ✓ | | ✓ | | |
| La Coruña | | | | | Various |
| **MADRID** | ✓ | ✓ | ✓ | ✓ | Video, Astronomy & various |
| **MURCIA** | | | | | |
| Cartagena | ✓ | | | | |
| **NAVARRA** | | | | | |
| Pamplona | ✓ | ✓ | | | |
| **RIOJA** | | | | | |
| Logroño | ✓ | | | | Film/Video |
| **VALENCIA** | | | | | |
| Alicante | ✓ | | | | Art, History, etc. |
| Benidorm | | | | | Social science |
| Denia | ✓ | | | | |
| Valencia | ✓ | ✓ | ✓ | ✓ | Translating |

## MODEL OF LETTER ASKING FOR INFORMATION ABOUT COURSES

> Londres, 20–VIII–89
> *(place and date: note that the month may be written in Roman numerals)*
>
> Secretaría de los Cursos para Extranjeros
> c/Nueva 42
> BILBAO
> *(addressee)*
>
> Muy Sr mío/Sra mía:
> *(Dear Sir/Madam)*
>
> Le agradecería mucho me mandara información sobre los cursos de español
> *(I would be very grateful if you would send me details of the Spanish courses)*
>
> organizados por esa institución, así como boletín de inscripción.
> *(run by your organization, together with an application form.)*
>
>     Atentamente
>     *(Yours faithfully)*
>
>     M. Cervantes
>
> *(Note that your name and address should be written on the back of the envelope.)*

## FIESTAS

Only the following are officially national holidays all over Spain:

| | |
|---|---|
| 1 January | — Día del año *(New Year's Day)* |
| 1 May | — Día del Trabajo *(Labour Day)* |
| 25 December | — Navidad *(Christmas)* |

Each region has its own fiestas besides, up to a total of 14 days per year. These are likely to include:

| | |
|---|---|
| 6 January | — Reyes *(Epiphany)* |
| 19 March | — San José *(St Joseph's Day)* |
| Maundy Thursday | — jueves santo |
| Good Friday | — viernes santo |
| Corpus Cristi | — variable date in June |
| 25 July | — Santiago *(St James's Day)* |
| 15 August | — Asunción *(the Assumption)* |
| 12 October | — Día de la Hispanidad *(Hispanic Day)* |
| 1 November | — Todos los Santos *(All Saints' Day)* |
| 8 December | — Inmaculada Concepción *(Advent)* |

If any of them happen to fall on a Tuesday or a Thursday, there is a great tradition of making a *puente* (literally bridge) or long weekend break. However, if they fall on a Sunday they're not passed over to the following Monday as in Britain, but are lost. It's a typically Spanish situation of win all or lose all.

## WHAT TO TAKE — A CHECKLIST

**Essentials**
Ticket
Passport
Insurance
Travellers' cheques and/or currency

**If Driving**
Driving licence
Green card

**If Working, etc.**
Special visa/work permit

**Also Useful**
Student ID card
YHA membership card
This guide
Maps
Phrase book
Dictionary
Birth certificate
Passport-sized photographs of yourself
Academic certificates, legalised for recognition in Spain (if applicable)
As much other certification as possible, from employer, host family, university, etc., giving details of what you're going to be doing in Spain
Two pin adapter
Alarm clock

## GLOSSARY OF USEFUL SPANISH WORDS

| | |
|---|---|
| acampada libre | camping rough |
| andaluz (pl. andaluces) | Andalusian |
| ayuntamiento | town hall |
| bacalao | salt cod |
| barcelonés | from Barcelona |
| barrio | district of a town |
| bodega | a place where wine is made, kept or sold |
| camino de Santiago | route to Santiago (see section on **Galicia**) |
| cañada | medieval trade route used by herders |
| casa de labranza | see sections on accommodation |
| clarete | light red wine, almost rosé |
| cocido | stew, usually with pulses |
| colegio mayor | university hall of residence |
| conde-duque | Castillian nobleman |
| coñac | Spanish brandy |
| corrida | bullfight |
| chigre | Asturian bar |
| chorizo | paprika and garlic sausage which comes either as small sausages for cooking, or large ones for slicing |
| dulce | sweet |
| encierros | bull running, as in Pamplona (see section on **Navarre**) |
| euskera | Basque language |
| gallego | Galician |
| farmacia | chemist |
| filete | steak, usually veal |
| fueros | traditional rights and privileges enjoyed by regions |
| gazpacho | raw soup of puréed salad vegetables |
| Generalitat | Catalan (and Valencian) autonomous government |
| hidalgo | (lesser) nobleman |
| huerta | lit. vegetable plot used to describe fertile areas in Valencia and Murcia |
| jai-alai | Basque word for *pelota* (see below) |
| jamón (serrano) | cured ham (like Parma ham) |
| jota | northern Spanish folk dance, typical of Aragón, Navarre and La Rioja |
| madrileño | from Madrid |
| malagueño | from Malaga |
| matador | lit. 'killer' — the highest grade of bullfighter |

| | |
|---|---|
| meseta | Spain's central plateau |
| moriscos | Moors living in Christian-occupied territory |
| mesón | pub or tavern |
| mudéjar | style of architecture developed by Moorish craftsmen working in Christian-controlled territory |
| navarro | from Navarre |
| paseo | pre-dinner stroll |
| paso | icons or floats in religious processions |
| pazo | Galician manor house |
| pelota | Basque ball game |
| plaza mayor | main square |
| portero | doorman |
| pueblo | village — a key concept in understanding a Spanish person's identity |
| ración | portion of food served in a bar — it's common to order several between a group and all dig in with bread |
| rastro | flea market |
| refugio de montaña | mountain hut (see sections on accommodation) |
| reserva | quality wine from a good vintage, aged for minimum periods in wood and bottle |
| romería | pilgrimage-cum-picnic |
| rosado | rosé wine |
| rúa | street (Galician) |
| salchichón | salami |
| seco | dry |
| seguro | insurance |
| semi-dulce | medium sweet wine |
| sierra | mountains |
| sindicatos | workers' unions |
| supermercado | supermarket |
| tablao | flamenco show |
| tapas | nibbles traditionally served on the house in bars as an accompaniment to drinks — nowadays often charged for |
| tasca | dive bar |
| terraza | pavement café |
| Tierra de Campos | Spain's 'prairie' |
| torero | bullfighter |
| turrón | sweet made from nuts and honey (see section on **Valencia**) |
| vega | fertile plain |
| zambras | flamenco performances |
| zarzuela | light operetta; Catalan fish stew |

## WHAT TO READ ABOUT SPAIN

### General reading
*The Spaniards: A Portrait of the New Spain*, John Hooper (Spanish correspondent for *The Guardian*), Penguin, 1987.
*The Transformation of Spain*, David Gilmour, Quartet, 1985. Detailed and enlightening analysis of Spanish politics during the transition from dictatorship to democracy.
*Spain: A Companion Guide to Spanish Studies*, P. Russell (ed.), Methuen, 1976. An invaluable reference work on all aspects of Spanish culture and history.
*Modern Spain, 1875–1980*, Raymond Carr, Oxford University Press, 1980. Good historical run-down.
*Spain*, Jan Morris, Penguin, 1982. A non-demanding and very readable account.
*Gatherings from Spain*, Richard Ford, Dent. First published in 1846, this is a riveting collection of observations on early nineteenth-century Spain.

### Guides
*Walks and Climbs in the Pyrenees*, Kev Reynolds, Cicerone Press, 1983. A serious walker's handbook.
*Picos de Europa*, *Sierra de Gredos* and *Pyrenees*. Walking/mountaineering guides, all by Robin Collomb and published by West Col.
*Landscapes of Gran Canaria* and *Landscapes of Tenerife* by Noel Rochford.
*Landscapes of Mallorca* by Valerie Crespi-Green. Guides for car tours, walks and picnics, published by Sunflower Books.
*España en Bici*, Paco Tortosa and Mª Mar Fornés, published by Tierra del Fuego, Madrid. 22 routes for cycletouring in Spain, including maps. One to look out for in bookshops in Spain.
*The Birds of Britain and Europe*, Collins, 1972.

### Food and drink
*The Wines of Spain*, Jan Read, Faber and Faber, 1982. Good solid information.
*Sherry*, Julian Jeffs, Faber and Faber, 1961. A classic.
*A Guide to the Wines of Spain and Portugal*, Jan Read, Pitman, 1977. A useful guide to touring *bodegas* and sampling the varieties.

### Good fiction
A Hemingway can make good reading matter when you're off to Spain: either *Fiesta* (largely set in Pamplona at the San Fermines), *For Whom The Bell Tolls* (his Civil War novel), or his bullfighting classics, *Death in the Afternoon*, and the posthumous *The Dangerous Summer*.
As an alternative Laurie Lee's *As I Walked Out One Midsummer Morning* and *A Rose for Winter* are spellbinding, and, less well known but equally enthralling, is Norman Lewis' *Voices of the Old Sea*, which brilliantly

captures the moment when tourism arrives in a Catalan fishing village. All are published by Penguin.

Good biographies include *My Last Breath*, film director Luis Buñel's ghosted 'autobiography', and *Or I'll Dress You in Mourning*, the melodramatic 'rags to riches' story of top 60s bullfighter El Cordobés, by Larry Collins and Dominique Lapierre and published by Weidenfield and Nicolson (1968).

The best contemporary Spanish novel currently available in English is possibly *Murder in the Central Committee*, by satirist and journalist Manuel Vazquez Montalban, published by Pluto (1984), or if you haven't read the timeless classic of Spanish literature, Cervantes' *Don Quixote*, this too is available in paperback, published by Penguin.

Also interesting if you're going to Galicia, or indeed anywhere in the north, is Edwin Mullins' quirky *The Pilgrimage to Santiago*, falling somewhere in between a travelogue and a historical account.

Finally, three of the most readable works by English authors on the Spanish Civil War: *Blood of Spain*, Ronald Fraser, Penguin 1981 (a fascinating oral history); *Homage to Catalonia*, George Orwell, Penguin; and *The Death of Lorca*, Ian Gibson, Paladin.

**Work**
See p. 54 for a list of useful publications.

**Welfare**
- *Young Visitors to Spain (Guía para Jóvenes Visitantes de España)*. A guide produced by the Instituto de la Juventud (see p. 36) and also published in English, available through the Central Bureau (see p. 42), price £2.00.
- *Guía de los Jóvenes*. Guide produced by the Instituto de la Juventud for Spanish people, but could be useful if you're going to live in Spain as it gives information on the rights of young people with regard to everything from unfair dismissal to military service, exhaustive lists of advice centres and welfare organisations, etc.

# PART TWO
# Portugal

MAJOR THROUGH ROUTES
AIRPORT
VIANA DO CASTELO
BRAGA
COSTA VERDE
BRAGANÇA
VILA REAL
PORTO
ATLANTIC OCEAN
MOUNTAINS
AVEIRO
VISEU
GUARDA
COIMBRA
FIGUEIRA DA FOZ
COSTA DA PRATA
SERRA DE ESTRELA
CASTELO BRANCO
LEIRIA
SPAIN
BATALHA
FATIMA
OBIDOS
PORTALEGRE
MAFRA
SANTAREM
LISBON
SINTRA
LISBON & REGION
ESTORIL
EVORA
PLAINS
SETUBAL
ALENTEJO
BEJA
30 Km.
30m.
SERRA DE MONCHIQUE
ALGARVE
PORTIMÃO
SAGRES
LAGOS
FARO
MADEIRA
10 km
10m
PORTO SANTO
PICO RUIVO
ATLANTIC OCEAN
FUNCHAL

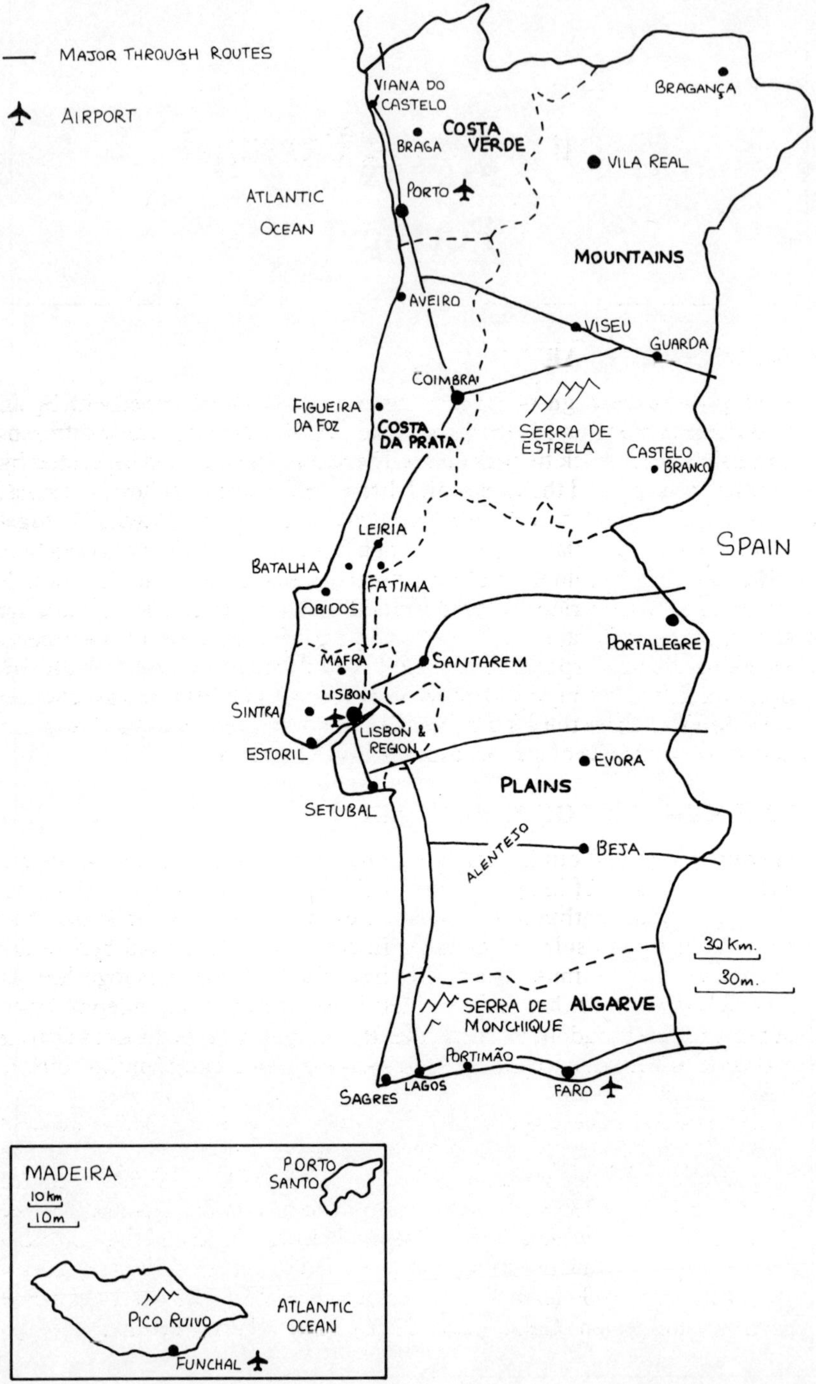

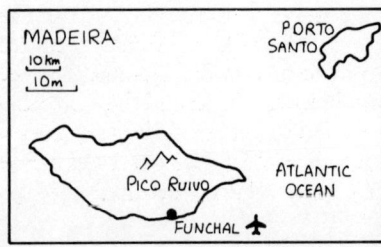

# Introducing Portugal

## A COUNTRY APART

Portugal — to the disgust of the Portuguese — is so often lumped with Spain that it needs pointing out from the start that they are two totally different countries, stuck back to back on the Iberian peninsula, and separated by remote tracts of land through which little traffic passes. Where Spain has traditionally looked towards the Mediterranean, or in on itself, Portugal turns towards the Atlantic, and although both maintain close relationships with their former colonies in Latin America, Portugal also looks towards its lost empire in Africa and even India. Portugal also has a long-standing association with Britain which has had a deep influence on its development, providing a counterpoint to the rigid Napoleonic structures which still predominate in Spain. The history Portuguese children learn in school is very different from the version Spanish children are taught, and Spanish and Portuguese are of course quite distinct languages.

## THE KINGDOM OF PORTUCALE

Having said this, though, there are a great many justifications for the existence of an area of interest which includes both countries, and for including Portugal within a book which is predominantly about Spain. Any study of the peninsula which takes into account the period before the twelfth century AD must necessarily treat the two countries together, as it wasn't until 1140 that Alfonso Henriques declared the independence of the separate kingdom of Portucale. Before this time, both areas shared the same history of successive occupations by Romans, Vandals, Suevi, Visigoths and Moors.

Galician-Portuguese was at that time just one of a number of dialects spoken in the peninsula, and it developed into a separate language as the kingdom of Portucale grew stronger and more stable, particularly under Dom Dinis (1279-1325), who was one of the first monarchs to rule over the complete area which is now Portugal. In Spain it was the Castilian dialect which became predominant, although the other variants were not lost, and a form of Galician-Portuguese is still spoken today in the extreme north-west of Spain (Galicia), bordering on northern Portugal.

## TOWARDS AN EMPIRE

In the fifteenth and sixteenth centuries both Portugal and Spain pursued their conquests for Christendom beyond the frontiers of the known world, and created overseas empires for themselves. Throughout this time the Portuguese nobility retained many links with their Spanish counterparts, reinforced by intermarriage between the two royal families. With the Reformation in northern Europe the Catholic countries were driven even closer together, and Spanish influence in Portugal increased both through the activities of the Jesuits and the establishment of the Inquisition there. Finally, in 1581, after a crisis over the Portuguese succession, the two crowns were united under Philip II of Spain, and Portuguese institutions were dominated by the Spanish for the next 60 years.

When the Portuguese monarchy was restored bitter resentment still remained against the Spanish. Despite this, however, Portugal very much took its lead from events in Spain during the years that followed, as both countries faced invasion from Napoleon's forces and similar struggles between absolutism and liberalism throughout the nineteenth century.

## DICTATORSHIP TO DEMOCRACY

In this century too, both countries suffered long dictatorships and the suspension of democratic freedoms, and were brought together by their shared neutrality in the second World War. Post war both underwent rapid economic expansion and modernisation, with the development of important tourist industries. The phenomenon of emigration to northern Europe and the Americas, although important in both countries, was more marked in Portugal which during the mid 70s sent over 14% of its workforce abroad, mostly to France.

Although Portugal's transition from dictatorship to democracy took a more revolutionary path than Spain's, both countries lost no time in electing socialist governments, to which they entrusted the task of bringing them into the mainstream of modern European currents, culminating in their entry together into the EEC in January 1986.

## PORTUGAL TODAY

Despite sharing so much history with Spain, Portugal has its own feel and character which set it apart. The first thing you notice is that it is a small country — the great open spaces of Spain are exchanged for intensively cultivated hillsides, dotted with houses in a density not seen across the border, giving the countryside a cosy, friendly, even claustrophobic air. The country has its contrasts, of course, mainly between north and south, and has been given variety and interest by the influx of immigrants from the African colonies since their independence, but the regional diversity which is so much a part of Spain today is less evident. With only one fifth of the land area of Spain, Portugal's resources are correspondingly smaller, and the impression is overall one of a poor country with nowhere near Spain's potential for development. Both economically and socially, the scale of change has been much more modest in Portugal — there are only six towns with more than 40,000 inhabitants, tourism is more understated, industrialisation very much restricted to small pockets, and the big multinationals are few and far between. Much of the country is still backward, and its attraction lies in its old-fashioned charm rather than in up-front style. The culture in general appreciates subtleties and shadings, rather than the great *sol y sombra* — all or nothing — contrasts of Spain.

If Portugal seems understated though, it certainly isn't because it hasn't got anything to shout about — it's perhaps just lacking the resources or the showmanship to promote itself. Its attractions are many: wonderful sandy beaches that make the Costa de Sol seem grim, beautiful countryside and mountains waiting to be explored, impressive monuments and buildings to see, and above all a rich and varied culture to get to know. The pleasures of discovering all this are perhaps all the greater because they are to such a large extent undocumented and unsung.

# 20
# Arriving & Surviving in Portugal

## PAPERWORK

### Passports
A British visitor's passport is sufficient to get you into the country as a tourist, but if you want to stay longer you'll need the full passport. For addresses of Passport Offices see p. 14.

### Visas
- **Portuguese Consulate,** 62 Brompton Road, London SW3 (tel. 01-581 3598).

No visa is required if you're just going as a tourist for up to 2 months, but if you want to stay longer you'll have to apply for a special residence visa to the Portuguese Consulate in London at least 3–4 months before you want to travel. You'll need to supply a character reference from someone legally resident in Portugal, several black and white passport sized photographs of yourself and a whole host of information such as where your parents were born. If all goes well, you will be given a temporary residence visa for 2 months, extendable twice for further periods of 2 months (a total of 6 months). This allows you to apply for permanent residence once you're in Portugal, which has to be done through the **Servico de Estrangeiros**, Av Antonio Augusto de Aguiar 18, Lisbon (tel. 01-8554047), which also has branches in other major towns. They will require a certificate of registration issued by a British Consulate in Portugal (see regional sections for addresses).

### Insurance
As in Spain, EEC agreements entitle British citizens to some free medical attention — if urgent — on production of **Form E111**, which you must obtain from the Department of Health before you leave this country.

Dental treatment and medicines are not covered by the agreement, so it's wise to take out extra medical cover. The **International Student Insurance Service** (ISIS) can be of help here — see p. 16.

No particular vaccinations are necessary for travel to Portugal, although if you're going on a dig it would be a good idea to have a tetanus jab.

## Other documentation
- **Identity Cards.** Once you have been in Portugal for 6 months, and obtained your permanent residence permit, you will need to apply for a *Bilhete de Identidade* or Portuguese ID card. Apart from being required by law, you will need this card for many official purposes, including applying for a Portuguese driving license.
- **International Student Identity Card.**
- **Federation of International Youth Travel Organisations Card** — see p. 15.

## Money
**Credit cards** are generally accepted in cities and tourist areas, but *not* at petrol stations. Take **currency** (a maximum of 5000$ is at present all you're allowed to take in), **travellers' cheques** or **Eurocheques** (see p. 16), or a combination of all three. **Girocheque** travellers' cheques are particularly useful if you're going to remoter areas as they can be exchanged at post offices rather than at banks.

**Banks** are open Monday to Friday 0830 to 1145 and 1300 to 1445, although there are a couple of banks in Lisbon which open in the evenings from 1800 to 2300
- **Banco Borges & Irmão,** Av de Liberdade 9–A
- **Banco Pinto & Sotto Mayor,** Pç dos Restauradores 11

You won't be allowed to open a proper bank account until you've got your residence permit, but you can open a special tourist account meanwhile.

Note that the escudo symbol ($) is written *after* the number of escudos and before the *fraction* (centavos), thus: 20$50 = 20 escudos 50 centavos and 4000$00 = 4000 escudos.

## Maps
Portugal is not a country that is particularly well documented, cartagraphically speaking or otherwise. You shouldn't have any difficulty getting large scale maps though — **Michelin** do one, or you can get a reasonable one free from the **Tourist Office** in London (1–5 New Bond St, London W1 (tel. 01–493 3873) ).

For smaller scale maps, there is a new series (1:200,000) under production called *Official Survey of Portugal*, available from Stanfords, 12 Long Acre, London WC2 (tel. 01–836 1321), or in Portugal try the **Instituto Geografico e Cadastral**, Praça de Estrêla, Lisbon.

For hiking or mountaineering, it might be useful to seek the advice of the **Clube Nacional de Montanhismo**, at Rua Formosa 303–2º, Porto.

Whatever map you use, bear in mind it might well be out of date.

## GETTING THERE

### By air
There are international airports in Lisbon, Faro and Porto, and Funchal for Madeira, and although flights tend not to be as cheap or as frequent

as to destinations in Spain, it's fairly easy to find a return flight for something in the region of £120, especially to Lisbon and Faro. Lisbon is the best served airport, with several flights daily.

Portugal's national airline is **TAP Air Portugal**, whose London office is at 38 Gillingham St, SW1 (tel. 01–828 2092) and they can help you with information on scheduled flights and special deals like their 'Sunrail' and 'Sundrive' offers. Sunrail is a 1, 2, or 3 week rail ticket valid all over Portugal which you can buy at a special rate at the same time as your flight, and Sundrive is a car-hire deal.

If you want cheap charter flights though, you should go to a specialist agent like the following (many other companies which offer cheap flights to destinations all over the world advertise in the press, and magazines like *Time Out*):

- **Abreu,** 109 Westbourne Grove, London W2 (tel. 01–229 9905)
- **Intercontinental Flight Services,** Morley House, 2nd Floor, Suite 8, 320 Regent St, London W1 (tel. 01–637 4676)
- **Owners Abroad,** Astley House, 33 Notting Hill Gate, London W11 (tel. 01–221 0535)
- **Portugalicia Travel,** 110b Ladbroke Grove, London W10 (tel. 01–221 0333)

If you're a student, the following student travel agencies offer discounted fares:

- **STA Travel,** 74 Old Brompton Rd, London SW7 (tel. 01–581 1022)
- **Worldwide Student Travel,** 37/8 Store St, London WC1 (tel. 01–580 7733)

Student travel agencies in Portugal are listed below, but in general it's advisable to book the whole trip from the UK:

- **Tagus Juvenil,** Pç de Londres 9–B, Lisbon (tel. 01-884957)
- **Turicoop,** R. Pascoal de Melo 15–1º–Dto, Lisbon (tel. 01-531804)

## By rail

It's an arduous journey overland to Portugal, and by rail it will take you a couple of days, changing trains and stations in Paris and in some cases in Madrid as well. Probably you'll only consider it if you want to visit other places on the way, or if you buy the **Interrail** card which for £139 gives you a month's unlimited travel on railways all over Europe. You can buy it (under 26s only) from any main BR station.

**Transalpino** (117 Euston Rd, London NW1 (tel. 01–388 2267) ) and **Eurotrain** (52 Grosvenor Gardens, London SW1 (tel. 01–730 8111) ) offer discounted rail fares for the under 26s, which work out at about £60–£70 single to destinations in Portugal. These tickets are also available through student travel agencies like the ones listed above.

It's also worth looking into the discounts offered by the **Rail Europ Family Rail Card** if 3 or more people are travelling together — you don't have to be necessarily members of the same family, just share the same address.

Full information on train times is available from any **BR Travel Centre**, or by ringing **British Rail Continental Enquiries** (tel. 01-834 2345).

### By coach
There are twice weekly coach services operating between London and Coimbra, Lisbon and the Algarve — phone **Victoria coach station** (01-730 3453) for details. Again, you're talking in terms of a couple of days travelling and you can expect to pay upwards of about £65 for the single fare.

### By car
Driving to Portugal is only really suitable for people who want to spend between 3 weeks and 6 months in the country — less than 3 weeks doesn't merit the time spent hauling through France and Spain (at least 48 hours each way and the same again to recover!), and if you're staying longer than 6 months you'll have to pay import duty on the vehicle, which is something to be avoided at all costs. Various alternatives exist if you want to move around by car: using the **Brittany Ferries sea crossing** to Santander in northern Spain — this cuts the driving time to perhaps one day — or **hiring a car** to use once you arrive in Portugal — you can do this on the spot (addresses given in regional section) or get your travel agent to arrange it for you at the same time as your flight. TAP Air Portugal offer a special 'Sundrive' package for example, which works out at from about £100 a week high season. Car hire in Portugal is cheaper than in Spain but petrol is more expensive. A third possibility would be to put your car on the train (details from British Rail) but this is definitely not a cheap option. For further information on driving in Portugal see p. 297.

### By sea
There are no passenger ferries from the UK to Portugal. The nearest you'll get by sea is Santander in northern Spain — see p. 20.

### Packages
There is a great variety of package tours to Portugal and a good range of interesting ones as well as the usual sun-and-sand deals, which are almost all to the Algarve (apart from the attractive 'winter sun' packages to Madeira). If you have an interest you want to follow up in Portugal a package can save time chasing up the contacts yourself. Here are some of the most interesting:

**Association for Cultural Exchange,** Babraham, Cambridge (tel. 0223-835977). 'Study tour' of Portugal taking in Lisbon, Tomar, Sintra, Porto and the North, and Evora, with emphasis on art and architecture.

**Blackheath Wine Trails,** 13 Blackheath Village, London SE3 (tel. 01-852 0025). Tours of the *vinho verde* and port-producing areas. Also Madeira.

**Caravela** (agents for TAP Air Portugal), 38 Gillingham St, 3rd floor, London SW1 (tel. 01–630 9223). Good selection of 'mainstream' packages throughout the country, tours, fly-drives, etc.

**Concertworld,** 6 Belmont Hill, London SE13 (tel. 01–852 2035) arrange tailor-made concert tours for orchestras and bands.

**Cox and Kings,** 21 Dorset Sq, London NW1 (tel. 01–724 6624). Natural history study holidays in northern Portugal. Their subsidiary **Countrywide Holidays** (same address) do walking holidays in Portugal and Madeira.

**Explore Worldwide,** High St, Aldershot, Hants (tel. 0252–319448). Small group expeditions to the Costa Verde and Gerês National Park via Santiago de Compostela in Spain.

**Fatima Travel,** 500 Bromley Rd, Downham, Kent (tel. 01–698 1234). Religious tours.

**Kestours,** Travel House, Elmers End, Beckenham, Kent (tel. 01–658 7316). 'City breaks' in Lisbon, and sports tours for clubs, as requested.

**Interchurch Travel,** 45 Berkeley St, London W1 (tel. 01–734 0942). Pilgrimage to Fatima and the cities of Portugal.

**Portugala Holidays,** 67 Outram Rd, London N22 (tel. 01–388 0162). Wide range of packages including sports holidays, wine tours, religious tours, city breaks, etc.

**Ramblers Holidays Ltd,** 13 Longcroft House, Fretherne Rd, Welwyn Garden City, Herts (tel. 0707–33133). Walking holidays in the Algarve, Douro Valley, Serra de Estrêla and Madeira (varying from year to year).

**Waymark Holidays,** 295 Lillie Road, London SW6 (tel. 01–385 5015). Small group walking holidays in the Azores and Madeira.

**Wexas International,** Travel Dept, 45 Brompton Rd, London SW3 (tel. 01–589 3315). Small group expeditions to Porto and the North with opportunities for walking, swimming, studying flora and fauna, etc.

See also the student travel agencies listed on p. 288 for the odd package at special student prices.

## WHERE TO STAY

### Hotels/pensions
*In the UK:*
- **Portuguese National Tourist Office,** 1 New Bond St, London W1 (tel. 01–493 3873)

*In Portugal:*
- **Tourist offices** — see regional sections later

It's fairly easy to find accommodation of this type on the spot, even at the height of the season. Lisbon and the Algarve are the places where you're likely to encounter the most difficulty, particularly in July and August. The tourist offices offer an excellent service, ringing round to find you accommodation if necessary. The following categories of accommodation exist:

- **Hotels.** Categorised from 1* to 5*. As a guide, a double room in a 1*

hotel is likely to cost around £5 a night, for which you'll get quite good facilities.
- **Pensões.** Pensions from 1* to 4*, many of which offer full board at very reasonable prices, enabling you to use them for short–medium term stays. Usually a 1* hotel is better and often cheaper than a 3 or 4* pension.
- **Estalagens.** Either 4* or 5*, these are high class tourist inns.
- **Pousadas.** State-run tourist inns, similar to the Spanish *paradores*, often in spectacular locations and serving good local food. Stays are limited to 5 days, and it's a good idea to book ahead through the following organisation: **Enatur,** Av Santa Joana Princesa 10–A, Lisbon (tel. 01–881221).
- **Moteis.** Motels, either 3* or 2* establishments.
- **Albergarias.** All 4* up-market establishments.

As in Spain, the letter R after any of these indicates there are no facilities for meals. Prices must be displayed on the back of the door of each room and rooms vacated by 1200 on the day of departure.

In addition to these, it's possible to find rooms (*dormidas*) in private houses for very reasonable prices. You see them advertised or get approached directly by people offering them as you arrive at the bus or train station.

## Youth hostels
- **Associação Portuguesa de Pousadas de Juventude,** R. Andrade Corvo 46, Lisbon (tel. 01–571054)
- **YHA (England and Wales),** Trevelyan House, 8 St Stephens Hill, St Albans, Herts (tel. 0727–55215)
- **International Youth Hostel Federation,** Midland Bank Chambers, Howardsgate, Welwyn Garden City, Herts.

There are only 14 youth hostels in Portugal, listed below. Except where indicated, all are open all the year round, and provide a very cheap way of staying in Portugal — between £2 and £3 a night for bed and breakfast, with meals priced at about £1.50 each on top of this.

As in youth hostels in Britain, you're expected to help with chores and to be in by around 2300. You will need to obtain an **International Youth Hostellers card** in order to use the facilities, and you can get this at any youth hostel, preferably in the UK in advance.

It's a good idea to book in advance, and the YHA here will give you advice on how to do this.

*Algarve*
**Pousada de Juventude de Vila Real de Santo António,** R. 1º de Maio 23, 8900 Vila Real de Santo António (tel. 081–44565)
**Pousada de Juventude de Sagres,** Promontório de Sagres, 8650 Vila do Bispo (tel. 082–64129)

*Costa da Prata*
**Pousada de Juventude da Areia Branca,** Areia Branca, 2530 Lourinha (tel. 061–42127)

**Pousada de Juventude de Leiria,** Largo Cándido dos Reis 7–D, 2400 Leiria (tel. 044–31868)
**Pousada de Juventude de S. Martinho,** Estrada de Alcobaça, 2465 Alfeizerão (tel. 062–99506)
**Pousada de Juventude de S. Pedro de Moel,** S. Pedro de Moel, 2430 Marinha Grande (tel. 044–59236). Open May to September.

*Costa Verde*
**Pousada de Juventude de Braga,** R. de Santa Margarida 6, 4700 Braga (tel. 053 78163)
**Pousada de Juventude do Lindoso,** Porto do Chão, Lindoso, Ponte da Barca, (tel. 053–47305). Open May to September.
**Pousada de Juventude do Porto,** R. Rodrigues Lobo 98, 4000 Porto (tel. 02–65535)

*Lisbon*
**Pousada de Juventude de Catalazete,** Estrada Marginal, 2780 Deiras (tel. 01–243 0638)
**Pousada de Juventude de Lisboa,** R. Andrade Corvo 46, 1000 Lisboa (tel. 01–532696)

*Plains*
**Pousada de Juventude de Evora,** R. da Corredoura 32, 7000 Evora (tel. 066–25043)
**Pousada de Juventude de Portalegre,** Antigo Convento de S. Francisco, Praça da República, 7300, Portalegre (tel. 045–23568)

*Mountains*
**Pousada de Juventude das Penhas da Saude,** Penhas da Saúde, Serra da Estrela, 6200 Covilhã (tel. 075–25375)

**Camping**
Portugal has 100 or so campsites, mostly up and down the coast, offering facilities varying from nought to 3★ at extremely low prices. You can get a full list and map from any Portuguese tourist office, or contact the **Federação Portuguesa de Campismo e Caravanismo** (R. Voz do Operário 1, Lisboa) who publish a detailed guide entitled *Roteiro Campista*.

Camping rough is not encouraged, but is permitted providing you are at least 1km away from an official site, beach (in practice only the popular ones) or centre of population, and provided your party does not exceed 20 people. If you are camping rough, do take care to avoid starting forest fires.

**Villas and holiday apartments**
A large number of companies offer villa and apartment holidays and you can pick up brochures in any travel agent. If you want to arrange a let privately, however — this sometimes has the advantage of getting away from the tourist areas — you could look for advertisements in the press, especially the Sunday papers, or in *TAPS*, the magazine of the Anglo-

Portuguese Society (see p. 303). In Portugal try the *Algarve News* or the *Anglo-Portuguese News*, published in Estoril.

**Manor houses**
It's possible to stay as a guest in *quintas* — country homes or farm houses, usually in very attractive rural areas. The **Ponte de Lima Tourist Board** offers a booking service, and can be contacted at Praça da República, 4990 Ponte de Lima (tel. 058-942334). For further general information contact the Head Tourist Office in Lisbon, at Av António Augusto de Aguiar 86.

**Renting/sharing**
Whereas short- to middle-term tourist accommodation is not too hard to find, long-term lets are very difficult to come by — there is an acute housing shortage in Lisbon and Porto, and in the Algarve such accommodation hardly exists, and what there is is very expensive. Be prepared for the time-consuming business of doing the rounds of property agents, asking around, and checking ads.

**Buying**
More and more British people are buying property in Portugal. You can get lists of estate agents through the **Portuguese Tourist Office** in London, and a lot of useful information and advice is contained in Susan Thackeray's book *Living in Portugal*, published by Hale. There is also a quarterly glossy news magazine on the subject entitled *Algarve Property*. As in Spain, beware of the time-share touts.

**Home exchange**
(See p. 26.) Although offers of home exchange from Portuguese people aren't anything like as common as in Spain, the following agencies are trying to extend their operations in Portugal and do carry some offers:

**Home Interchange Ltd,** 8 Hillside, Farningham, Kent (tel. 0322-964527)
**Homeswop,** 15 Benyon Gardens, Culford, Bury St Edmunds, Suffolk (tel. 0284-84315)
**Intervac,** 6 Siddals Lane, Allestree, Derby (tel. 0332-558931)

**Student exchanges**
As so little Portuguese is taught in British schools, there are no formal structures for arranging student exchanges. However, the following organisations may be able to help:

**The Central Bureau for Educational Visits and Exchanges** (see p. 42)
**The Youth Exchange Centre,** Seymour Mews House, Seymour Mews, London W1, (tel. 01-487 5961). Can provide funding and assistance in arranging group exchanges.
**The Portuguese Consulate** (Educational Co-ordinator), 62 Brompton Rd, London SW3 (tel. 01-581 8722)
**The Hispanic and Luso-Brazilian Council** — see p. 41.

**Intervac** and **Homeswop** (above) can put potential exchangees in contact with each other through their home-exchange advertising service.

**Homestays**
*Home from Home*, published by the Central Bureau (see p. 42), price £3.50.

**The Experiment in International Living,** Upper Wyche, Malvern, Worcs (tel. 06845-62577) — see p. 28. Costs for Portugal are about £140 for 2 weeks, quite a lot cheaper than Spain.

**Servas,** 6 Addison Rd, Hove, E. Sussex (tel. 0273-7287763); also at 77 Elm Park Mansions, Park Walk, London SW10 (tel. 01-352 0203) — see p. 29. There are about thirty 'hosts' in Portugal.

**Euroyouth,** 301 Westborough Rd, Westcliff-on-Sea, Essex (tel. 0702-341434). *En famille* accommodation combined with language courses in Lisbon throughout the year. Also the possibility of 'holiday guest stays' whereby applicants receive free accommodation with a family in return for making conversation in English with the host/host's children for several hours daily.

**En Famille Agency,** Westbury House, Queens Lane, Arundel, Sussex (tel. 0903-883266). Accommodation with Portuguese families arranged for groups, families or individuals for any length of time at any time of the year. There is a £30 fee to the agency, and costs are approximately £85 per week full board.

## FOOD AND DRINK

**Eating out**
The major thing to remember when eating out in Portugal is to order about half as much as you think you'll need — the portions are enormous! In most restaurants you'll have the choice between ordering a *dose* (full portion) or a *meia dose* (half portion). Alternatively it's quite acceptable to order one dish between two. With such generous servings you don't really need anything except a main dish, but in the everyday restaurants at least everything is so cheap it seems churlish not to order other courses as well.

The basic ingredients of Portuguese cooking are seafood, including the ubiquitous *bacalau* (salt cod), olive oil, wine, and fresh fruit and vegetables. Rice is grown in well-irrigated areas of the plains, but you'll also see pasta and potatoes in more or less similar proportions. Meat very definitely takes second place to fish, and is more often than not pork. Noteworthy dishes are:

- *caldo verde*: potato and cabbage soup similar to that found in Galicia.
- *grão*: chick pea soup
- *sopa da peixe*: fish soup
- *gaspacho*: similar to the Andalusian *gazpacho* — a soup of raw puréed salad vegetables
- *amêijoas na cataplana*: clam stew with ham and sausage

- *bifes a Portuguesa*: beef in mustard sauce
- *carne de porco a Alentejo*: pork with clams
- *cabrito assado*: roast kid
- *leitão*: roast sucking pig

To finish your meal, there is an enormous range of locally made sweets and cakes which vary according to the region — often made out of eggs, nuts and sugar — all of which can be relied on to be sweet, sticky and delicious. Alternatively there is always fresh fruit, or various cheeses, of which the best are *queijo Serra da Estrêla*, a sheeps cheese from the Serra da Estrêla, and *cabreiro* — goats cheese.

The Portuguese eat at more 'normal' times than the Spanish — 1230 to 1400 for lunch (*almoço*), and 1930 to 2130 for dinner (*jantar*) — except in the *fado* restaurants (see p. 341). A great Portuguese institution is the habit of popping off at any time of the day for a coffee or tea and cakes in a *salão do cha*, some of which are wonderful old art nouveau places. Portugal does excellent coffee and tea and its *patisserie* is superb.

## Portuguese wines

The British have appreciated Portuguese wines for centuries, and played an important part in developing Portugal's finest and best known variety — port. Vintage port is as expensive in Portugal as it is in Britain, since only one year in five on average produces wine considered good enough for this designation, and the ageing process takes many years. However, there are many other types of port worth sampling — crusted port (a blend of different vintages which is matured more quickly) and late bottled vintage (matured for longer in wood before bottling) compare well with vintage port. Tawny port is lighter coloured and has a more delicate flavour, and ruby port is well known in Britain. The white ports, however, are hardly ever seen in Britain, and are well worth trying — there is a dry version that may be drunk as an aperitif. If you're at all interested in sampling the delights of port, the best places to go are the **Port Wine Institute** in Lisbon (R. São Pedro de Alcantara 45) and the **Solar do Vinho do Porto** in Porto, in the R. Entre-Quintas. It's also possible to visit the port lodges in Vila Nova de Gaia during normal working hours, and get a free tasting! Portugal's other great dessert wine is the luscious Moscatel de Setúbal — another one to look out for.

Madeira has of course been enjoyed by the British for centuries and is widely available on the mainland as well as on its island of origin. It comes in four varieties which, in increasing order of sweetness, are Sercial, Verdelho, Bual and Malvasia. The drier varieties are generally drunk as an aperitif, while the sweeter versions make good after-dinner drinking, although all may be sampled with impunity (and enjoyment) at any time of the day.

Mateus Rosé is produced in an undemarcated area of the Upper Douro, mainly for export (in huge quantities), so if you want a fresh young wine with a hint of sparkle, the *vinhos verdes* are the ones to go for. The whites, low in alcohol and delicately flowery or fruity, are fairly well-known in

Britain, but in fact 70% of *vinhos verdes* are red, and these are much more of an acquired taste, but nonetheless a good accompaniment to Portuguese food.

It's the Dão wine region around the city of Viseu that perhaps produces Portugal's finest table wines, however — mostly dry, full bodied reds, but also a proportion of clean dry whites. Around the city of Lisbon there are three other demarcated areas which produce table wine, Bucelas, Carcavelos and Colares — all worth looking out for.

Wine from outside the denominated areas is called *consumo* wine and is generally very drinkable. The area around Torres Vedras produces a lot of Lisbon's everyday wine, while almost every other region produces some, although vines become less frequent the further south you go.

## GETTING ABOUT

In Portugal you don't have the problem of enormous distances that exists in Spain and getting around does not present any great difficulty. Public transport is cheap and most places are well served by both road and rail networks.

### By rail

The British were responsible for building Portuguese railways, now run by the national company **CP** (Head office: Calçada do Duque 20, Lisboa (tel. 01–363181)). There are over 4,000 kilometres of track, roughly forming a main north to south route down the coast with various spurs crossing the country from east to west. Thus over 700 towns and villages are linked into the network, although frustratingly their stations are often several miles out of the centre. The Douro line, which follows the Douro valley up from Porto to Barco de Alva through some fantastic scenery can be counted among the great railway journeys of the world and the little narrow gauge lines off it are a great way of exploring the villages of the north.

Trains which stop everywhere are classed as **regional** and are quite cheap — cheaper than the bus in most cases. However, the faster trains, **rapidos** and **expressos**, are more expensive and if you have an Interrail card you may have to pay a supplement. You'll need to turn up at the ticket office well in advance and may have to book a seat.

Cycles can be carried on most trains as long as they are checked in in advance. On longer journeys they might not be carried on the same train as the one you're travelling on.

If you're interested in travelling around by train, you might consider buying **TAP Air Portugal**'s 'Sunrail' package, which costs an extra £58 for 2 weeks on top of your air fare (£36 for 1 week, £83 for 3), and allows you unlimited rail travel throughout your stay.

### By coach and bus

Most bus services are run by the national company **Rodoviaria Nacional** and provide a good way of getting around. Bus stations are normally centrally located in towns. In Lisbon most buses leave from the Praça Restauradores.

## By car
For driving in Portugal you'll need either an **International Driving Licence**, obtainable from the **AA** or **RAC** in the UK, or from the Portuguese motoring organisation, the **Automovel Club de Portugal**, Rua Rosa Araújo 24, Lisbon (tel. 01-563931), or one of the new EEC format driving licences. You'll also need extended insurance in the form of a **green card** from your insurance company — it's worth taking out as much insurance as possible as the accident rate is frighteningly high in Portugal.

The International Highway Code is used, and traffic drives on the right. It's compulsory to wear seat belts in the front seats, and to carry a red warning triangle for use in case of break down or accident. If you do break down, you can get assistance from the **Automovel Club de Portugal** at the address given above, or from one of its regional offices:

**Porto:** R. Gonçalo Cristóvão 2 (tel. 02-29271)
**Aveiro:** Av Dr. Lourenço Peixinho 89-D (tel. 034-22571)
**Braga:** Av da Liberdade 466-1º-D (tel. 053-25004)
**Coimbra:** Av Navarro 6 (tel. 039-26813)
**Faro:** Praça D. Francisco Gomes (tel. 089-24753)

The speed limit is 120 kilometres per hour on main roads, 90 kmph on other roads, and 60 kmph in towns — you can be fined on the spot for traffic offences.

A north-south motorway is under construction which should eventually go from Braga to Setubal and on to Sines — the busiest stretches around Porto, Coimbra, Lisbon and Setubal are already in use. Petrol is currently more expensive in Portugal than anywhere in Europe, and petrol stations tend to be few and far between, so keep an eye on the fuel gauge if you're touring around.

It's important to bear in mind that Portuguese residents of any nationality are forbidden from driving a foreign registered car and must also have a valid Portuguese driving licence as opposed to an international one. This means effectively that if you're thinking of staying for longer than 6 months, it will be cheaper to buy a car in Portugal rather than fork out the import duty necessary to re-register your own car. Getting a Portuguese driving licence is a complicated business and you won't be able to do it until you've got your residence papers, by which time you should have some experience in dealing with the Portuguese bureaucracy! The **Automovel Club de Portugal** are the people to contact for full information.

## Hitching
This is illegal on motorways and although not officially encouraged elsewhere is at least possible.

## Taxis
Official taxis are black and green, and provide a cheap service compared

to UK prices, although they charge supplements after normal working hours or for carrying baggage and expect at least a 10% tip.

## COMMUNICATIONS AND THE MEDIA

### Telephones
The Portuguese telephone system is not renowned for its efficiency, and although it has improved a lot in recent years, be prepared for plenty of strange noises. Telephone booths take 2$50, 5$, and 25$ coins.

You can dial Britain direct from phone booths marked *internacional*, the code is 00 44 plus the British area code without the initial 0 (eg 00 44 1 for a London number, 00 44 61 for a Manchester number, etc.). International booths are few and far between outside the main cities, but if you're elsewhere in the country you can get a call put through for you at any main post office (*correio* — see below). If you're phoning from a private number, you can usually dial direct, otherwise dial 3295 for international operator service, or 3299 for calls outside Europe.

For calls within Portugal, the area code for Lisbon is 01, and for Porto 02. Other codes are:

| | |
|---|---|
| Albufeira 089 | Amarante 055 |
| Barreiro 01 | Beja 084 |
| Braga 053 | Castelo Branco 072 |
| Chaves 076 | Coimbra 089 |
| Guarda 071 | Leiria 044 |
| Loule 089 | Santarem 043 |
| Setubal 065 | Torres Vedras 061 |
| Viana do Castelo 058 | Viseu 032 |

For information on any other area codes, dial 091. In case of emergencies the number to dial, wherever you are in the country, is 115.

If you're calling Portugal from Britain, the number to dial is 010 351 plus the area code (minus the initial 0), and subscriber's number.

Telex is widely used in Portugal for business purposes.

Telephone directories (available at post offices) contain all this information and more — each area directory comes with its own Yellow Pages.

### Post
Post offices (*correios*) are to be found everywhere, and also provide telephone and telegraph services. Normal opening hours are 0900 to 1900, Monday to Friday, although some close a little earlier and you may find some closed for lunch between 1230 and 1400. The main post offices in Lisbon and Porto operate extended hours until late at night.

### Television and radio
**Radiotelevisão Portuguesa** is state owned and operates two channels — the main one is on air from 1300 to 2300 approximately. There are a lot of foreign programmes, including subtitled English and American films, and some wonderful Brazilian soap operas, interspersed with a fair sprinkling of commercials.

Radio is provided by both the state-owned **Radiodifusão Portuguesa** and private stations, and it's also possible to pick up the BBC World Service.

## The press
The main Portuguese daily papers are:
- **Lisbon:**
— Diario de Noticias
— O Dia
— O Diario
— Correiro da Manhã
**Porto:**
— O Comércio do Porto
— O Primeiro de Janeiro
— Jornal do Noticias

plus several evening papers. There are also weekly publications such as *Expresso, O Jornal, Tempo* and *O Pais*, and a range of regional papers. In Lisbon the best guide to what's on is the weekly *Se7e* (Sete).

## LIBRARIES

The best libraries are in Lisbon, Porto and Coimbra, and addresses are given in the regional sections later.

## SHOPS AND SHOPPING

Opening hours are normally 0900–1300 and 1500–1900, Monday to Friday and Saturday mornings. One of the great delights of Portugal is its proliferation of small specialist shops selling odd combinations of goods (like port and fruit for example) rather than big chains or department stores. Best buys are from Portugal's textile industry — fabrics, hand embroidered tablecloths or shawls, woven rugs and blankets, and clothing of all kinds. Leatherware is amazingly cheap and of very good quality, so don't buy any new shoes before you go!

In the food line, wine, port and madeira are of course all excellent and cheap as well as other home produce like nuts (especially almonds), fruit, vegetables and fish, but imported food and other items are expensive.

## GOVERNMENT MINISTRIES

If you've got a specific problem or enquiry, it's far better to approach the relevant Ministry directly, rather than trying to squeeze information out of intermediary sources (Embassies etc.), who are probably not very well informed themselves anyway:

**Prime Minister's Official Residence:** S. Bento, 1200 Lisboa
**Ministro de Estado** (Minister of State), R. Prof. Gomes Teixeira, 1300 Lisboa (tel. 01–673930)
**Ministro de Defesa Nacional** (Defence), Av Ilha da Madeira, 1400 Lisboa (tel. 01–610409)

**Ministro da Administração Interna** (Home Office), Praça do Comercio, 1100 Lisboa (tel. 01-364421)
**Ministro dos Negócios Estrangeiros** (Foreign Office), Largo do Rilvas, 1300 Lisboa (tel. 01-602076)
**Ministro da Justiça** (Justice), Praça do Comércio, 1100 Lisboa (tel. 01-360786)
**Ministro das Finanças e do Plano** (Finance and Planning), Av Infante D. Henrique, 1100 Lisboa (tel. 01-877555)
**Ministro da Educação** (Education), Av 5 de Outubro 107, 1000 Lisboa (tel. 01-734775)
**Ministro do Trabalho e Seguranca Social** (Employment and Social Security), Praça de Londres 2, 1000 Lisboa (tel. 01-802010)
**Ministro da Saúde** (Health), Av João Crisóstomo 9, 1000 Lisboa (tel. 01-544560)
**Ministro da Agricultura** (Agriculture), Praça do Comércio, 1100 Lisboa (tel. 01-327106)
**Ministro da Indústria e Energia** (Industry and Energy), R. da Horta Seca 15, 1200 Lisboa (tel. 01-372823)
**Ministro do Comércio e Turismo** (Trade and Tourism), Av da República 79, 1600 Lisboa (tel. 01-779893)
**Ministro da Cultura** (Culture/Arts), Av da República 16, 1000 Lisboa (tel. 01-579037)
**Ministro do Equipamento Social** (Social Services), Praça do Comércio, 1100 Lisboa (tel. 01-879541)
**Ministro da Qualidade de Vida** (Quality of Life), R. Do Século 51, 1200 Lisboa (tel. 01-322812)
**Ministro do Mar** (Sea), R. da Prata 8-1º, 1100 Lisboa (tel. 01-878541)

OTHER KEY CONTACTS

Political parties
**Partido Socialista (PS)** (Socialist Party), R. da Emenda 46, 1200 Lisboa (tel. 01-326171)
**Partido Social Democrata (PSD)** (Social Democratic Party) R. Buenos Aires 39, 1200 Lisboa (tel. 01-602415)
**Centro Democratico Social (CDS)** (Centre Social Democratic Party) Largo do Caldas 5, 1100 Lisboa (tel. 01-861171)
**Partido Comunista Portugés (PCP)** (Communist Party) Av Soeiro Pereira Gomes, 1600 Lisboa (tel. 01-766435)
**Movimento Democrático Portugués (MDP/CDE)** (Portuguese Democratic Movement (allied to Communist Party)), R. Artilharia Um 105-2º, 1000 Lisboa (tel. 01-680809)
**União de Esquerda para a Democracia Socialista (UEDS)** (Left Alliance) R. Manuel Bernardes 23, 1200 Lisboa (tel. 01-601960)
**Associação Social Democrata Independente (ASDI)** (Independent Social Democratic Association), Travessa do Fala-Só 9, 1200 Lisboa (tel. 01-376425)

Arriving & Surviving in Portugal                              301

**Partido Renovador Democrático (PRD)** (Democratic Renewal Party) R. M de Albuquerque, 1100 Lisboa

**Sports federations**
The Portuguese equivalent of the Sports Council is the **Instituto Superior de Educação Fisica**, and may be contacted at Centro de Documentação e Informação, Cruz Quebrada, Lisboa. For information about other sports — where to practise them, how to get in touch with clubs to arrange matches, general advice, etc. — contact the relevant sports federation, as follows:

**Arqueiros** (Archery), Estádio Nacional, Carreira de Tiro, 2780 Cascais
**Act. Subaquáticas** (Subaqua), Estádio Nacional, 2780 Cascais
**Aeronautica** (Flying), Av da Liberdade 226–2º, 1200 Lisboa
**Atletismo** (Athletics), Av Infante Santo 68–7º, 1300 Lisboa
**Automobilismo** (Driving), R. Rosa Araújo 24–6º, 1200 Lisboa
**Badminton**, Av Duque de Avila 9–4º, 1000 Lisboa
**Basquetbol** (Basketball), R. da Madalena 179–2º, 1100 Lisboa
**Bilhar** (Snooker), R. Gonçalves Crespo 28, 1100 Lisboa
**Boxe** (Boxing), Av Duque de Avila 9–5º, 1000 Lisboa
**Bridge**, R. Antonio Augusto de Aguiar 163–4º, Lisboa
**Campismo e Caravanismo** (Camping and Caravanning), Av 5 de Outubro 15–3º, 1000 Lisboa
**Canoagem** (Canoeing), R. Antonio Pinto Machado 50, 4100 Porto
**Ciclismo** (Cycling), R. Barros de Queirós 39–1º, 1100 Lisboa
**Columbofilia** (Racing Pigeons), R. Padre Estevão Bamal 79, Coimbra
**Damas** (Draughts), R. Soc Farmaceutica 56–2º, 1100, Lisboa
**Esgrima** (Fencing), R. do Quelhas 32, 1200 Lisboa
**Equestre Port** (Riding), Av Duque de Avila 9–4º, 1000 Lisboa
**Futebol** (Soccer), Pç da Alegria 25, 1200 Lisboa
**Ginástica** (Gymnastics), Av Duque de Avila 9–1º, 1000 Lisboa
**Golf**, R. Almeida Brandão 44, 1200 Lisboa
**Halterofilismo** (Weightlifting), R. do Quelhas 32, 1200 Lisboa
**Hoquei em Campo** (Hockey), R. Antonio Pinto Machado 60, 4100 Porto
**Judo**, R. do Quelhas 32, 1200 Lisboa
**Lutas Amadoras** (Wrestling), R. do Quelhas 32, 1200 Lisboa
**Minigolfe** (Mini golf), R. Gonçalo Sampaio 164, 4100 Porto
**Karaté**, R. do Dr Alfredo Costa 20–1º, Sintra
**Montanhismo** (Mountaineering), R. Formosa 303–2º, 4000 Porto
**Motociclismo** (Motorcyling), Av Duque de Avila 9–5º, 1000 Lisboa
**Motonautica** (Speedboating), R. Almeida Brandão 39, 1200 Lisboa
**Natação** (Swimming), Estadio Nacional (Piscina), 2780 Cascais
**Patinagem** (Skating), R. Duque de Palmela 27–6º, 1200 Lisboa
**Pesca Desportiva** (Fishing), R. Soc Farmaceutica 56–2º, 1100 Lisboa
**Pesca Desportiva Alto Mar** (Deep sea fishing), Largo Dr David Alves 14–2º, 4491 Póvoa de Varzim
**Remo** (Rowing), Doca de Sto Amaro Alcântara Mar, 1300 Lisboa
**Rugby**, R. Soc, Farmaceutica 56, 1100 Lisboa

**Ténis** (Tennis), Centro de Ténis de Monsanto, 1500 Lisboa
**Ténis de Mesa** (Table Tennis), Pça da Alegria 65–2º, 1200 Lisboa
**Tiro** (Target Shooting), R. Luís Derouet 27–3º, 1200 Lisboa
**Tiro com Armas de Caça** (Clay Pigeon Shooting), Av Júlio Diniz 10–4º, 1000 Lisboa
**Vela** (Sailing), Doca de Belém, 1300 Lisboa
**Voleibol** (Volleyball), R. Antonio Pinto Machado 60, 4100 Porto
**Xadrez** (Chess), R. Soc Farmaceutica 56–2º, 1100 Lisboa

**Other contacts**
**British Embassy and Consulates** — see regional sections.
**British Chamber of Commerce:** R. da Estrêla 8, Lisboa
**British Hospital:** R. Saraiva da Carvalho 49, 1200 Lisboa (tel. 01–602020)
**British Institute (British Council):** R. de Luis Fernandes 3, 1200 Lisboa
**British Churches:**
— Church of England, R. da Estrêla 4, Lisbon
— St Pauls, Estoril
— Church of Scotland, R. Arriaga 13, Lisbon
— Irish Dominican Church, Lg do Corpo Santo, Lisbon
**Instituto de Cultura e Língua Portuguesa,** Praça do Príncipe Real 14–1º, Lisboa. Portuguese government organisation responsible for promoting Portuguese language and culture throughout the world. Provides funding for studies and research, supplies Portuguese language assistants, supports mother-tongue classes and cultural activities for Portuguese emigrants abroad, gathers, collates and publishes information in the area of Portuguese studies, etc.
**Fundo de Apoio aos Organismos Juvenis (FAOJ),** Ministro de Educação, Av Duque de Avila 137, 1097 Lisboa. Youth department. Organises work camps — see regional section for addresses of regional offices.
**Instituto Portugés de Cinema,** R. São Pedro de Alcântara 45–2º, Lisboa (tel. 01–367395) Official Film Institute.
**Tourist offices** — see regional sections.
**Associação Portuguesa de Agências de Viagens e Turismo,** R. Duque de Palmela 2–1º, 1200 Lisboa. Portuguese association of travel agents and tour operators.
**Comisão da Condicão Feminina,** Av da Republica 32–2º, Lisboa. Leading Portuguese feminist association.
**Comité Anti-Nuclear,** R. São Bento 672, Lisboa. Leading anti-nuclear group.

## PORTUGUESE CONTACTS IN THE UK

**Official departments**
**Portuguese Embassy:** 11 Belgrave Square, London SW1 (tel. 01–235 5331)
**Portuguese Consulate:** 62 Brompton Rd, London SW3 (tel. 01–581 8722, Visa Dept: 01-581 3598)

**Portuguese Tourist Office:** 1–5 New Bond St, London W1 (tel. 01–493 3873)
**Portuguese Chamber of Commerce** — as tourist office above.

### Other contacts
**Anglo-Portuguese Foundation,** 2 Bedford Sq, London WC1.
**Anglo-Portuguese Society,** Canning House, 2 Belgrave Square, London SW1 (tel. 01–245 9738). Rather staid society fostering links and friendship between the two countries — meetings, lectures, exhibitions, social events, etc.
**The Calouste Gulbenkian Foundation UK Branch,** 98 Portland Place, London W1 (tel. 01–636 5213).
**Association of Teachers of Spanish and Portuguese,** 50 Markham St, London SW3, and 33 North Lane, Huntington, Yorks (tel. 0904–769608). See p. 41.
**Association for Contemporary Iberian Studies** — see p. 42
**Central Bureau for Educational Visits and Exchanges** — see p. 42
**Cyclist Touring Club,** 69 Meadrow, Godalming, Surrey (tel. 04868–7217). Can supply an information sheet on cycletouring in Portugal.
**Grant and Cutler,** 55–57 Gt Marlborough St, London W1 (tel. 01–734 2012). Foreign booksellers with large Portuguese/Brazilian section. Postal service.
**Hispanic and Luso-Brazilian Council,** Canning House, 2 Belgrave Square, London SW1 (tel. 01–235 2303). See p. 41
**Portugalia Wine Club,** PO Box 200, Crowborough, E. Sussex (tel. 08926–2393). Portuguese wine club.
**Taps Magazine,** Forest Holme, Friars Gate, Crowborough, E. Sussex. The quarterly magazine of the **Anglo-Portuguese Society,** full of snippets of news on Portugal, details of events, and carrying useful advertisements for villas for rent/sale, private Portuguese classes, penfriends, etc.

# 21
# Study & Work Opportunities

## STUDY

### 'PORTUGUESE FOR FOREIGNERS' COURSES

These take place in Portuguese universities, either during the summer vacation, or as courses which last the full academic year. Grants are available from the **Instituto de Cultura e Língua Portuguesa** to cover tuition fees, but not other expenses (see **Grants and Scholarships** below).

People come from all over the world to attend the courses, and are mostly students of Portuguese in their own countries, but this is by no means an entrance requirement — anyone can enrol provided they are over 17. Although only a handful of institutions offer courses, in Lisbon last year over 500 people attended the summer course, so it's definitely not a small-scale operation, and courses of this sort have been running for over 60 years.

Below is a summary of courses available — you should write directly to the institution concerned for further details and *Ficha de Inscricão* — clear English is generally understood, but it might be a good idea to mark clearly on the envelope *Cursos para estrangeiros*.

### University of Lisbon

Offers a month's summer course in July and a year-long course from mid-October to the beginning of June. The latter is divided into two semesters (October – mid February and mid February – June) and it is possible to enrol for just one of them, although preference is given to people intending to stay for the whole academic year.

The summer course costs approximately £140 and the annual course approximately £200–£250 per semester. On top of this you'll have to meet food and accommodation expenses — no accommodation is provided but help is given in finding rooms. You do have the advantage of being able to use the university canteen, sports facilities, etc.

Both the summer course and the year-long course cater for four different levels of ability, from complete beginners to university level, and there are 4 hours of classes each day from Monday to Friday, with excursions, lectures, etc. in the afternoons and evenings, so you are completely immersed in Portuguese culture.

The address to write to is: Departamento de Língua e Cultura Portuguesa, Faculdade de Letras de Lisboa, Cidade Universitária, 1699 Lisboa.

### The New University of Lisbon
This institution offers a summer course for students of Portuguese in British and American universities. It's normally run from mid-June to mid-July, with a maximum of 50 students. The course consists of five areas of study: language work in small groups, history of the Portuguese language, Portuguese history, Portuguese art history, and Anglo-Portuguese studies, tracing the history of relations between Britain and Portugal. Applicants must be students of Portuguese at a British or American university, and should apply by the end of March.

The course costs £100, excluding accommodation. Write to: Departamento de Estudos Anglo-Portugueses, Faculdade de Ciências Sociais e Humanas, Av de Berna 24, 1000 Lisboa.

### The University of Coimbra
There is the possibility of doing either a summer course or a year-long course here. The year-long course lasts from mid-October to mid-June and consists of three levels of ability from beginners up. The lower grade is mostly language work while the advanced grade includes lectures in history, art, contemporary Portugal, etc. At the beginning of the second term it's possible to transfer up to the next grade.

The course costs £65 a semester, excluding accommodation, but including various visits and excursions. Again, no accommodation is provided, but help is given finding rooms. The summer course — which has been running for over 60 years — is held under similar conditions and lasts for the whole of July.

The address to write to is: Universidade de Coimbra, Faculdade de Letras, Gabinete de Relaçãoes Internacionais, 3049 Coimbra (tel. 039–34613 and 039–25551).

### The University of Aveiro
Summer courses take place here under similar conditions to those in Lisbon and Coimbra. If you're interested, try writing to: Faculdade de Letras, Universidade de Aveiro, R. Dr Mario Sacramento 62, Aveiro.

### Private-sector courses
In Lisbon there are one or two private language schools which can offer Portuguese for foreigners — useful if you want classes at some time other than over the summer holidays:

- *Centro Audio Visual de Linguas*, Pça Luis de Camóes 36–3º (tel. 01–364988)
- *Centro de Linguas*, Av da Republica 14 (tel. 01–533733)

The organisation **Euroyouth** (see **Homestays** on p. 294) can arrange language courses in Lisbon as a package including accommodation with Portuguese families.

## GRANTS AND SCHOLARSHIPS

The **Instituto de Cultura e Língua Portuguesa** offers grants covering the cost of tuition fees of all the above courses. Applications should be made by the end of May, both for summer courses and for the year-long courses, and preference is given to people already studying Portuguese in their own country. Write to: Instituto de Cultura e Língua Portuguesa, Praça do Príncipe Real 14–1º, 1200 Lisboa (tel. 01-364508 and 01-363885).

The same institution also has funding available for the following:

- **Teacher-training** for non-Portuguese nationals who wish to become teachers of Portuguese. Grants are awarded to follow a course of study in Portugal for up to 3 years, provided there is a sponsoring institution in Britain or elsewhere which guarantees you a post as a teacher of Portuguese on completion.
- **Research.** Grants for an initial period of 12 months for research projects in the area of Portuguese language and culture. These are generally awarded to PhD students, or to teachers and researchers intending to publish their work.

The **Calouste Gulbenkian Foundation** funds research projects in the area of Portuguese studies, again, normally at the level of university teachers or researchers. For details write to: International Department, Fundação Calouste Gulbenkian, Av de Berna 45A, 1093 Lisboa.

The **Instituto Nacional de Investigação Científica** makes awards to postgraduates or last-year university students with some knowledge of Portuguese for study in any branch of science or the arts in Portugal for one academic year. The awards are worth about £220 a month for 9 months, plus the cost of any tuition fees. (This would probably need to be supplemented in order to live comfortably in Portugal.) Applications should be submitted through the Portuguese Embassy in London and need to be returned by 31 March each year. The address to write to is: Portuguese Embassy, 11 Belgrave Square, London SW1. Forms are available.

For details of scholarships awarded by international organisations such as the **Council of Europe**, **NATO** and the **European Communities Commission**, see p. 50 and p. 48 for a list of useful publications about sources of funding for study abroad.

## STUDY WITHIN THE STATE SYSTEM

If you are legally resident in Portugal you enjoy the same rights as Portuguese nationals as regards access to education. However, as in Spain, you will have to satisfy the authorities of the validity of your previous education — whatever level. This need not necessarily be a complicated procedure, but you will need to provide documentary evidence of the years of schooling you have undertaken, qualifications obtained, etc., so be prepared to dig out every conceivable bit of paper you've got relating to this and write to: **Ministry of Education**, Av 4 de Outubro 107, Lisboa. A useful source of information is a UNESCO publication entitled *Study Abroad*, available from HM Stationery Office, PO Box 569, London SE1.

Education is provided free and non-selectively in state schools at Basic and Lower Secondary levels — 9 years of schooling in all. University education is not free, but as an EEC national you should have access to it on equal terms with Portuguese students. A normal university degree course (*licenciatura*) lasts 4–6 years, although courses at other institutions (polytechnics and university institutes) offer *bacharelato* degrees in technical subjects after 3 years. At postgraduate level, provided your first degree has been recognised as equivalent to a *licenciatura*, the *mestrado* or Masters degree will be open to you, followed after 1–2 years by the *doutoramento* or PhD. A high level of proficiency in Portuguese would obviously be required. The major reasons for wanting to do a degree at a Portuguese university would be either to specialise in Portuguese studies or to be able to live and work in Portugal afterwards.

There are four traditional state universities in Portugal: two in Lisbon, one in Porto and one in Coimbra, and these are listed in the regional sections. In addition there are a number of new universities and university institutes which have been set up since 1973 in each of the other regions (Minho, Algarve, etc.), as well as several private higher education institutions.

# WORK

## GENERAL SITUATION

Work prospects in Portugal for British people are pretty poor. Everywhere you enquire you find the same story, so it's not just a lie put about by the authorities to discourage people. The country is small, relatively undeveloped and poor, so offers few opportunities in industry or business. It has also an ample labour market to fill vacancies for casual or unskilled staff. Add to this the fact that very few British people thinking of looking for jobs in Portugal are likely to speak much Portugese, and you're talking about substantially less opportunity than in Spain. The possibilities and leads that do exist are covered after the section on **Finding a job**.

## WORK PERMITS AND OTHER MATTERS

**Work permits**
- **Portuguese Consulate,** Silver City House, 62 Brompton Rd, London SW3 (tel. 01–581 8722)

Portugal became a member of the European Community in January 1986, along with Spain, but as in the case of Spain, free labour market mobility does not come into effect until after the seven year transitionary period, which means that until then you'll have to go through the difficult process of getting a work permit if you want a job in Portugal. The only exception to this are temporary jobs which last for less than 30 days — in this case you only have to inform the Ministry of Labour (Praça de Londres 2) of your intentions.

If you want to work for longer you must first find your job, then the onus is on your employer to satisfy the Ministry of Labour that the post couldn't be equally well filled by a Portuguese national. Obviously this excludes all but a very narrow range of activities. In any case, you'll need a residence permit (see p. 286), and you'll have to initiate proceedings to get this at the same time as your employer is trying to get the contract approved, and hope the whole thing falls into place. Once you do get a permit though — and it will be for 6 months assuming the job lasts that long — you shouldn't have any trouble renewing it provided your employer still wants to keep you on.

Some people try to beat the authorities and just turn up hoping to pick up temporary casual work. You may be successful, and the method is fine if you don't care whether you work or not, but in the present climate it would be silly just to turn up with no money and bank on finding something without the authorities finding out.

Self-employed people don't need a work permit at all (see below), and this goes for professional people setting up in practice in Portugal, although the latter will need to satisfy strict conditions as regards their qualifications to do so (see p. 312).

## Tax

Portugal has a double taxation agreement with Britain, which means that if you pay tax in Portugal (at considerably less than the British rate) you can't be taxed again on the same income. However, to be exempt from paying tax in Britain you have to be resident abroad for at least 6 months in any tax year. Tax payments in Portugal are horrendously complicated, and have to be paid strictly at certain times of the year or a fine is payable, so if you are self-employed or have any income from which tax is not deducted at source, it's well worth getting an accountant. The British Embassy in Lisbon can supply a list.

For information about tax matters in Portugal contact: **Direcção Geral das Contribucões Impostos**, R. da Alfandega, 1100 Lisboa. In Britain write to: **Inland Revenue**, Inspector of Foreign Dividends, Lynwood Road, Thames Ditton, Surrey.

## Social security

Urgent medical treatment is provided free to British nationals in Portugal, whether employed or not, and as stated before you'll need extra insurance as well. If you're working this should be provided by the Portuguese social security and you will need to make sure that your employer is making the necessary monthly contributions to the **Caixa de Previdência**, enabling you to receive free or practically free medical attention as required and to get discounts on medicines. If you're self-employed you will probably have to make your own contributions into the Caixa.

Unless you're working for a company based in Britain, you aren't obliged to continue paying social security contributions in this country, although in many cases it is a good idea to do so, in order not to lose your entitlement to benefits when you return. If you want advice on this, write to the

**DSS Overseas Branch**, Newcastle-on-Tyne, NE98 1YX

## FINDING A JOB: GENERAL HINTS

Newspaper advertisements are of course an obvious source of information as to vacancies. A few posts, mostly for teachers, are advertised in the British press, but a better source is likely to be newspapers published in Portugal. These include the main Lisbon daily, the *Diario de Noticias*, Porto's *O Comercio*, and English language papers *The Anglo-Portuguese News*, published fortnightly in Estoril, *The Algarve News* and *The Algarve Magazine*, both monthly and published in Lagos.

You could also consider advertising your services in these publications. The following agencies will place advertisements for you in the Portuguese press:

- **Media Universal Services,** 34–35 Skylines, Lineharbour, Docklands, London E14 (tel. 01–538 5505)
- **Publicitas Ltd,** 525/527 Fulham Road, London SW6 (tel. 01–385 7723)

If you want to advertise in the English-language publications, you should write to them at the following addresses:

- *Anglo-Portuguese News*, Av de São Pedro 25, Monte Estoril.
- *The Algarve Magazine and News*, R. 25 de Abril, 8400 Lagos.

Employment agencies which deal with overseas appointments handle very few vacancies in Portugal, nonetheless some of the most likely ones to contact are listed on p. 70. The **Federation of Recruitment and Employment Services** (10 Belgrave Square, London SW1) can supply a list of agencies which handle overseas appointments.

Approaching potential employers directly may produce some results, and a list of British companies with dealings in Portugal is given on p. 313. The British-Portuguese Chamber of Commerce (R. da Estrêla 8, Lisbon) may also be able to help put you in touch with companies likely to be interested in employing people in your particular field, although the British Embassy in Lisbon stress that even the old-established British firms in Portugal are employing fewer and fewer British staff.

A list of publications likely to be of use in researching further job opportunities is given on p. 54.

## AU PAIRING

Very few opportunities exist for this type of arrangement — the demand doesn't exist either in Portugal, or indeed from British people looking for au pair posts in Portugal. Of the agencies here which arrange au pair placements abroad, none deal specifically with Portugal, but you may be able to persuade them to go out of their way to find you something if you are really interested. The most likely ones to contact would be:

- **Anglia Agency,** 154 Fronks Rd, Dovercourt, Harwich (tel. 0255-503717)
- **Jolaine Au Pair and Domestic Agency,** 171 High St, Barnet, Herts (tel. 01-449 1334)

Listed below are two Portuguese organisations which might be of help. Try writing in Portuguese and enclosing an international reply coupon and self-addressed envelope. Better still, call in on them in person if you're in Lisbon:

- **Centro de Intercambio e Turismo Universitario,** Av Defensores de Chaves 67–6º–D, Lisboa
- **Turicoop,** R. Pascoal de Melo 15–1º–D, 1100 Lisboa

If you're really struck on the idea of au pairing in Portugal, you could try advertising your services through the Portuguese press (see p. 309), stressing the advantages to families of having an English speaking person to look after their children! If you do get a post, you'll be glad to note that you don't need a work permit, but do bear in mind the comments on au pairing in Spain on p. 55 which hold good equally for Portugal.

## TEACHING ENGLISH AS A FOREIGN LANGUAGE

This is a more fertile area, and one worth investigating, although opportunities are far fewer than in Spain. You'll need a teaching qualification of some sort, even if it's only a week's crash course like that run by **Linguarama** (see p. 56). The British Council can supply a free leaflet listing courses of training entitled *Academic Courses in the United Kingdom relevant to the teaching of English to speakers of other languages,* which is available from: **English Teaching Information Unit,** The British Council, 10 Spring Gardens, London SW1A 2BN.

For details of posts with the British Council abroad, including Portugal, the **Overseas Educational Appointments Department,** 65 Davies St, London W1, is the office to contact. Their Institute in Portugal, where the teachers are employed, is at R. Luis Fernandes 3, 1200 Lisboa, and if you're on the spot this might make a useful source of contacts for finding out about other teaching opportunities.

Private language schools are nothing like as numerous as in Spain:

**Lisbon:**
**Centro Internacional de Linguas,** R. Mouzinho da Silveira 25, 1200 Lisboa
**Academia Comercial Tecla,** Av Almirante Reis 106–5º–E, 1100 Lisboa
**American Secretarial School,** Rua Castilho 38–1º–E, 1200 Lisboa
**Centro Sight and Sound,** Rua Filipe Folque 46–4º, 1000 Lisboa
**Berlitz,** Escadinhas da Barroca 2–1º, 1100 Lisboa
**Cambridge School,** Av Guerra Junqueiro 8–1º–D, 1000 Lisboa
**Oxford School,** R. D. Estefania 165–1º, 1000 Lisboa
**Centro Audio-Visual de Linguas,** Pç Luis de Camões 36–3º–E, 1200 Lisboa

**CIAL,** Av da República 14–2º, 1000 Lisboa
**Instituto Británico em Portugal,** Rua Luis Fernandes 3, 1200 Lisboa
**Instituto de Línguas de Algés,** R. dos Bombeiros Voluntários 29–2º, Algés, 1495 Lisboa
**Instituto de Novas Profissões,** Av Duque de Loulé 47–1º, 1000 Lisboa
**Instituto Superior de Línguas e Administração,** R. Sacramento á Lapa 14/6, 1300 Lisboa

**Porto:**
**Inlingua,** R. Gonçalo Cristovão 217–12º, Edificio Jornal de Noticias, Porto
**Cambridge School,** R. Duque da Terceira 381–1º–C, Porto
**Instituto de Inglés do Porto,** R. Sá da Bandeira 522–1º, Porto
**Tematron-Novos Laboratórios de Ensino Programado,** Av Boavista 292–5º, Porto.

There are also:

**International House:** An organisation with schools in Lisbon (R. Marques Sa da Bandeira 16, 1000 Lisboa), Barreiro, Coimbra, Figueira da Foz, Porto and Viseu — for further information contact the London office: 106 Piccadilly, London W1 (tel. 01–491 2598).

**Linguarama** have six language schools in Portugal: their Head Office is at 53 Pall Mall, London SW1 (tel. 01–930 7697).

Look out for advertisements that these organisations may place in the British or Portuguese press (see p. 309) or contact them directly.

There are reasonable possibilities of finding private classes, especially over the summer months. You might even be taken on as a governess or tutor by a family for July, August or September, when children have their school holidays. Again, look out for ads, especially in the Portuguese papers, or place your own. You could also contact: The Honorary Secretary, Home International, R. Gustavo de Matos Sequeira 35–2º, 1200 Lisboa. You don't need a work permit for this type of employment.

## OTHER TEACHING OPPORTUNITIES

Fully qualified British **teachers** are sometimes required to fill vacancies in the handful of English-medium schools in Portugal — mostly around Lisbon or in the Algarve — which are listed in the regional sections.
There are no opportunities to teach in state schools, however. The **Central Bureau for Educational Visits and Exchanges** doesn't operate either the language assistants programme or the teacher exchange scheme with Portugal.

## COURIERS

This is a possible area, and also one where opportunities are likely to increase. It's something you should arrange from Britain by contacting one of the following:

- **Club Cantabrica Holidays Ltd,** 146–148 London Rd, St Albans, Herts (tel. 0727–33141)
- **Club 18–30,** Overseas Personnel Dept, Academic House, 24–28 Oval Rd, London NW1 (tel. 01–267 7044)
- **Thomson Holidays,** Overseas Personnel Dept, Greater London House, Hampstead Rd, London NW1 (tel. 01–387 9321)

## CASUAL WORK

Not worth considering except possibly on the Algarve at the height of the season. Then you might pick up a few escudos selling timeshares, leafletting, street vending, working in bars or discos, scrubbing out boats at Vilamoura marina, etc., but be prepared for the outcry from the locals if you're found out — especially doing bar work.

## FARM WORK

You may possibly be able to get work of this type through the **Ministry of Agriculture** (Av da Republica 84–3º, 1600 Lisboa), which produces a list of regional offices and fruitgrowers' associations. The national fruitgrowers' association is the **Junta Nacional das Frutas**, R. Rodrigo de Fonseca 8, 1200 Lisbon. Prospects are not good though, even for getting a reply! Enclose an International Reply Coupon to encourage some response.

On a brighter note, the **International Farm Experience Programme** (YFC Centre, National Agricultural Centre, Kenilworth, Warwicks (tel. 0203–58704) may be able to find short placements in Portugal for young people with experience of agricultural work to help them broaden their knowledge of agricultural methods.

## SELF-EMPLOYMENT

You don't need a work permit to be self-employed in Portugal, but you will have to go through all the residence formalities, and to have a special stamp put in your passport by the **Serviço de Estrangeiros** (Av Antonio Augusto de Aguiar 18, Lisboa). You may also need a licence from the relevant authorities, depending on what you intend to do.

In the Algarve especially there are many well-established small businesses operated by Britons and other northern Europeans — both directly related to the tourist industry (bars, discos, boutiques, etc.) and serving the ex-patriate communities (property consultants, builders, etc.). Similarly, there are many cases of failed businesses — people who have had idealistic ambitions of running a business about which they know little, or expected life to be one long holiday.

Doctors and dentists can open a practice in Portugal provided they have either become a member of, or obtained an entitlement to practise from, the **Ordem dos Medicos**, Av da Liberdade 65–1º, 1200 Lisboa. In either case they must produce a legalised copy of their degree, and a declaration from the BMA that they have a clean record of service.

## OTHER OPPORTUNITIES

### Secretarial/commercial
No real opportunities unless you are bilingual in Portuguese. See p. 309 for general comments on finding vacancies.

### Opportunities in international organisations
Opportunities may sometimes occur in Portugal with the **Organisation for Economic Co-operation and Development** for experts in various fields (regional planning, economics, finance, agriculture, industrial development, etc.) to undertake short assignments. The following office keeps a file of suitable applicants whom they can contact when suitable vacancies arise: **International Recruitment Unit**, Overseas Development Administration, Abercrombie House, Eaglesham Rd, East Kilbride, G75 8EE.

### EEC young worker exchanges/exchange of students for technical experience
The possibility of short-term work placements in Portugal for young workers or students on technical courses in need of work experience, arranged through the **Central Bureau for Educational Visits and Exchanges**, Seymour Mews House, Seymour Mews, London W1 (tel. 01–486 5101).

## BRITISH COMPANIES WITH OFFICES IN PORTUGAL

### Lisbon
**Barclays Bank International Ltd,** Av de Republica 9–1º
**Bank of London and South America,** R. do Ouro 40–48
**Beecham Portuguesa Produtos,** R. Mem Rodrigues 4–A
**Bells & Cía,** Av de Roma 42
**Berec Portuguesa,** R. Goncalves Zarco 6
**Blackwood Hodge,** Av Infante D. Henrique 306, Cabo Ruivo
**BP Ltd,** Praçqa Marques de Pombal 13
**Coopers & Lybrand Ltd,** Av 5 de Outubro 33–3º–E
**Commercial Union Assurance,** R. Artilharia Um 39–1º
**Companhia de Seguros Prudential,** R. Madalena 191–4º
**Deloitte Haskins & Sells,** R. Silva Carvalho 234–4º
**Ernst & Whinney,** Av Antonio Augusto de Aguiar 19–4º
**Eastencia Electronic e Tecnica,** Praça Prof Santos Andrea
**Hoover Electrica Portuguesa,** R. D. Estfania 90–A
**ICL Computadores,** Av Estados Unidos de America 57–A/B
**Industrias de Alimentação (Heinz),** Av da Republica 57–7º
**James Rawes & Cia,** R. Bernardino Costa 47
**Laing Portuguesa,** R. Augusto dos Santos 4–4º

**Laboratorios Wellcome de Portugal,** R. Visconde de Seabra 4–4º
**Lloyds Register of Shipping,** Av 24 de Julho 60–2º
**Metal Box of Portugal,** Av Conselheiro Fernando de Sousa 19–5º
**PA Consultores,** R. Castilho 211–5º
**Peat Marwick Mitchell & Co,** Av do Brasil 1–8º
**Price Waterhouse & Co,** Av 5 de Outubro 35–8º
**Rank Xerox Ltd,** Av Antonio Augusto de Aguiar 106
**Robbialac Portuguesa,** R. do Conde Redondo 46
**Reckitt Portuguesa,** R. S. Sebastião da Pedreira 122– 1º
**Reuter Portuguesa,** Praça da Alegría 58–1º
**Royal Exchange Assurance,** R. Jose Estevão 87, Caixa Postar 1234
**Shell Portuguesa,** Av da Liberdade 249
**Arthur Young & Co,** R. Marqués Subserra 10–1º

**Elsewhere in the country**
**Building Design Partnership,** Sitio do Castelo 1–1º, Cascais
**Black & Decker,** Quinta Carreira Lote 78, S. João do Estoril, Estoril
**British Leyland,** Quinta de Vitoria EN10, 2685 Sacavem
**Cía de Linhas Coats & Clark,** Santo Ovidio, 4401 Vila Nova de Gaia
**ICI Finicisa,** Quinta do Ribeiro de S. Vicente, EN246, 7300 Portalegre
**Pillar Portuguesa (RTZ),** S. Marcos, Apartado 23, 2736 Cacem

In addition to these there are also plenty of American firms operating in Portugal — Citibank, Texas Instruments, etc.

## VOLUNTARY WORK

### WORK CAMPS

Work camps offer the opportunity of working with other young people of different nationalities on worthwhile projects of value to local communities — in Portugal this usually means conservation, archaeological digs, construction or renovation work. Camps are normally in the summer months and last 2–3 weeks, during which 10–20 volunteers organise work, share chores, exchange ideas, and have a chance to learn about and become involved in the host community — in this case Portugal. The following organisations run work camps in Portugal:

- **Christian Movement for Peace,** British Secretariat, Hilton's Chambers, Roushill, Shrewsbury, Shropshire (tel. 0743–66542). The year's programme is available in the spring, and applications should be in by June. Knowledge of Portuguese is helpful, but not essential. There is a £22 fee payable to the organisation. Accommodation is provided but other expenses including travel are the responsibility of the individual.

- **United Nations Association,** Youth Service, Temple of Peace, Cathays Park, Cardiff (tel. 0222–28549). Accepts applications for work camps organised by **Turicoop** (see below). Applicants should be aged at least 18 and have previous voluntary work experience (it's useful to gain this on some project in the UK first — the same organisation can help here). Fees total £17, and a knowledge of French, together with skills such as woodwork, electrics, etc., is useful. Food and accommodation are provided.

- **Turicoop,** Turismo Social e Juvenil, R. Pascoal de Melo 15–1º D, Lisboa (administered by the United Nations Association in the UK — see above). This organisation runs fifteen or so camps each year for volunteers from different countries, and produces a wonderful programme full of useful information in terrible English! Unless you're on the spot I'd definitely recommend booking through the UN Association. The organisation is also a youth travel agency, and does as a special offer a week's bed and breakfast at the seaside for £20 to help you recover from your labours!

- **Fundo de Apoio aos Organismos Juvenis (FAOJ),** Av Duque d'Avila 135/7, 1097 Lisboa (tel. 01–535081). Run 40 or 50 work camps each year throughout the country, both for Portuguese nationals only, and international. Again, accommodation and food are provided, but not travelling expenses. Maximum age 25. Knowledge of Portuguese very useful. The organisation makes a useful contact if you're in the country already, as it has offices in every region (listed in the regional sections), through which bookings should be made.

- **Associação de Turismo Estudantil e Juvenil,** R. do Breiner 65–2º, 4000 Porto. Organises a variety of workcamps.

- **Companheiros Construtores,** R. Pedro Monteiro 3–1º, 3000 Coimbra. Camps mostly involving renovation and building work — part of an international organisation.

For further details on work camps generally, see pp. 71–2.

## OTHER VOLUNTARY WORK

Other organisations which may require volunteers for Portugal are as follows:

**Archaeology Abroad,** 31–34 Gordon Square, London WC1. Occasionally have details of archaeological sites in Portugal requiring experienced volunteers.

**The Institute of Cultural Affairs,** 277 St Ann's Rd, London N15 (tel. 01–802 2848). Involved in community development schemes and development education.

**The People to People Health Foundation Inc,** Project House, Health Sciences Education Centre, Millwood, VA22646, USA. Vacancies for short-term teaching fellows in medical and nursing schools.

**Co-ordinating Committee for the International Voluntary Service,** 1 Rue

Miollis, 75015, Paris. Clearing house for information on voluntary work throughout the world.

## MISSIONARY WORK

Very limited opportunities in Portugal, but the following organisations have some involvement:

**The Bible Churchmen's Missionary Society,** 251 Lewisham Way, London SE4 (tel. 01-691 6111).

**Christians Abroad,** Livingstone House, 11 Carteret St, London SW1 (tel. 01-222 2165).

**Evangelical Missionary Alliance,** Whitefield House, 186 Kennington Park Rd, London SE11 (tel. 01-735 0421). Clearing house for information on missionary work throughout the world.

**The Medical Missionary Association,** 6 Cannonbury Place, London N1 (tel. 01-359 1313). Missionary work for medical practitioners.

# 22
# Portugal in Detail

**PORTO AND THE COSTA VERDE**

This region incorporates one of Portugal's most picturesque provinces, the green and verdant Minho, and the country's second city, Porto. It is and always has been a densely populated area, and the neatly tilled and terraced hillsides come as a bit of a surprise if you've come across the border from the wilds of Galicia in northern Spain. Every bit of cultivatable ground is pressed into service, with the *vinho verde* vines trained high above the ground on granite pillars — or even trees — in order to grow other crops such as cabbages or maize below. Elsewhere pines and eucalyptus form an important part of Portugal's timber industry, and in the north an enormous tract of land has been set aside to form the Peneda-Gerês National Park.

With such a large section of the population involved in agriculture, rural concerns predominate and there are some wonderful country markets selling local produce, livestock and handicrafts. The land is divided into

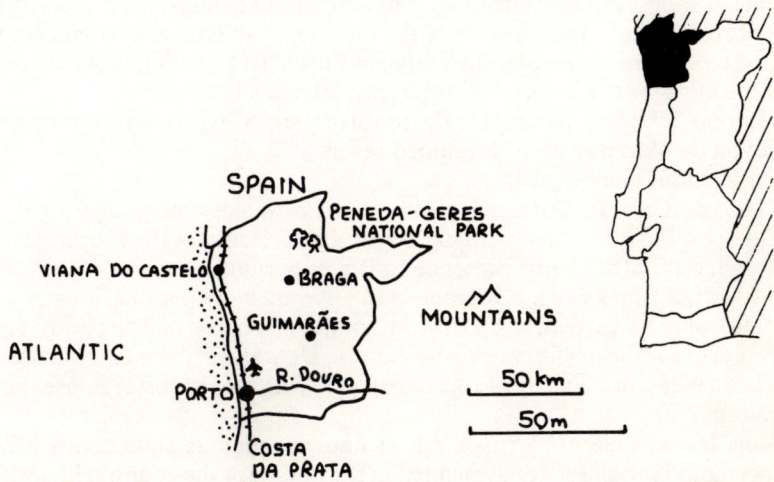

smallholdings rather than large estates which is perhaps why the countryside has a reputation for being intensely conservative. As a counterbalance to this the city of Porto has always been the great stronghold of Portuguese liberalism and has seen numerous uprisings against the traditional order, including the Revolution of 1820, when a new liberal constitution was proclaimed.

Historically the region had a crucial role in the very birth of Portugal as a nation. It was these lands, between the great rivers the Minho and the Douro, over which Alfonso Henriques pronounced himself king in the early twelfth century, splitting away from his nominal suzerain, King Alfonso of Castile. Guimarães was the first capital of the new kingdom of Portucale but the focus of power soon shifted south as new territory was captured from the Moors.

Today the region has a considerable amount to offer in terms of historic interest, great countryside for exploring by car or on foot, a long stretch of sandy beaches — although watch out for sea mists — and in Porto, the country's second city, a bustling commercial centre.

## WHAT TO SEE

**Porto** (Oporto in English). A city of about 350,000 sprawled attractively along the north bank of the Douro. Wine has been shipped to Britain for centuries from Porto, and was traditionally brought downstream from the vineyards of the upper Douro in boats called *barcos rabelos*. The port lodges are all on the opposite bank, in **Vila Nova de Gaia**, which is connected to the city via the spectacular two-tiered **Ponte Dom Luis**. The railway bridge, the **Ponte Maria Pia** was designed by Eiffel and is perhaps Porto's greatest landmark.

The old quarter is a tangle of fascinating alleyways crammed with bars and old shops, but apart from a few museums (see listings) the city's a little short on 'sights'. Perhaps one of the most enjoyable ways to spend some time would be in the **Solar do Vinho do Porto** (R. Entre-Quintas), where you can sample hundreds of different varieties of port.
**Espinho.** Windswept resort to the south of the city, with enormous beach.
**Póvoa de Varzim.** Well-developed resort.
**Esposende.** Good beach.
**Viana do Castelo.** Attractive resort-town with a certain graceful air.
**Valença.** Frontier town with massive walls overlooking the Minho river.
**Braga.** Capital of Minho province and an important religious centre from the earliest times when it was one of the five ancient episcopal sees in the Peninsula. Its cathedral houses the tombs of Henry of Burgundy and Teresa of Castile, its founders, and Alfonso Henriques' parents. Nowadays it has a pleasant, slightly old-fashioned air, with its old coffee houses and monuments.
**Bom Jesus.** One of Portugal's best known religious sights, this is an enormous baroque stairway planted in the middle of the countryside, with representations of the life of Christ at each stage on the way up. At the top of course, you have a picnic! — it's really just an excuse for a day out.

**Guimarães.** Attractive old medieval town, lively despite its small size.
**Barcelós.** Market town (its Thursday market is one of the best in Portugal) where the famous Portuguese cockerel originated.
**Citânia de Briteiros.** Impressive Celtic hill settlement which has been extensively rebuilt and restored.

## WHAT TO DO

### ART GALLERIES AND MUSEUMS

**Porto**
**Museu Nacional de Soares dos Reis,** Rua D. Manuel II. Good art collection housed in a former Royal Palace.
**Museu etnográfico,** Largo de S. João Novo. Interesting ethnographic collection, again housed in a beautiful old house.
**Casa-Museu de Guerra Junqueiro,** Rua de Dom Hugo. House of the poet Guerra Junqueiro, including his collections of art works.

**Vila Nova de Gaia**
**Casa-Museu de Teixeira Lopes.** Former house of contemporary sculptor.

**Braga**
**Casa dos Biscainhos.** Seventeenth-century building housing small museum.

**Guimarães**
**Museu Martins Sarmento.** Interesting Celtic finds housed in a former convent.

### CINEMA

Festival of Cartoon Films (**Cinanima**) held at Espinho during November.
Festival of Fantasy Films (**Fantas Porto**) held in Porto in February.
Amateur Film Festival held in November at Guimarães.

### FESTAS

St John's Eve (23/24 June) in **Porto.** Much merrymaking lasting all night. Similar celebrations also take place in **Braga.**
A big pilgrimage to **Bom Jesus** takes place at Whitsun.
Important religious Easter celebrations in **Braga,** with hooded penitents and torchlit processions.
**Viana do Castelo** has an important *romaria* lasting for several days around 20 August each year, with big parades, carnival figures, bands and dancing.
The 'New Fairs' in **Ponte de Lima** in mid-September are also a big event, with fireworks and brass-band competitions.
Festival in early August and *romaria* on the first weekend in July at **Guimarães.**

## LIBRARIES

**Porto:**
**Municipal Library,** Largo de S. Lázaro
**City Archives,** Terreiro de D. Alfonso Enriques
**American Library,** Rua da Firmea 521.

## MUSIC

An international music festival is held during July in **Póvo de Varzim**.

## SPORTS

There is a big Sports Centre, the **Palácio de Cristal**, at Rua Dom Manuel II, Porto (tel. 02-29906). Other sports facilities, apart from sea bathing, walking (especially in the **Gerês National Park**) and the occasional tennis court, are:

- **Fishing.** For salmon and trout (1 March to 31 July for both) in the **Minho** and **Lima rivers**, and also in the **Caniçada** and **Venda Nova dams**, just outside the Gerês National Park area (you can't fish within the park, which is a protected area). There is also sea fishing from places along the coast, especially **Póvoa de Varzim**, which is supposed to be good for bass.
- **Golf.** There is an 18 hole golf course at Espinho, serving the Porto Golf Club, whose address is Pedreira, Silvalde, Espinho.

## THEATRE

In **Porto** an **international festival of Iberian Theatre** is held every November and other events during May.
An **amateur theatre festival** is held in March in **Guimarães**.

## UNIVERSITIES

**Universidade do Porto,** R. D. Manuel II, Apartado 211, Porto (founded early this century)
**Universidade do Minho,** Lgo do Paço, Braga (new university)

## USEFUL ADDRESSES

**Tourist offices**
**Porto:** Pr D. João I, 43 (tel. 02-317514)
**Braga:** Av Central
Tourist offices also located in Barcelos, Esposende, Espinho, Caldas do Gerês, Monçao, Póvoa de Varzim, Valença and Viana do Castelo.

**FAOJ Regional Offices**
**Porto:** R. Júlio Dinis 604–1º (tel. 02–695434)
**Viano do Castelo:** R. de Sto António 149–2º (tel. 058–23583)
**Braga:** R. de Sta. Margarida 6 (tel. 053–22835)

**Government offices**
**Serviço de Estrangeiros:** R. Almada 526, 4º, Porto (tel. 02–319982)

**Travel agents**
**Melia Tours,** Pç. Humberto Delgado 269, Porto (tel. 02–310034)
**Wagons-Lits,** Rua Dr. Artur Magalhães Basto 12, Porto (tel. 02–25040)

**Car hire**
**Europcar,** R. de Sta. Catarina 1158–1164, (tel. 02–318398) — also a branch at the airport.
**Interrent,** Rua do Bolhão 182, Porto (tel. 02–381964)

**British representation**
**British Consulate:** Avda da Boavista 3072, Porto (tel. 02–684789)
**British Council:** Rua do Breyner 115, Porto
**British hospital:** Rua da Bandeirinha 12, Porto
**British schools:** The Oporto British School, Foz do Douro

## THE COSTA DA PRATA

The Portuguese tourist authorities certainly knew what they were doing when they created this particularly attractive tourist region, which takes in the province of Beira Litoral and part of Estremadura, and manages to

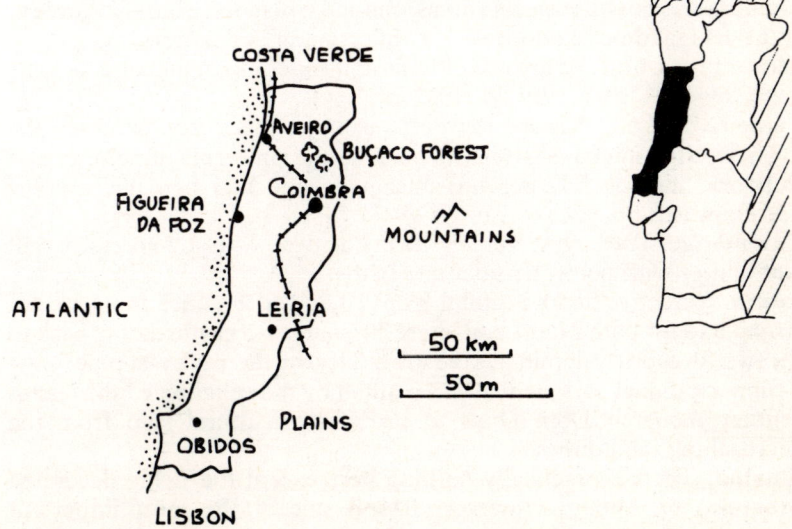

combine good beaches and resorts, beautiful rolling countryside, the ancient city of Coimbra, and some of Portugal's most interesting monuments within a fairly narrow and manageable coastal strip.

It's a region which has seen some of the most momentous events in Portuguese history — and the monuments are there to remind you, from the show-case medieval town of Obidos to a museum commemorating Wellington's role in the Peninsular War.

Despite the fact that there are no large cities, the region has quite a lot to offer, with Portuguese language courses for foreigners at Coimbra, thousands of pilgrims visiting the Basilica at Fatima each year, and plenty of activity at Figueira de Foz.

## WHAT TO SEE

**Coimbra.** Portugal's capital for 200 years, with the country's oldest and most prestigious university — founded in Lisbon in 1290 and transferred here in 1310 — which produced among others Luis de Camões, Portugal's greatest writer, and Dr Salazar himself, who taught economics here before devoting himself to politics. Coimbra today is just a small provincial capital, but nonetheless with a pleasant student atmosphere, and a reasonable amount to see and do.

The **university** itself is one of the main sights, perched on a hill on the banks of the Mondego river. Most of the older buildings date from the sixteenth century, when it was endowed by João III who was keen to leave the Dark Ages behind and promote a renaissance of culture and learning. At his instigation the Jesuits became a powerful teaching force both here and in Portuguese territories overseas. There is also a fantastically rich **library** in heavy Portuguese baroque style.

Coimbra's **cathedral**, the rather solid Sé Velha, was started in 1162, and is one of the most important examples of Portuguese Romanesque. Coimbra also boasts some fine **mansions** and **convents**, a **botanic garden**, and **Portugal dos Peguenitos** — a collection of scaled down replicas of many of the country's great buildings and styles of architecture — as its name suggests, especially for children.

**Figueira da Foz.** Perhaps the best resort on this coast, certainly the liveliest, with some real attempts made to put on events of cultural and 'folkloric' interest. The beach is amazingly wide, and there is also a port and shipyards.

**Conimbriga.** The largest Roman site in Portugal, with an impressive wall and houses with pools, mosaics and baths.

**Leiria.** Attractive district capital (pop. 10,000 or so), once an important stronghold for both Moors and later Christians — a **castle** dating back to the twelfth century dominates the town. Nearby there is a vast pine forest — now a national park, which was planted by the enlightened thirteenth century monarch Dom Dinis to protect agricultural land from the encroaching sand dunes.

**Batalha.** There's practically nothing here except the richly decorated **Mosteiro** or Abbey. However, this is one of the most important monuments in Portugal, built in fulfilment of a vow made to the Virgin by João I before the decisive battle of Aljubarrota against Castile in 1385.

The historic friendship between England and Portugal dates from the period immediately following this battle, when the two countries signed the Treaty of Windsor, and João I married John of Gaunt's daughter Phillipa. Their joint tomb is contained within the Abbey, as is that of their most famous son, Henry the Navigator, whose furtherance of Portuguese seamanship and exploration paved the way for the growth of a worldwide Empire.

The Abbey then, quite apart from being a fantastic piece of architecture (the later Manueline embellishments are especially fine), is also of considerable symbolic importance, recalling this crucial period in the country's history when, freed from the spectre of dependence on Castile, Portugal embarked on an era of self-confidence and greatness.

**Grutas de Mira de Aire.** Spectacular caves with stalagtites, stalagmites and an underground lake. There are also other caves in this vicinity, at **São Mamede, Alvados** and **Santo Antonio.**

**Fatima.** An insignificant spot which has become an important place of pilgrimage for Catholics after the famous apparitions of the Virgin Mary here in 1917 to three peasant girls. An immense **Basilica** has been built to accommodate the thousands of pilgrims which come here every year on the anniversaries of the apparitions — the 13th of every month between May and October — when there are open-air masses and candlelit processions.

**Alcobaça.** Like so many others, a place which owes its *raison d'être* to its great monument — the immense **Cistercian abbey**. Once extremely powerful it was dissolved in the nineteenth century, but much remains to be wondered at, including some beautiful Manueline cloisters, its church which is the largest in Portugal, and its kitchens, which probably also are! It also contains the tombs of Dom Pedro and Inês de Castro — a fourteenth-century crown prince and his Spanish bride who was murdered in an attempt to prevent foreign influence over Portuguese affairs. Later when Dom Pedro became king he had the body of Inês de Castro exhumed and crowned queen beside him.

**Nazaré.** Fishing village with a good beach which has adapted attractively to development as a tourist resort.

**S. Martinho do Porto.** Resort, beaches, etc.

**Peniche.** Important fishing port on a rocky promontory. Its old fortress was used as a political prison by Salazar.

**Obidos.** Self-consciously picturesque medieval town with a spectacular castle now converted into a *pousada*. Its greatest contribution to Portuguese history, though, is perhaps having been the home of the great seventeenth-century woman miniaturist Josefa de Obidos (actually born in Seville), whose work can be seen in the parish church and in the small museum.

**Torres Vedras.** A modern town which owes its fame to having lent its name to Wellington's chain of defences (stretching over 25 miles from the sea to the Tagus estuary) constructed in the Peninsular War to prevent

Napoleon's troops from advancing on Lisbon.

**Aveiro.** An ancient district capital of some importance on the Vouga delta of saltmarshes, waterways and canals, traditionally navigated in distinctive flat-bottomed boats called *barcos moliçeiros*. A sizeable lagoon, the **Ria de Aveiro**, is the main feature of the coast just here.

**Buçaco Forest.** Just north of Coimbra, this is a very ancient forest which can boast over 700 varieties of tree. Today it is treated as a national park, and there are walks laid out through the woods, a beautiful lake, and a military museum commemorating the Battle of Buçaco — another of Wellington's victories against Napoleonic forces in the Peninsular Wars.

## WHAT TO DO

### ART GALLERIES AND MUSEUMS

Most of the places of interest in this region are museums in themselves, or have small museums attached to them, but the following is of particular interest:

**Museu Machado de Castro,** Coimbra (next to university). An extremely rich collection of paintings, sculpture, furniture, ceramics and other treasures, housed in the former Archbishop's Palace and named after an eighteenth-century sculptor.

### CINEMA

There is an international film festival held every September in **Figueira da Foz**, usually with an excellent selection of films. An international film festival for non-professional film-makers is also held in **Coimbra** in April.

### FESTAS

Apart from the Fatima pilgrimages already mentioned, carnival is celebrated with some gusto in this region, especially in **Nazaré** and **Ovar**. **Coimbra's student celebrations** at the end of the academic year in May are worth witnessing — they are called the *queima das fitas*, which means 'the gown-burning'! There are **regattas** in **Aveiro** in July and August, and a *romaria* in **Nazaré**, with bullfights, on 8–10 September.

### LIBRARIES

**University Library,** Coimbra. Important for the rarity of some of its volumes as well as for its spectacular decoration.

### MUSIC

An important **music festival** is held in **Figueira da Foz** each year during June and July, and the **Obidos Early Music Festival** takes place in August.

## UNIVERSITIES

**Universidade de Coimbra,** Pça da Universidade, Coimbra
**Universidade de Aveiro,** R. Dr Mario Sacramento 62, Aveiro (newly established)

## USEFUL ADDRESSES

**Tourist offices**
Av 25 de Abril, Figueira da Foz (tel. 033–22610)
Offices are also located at Alcobaça, Aveiro, Batalha, Buçaco, Coimbra, Fatima, Leiria, Nazaré, Torres Vedras, etc.

**FAOJ Regional Offices**
**Aveiro:** Av 25 de Abril 24 (tel. 034–28625)
**Coimbra:** R. Alexandre Herculano 52 (tel. 039–28191)
**Leiria:** Lgo Cândido dos Reis 9 (tel. 044–23378)

**Travel agents**
**Abreu,** Rua da Sota 2, Coimbra
**Visa,** Av Fernão de Magalhaes 11, Coimbra

**British representation**
**British Embassy/Consulate** — see Lisbon
**British schools** — none in the region.

## THE MOUNTAINS OF PORTUGAL

The whole of the northern half of interior Portugal, that is the provinces of Tras os Montes, Alto Douro, Beira Alta and Beira Baixa, is extremely mountainous. There are some small but noble old towns like Viseu, Guarda and Bragança, and endless unspoilt scenery with some spectacular views. It is also rough country though, freezing in winter and burning in summer, and the neatly terraced mountainsides of the Upper Douro are a tribute to the tenacity of the people in making such harsh land work for them. It's in this region you'll find Portugal at its most basic, carrying on a simple agricultural routine which is great if you like to get off the beaten track, but not somewhere to consider if you're looking for anything more than this.

## WHAT TO SEE

**Bragança.** The Braganças were the royal house of Portugal from the Restoration in 1640 till the abolition of the monarchy in 1910. Catherine of Bragança married Charles II and is supposed to be responsible for introducing the custom of afternoon tea to Britain. Bragança today is an attractive place, preserving its medieval ramparts and a wonderful old town hall from the twelfth century, but despite its contribution to Portuguese history offers little else.

**Chaves.** Little spa town in a valley — a real contrast to the forbidding mountain scenery all around. It is noted for its hams, its spectacular Roman bridge, and its castle — it was in former times an important frontier stronghold.

**Miranda do Douro.** A remote frontier town whose inhabitants (all 2,000 of them) speak a separate dialect of Portuguese. It's a pretty little place, looking out from its medieval walls over the Douro river and a huge hydroelectric dam.

**Vila Real.** Provincial capital noted for its black pottery, and more especially for the **Solar de Mateus** — the pinnacled baroque mansion that appears on every bottle of Mateus Rosé. It's here that the wine is made, and it's possible to visit the house and gardens for a small fee.

**Régua.** Busy provincial town on the Douro and an important rail crossroads.

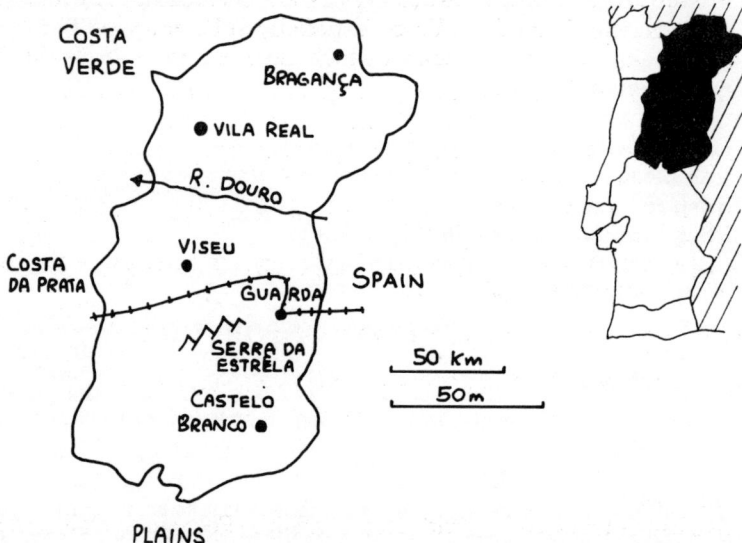

**Lamego.** Prosperous little agricultural town producing *raposeira* — Portugal's 'champagne'. Nearby is the sanctuary of **Nossa Senhora dos Remedios** — an elaborate stairway similar to Bom Jesus (see section on Costa Verde).

**Caramulo.** Centre for the surrounding **Serra do Caramulo**, where there's good climbing and walking. It has two great museums (see below).

**Viseu.** The most notable town in the region with quite a lot to offer. It's basically a medieval city — its cathedral is sixteenth century on a Romanesque base — and today is important as an agricultural centre, most especially for the Dão wines produced locally. In the sixteenth century an important Portuguese school of painting flourished in Viseu, led by Grão Vasco, whose works can be seen in the museum of the same name (see below).

**Guarda.** The highest town in Portugal at over 3,000 feet — good views but rather windswept.
**Serra da Estrêla.** Portugal's highest mountain range, with some stunning views, some good local sheep's cheese, and even a ski resort (see below).
**Covilhã.** Good base for exploring the **Serra** and quite a sizeable town.
**Castelo Branco.** Capital of Beira Baixa, where the mountains subside into the flat plains of the Alentejo. The town is known for its beautiful embroidered bedspreads and its agricultural produce. The former **Bishops' Palace** (containing a museum) and gardens is its major attraction.

## WHAT TO DO

### ART GALLERIES AND MUSEUMS

**Viseu**
**Museu Grão Vasco,** Paço dos Tres Escalões. A museum including some important works by Grão Vasco (especially St Peter on his Throne), and other paintings from his school which include a particularly interesting Adoration of the Magi.

**Caramulo**
**Fundação Abel Lacerda.** A wonderfully heterogeneous collection ranging from sixteenth-century Brussels tapestries to sketches by Dali and Picasso, by way of a Grão Vasco.
Caramulo also has (unexpectedly) a **vintage car museum** — the only one of its kind in Portugal.

**Lamego**
**Museu Regional.** Mixed collection including paintings by Grão Vasco and *azulejos* and other items taken from local churches which have now been demolished.

**Amarante**
**Museum of modern art,** with a lot of works by Portuguese Cubist, Amadeo de Soussa Cardoso.

**Bragança**
**Museu Abade Baçal.** Chiefly notable for the prehistoric granite sculptures of pigs in its gardens which have been found on several sites in Tras os Montes.

---

### FESTAS

**Viseu**
**Feira de San Mateus.** Lasts throughout September. Agricultural show with bullfights, folk dancing, etc.
**Vil de Moinhos.** In June, processions and cavalcades, again with folk dancing and singing.

### Lamego
Pilgrimage to *Nossa Senhora dos Remedios* on 8 September each year, providing an excuse for general festivities, concerts, and a 'flower battle'.

### Covilhã
Big procession to *Nossa Senhora da Boa Estrêla* (near the high peak of Torre) on the second Sunday in August.

## SPORTS

**Fishing.** Probably the best place for this is at **Chaves** on the river Tamega.
**Hiking and climbing.** Good prospects throughout the region.
**Skiing.** Portugal's only winter sports station is at **Malhão da Estrêla**, where there is basic lifting equipment and a range of accommodation. For further information contact the **tourist office** in **Covilhã**.

## USEFUL ADDRESSES

**Tourist offices**
**Covilhã:** Praça do Municipio (tel. 075–22170)
**Guarda:** Praça Luis de Camões
**Castelo Branco:** Alameda da Libertade
Other tourist offices are located at Bragança, Chaves, Lamego, Vila Real and Viseu.

**FAOJ Regional Offices**
**Bragança:** R. dos Combatentes da Grande Guerra 50 (tel. 0503–22775)
**Guarda:** R. General Povoas 3 (tel. 071–22210)
**Viseu:** R. Capitão Silva Pereira 117 (tel. 032–22793)

**British representation**
**British Embassy/Consulate** — see Porto or Lisbon.
**British schools** — none in the region.

## THE PLAINS

This region takes up a huge slice of Portugal in terms of land area, and the provinces of Ribatejo and Alta and Baixa Alentejo in administrative terms. Ribatejo, as its name suggests, is to be found alongside the River Tagus, and is a province of rich green meadows where horses and fighting bulls are bred. There are also rice paddies and cultivated land, interspersed with windmills and little white cottages. In the Alentejo, agriculture is also to the fore and in contrast to the North, it consists of vast estates of wheatfields or olive and cork plantations.

The region was important in Roman times as part of the province of Lusitania, and later both Beja and Evora were important towns under the Moors. It was never very densely populated, however, and as the Christians advanced on Moorish strongholds in the south, it became a sort of buffer zone, constantly being captured and reclaimed. When the land finally came under Christian control it was given in huge tracts to knightly orders such as the Templars as a means of ensuring its defence. These large estates have never effectively been broken up and land reform in the Alentejo was an important issue during the 1974 Revolution. However, little progress has been made in breaking up these traditional *latifundia*, and in the main agriculture has stagnated. The population remains sparse and for the most part impoverished.

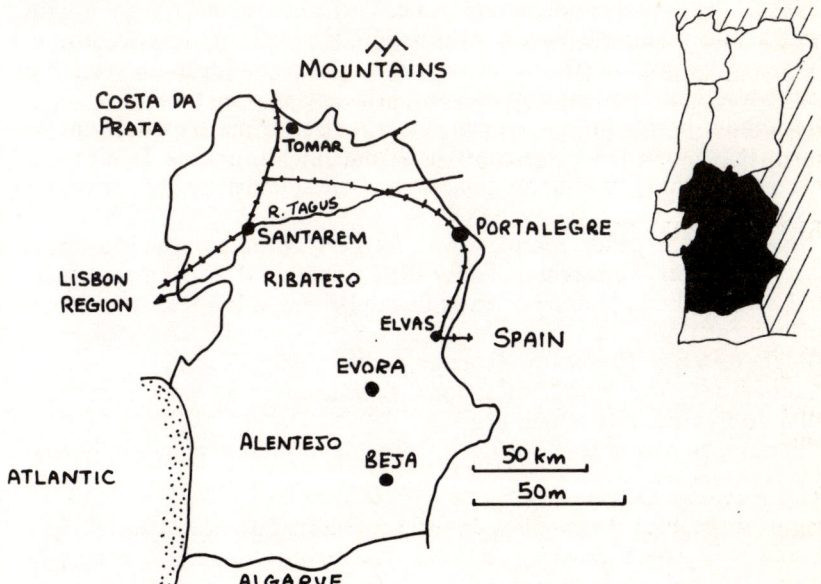

## WHAT TO SEE

**Santarem.** The historic capital of the Ribatejo province, looking out over the rich plains. Today it is a market town and centre for bull-breeding, and is most remarkable from the impressive view to be had from the **Portas do Sol**.

**Abrantes.** Pretty town with a castle on the banks of the Tagus. Nearby is the Knights Templars' castle of **Almourol**, built on an island in the river and inspiration for a whole body of romantic legends and tales.

**Tomar.** One of the most rewarding towns in the region with plenty of traditional charm. It is made outstanding, however, by the **'Convent of Christ'** which was headquarters of the Knights Templars from the time the Moors were driven out in the mid-twelfth century until the Order was dissolved a century and a half later. It was subsequently taken over by the Order of Christ, a new order founded by the Portuguese King Dom Denis which inherited all the Templars' property and was to play a leading role in overseas exploration and conquest in the fifteenth and sixteenth centuries.

It was during this period that many of the architectural highlights of the monastery were added, including a fantastic manueline window of nautical motifs — a tangible reminder of the way that the urge to discover and conquer new lands was tied up with religious belief.

The monastery boasts a total of seven cloisters, and at its heart is a twelfth-century Templars' church, the **Charola**, modelled on the Holy Sepulchre in Jerusalem.

**Portalegre.** District capital with traditional industries based on cork and textiles. Some attractive old mansions and convents.

**Evora.** The capital of the Alentejo, once Portugal's second city, now with 40,000 inhabitants the biggest in the region. It's pleasant, historic, attractive, yet very provincial. It boasts a Roman temple, a Jesuit university, a cathedral, and number of interesting palaces and mansions.

**Estremoz.** Lively little town which is a centre for marble quarrying — much of the town is actually constructed out of white marble. It has a vast main square and is famous for its *moringues* — traditional earthenware water coolers.

**Vila Viçosa.** Another 'marble town', formerly the seat of the Braganças (see section on **Mountains**). Today their palace (and its contents left by the last king Dom Manuel when he fled to Britain in 1910) are the town's main attraction.

**Alcacer do Sal.** Pretty town surrounded by rice paddies.

**Santo Andre** and **Melides Lagoons**. Beaches.

**Ilha do Pessegueiro.** Good beaches.

**Vilanova de Milfontes.** The nearest the Alentejo coast comes to having a seaside resort.

**Sines.** Big oil refinery and development area.

**Beja.** Capital of lower Alentejo, and an important centre under the Romans, and later the Moors. Its walls, still largely extant, are of Roman origin and sights include a castle with an impressive watchtower overlooking the plains, and a fifteenth-century convent.

**Elvas.** Heavily fortified town on the Spanish border, still a military garrison. It's also extremely attractive, huddled inside its town walls and boasts a castle of Moorish origin. Outside the town is an impressive fifteenth-century aqueduct with 700 arches, measuring over 4 miles in length!

## WHAT TO DO

### ART GALLERIES AND MUSEUMS

**Evora**
**Museu Regional.** Important collection of fifteenth- and sixteenth-century Flemish and Portuguese paintings.

**Estremoz**
**Museum of Rural Handicrafts.** Some noteworthy ceramics.

**Portalegre**
**Municipal Museum** containing some interesting religious pieces, plus more ceramics.

**Beja**
**Museu Regional** with some excellent *azulejos*.

## CINEMA

A **festival of children's films** is held at **Tomar** each January.

## FESTAS

The **Ribatejo Fair** is held at **Santarem** each year starting at the end of May and lasting 2 weeks. Bullfighting is the main attraction here, together with folk dancing. Santarem also sees bullfights and festivals during the second half of April (**Milagre Fair**) and the second half of October (**Piedade Fair**), plus other festivities during August.

**Tomar** has an especially interesting folk festival — the **Festa dos Tabuleiros** — which takes place on alternate years during July.

**Evora's** festivities coincide with St John's Day (23 June) and **Beja** has its, including bullfights, in August.

## SPORTS

**Bullfighting.** The best region in Portugal for this.
**Hunting and shooting.** Both are popular sports in the region.

## THEATRE

An **amateur theatre festival** is held at **Evora** each June.

## USEFUL ADDRESSES

**Tourist offices**
**Evora:** Praça do Giraldo
**Vila Viçosa:** Praça da Republica
**Estremoz:** Largo da Republica
**Elvas:** Praça da Republica
**Portalegre:** Rua 19 de Junho
**Beja:** Rua Capitão J F de Sousa

**FAOJ Regional Offices**
**Santarem:** Lgo Padro Francisco Nunes da Silva 3 (tel. 043–22292)
**Evora:** R. Miguel Bombarda 43 (tel. 066–22959)
**Beja:** R. Pedro Alvares Cabral 8 (tel. 084–22672)
**Portalegre:** Pça da Republica 17 (tel. 045–22776)

**British representation**
**British Embassy/Consulate** — see Lisbon.
**British schools** — none.

## THE ALGARVE

The Algarve is Portugal's major tourist area, and although there is a lot of timeshare and villa development, there is nothing on the scale of the Costa del Sol.

There are parallels with the Spanish region of Andalucía, however. The region formed the Moorish kingdom of Al Gharb and many Moorish elements remain in the layout of towns and villages and in traditional crafts practised — especially the characteristic *azulejos*. However, the Moors were expelled from the area in 1249, which was 250 years before they lost their last stronghold in Andalucía. It was during this latter period that the great Moorish monuments of Spain were constructed, and which Portugal has therefore missed out on.

Today the region is lavish in its natural offerings — beautiful beaches, exotic shrubs and fruit trees and a wonderful climate. It combines these with the facilities necessary for a good holiday — cheap bars and restaurants, discos, pockets of excellent sports facilities, etc. However, in terms of lengthier stays its possibilities are more limited, unless, like so many British ex-patriates, you can afford to buy your own business or retirement home.

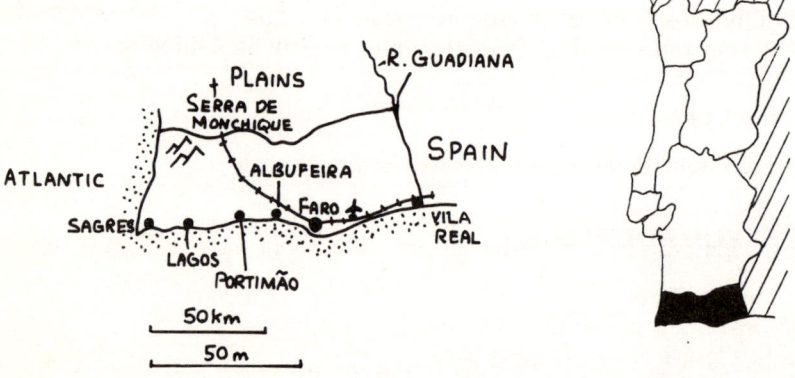

## WHAT TO SEE

**Sagres.** Windswept headland on the very south-western tip of Europe. It was here that Henry the Navigator founded his **School of Navigation**, surrounded by strong walls, which you can visit today. There is a **youth hostel** in what is supposed to be the house in which he stayed.
**Lagos.** A major resort and a centre for the western Algarve. There are some really beautiful beaches and cliffs here, eroded into dramatic shapes and

arches by the sea. Most of the old town was destroyed by the Great Earthquake of 1755, and Lagos now looks very definitely towards tourism for its inspiration.

**Portimão.** Big port with important fish-canning industry.

**Praia da Rocha.** The first and finest of the Algarve's tourist resorts.

**Silves.** The capital of the Moorish kingdom of Al Gharb, situated inland among orange and almond groves. In those days it must have been a place of some splendour, as it was a river port, but today is much reduced in status, although it still gives the impression of a Moorish city with its Arab fortifications and winding streets.

**Monchique.** Market town — little more than a village — in the lovely **Serra de Monchique**, a wooded mountain area with good views, good hiking and flourishing local crafts. Nearby at **Caldas de Monchique** the mineral waters are bottled and sold all over the country.

**Albufeira.** One of the region's most important tourist developments, and an attractive, lively town, with good beaches.

**Vilamoura.** More tourist developments including a marina.

**Faro.** Regional capital on the southernmost tip of Portugal, given key importance through its international airport. It's not a big place, but has some life of its own besides tourism as a commercial, agricultural and fishing centre.

**Olhão.** Busy fishing port with excellent beaches on *ilhas* (long sandbanks providing sheltered waters) nearby.

**Tavira.** Exceedingly pretty port with important tunny fishing industry.

**Vila Real de Santo Antonio.** Frontier town on the Guadiana river which you can cross by ferry into Spain. It was built by Pombal (who redesigned Lisbon), on a smart grid-pattern around an attractive main square.

## WHAT TO DO

## ART GALLERIES AND MUSEUMS

**Lagos**
**Municipal Museum.** Mixed collection of archaeological and ethnographic exhibits.

**Faro**
**Ethnographical Museum.** Interesting collection including costumes, crafts, and photographs depicting traditional Algarve customs.
**Archaeological Museum.** Particularly good on Roman material found locally.

## CINEMA

An **international festival of films** produced by non-professionals takes place in **Praia da Rocha** during May.

## FESTAS

Carnival time (usually late February-early March) is celebrated in **Loulé** with parades, folk music and dancing and 'flower battles', and there is also a festival 2 weeks after Easter in honour of **Nossa Senhora de Piedade**.
The beginning of August sees carnival-type celebrations in **Praia da Rocha**, and **Faro** celebrates its **Festa da Santa Iria** in October.

## MUSIC

The **Algarve Music Festival** is held in **Lagos** in May and June, and usually includes concerts, recitals and ballet by internationally known performers.
In the resorts you'll find discos and here and there live jazz or rock music.

## SPORTS

Sports have been promoted in the Algarve as a tourist attraction, and facilities for certain types of sport are extremely good:

**Fishing.** When non-commercial it is mostly done from the cliff edge — quite efficient but rather dangerous.
**Golf.** There are courses at **Penina, Vilamoura, Vale do Lobo** and **Quinta do Lago**.
**Horseriding.** Generally available, especially around **Almansil** and **Penina**.
**Sailing.** There is an important marina at **Vilamoura**.
**Tennis.** There are courts available in all the resorts and a big tennis centre at **Vale do Lobo**.
**Windsurfing, waterskiing, etc.** At various points along the coast. There's a windsurfing school at **Ferragudo**.

## USEFUL ADDRESSES

### Tourist offices
**Faro:** Rua de Misericórdia 8–12 (tel. 089–25404); also at airport.
**Silves:** Rua Dr Franesco Vieira
**Albufeira:** Av 5 de Outubro
**Olhão:** Largo da Lagoa
**Tavira:** Praça da Republica
**Vila Real de Santo Antonio:** Rua da Princesa
**Sagres:** In the Navigational School

### FAOJ Regional Offices
Rua dos Bombeiros Portugueses 4–1º, Faro (tel. 089–22932)

### Travel agents
Faro:
**Abreu:** Av da Republica 124, (tel. 089–25035)
**Viagens Rawes:** Rua Conselheiro Bivar 72, (tel. 089–23017)

Portimão:
**Capristanos:** R. Mouzinho de Albuquerque 47, Portimão (tel. 082–23136)
**Melia Tours:** R. Machado dos Santos 11, Portimão (tel. 082–25152)

**Car Hire**
**Europcar:**
— Faro airport
— R. Aboim Ascensão 111, Faro (tel. 089–23777)
— Estrada Nacional 120, Lote 1, Lagos (tel. 082–63173)
**Avis:**
— Faro airport
— R. Igreja Nova 13, Albufeira (tel. 089–52678)
— Hotel Algarve, Praia da Rocha (tel. 082–22029)
**Guerin Rentacar:**
— Av Republica 156, Faro (tel. 089–24763)

**British representation**
**British Consulate:** Rua de Santa Isabel 21–1º esq, Portimão (tel. 082–23071)
**British schools:**
— Algarve International School, Porches
— Prince Henry International College, Vale do Lobo, Almansil
— Barlavento English School, Espiche, Lagos

## LISBON AND REGION

This is the region you'll most probably choose if you're interested in anything other than straight tourist pursuits. A tenth of Portugal's population live in the capital — a city of 1 million and by far the biggest in the country. Setúbal is another major centre, and Estoril and Cascais are the country's most cosmopolitan resorts, with excellent facilities of all kinds.

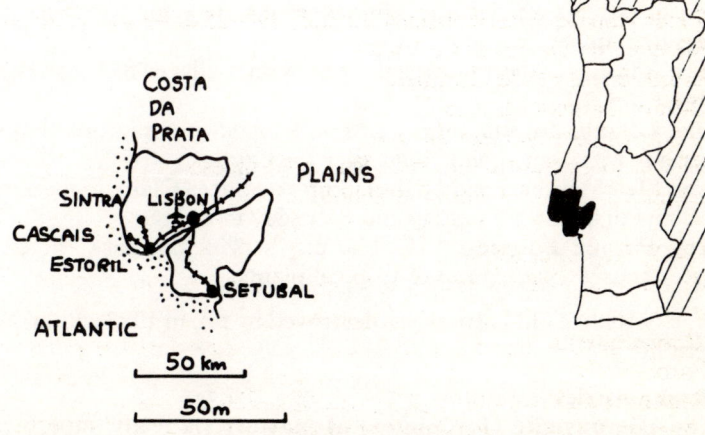

Contrasts with the rest of the country are dramatic and here more than anywhere you can follow up interests and get involved in life at the same level as you would at home.

## WHAT TO SEE

### Lisbon
Portugal's capital has real character — all the old-world charm common to so many Portuguese towns combined with the pace and variety that only a big city can provide. Situated among hills at the mouth of the Tagus the ancient city (pre-Roman in origin) was attractively remodelled in a manner befitting an eighteenth-century European capital by the Marques of Pombal after a tremendous earthquake in 1755 which destroyed most of the city centre. Despite the elegance of these streets, collectively known as the Baixa, and despite more recent attempts at modernity like the great suspension bridge built by Salazar, it's a city with a distinct earthiness and old-fashioned air with its antique tearooms, its trams, its fishwives, its shoeshine boys, its cobbled alleyways of the Alfama district and the *fado* houses and bars of the Bairro Alto. Here are some of its 'sights' in more detail:

**The Praça do Comercio.** Known in English as 'Black Horse Square' and by Lisboans as **Terreiro do Paço** this is the starting point for Pombal's rational city, backing onto the river with the main streets of the **Baixa** leading off it.
**The Rossio.** Three squares in one marking the other extreme of the Baixa and a great focus of activity in the city. Nearby is the main railway station.
**The Chiado.** The city's most affluent shopping area.
**The Sé.** Lisbon's great old cathedral, built in the twelfth century as soon as the city came under Christian control.
**The Elevador.** A wonderful old lift, designed by Eiffel, which takes you up to the Chiado and the Bairro Alto.
**The Bairro Alto.** Lisbon's Soho — a district of dark narrow seventeenth-century streets which comes alive at night — good for places to eat, drink, and hear music.
**The Alfama.** Lisbon's oldest district, with a villagey feel of an Arab town about it.
**The Castelo do São Jorge.** Lisbon's castle — a mixture of styles and periods with some good views over the city.
**The Flea Market.** Held on the **Campo de Santa Clara** on the edge of the Alfama district on Tuesday and Saturday mornings.
**The Parque Eduardo VII.** The city's principal park, noted for its greenhouses (*estufas*) full of tropical plants.

*Note:* Much of old Lisbon was destroyed by fire in 1988 and has yet to be rebuilt.

### Belem district
**The Hieronymite (Jerónimos) Monastery.** A really superb piece of

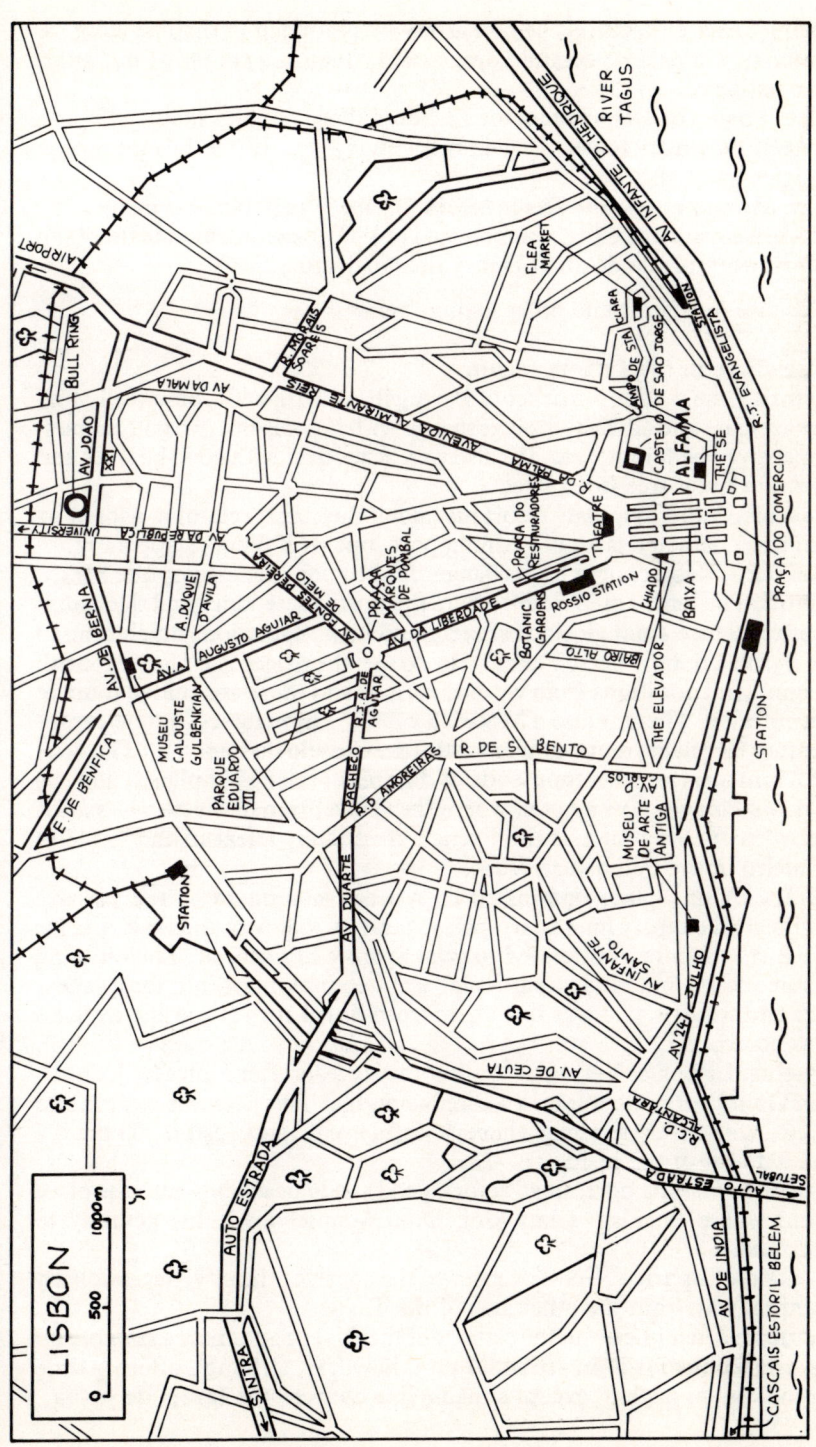

manueline architecture, the monastery was founded in thanksgiving for Vasco de Gama's successful voyages and contains a couple of museums (see listings).
**The Tower of Belém.** One of Lisbon's most famous sights, this is a sixteenth-century tower — again manueline — guarding the entrance to the port.
**The Monument to the Discoverers.** Again, a very familiar image, this modern concrete sculpture was erected in 1960 to commemorate the 500th anniversary of the death of Henry the Navigator.

(See also museums and other listings below)

### Elsewhere in the Lisbon region
**Estoril.** The most up-market of Portugal's resorts with some really luxurious villas and all the trappings that go with it — casino, two golf courses, expensive restaurants, etc. It's also very attractive, with good beaches and pleasant quiet tree-lined streets.
**Cascais.** More 'popular' resort just along the coast, retaining a lot of its original character as an old fishing port, but with plenty happening.
**Guincho.** Resort noted for its dangerous but nonetheless popular beach.
**Sintra.** The 'enchanted Eden' where the Portuguese kings had their summer residence amid glorious scenery and lush vegetation, much praised by Byron among others. There's a lot to see: the palace itself is of Moorish origin, with additions from various periods and there are guided tours of the interior. There is also a **Moorish castle**, a **monastery**, a nineteenth-century Germanic **mock-gothic castle** (the **Castelo da Pena**), the **Gardens of Montseratte**, with thousands of different varieties of plants, and the **Seteais Palace**, now a hotel, where the Convention of Sintra was signed between Wellington and the French after their defeat in the battle of Vimeiro in the Peninsular Wars.
**Mafra.** A tiny place dominated by a great monument — the massive eighteenth-century monastery-palace built by João V in thanksgiving for the birth of an heir, intended to rival Spain's El Escorial. The building is remarkable not for any particular architectural merit, but for its sheer size and scale — gold was flowing in from Brazil at the time and expense was no object.
**Queluz.** Lisbon's 'Versailles' built some 30 years after Mafra by João V's son Dom Pedro — comparisons are inevitable. This palace is elegant and pretty with lovely gardens whereas Mafra is cold and austere. There is a guided tour of the inside.
**Ericeira.** Fishing port, small resort, good sandy beaches — also the place from where Portugal's last king Dom Manuel made his getaway to England.
**Costa da Caparica.** Good beaches to the south of the city, accessible by mini railway from the other side of the Tagus.
**Sétubal.** Ancient city on the estuary of the River Sado, now a sizeable industrial centre. It is an attractive city, however, although offering little in the way of 'sights' except a manueline church, the **Igreja de Jesus.**

**Troia.** Sétubal's beach and a well-appointed holiday resort, on the opposite bank of the river.
**Sesimbra.** Popular holiday resort, noted for swordfish and tunny fishing. There is a good sheltered beach and a Moorish castle nearby.

## WHAT TO DO

### ART GALLERIES AND MUSEUMS

Note that closing day is normally Mondays.

**Lisbon**
**Museu Calouste Gulbenkian,** Av de Berna (opening hours vary according to the time of year). Calouste Gulbenkian was an Armenian art collector, who during the last war found refuge in Portugal, bringing with him this amazing selection of treasures which was acquired for the Portuguese nation. The Gulbenkian Foundation plays an important part in other aspects of cultural life, supporting among other things an orchestra, concert halls, and temporary exhibitions. The museum is situated with the rest of the Gulbenkian complex, in purpose built accommodation off the Praça de Espanha, and as the most important art collection in Portugal contains some superb pieces, ranging from Ancient Greek to Lalique.
**Museu de Arte Antiga,** R. das Janelas Verdes 95 (open all day). Portugal's major collection of national art. The highlights are paintings from the Nuno Gonçalves school (fifteenth and sixteenth centuries), which was much influenced by Flemish art of the period. There are also a few works by more internationally known figures (Bosch, Zurbarán, Rafael), and collections of ceramics and silverware.
**Museu de Azulejos,** R. Madre de Deus (open 1100 to 1300 and 1500 to 1700). Beautiful collection of *azulejos*, housed in a church.
**Museu da Cidade,** Palácio do Pimenta, Campo Grande (open afternoons only). Well thought-out city museum.
**Museu do Trajo,** Palácio Palmela, Largo S. João Baptista (open 1000 to 1300 and 1430 to 1700). Good collection of costumes.

Other museums, of perhaps less interest, are as follows:

**Military Museum,** L. do Museu de Artilharia
**Overseas Museum,** R. Portas Sto. Antão.
**Contemporary Art Museum,** R. Serpa Pinto 6

**In Belém**
**Museu de Arte Popular,** Av Brasília (open 1000–1230 and 1400–1700). Museum of folk art situated just next to the Monument to the Discoverers.
**Museu de Marinha** (in the Jerónimos Monastery; open 1000–1230 and 1400–1700). Maritime museum.
**Museu de Arqueologica.** Archaeological collection, also housed within the Jerónimos Monastery.

**Museu dos Coches,** Praça Alfonso de Albuquerque (open all day). One of Lisbon's most vaunted attractions — a collection of baroque coaches and carriages, heavily gilded and mostly commissioned by absolute monarch João V with proceeds from Brazilian gold.

**Elsewhere**
Other museums in the Lisbon region (see also What to See):
**Sintra:** Palácio Nacional; Palácio da Pena
**Mafra:** the monastery
**Queluz:** the palace
**Sétubal:** Municipal Museum with good collection of fifteenth- to sixteenth-century paintings housed in the cloisters of the Igreja de Jesus, Av 5 de Outubro.

## BULLFIGHTS

The bullfight in Portugal developed differently from in Spain — here the mounted bullfighters play a more important role, and the bull is not killed, merely worn down, to be killed out of the public eye. The best *corridas* are without doubt to be seen in Lisbon's bullring, the **Campo Pequeno.** The season lasts from April to October and fights usually take place on a Thursday afternoon.

Outside the capital, the town of **Vila Franca de Xira** on the Tagus is a big bullfighting centre, and has an important fair during July (see section on Festas).

## CINEMA

Lisbon is a great place to see films — foreign films are usually only subtitled in Portuguese, not dubbed, so you don't require any proficiency in the language in order to enjoy them! There are plenty of cinemas, and tickets, which are cheap anyway, are often half price on Mondays. You can find out what's on through the press, or the weekly publication *Sete*. Portugal's **National Film Theatre** (Palácio Foz, Praça Restauradores) has some especially interesting programmes.

## CRAFTS

There is a **crafts fair**, with a wide range of articles produced from all over the country, in **Estoril** throughout July and August.

## FESTAS

**Lisbon** has its big celebrations in June, in honour of the **Santos Populares** which are St Anthony (12/13th), St John (23/24th) and St Peter (28/29th). The streets are decked out with flags, there are fireworks, and everyone has a good time. **Sintra** also celebrates the latter in good folk style.

**Sesimbra** fishermen celebrate the **Festa do Senhor das Chagas** in May, and **Sétubal** has its **Feira de Santiago** in July, which takes the form of a traditional agricultural and craft show.

Perhaps the most interesting festa, though, is the so-called '**Red Waistcoats Festival**' (Festa da Colete Encarnado) which is held in **Vila Franca de Xira** on the first and second Sundays in July. It's a real folk festival — the red waistcoats are the traditional costume worn by the mounted *campinos* who watch over the herds of cattle in the Ribatejo — and there is music, dancing, bull-running in the streets, and big *corridas*.

## LIBRARIES

**National Library,** R. Ocid. do Campo Grande, Lisbon (open all day Mondays to Fridays, and Saturday mornings). Ancient and valuable collection in a new building.
**Overseas Archives,** Calçada da Boa Hora, Lisbon. A wealth of documentation relating to Portugal's colonial history.
**Municipal Library,** Praça do Município, Lisbon (open Monday to Friday 0900–1200 and 1330–1730). Contains a complete collection of books published in Portugal since 1932, plus a newspaper archive.
**Library of the Palace of Ajuda,** Calçada da Ajuda, Lisbon. Formerly the royal family's library.

## MUSIC

(See press for programmes.)
The main venue in **Lisbon** for opera, classical and ballet is the **Teatro São Carlos** in R. Serpa Pinto — most events are sponsored by the Gulbenkian Foundation (Av de Berna), where you can pick up a programme. **Estoril** has a **music festival** every June and July, with numerous concerts and recitals by internationally known performers.

One of the great attractions of **Lisbon** is its **fado houses.** *Fado* is Portugal's version of the blues or flamenco — a strange haunting popular music which shows marked African influences, supposed to have reached Portugal via Brazil through the slave trade. It's the dirge-like singing — usually by a woman — that stands out, although there is usually a guitar accompaniment. The places to go to hear this music are small bar/restaurant type places called *casas de fado* or *adegas tipicas* to be found mainly in the Bairro Alto. They open around 2100 or 2200 and go on until the early hours. Prices vary widely depending on the type of place you go to — some are getting too up-market for their own good — but anywhere you can expect to pay a minimum charge of about 1,500$.

Lisbon has its fair share of the usual discos and clubs, and also venues for live music. Look out especially for African bands at **Lontra** (R. de São Bento) and **BonTom** (R. São João da Praça) and also Brazilian bands — two great plusses from Portugal's colonial past.

There is also an **international jazz festival** held in **Cascais** in November.

## SPORTS

This region has some of the best sports facilities in the country, not only in **Lisbon** itself but also in **Estoril** and **Cascais**. The **National Stadium** is in **Cruz Quebrada**, on the road to Estoril, and there is a good **sports pavilion** in the **Parque Eduardo VII**. Look out too for the **university sports facilities** (Av Prof. Egas Moniz) which if you have a student card you may be able to use. Other sports possibilities are as follows (if you're particularly interested in any sport not mentioned, contact the relevant sports federation, as listed on p. 301 and they'll put you in touch with a club):

**Deep sea fishing.** From Sesimbra (tunny, shark, swordfish, etc.).
**Scuba-diving/underwater fishing.** Sesimbra again, also Troia.
**Windsurfing.** There is a windsurfing championship on the beach at Guincho in August — watch out for the undertow if you're swimming or windsurfing here at any other time.
**Sailing.** Marinas at Estoril and Cascais.
**Golf.** Courses at Vimeiro, Estoril, Troia, and two in the Lisbon area at Belas and Aroeira.
**Tennis.** Lisbon Tennis Club is in the Parque F. de Monsanto, to the west of the city, and Estoril Tennis Club is in the Av Amaral.
**Swimming.** Some swimming pools in the city are:
— Areeiro, Av de Roma
— Atenue, R. das Portas de Sto Antão
— Campo Grande
— Olivais Av Dr Francisco Luis Gomes
— Parque de Camping
— Parque F. de Monsanto
— Penha de França, Trav do Calado.
**Riding.** There is a big horseriding centre, the Leziria, at Vila Franca de Xira.
**Football.** You can watch Sporting Lisbon play at the Estadio Jose Alvalade, or Lisbon's other, perhaps more famous team, Benfica, at the Estadio da Luz.

## THEATRE

**Lisbon's** big theatres are the classical **Teatro Dona Maria II** in the Praça D. Pedro IV, which puts on both Portuguese and foreign plays, and the municipal **Teatro São Luis** (R. António Maria Cardoso) where some surprisingly *avant-garde* productions are staged.

There is an **international theatre festival** which takes place each July and August in **Sétubal**, and a **youth theatre festival** in **Lisbon** during June.

## UNIVERSITIES

**Universidade de Lisboa,** Praça da Universidade, 1600 Lisboa. Classical style university founded early this century.

**Universidade Técnica de Lisboa,** R. do Quelhas 6–A, Lisboa. Technical university.
**Universidade Nova de Lisboa,** Praça do Príncipe Real 26, 1200 Lisboa. New university founded since the 1974 revolution.

## USEFUL ADDRESSES

### Tourist offices
Lisbon:
Av Antonio Augusto de Aguiar 86 (tel. 01–575086) (National Tourist Board)
Praça dos Restauradores (tel. 01–363624)
R. Jardim do Regador 50 (tel. 01–325527)
Av Duarte Pacheco (tel. 01–655699)
Also at·airport, Parque Eduardo VII, Rocha and Alcantara docks, and Santa Apolónia station.

### FAOJ Regional Offices
R. D. Estefânia 14, 1400 Lisboa (tel. 01–573345)
Praça Marquês de Pombal 10, 2900 Sétubal (tel. 065–28834)

### Government offices
**Serviço de Estrangeiros:** Av Antonio Augusto de Aguiar 18 (tel. 01–554047)

### Travel agents
Lisbon:
**Abreu:** Av da Liberdade 160 (tel. 01–371341)
**Capristanos:** Av Duque de Loulé 47–A (tel. 01–360171)
**Tagus Travel** (youth travel): R. Camilo Castelo Branco 20 (tel. 01–548685)
**Transalpino:** Av Guerra Junqueiro 28–C (tel. 01–807472)
**Wasteels-Expresso:** Av Antonio Augusto de Aguiar 88–C (tel. 01–579180)
**Turismo Social e Juvenil — Turicoop** (youth travel and exchange): R. Pascoal de Melo 15–1º–Dto (tel. 01–531804)
**Tagus Juvenil** (youth travel): Praça de Londres 9–B (tel. 01–884957)

### Car hire
**Turicar:** Rua Filipe de Mata 26–A, Lisboa (tel. 01–733148); also at airport.
**Europcar:**
— Av Antonio Augusto de Aguiar 24–C, Lisboa (tel. 01–535115)
— Av Marginal, Cascais (tel. 286 7295)
**Avis:**
— Av Praia de Vitoria 12–C, Lisboa (tel. 01–561177)
— Pça dos Restauradores 47, Lisboa (tel. 01–361170)
— Also branches at airport and Hotels Ritz and Tivoli.
— Estação Tamariz, Estoril (tel. 01–268 5728)

**Kenning Car Rental:** R. Luciano Cordeiro 6–A, Lisboa (tel. 01–534627)

**British representation**
**British Embassy:** R. de S. Domingos a Lapa 35–37, Lisboa (tel. 01–661191)
**British Council:** R. Luis Fernandes 3, Lisboa
**British Chamber of Commerce:** R. da Estrêla 8, Lisboa

**British and International Schools**
**St Julian's School,** Quinta Nova, Carcavelos, 2775 Parede
**St Antony's International Primary School,** Av de Portugal 11, Estoril
**St George's School,** Vila Conçalves, Quinta das Loureiras, Estrada Nacional 2750, Cascais
**St Dominic's College,** Rua Outeiro da Polima, 2780 Arneiro
**Casa dos Santos Infant School,** Quinta do Relógio, 2710 Sintra
**Nursery Class,** Rua da Arriaga 39, Lisboa
**O Pincho Kindergarten,** Quinta de S. João, Rebelva, Carcavelos
**American International School,** Apartado 10, Carnaxide, Linda-a-Velha

# MADEIRA

The island of Madeira, 600 miles out into the Atlantic south-west from Lisbon, is in many ways a half-way house bridging the Old and New Worlds. Discovered totally uninhabited in 1419 by the Portuguese explorer João Gonçalves Zarco, it was immediately claimed for the Portuguese crown. Its dense forests were cleared to make room for profitable crops — first sugar cane until the mid sixteenth century when it was outstripped by produce from Brazil and later vines producing the distinctive Madeira wine beloved for centuries by the British.

Although mountainous — the highest peak is Pico Ruivo at 6,000 ft — Madeira's plentiful sunshine, rich volcanic soil and abundant water chan-

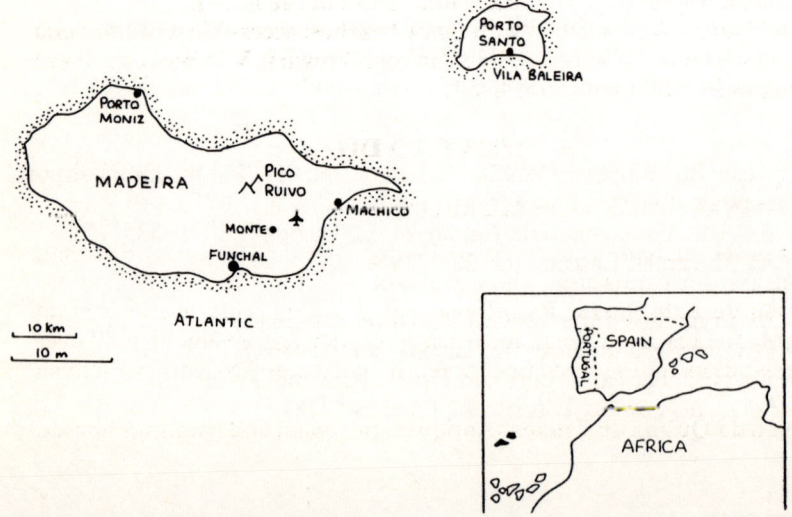

neled through an ingenious irrigation system combine to make the island highly fertile, a delight for gardeners and botanists. The vegetation is green and lush everywhere, the hillsides are terraced to produce a wide variety of fruit and vegetables, and the island's public gardens are a major attraction.

The island is small — only 35 by 13 miles — and is an ideal destination for a peaceful, away-from-it-all holiday but offers little scope for organised study or, indeed, employment.

## WHAT TO SEE

**Funchal.** The capital, with a population of 100,000, is situated on a breathtakingly beautiful bay to the south of the island. It consists of a main promenade along the sea front, the **Avenida das Comunidades Madeirenses** (Avenida do Mar), with a combination of narrow cobbled streets and attractive avenues going up the hillside behind it. It has some interesting buildings which make undemanding sightseeing and beautiful gardens. The two deep ravines or *ribeiros* which carry excess water down from the mountains to the sea are a distinctive feature of the town. An essential stop for those interested in wine is the *armazen* or **old wine lodge** on the Av Arriaga, which as well as offering the chance to sample all four varieties of Madeira (see p. 295) is something of a museum dedicated to the island's eponymous product.

**Monte.** Pretty, much visited hill town above Funchal. 'Toboggan' rides are offered down to the capital on upholstered wicker chairs.

**Pico Ruivo.** The highest peak, offering some spectacular views over the island.

**Câmara do Lobos.** Picturesque fishing village.

**Cabo Girão.** Beauty spot with spectacular cliffs.

**Machico.** Historic town.

**The Levadas.** There are 600 miles of these irrigation channels on the island, painstakingly constructed over the years to prevent water from the mountains gushing out to sea. Alongside are footpaths which provide a delightful way of exploring the wilder parts of the island.

**Porto Santo.** Nearby island with sandy beaches, accessible from Madeira by air or by boat (1½ hours). Its main (only) town is **Vila Baleira**, where Christopher Columbus once lived.

## WHAT TO DO

## ART GALLERIES AND MUSEUMS

**Museu Municipal,** Palácio de S. Pedro, Rua da Mouraria, Funchal. Natural history museum, with aquarium.

**Museu de Arte Sacra,** Paço Episcopal, Funchal (entrance in Rua do Bispo). Religious paintings and other items taken from churches all over the island, including some fine fifteenth- and sixteenth-century Flemish works.

**Museu da Quinta da Cruzes.** Antiques, porcelain and paintings housed in a manor house where Zarco (discoverer of Madeira) is thought to have lived.

## CINEMA

The **Cine-Jardim** is on the Rua do Carmo, and the **Cine-Parque** on the Rua Ivens. Both have varied programmes of original-version films.

## FESTAS

**20–30 June**. St Peter's day festival at **Ribeira Brava** with processions and dancing.
**14–15 August**. Festival of **Nossa Senhora do Monte** in **Monte**, celebrating the Feast of the Assumption.
**New Year's Eve**. Celebrated in great style in Funchal with fireworks, singing and dancing.

## SPORTS

Madeira has no sandy beaches; however, it makes up for this with good facilities for the whole range of **water sports**: snorkelling, scubadiving, sailing, water skiing and fishing. There is good **sea swimming** too, especially in the many semi-natural pools created by rock formations.

**Golf** (the Santo da Serra nine-hole course is about 15 miles north of Funchal) and **tennis** are well provided for, **walking** the *levadas* is a great attraction for hikers and naturalists as well as less earnest amblers and strollers, and the Pico Ruivo at 6,000 ft offers good scope for **mountain climbing**.

## THEATRE

Madeira's theatre is on the Av Arriaga.

## USEFUL ADDRESSES

**Tourist office:** Av Arriaga 18, Funchal (tel. 094–29057)
**British Consulate:** Av do Zarco 2, Funchal 9000 (tel. 094–211221)
**Travel agent:** Wagons-Lits, Av Arriaga 44, Funchal

# MORE USEFUL INFORMATION

## SUMMARY OF COURSES FOR FOREIGNERS

|  | Summer | ½ year | Full Year |
|---|---|---|---|
| University of Lisbon | ✓ | ✓ | ✓ |
| New University of Lisbon | ✓ |  |  |
| University of Coimbra | ✓ |  | ✓ |
| University of Aveiro | ✓ |  |  |

## WHAT TO READ ABOUT PORTUGAL

It's amazing how few books on Portugal exist in English, but here is a brief selection worth looking out for:

*Portugal, A Short History*, H. V. Livermore. Short yes, but very dry. Also extremely informative if you can plough your way through, from the Suevi to Salazar.

*Portugal, A Bird's Eye View*. Useful handbook on Portuguese society and institutions. It's an official publication, so you may be able to get a copy through the Portuguese Embassy in London.

*Port*, George Robertson, Faber and Faber, 1978. Another classic which is also good on the history of Porto and the Douro — if rather opinionated!

*Portugal, A 20th Century Interpretation*, Thomas Gallagher, Manchester University Press. A serious and scholarly contribution to the field of Portuguese studies.

*Living in Portugal: A Complete Guide*, Susan Thackeray, Hale, 1985. Aimed mainly at people retiring or buying a second home.

*The Lusiads*, Luis de Camões. Portugal's national epic, available in English and published by Penguin.

# Index

Abrantes, 329
accommodation,
   Portugal, 290–94
   Spain, 22–6, 81, 100, 109, 118,
      130, 145, 158, 174–5, 186,
      195, 206–7, 220, 226, 232,
      250, 252, 264
ACIS (Association of Contemporary
   Iberian Studies), 42
airports, *see* travel
air sports, 38, 112, 268, 301
Alava, 173
Albufeira, 333
La Albufera (Valencia), 238
Alcalá de Henares, 205
La Alcarria, 144, 148
Alcobaça, 323
Alfama, *see* Lisbon
Alicante, 238
Almería, 80
Alto Douro, *see* Mountains
Aranjuez, 205
archaeological sites, 83, 109, 197, 221,
   233, 317, 322
archaeology, 73, 111, 176, 253, 265
archery, 39, 301
architecture, 77, 78, 79, 84, 98, 142,
   160
art galleries, *see* museums and art
   galleries
athletics, 38, 301
ATSP (Association of Teachers of
   Spanish & Portuguese), 41
au pairs, 55, 309–10
Aveiro, 324
Avila, 126
Avilés, 107

Badajoz, 184
badminton, 38, 301
ballet, *see* music
banks, 16, 287
Barcelona, 153–5
baseball, 38
basketball, 38, 301
Batalha, 322
Beira, *see* Mountains
Beja, 330
Belem, *see* Lisbon
Bilbao (Bilbo), 174
Bizkaia, *see* Vizcaya
Bom Jesus, 318
bowls, 38
boxing, 38, 301

Braga, 318
Bragança, 325
bridge, 301
British companies, 63–70, 313–4
British representation, 40, 302
bullfighting (*see also* Pamplona, San
   Fermines),
   Portugal, 331, 340
   Spain, 84, 161, 177, 228, 241, 254
bureaucracy, 35
Burgos, 126
buses (*see also* coach travel), 30, 296–7

Cáceres, 185
Cádiz, 76
camping, 25, 292
canoeing, 38, 111, 167, 301
Cartagena, 219
Castellón, 238
car hire (*see also* driving), 20, 289
caravanning, 301
Cascais, 338
Castelo Branco, 327
caves,
   Portugal, 301, 323
   Spain, 38, 102, 110, 119–20, 177,
      234, 241
caving, 38, 301
Central Bureau for Educational Visits &
   Exchanges, 42
chess, 38, 302
children's entertainment, 161, 209, 242
Chinchón, 205
cinema and film,
   Portugal, 302, 319, 324, 331, 333,
      340, 346
   Spain, 85, 102, 110, 133, 161, 177,
      197, 209, 233, 242, 266
Ciudad Real, 143
climbing, *see* hiking, mountaineering
coach travel,
   to Portugal, 289
   to Spain, 19–20
   within Spain, 30, 108, 118, 130,
      239
Coimbra, 305, 322
conservation, 72
cookery (*see also* food and drink), 120,
   178
Córdoba, 78
La Coruña (Corunna), 193
Costa Blanca, 238
Costa Brava, 157
Costa de la Luz, 77

Costa del Azahar, 238
Costa del Sol, 76
Coto Doñana, 78, 93
couriers, 59, 311–12
crafts, 88, 111, 163, 198, 340
Cuenca, 144, 147
cycling, 38, 88, 113, 166, 256

Dalí, Salvador, 157, 161
dance (*see also* flamenco), 163, 178, 243
disabled, sport for (Spain), 38
dog racing, 38, 256
Donostia, *see* San Sebastián
draughts, 301
driving,
    Portugal, 289, 297
    Spain, 20, 31

education, 41, 46, 307
Elche, 238, 244
El Escorial, 205
El Greco, 142–3, 146
El Maestrazgo, 99, 239
Elvas, 330
embassies,
    British, 40, 344
    in London, 41, 302
employment agencies, 70
employment law, 53
Estoril, 338
Estremoz, 330
Evora, 330
exchanges,
    catering, 62
    homes, 26, 293
    student, 27, 293
    teacher, 59
    young worker, 63, 313

fado, 341
fallas (Valencia), 243–4
farmhouse holidays, 25, 293
Faro, 333
fashion, 254
Fatima, 323
feminist organisations, 40, 302
fencing, 38, 301
ferries, 20, 80–81, 158, 239, 251, 264
festas (*see also* fiestas), 319, 324, 327, 331, 334, 340–41, 346
fiestas (*see also* festas), 88–9, 102–3, 111, 120, 135–6, 148, 163–4, 178, 187, 198, 212, 221, 228, 234, 243–4, 255, 266–7, 274–5
Figueira da Foz, 322
film, *see* cinema and film
fine art (*see also* museums and art galleries), 164, 198–9, 228

fishing,
    Portugal, 301, 320, 328, 334, 342
    Spain, 113, 122, 137, 149, 167, 188, 200, 228. 234, 256–7, 268
flamenco, 83, 87, 91, 213, 221, 256
Formentera, 251
food and drink,
    Portugal, 294–5
    Spain, 81–2, 101, 109, 118, 131, 145, 158–9, 175, 186, 195–6, 207, 220, 226, 232, 240, 252, 265
football, 38, 92, 167, 179, 215, 301, 342
Fuerteventura, 262–3
Funchal, 345
Fundo de Apoio aos Organismos Juvens, 302

Gandía, 238
Gasteiz, 173
Gaudi, Antonio, 155
Gerona, 156
Gijón, 107
golf,
    Portugal, 301, 320, 334, 342, 346
    Spain, 38, 92, 121, 179–80, 245, 257, 268
Gomera, 262
government ministries, 36, 299–300
Goya, Francisco de, 98, 101, 202, 208
Granada, 79
Gran Canaria, 262
grants and scholarships, 48, 306
Guadalajara, 144
Guadalupe, 185
Guanches, 260, 262, 265
Guarda, 327
Guernica, 173
Guipúzcoa (Gipuzkoa), 173
gymnastics, 38, 301

Haro, 231
Hierro, 262
hiking, 89, 103, 112, 121, 136, 148–9, 164, 178–9, 188, 199, 244, 267, 346
Hispanic & Luso-Brazilian Council, 41
hitch-hiking, 31, 157, 297
hockey, 38, 301
Holy Week, *see* fiestas
homestays, 28, 294
horseriding (*see also* pony trekking), 38, 39, 89, 90, 180, 257, 268, 301, 334, 342
hotels, 22, 290–91
hovercraft, 80, 81, 264
Huelva, 77
Huesca, 99
hunting (*see also* shooting), 38

IASTE (International Association for the Exchange of Students for Technical Experience), 45
Iberia Airlines, 18
Ibiza, 250
ICONA (Instituto para la Conservación de la Naturaleza), 40
INICE (Instituto Nacional de Investigaciones Cientificas y Ecológicas), 46
Instituto de Cultura e Lingua Portuguesa, 302
Instituto de la Juventud, 36
insurance (*see also* social security), 15, 286
international organisations,
  grants from, 50
  work with, 62, 313

Jaen, 79
jazz, 179, 213, 256, 341
Jérez de la Frontera, 76
Jewish quarters, 78, 143, 193
judo, 38, 301

karate, 38, 301

Lagos, 332
language assistants, 58
language courses,
  Basque (Euskera), 178
  Catalan, 162
  Portuguese, 304–5, 324
  Spanish, 43–5, 85–7, 102, 110–11, 120, 133–5, 147, 162, 197, 210–11, 221, 227, 233, 242–3, 254, 266
  tabular summary (Portuguese), 347
  tabular summary (Spanish), 272–3
Lanzarote, 263
Leiria, 322
León, 127
Lérida, 156
letter-writing, 33, 274
libraries,
  Portugal, 299, 320, 324, 341
  Spain, 34, 90, 103, 119, 165, 212
Lisbon,
  city, 336–8
  language courses in, 304–5
  region, 335–44
Logroño, 231
Lorca, 220
Lugo, 193

Madeira,
  island, 344–6
  wine, 295

Madrid,
  city, 203–5
  region, 202–18
Mafra, 338
Mahón, 250
Málaga, 75
Mallorca, 249–50
Marbella, 75–6
markets (*see also* Rastro, shopping), 91, 214, 255, 336
maps, 17, 287
Menorca, 250
Mérida, 184, 189
minigolf, 301
ministries, *see* government ministries
missionary work, 73, 316
monasteries,
  accommodation in Spanish, 24, 101, 130–31, 175, 186, 195, 207, 220, 226
  to visit, 155, 185, 226, 252, 336–8
money, 16–17, 287
motorboating, 38, 301
motorcycling, 38, 301
Mountains (region of Portugal), 325–8
mountains, *see* serra, sierra
mountaineering, 24, 38, 87, 100, 301
museums and art galleries,
  Portugal, 319, 324, 327, 330–31, 333, 339–40, 345–6
  Spain, 83–4, 101, 110, 119, 132, 146–7, 160, 176–7, 187, 197, 208–9, 221, 227, 233, 241, 253–4, 265–6
music (*see also* fado, flamenco, jazz, opera),
  Portugal, 320, 324, 334, 341
  Spain, 91, 103, 121, 149, 165, 166, 179, 199, 212, 222, 245, 256, 267

national parks,
  Portugal, 317, 324
  Spain, 100, 112, 144, 166, 183, 189, 261, 262, 263
newspapers, *see* press
nightlife, 213

Obidos, 323
opera, 165, 212, 267, 341
Oporto, *see* Porto
Orense, 193
Oviedo, 107

package tours,
  Portugal, 289–90
  Route to Santiago, 195

Spain, 21, 81, 158, 195, 252
  with language courses (*see also*
    language courses), 44–5
painting, 87, 100, 102
Palencia, 127
La Palma, 261
Palma de Mallorca, 249–50
Las Palmas, 262
Pamplona (*see also* San Fermines), 225
parachuting, *see* air sports
parador holidays, 21
paradors, 24
parks and gardens (*see also* national
  parks), 214, 238
passports, 14, 286
pelota, 39, 180, 228
Picasso, Pablo, 160, 208
Picos de Europa, 107, 112, 121
Picos de Urbión, 129
pigeon breeding/racing, 38, 301
Plasencia, 185
political parties, 37, 300–301
Pontevedra, 194
pony trekking, 90, 113, 137, 185
port, 295
Portalegre, 330
Portimão, 333
Porto,
  city, 318
  region, 317–21
post, 33, 298
pottery, 147, 163, 241, 243
pousadas, 291
Prado Museum, 208
Praia da Rocha, 333
press,
  Portuguese, 299, 309
  Spanish, 33, 91, 103, 112, 137,
    165, 179, 188, 199, 222, 228,
    234, 244, 255, 267
professional organisations, 61
property purchase, 26, 293
public transport (*see also* travel), 29
Pyrenees, 100, 156–7

quintas, 293

rail travel (*see also* travel),
  in Portugal, 296
  in Spain, 29
  to Portugal, 288–9
  to Spain, 18–19
rally driving, 38, 301
Rastro, 214, 255
Rías Gallegas, 192
Rioja,
  region, 231–5
  wine, 233

Romería del Rocío, 89
Roncesvalles, 224
Ronda, 75
rowing, 38, 301
rugby, 39, 301
running, 257

Salamanca, 127, 133–4
sailing, 39, 167, 222, 257, 268, 302,
  334, 342
San Fermines, 228
San Sebastián, 173, 179
Santander (*see also* ferries), 117, 120–21
Santarem, 329
Santiago de Compostela, 191–2, 193
  Route to, 195, 199
Santo Domingo de la Calzada, 231
scholarships, *see* grants and scholarships
schools,
  addresses of, *see* useful addresses
  study in, 46, 306–7
  work in British, 59, 311
secretarial work, 62, 313
Segovia, 128
self-employment, 61, 312
Sétubal, 338
Seville, 77
sherry, 76, 82
shooting, 38, 39, 138, 302, 331
shopping (*see also* markets, Rastro), 34,
  121, 179, 199, 214, 299
shot putting, 39
Serra da Estrêla, 327
Serra de Monchique, 333
Serra do Caramulo, 326
Serranía de Cuenca, 144
Sierra de Alcaraz, 144
Sierra de Ancares, 193
Sierra de Béjar, 128
Sierra de Cazorla, 79, 89, 93
Sierra de Guadarrama, 205
Sierra de Segura, 79
Sierra Morena, 79, 89
Sierra Nevada, 79–80, 90, 92
Sintra, 338
Sitges, 156
skating, 39, 301
skiing, 38, 92, 103–4, 113, 122, 138,
  167, 200, 215, 234, 328
snooker, 38, 301
social security, 52, 308
Soria, 205
sport (*see also individual sports*), 92, 166,
  200, 215, 245, 258, 268–9, 320, 342
sports federations, 37–9, 301–2
squash, 39

student,
    ID card, 15
    TIVE offices, 39
    travel agencies, 17, 288
study visits, 45
sub aqua, 37, 301
swimming, 39, 215, 301, 342, 346

table tennis, 39, 302
TAP Air Portugal, 288
taxation, 52, 308
taxis, 206, 297
teacher exchanges, 59
teaching, 56–8, 310
Teide, 261
telephones, 32, 298
television, 33, 298
tennis, 39, 92, 302, 334, 342
Tenerife, 261
Teruel, 99
theatre,
    Portugal, 320, 331, 342, 346
    Spain, 92, 104, 122, 138, 143, 149–50, 167–8, 180, 189, 215–6, 222, 229, 244, 245, 258, 269
Toledo, 142
Tomar, 324
Torres Vedras, 323
tourist offices, London, 41, 303
trade unions, 39–40
translating, 62
Tras os Montes, *see* Mountains
travel (within regions), 17–21, 80–81, 100, 108, 117–8, 130, 144–5, 157, 174, 185–6, 194, 205, 220, 226, 232, 239, 287–90
travel agencies, 17, 18, 21, 39, 288
Trujillo, 185

useful addresses,
    Portugal, 320–21, 325, 328, 331–2, 334–5, 343–4, 346
    Spain, 93–6, 104–5, 114–5, 122–3, 139–40, 150–51, 168–70, 181–2, 189–90, 200–201, 216–18, 222–3, 229–30, 235, 246–7, 258–9, 269–71
universities,
    Portugal, 304–5, 307, 320, 325, 342–3
    Spain, 25, 43, 46–7, 93, 104, 113–4, 120, 134, 138, 168, 180–81, 189, 200, 216, 222, 229, 254, 269

Valencia,
    city, 237
    region, 236–47
validation of qualifications, 47, 306
Valladolid, 129
Valle de los Caídos, 205
Viana do Castelo, 318
Vigo, 194
Vila Real de Santo Antonio, 333
visas, 14, 286
Viseu, 326
Vitoria, 173
Vizcaya, 173
volleyball, 39, 302
voluntary work, 71–3, 314–6

waterskiing, 38, 245
weightlifting, 38, 301
wildlife, 93, 104, 114, 189, 200, 246
windsurfing, 92, 167, 245, 334, 342
wines (*see also* madeira, port, sherry, Rioja), 82, 89, 101, 131, 145, 159, 181, 196, 220, 227, 233, 234, 240, 295
work, 59–73, 307–16
work camps, 71–2, 314–5
wrestling, 38, 301

youth conferences, 114, 269
youth hostels, 23, 291–2

Zafra, 184
Zamora, 129
Zaragoza, 98
zarzuela, 213